Crossing Borders
Re-mapping Women's Movements at the Turn of the 21ˢᵗ· Century

Crossing Borders

Re-mapping Women's Movements at the Turn of the 21st century

Edited by
Hilda Rømer Christensen
Beatrice Halsaa
Aino Saarinen

University Press of Southern Denmark

© The authors and University Press of Southern Denmark 2004
University of Southern Denmark Studies in History and Social Sciences vol. 280
Printed by Narayana Press

ISBN 87-7838-859-7

Cover design by Anne Charlotte Mouret
Front cover: Women in Black. Demonstrating against violence at the 4th World Conference on Women.
Beijing 1995. Courtesy of the Women's History Archives, Denmark.
Back Cover: Voters from Norway. Courtesy of the Norwegian Association for Women's Rights.
P. 294: © Dea Trier Mørch / Copy-Dan Billedkunst 20040214

Thanks to Eva Lous at the Women's History Archives in Denmark for providing numerous
illustrations for this book.

This book has been published in the context of the Thematic Network
Women's Movements and Internationalisation, financed by NORFA, the
Nordic Academy for Advanced Study and with financial support from NIKK,
the Nordic Institute for Women's Studies and Gender Research.

University Press of Southern Denmark
Campusvej 55
DK-5230 Odense M
Phone: +45 6615 7999
Fax: +45 6615 8126
Press@forlag.sdu.dk
www.universitypress.dk

Distribution in the United States and Canada:
International Specialized Book Services
5804 NE Hassalo Street
Portland, OR 97213-3644 USA
Phone: +1-800-944-6190
www.isbs.com

Contents

Part IV. Addressing Violence and Care

Part V. Multiculturalism – globalisation

Reflections

Abstracts 355

Biographical Statements 363

Index of names 369

Crossing Borders

Re-mapping Women's Movements at the Turn of the 21st Century

Hilda Rømer Christensen, Beatrice Halsaa, Aino Saarinen

> *"It does not give any meaning to look at young feminists as a generation without history. (...) But it does give meaning to relate to the fact that the problems young women are up against are by and large the same as the problems feminists struggled with 30 years ago."* [1]

The Nordic countries have recently witnessed a new wave of activity in the area of feminist critique and organising. The move has substantiated in a range of books and journals, expressing the experiences of young women and men in late modernity and their striving to create a new collective "we" prepared for feminist struggle. The new wave has been coined *third wave feminism*. A generational term that refers to theories, activism and the launching of a more diverse and inclusive agenda for feminism; and an institutional term that includes the flourishing of international networking and campaigning at the dawn of the 21st century. The new generation or third wave feminism presents a many-facetted picture of feminisms today and also invites a re-narration of the history of feminism and of women's movements. Third wave feminism refers to the idea of feminist genealogy as consisting of waves and implies a *second wave* that took off in the 1960s and the 1970s and a *first wave* around the turn of the last century.

Nordic feminist activists in this new third wave discourse have positioned themselves as successors and critiques of second wave feminism. Expressed in the wish for a more easygoing feminism and a deconstruction of women as anything but a uniform category. Some take a more critical stance to second wave feminism, and what they see as restricted notions of race, sexuality, class, fashion and beauty.[2] A common project has been to insist on analytical renewal and to define gender and heterosexual normativity as constructed categories.

The main aim of the anthology is to pay tribute to the scholarly and historical canon of women's movements and of feminist genealogy. And to make visible both continuities and breaks in the collective feminist voices and other 'we's' that have united women, and some men, in the fight and efforts of creating a better world for humanity during the 19th and 20th centuries.

In doing so it is substantiated that even historical waves have been marked by more diverse compositions and goals than is revealed in the portraits offered by the latest – often media mediated accounts of feminism. The volume seeks to comment and confront the question of waves in the history of women's movements, by widening the historical and geographical frameworks. Accordingly, notions of crests and abbeys in 20th century women's movements are beeing approached from new and different perspectives, through which the idea of waves are being questioned and moulded into new perspectives. The volume endeavours that feminism and women's movements in a broader sense make up a fruitful scholarly Klondike and a dynamic field of conflicts, competitions and co-operations.

The network of scholars that have produced the book at hand was launched with the working title: *Women's Movements and Internationalisation: the "Third Wave"?* in the late 1990s. The aim was to explore the scope and character of mobilisation in a historical and methodologically new context. The network has of course been fuelled and inspired by the emerging "third wave" during the very same period.

This gainful process of research networking was initiated at NIKK, the Nordic Institute of Women's Studies and Gender Research at the University of Oslo in 1996. It was made possible by the generosity of NORFA, the Nordic Academy of Advanced Studies in 1997-2002. Both institutions form parts of the joint Nordic arrangements that have been developed intensively since the 1950s, when the Nordic Council was founded. The WMI network: *Women's Movements and Internationalisation: the "Third Wave"?,* comprised of doctoral students and senior researchers and represented thus multiple research generations from the 1970s till the 1990s. Though rooted in the Nordic countries, it contained a broad geographical distribution of scholars from the Baltic area, Russia, China and Britain, thereby crossing usual lines between the East and the West. The multidisciplinary composition of the group, with scholars from anthropology, sociology, political science, cultural studies and history gives evidence of the diverse approaches and thematic issues that are represented. During its active period the network progressed into a multi-voiced and productive community that has given contributions to several doctoral dissertations and led to one previous joint publication.[3]

The anthology is the outcome of both intellectual and territorial journeys. The network seminars were rotating in all the five Nordic countries, profiting from meetings with invited scholars from outside the network and activists in the form of visits paid to local women's organisations and projects. Together these journeys challenged, unified and centralised perspectives on the women's movements and generated new and innovative approaches, themes and problems. Hidden dialectics were spelled out: linking the current and the historical perspectives, linking hard core and soft versions of feminism, linking Eastern and Western perspectives and high politics with grass roots activities.

Crossing borders and re-mapping women's movements

The title, *Crossing Borders. Re-mapping Women's Movements at the Turn of the 21ˢᵗ Century,* indicates the multi-layered ways in which women's movements have developed over the past and the many challenges facing women's movements today. In addition to mapping a broad range of issues the anthology strives for re-narrations and re-locations of one of the major social movements of the 20ᵗʰ century and for fresh analysis of its latest trends.

The framework for the texts has been set by recent structural, ideological and cultural changes towards globalisation – including the end of the Cold War bipolarisation – and immigration and multiculturalism intertwined with it. Globalisation and multiculturalism have produced new fields of co-operation and conflicts for women's movements and generated new questions: How has globalisation in its multiple forms influenced women's movements, their practices and key notions? What kind of hegemonies are in play – empirically and conceptually – and how are they negotiated and displaced in today's more and more complex political and intellectual settings? What are the roots of international and transnational networking and how have different levels of politics interacted, from the grass-root level to international politics during the 20ᵗʰ century? What are the new strategies for coping with the increasing amount and influence of multilateral political institutions, for building up more solid grounds for a global civil society? What role do new and old women's movements play for the (re)foundation of women's movements in the former socialist countries in Europe, and what are the conditions in China still under communist rule? How have the relationships of women on the move across the global East-West divides been changing in the last decades?

Besides confronting these questions and issues common not only to scholars but to all with an interest in women's and other social movements, the specific aim of the anthology has been to approach critically research done on women's movements in the Nordic countries both empirically and conceptually. The anthology aims at exploring the links between Nordic and inter- and transnational women's movements, and at looking with new eyes at Nordic movements themselves in order to reappraise women's struggles and activities.

Recent comparative studies have argued that the Nordic countries have been marked by a collective and co-operative ideology where discourses of gender quality have emphasised common interests between men and women. This social paradigm has created a benevolent climate for social change including gender equality issues, and has stimulated a Nordic forum for discussion where also men participate. At the same time the gender neutral discourse might explain the resistance to women's organising in separate and autonomous structures and the reluctance to address power and privileges in gender specific perspectives.[4] The neutral discourse including the hegemonic position of Protestantism might also explain the difficulties of the Nordic countries in dealing with race and multiculturalism. The doubleness of benevolence and resistance is touched upon in several chapters in both current and historical perspectives.

The goal has been to widen the scope of former and contemporary scholarly debates and focus points in the community of Nordic women's and gender studies.[5] Not least through the rethinking of key concepts in the histories and genealogies of women's movements, inspired by the challenges spelled out by diverse post-modern and post-structuralist approaches and epistemologies.

The discursive re-mapping and re-narration of the women's movements is all in all an exercise that is complicating the field a great deal. Even though there might be a dialectic relationship between the different positions presented in this volume it is also clear that the re-assessments are by no means univocal. Contrasting on one hand a position that argues from within the logic of modernist feminism in favour of identifying a common core in feminism as a precondition for the formation of a separate analytical body, and for the identification of feminism as something independent from Liberalism and Marxism. And on the other hand a position informed by postcolonial thinking, suggests a different beginning by critically looking at unifying concepts such as feminist movements and women and the processes of constructing categories. What are the reasons for processes of definitions, identifying and naming? Who constructs meanings and boundaries of meanings? These questions imply a fresh focus on relations between women, highlighting ways in which feminists and feminist scholars are also involved in the production of power-structures, of insiders and outsiders. The claim is that focusing on waves and on continuity and change often invites an approach focusing on mainstream activists. An approach that is blind to activists who act in other areas and arenas, such as black, migrant and refugee women.[6]

In this way re-mapping consists of an intellectual enterprise aimed at elucidating the borderlands of past and present production of meaning, knowledge and concepts. Or the ways in which the women's movements have been talked about, thought about and represented.

International feminism in the 20th century:
The long march through the institutions

When looking at the 20th century women's movements from a contemporary globalising angle, several discourses are in play.

During the 20th century women's movements have undergone profound changes both at national and international levels due to and intertwined with general political and economical changes. These changes have been generalised in a set of post-labels, such as post modernity, post industrialism, post colonialism, post feminism and so on. This all in all mirrors moves at many levels and forms that can be subsumed under the contested label globalisation.

The major shifts occur to the women's movements and feminism at several and parallel levels: On one hand the transformation of delimited women's movement at national and international levels in the early decades of the 20th century into today's looser networks. Typified in Non Governmental Organisations, NGOs – with feminist, social or other goals. On the other hand the institutionalisation of feminist goals in transnational organisations such as the United Nations, the International labour Organisation and The World Bank.

Seen in a longitude 20th century perspective it is obvious that one important branch of international feminism has been closely related to the negotiations and integration of key issues in major institutions making the feminist endeavours identical with the long march through the international institutions.

Right from the end of the 19th century international cooperation in this area was mainly conducted in the framework of international women's organisations. Along with the launching of the nation states in the 19th and early 20th centuries, first wave feminism took off in the form of women's organisations that mushroomed at both national and international levels. Even though first wave feminism has often been made identical with suffrage, the goals of early women's organizing were broader and mirrored nation class, religion, as well as social and political issues. Huge international conferences made up sites for proliferation of the international women's organisations and for addressing burning issues, such as trafficking and prostitution, protective labour legislation and suffrage.[8]

From the beginning the international women's organisations played a double role. In their ideal form they composed transnational umbrella structures and acted as melting pot for different national organisations and committees. As such they initiated and mediated between different geopolitical cultures and emphasies. During the first decades of the 20th century some of the international women's organisations also acted as channels for the consolidation of Anglo-American hegemonies. A situation that was somehow changed with the new structures of international co-operation after World War II.[7]

Following World War I and the Versailles Treaty of 1919 new institutions such as The League of Nations and the International Labour Organisation enhanced new frameworks for international co-operation. They were situated in Geneva which in the interwar years succeeded London as the new international Capital of the World.

Geneva during the 1920s and 1930s also became a unique place for women's co-operations. Here women's international organisations managed for the first time in history to co-ordinate international aspirations on a continuous and semi-professional basis. The co-operation was formalised in 1925 in the *Joint Standing Committee of Women's International Organisations*, launched at the initiative of the old and respectable *International Council of Women*. The members consisted of the associations considered as feminist or at least as catering for women's interests: such as *The World's Women's Christian Temperance Union, The International Council of Women, The World's Young Women's Christian Association, The International Council of Nurses, The International Alliance of Women for Suffrage and Equal Citizenship, The Women's International League for Peace and Freedom, The World's Union of Women for International Concord,* and *The International Federation of University Women.* It is thought provoking that the charmed circle did not comprise of labour, Catholic or Jewish women's organisations; they either refused to join or were not invited. [9]

The aim of the Joint standing committee was to push for the appointment of women to the League of Nations and to take up the issues of the promise of gender equality. Expressed in the Covenant of the League, saying in article 7 that "all positions under and in connection with the League, including the Secretariat, shall be open to men and women."[10] The promise of gender equality, however, became a great disappointment in the League context. Women were never appointed to the League Council and only a few women took prominent offices and were appointed as League delegates by their governments. Nevertheless Geneva became the nexus and laboratory for international networking and for making women and women's organisations visible.

During the 1920s and the 1930s the goals of international co-operation among women widened. The work was now carried on in several cooperative bodies, such as the *Liaison committee of the Women's International Associations* and in specific Committees such as the *Women's Consultative Committee on Nationality* and the *Peace and Disarmament Committee.* The joint efforts of the committees were altogether to create and strengthen international feminism and to push for change in the field of foreign policy and international relations to also include social issues, peace and gender equality.

Already at this point in time it became clear that feminism or women's issues were by no means univocal and the international community in and around Geneva also made up a space for the spelling out of different priorities and strategies. One central conflict of the interwar years crystallised around the issue of protective labour legislation. The question was whether it protected or discriminated against women. The conflict even produced a new organisation, the *Open Door International* in 1929 aimed at lobbying against measures of protective labour legislation and the ILO, regarded as the "chief enemy" in relation to equal working rights for women.[11] Another – related – conflict culminated around the debate for and against a general resolution on Equal Rights. The Equal Rights Treaty was initiated by equal rights proponents and put onto the agenda of the League of Nations in 1935. The aim of the Treaty was to force national

Pioneering Community, Geneva 1920. Nordic women were among the first women delegates in the League of Nations. From left to right, Professor Kirstine Bonnevie, Norway, Anne Bugge Wicksell, Sweden and Henni Forchammer from Denmark.

Henni Forchammer was one of the few women delegates to the Leaugue assemblies from 1920 till 1938. She pioneered as the first woman speaker at the League General Assembly in 1920. At this occasion she spoke on the issue of trafficking and refugee women as a member of the Social committee of the League. Like several active women in her generation, she held an impressive record in national and international women's organisations: She was president of the Danish National Council of Women from 1913-31 and vice president of the International Council of Women from 1914-1930. Also peace issues had her attention and she was an eager member of Women's International League for Peace and Freedom.

governments to make laws complying with the principle of equal rights. Meaning that the countries that signed the Treaty were to work towards equal rights or gender-neutral legislation. While the Treaty was turned down, the initiative forced the League to commission a more moderate and gradual step. In the form of a general inquiry into the status of women at an international level.[12]

So the phrasing *Status of Women* became a central metaphor for women's issues and equality aims also in the following years and was institutionalised in the new United Nation structures as the *Commission on the Status of Women* after World War II.

It is interesting that a handful of Nordic women were very active from the very beginnning of the League of Nations and later on in the launching of equality issues in the United Nations. [13] Due to early enfranchisement and the somehow more democratic traditions in the field of foreign relations, Nordic women were among the first official delegates in the League of Nations.

The lengthy international traditions are thoroughly documented in this anthology, not least in the focus on the UN conferences on women from 1975 and onwards.

The very priorities and outlooks in many current feminist activities and goals resemble the old issues and agendas, launched along with first wave feminism during the latter part of the 19th century, and the international social orientated feminism of the 1930s. In several ways the international scene of Geneva in the 1930s made up a laboratory and a learning process for current issues and discussions – yet voiced and unfolded and contested in new settings.

As such the co-operation between the international women's associations during the interwar years makes up an important take-off for international feminism and for maintaining and translating feminist goals into new organisational structures from the first to the second half of the 20th century.

Late 20th century: The era of NGOs and gender mainstreaming

During the last decades of the 20th century the hierarchical structures of international co-operation have been moulded into new forms and extended into a multitude of issues, clearly demonstrated in the numerous UN initiatives related to women and gender.[15] International co-operating bodies now tend to present themselves as diversified, de-centred and closely integrated in the framework of a new policy agenda. The focus on new and more diverse processes have been nurtured by the evolving globalisation and neo-liberalised economies and the development of modern communication technologies.

At the political level governance has materialised as the postmodern political form that transcends the nation state. Governance processes now take centre stage as policy committed to diverse structures and institutions that interact with each other in dynamic and complex decision processes; from nation states over international institutions, to the inclusion of NGOs and social movements at both national and international levels. Accordingly the last decades of the 20th century have witnessed a restructuring of women's organisations into a diversified body of Non Governmental Organisations. They might consist of old surviving women's organisations (e.g. The International Council of Women, the International Alliance of Women, the World's Young Women's Christian Association and the International Federation of University Women) as well as of new organisations and networks.

Women's NGOs or social movements have been recognised as vital actors in both Western and Non-western societies. By now they carry out a broad spectrum of activities including the launching of social and development programmes, promoting social justice and human rights, monitoring governments and numerous other functions.

The new forms and scopes of international networking and transnational organising have produced and emphasised a whole new range of burning issues and critical points. This new style of women's movements have for instance been criticised for the role of facilitating the consolidation of hegemonic, neo-liberal principles and priorities that substitute or undermine state subsidised facilities.[16]

The accounts in this volume both underpin and undermine this criticism. Regional approaches, like the Nordic intervention in the Barents region, might stand for a more diverse and complicated picture. As well as the application of new middle range principles such as transversal dialogue and processes of rooting and shifting as useful instruments for bridging the differences and as a way of taking institutional and territorial divergences seriously.[17]

During the 1990s *gender mainstreaming* has been launched as the overall strategy to implement gender equality. Not least the United Nations and the latest UN Fourth World Conference on Women in Beijing in 1995 have been the nexus and the channel for the mainstreaming strategy. Mainstreaming is a strategic concept that derives from different geopolitical and institutional settings including NGOs and today gender mainstreaming makes up the often contested framework for development of international and global implementation of equality. The volume presents how the Beijing meetings have influenced the stage both at international, regional and national levels.

Today, actors press, in many ways, for the integration and the accountability of gender in international relations and agreements. They have launched the need for a global feminist response to counteract the many types of oppression still facing women around the world. So far it seems as if gender issues has had the highest legitimacy in relation to bodily issues such as the prevention of bodily harm, and in relation to human rights committed to liberal democratic institutions and constitutions such as suffrage, violence against women and trafficking.[18]

Contested issues

International feminism has constantly made up a contested space for the spelling out of conflicts and for the making of political strategies as part of enhancement and consolidation. Today not only the actors themselves but also gender research make up parts of the agenda and are implicated in the issues at both conceptual and strategic

Springtime in New York 1946. Members of the first Commission of the Status of Women. From left to right: Bodil Begtrup, Denmark, (chair), Hansa Metha, India, Minerva Bernadino, The Dominican Republic and Angela Jurdic from Libanon. Besides bringing about the Status of Women's Commission they influenced the contents of the Universal Declaration of the Human Rigths in 1947-48, to include both men and women.

levels. Current debates seems to crystallise around the idea of a universal conception of justice, equality and human rights built on liberal universalism. Is there one set of defining human rights and justice that applies to all women? The cosmopolitan concept of global feminism has been opposed to by various concepts such as international feminism or post (colonial) global feminism, regarded as more sensitive to cultural variation to local particularity and culture, as well as to history and the impact of colonialism. Accordingly it is argued that connections across national and cultural differences are necessary, but must be treated with caution and an awareness of the history, especially of Western interventions in developing countries. Universal moral principles have one set of benefits, while the cultivation of differences offers new ethical and political opportunities for global activities.[19]

This volume in all its diversity takes issue of a kind of middle range approach that links local, regional and global levels. It pays attention to the women's movements as important social movements of the 20th century – regarding both the advancement of women's and gender issues at the international agenda, and the unfolding of new strategies and practices. [20]

It seems as if the Nordic countries stand out in the making of gender research and of women's movement tools for successful political interventions throughout the second half of the 20th century. Notably in Sweden, Finland and Norway a pioneer generation of women social scientists launched path-breaking analysis of women's work and family life already in the 1960s. One generation before the breaktrough of gender studies in the Western university world.[21] Today it seems as if gender studies are more institutionalised and rooted in the Nordic countries compared to the European level.[22] Meaning that the struggle for gender equality and the recognition of power and gender in the scientific discourses have been moved, but by no means overcome.

All in all, the volume points to the importance of empirical and strategic gene-ralisations of women and of women's movements. They have formed a wide range of discursive communities that have gradually unfolded at the global level during the 20th century. As such the volume invites to recognise the integrated nature of research, reflection and differentiation.[23] At both a literal and a general level it is a manifestation of the links between women's movements and gender studies. And the struggle of how to come to terms with new challenges and new interpretations.

References

Andreasen et al. (1991). *Moving On. New Perspectives on the Women's Movement,* Acta Jutlandica LXVII: 1. Humanities Series 66. Aarhus University Press

Bergman, Solveig (1999). "Women in New Social Movements", in Christina Bergqvist *et al.* (eds.) *Equal Democracies? Gender and Politics in the Nordic Countries.* Oslo Universitetsforlaget.

Bergman, Solveig (2000). "Women's Studies in the Nordic Countries – Organisations, Strategies and Resources", in Rosi Braidotti, Esther Vonk & Sonja van Wichelen (eds.). *The Making of European Women's Studies.* Vol. II. Athena. Utrecht University.

Bergqvist, Christina & Borchorst, Anette, Christensen, Ann-Dorte, Raaum, Nina C, Ramstedt-Silén, Viveke and Styrkársdóttir, Audur, (eds.) (1999). *Equal Democracies? Gender and Politics in the Nordic Countries.* Universitetsforlaget, Oslo.

Bertone, Chiara (2002). *Whose Needs? Women's Organisations, Claims on Child Care in Italy and Denmark.* FREJA, Aalborg University.

Björnsdóttir, Birna Anna & Sturludóttir, Oddný & Hauksdóttir, Silja (2000); *Dís.* Reykjavík, Forlagið.

Briskin, Linda (1999). Mapping women's organizing in Sweden and Canada: Some Thematic Considerations. In Briskin, Linda & Eliassson, Mona (eds.). *Women's Organizing and Public Policy in Canada and Sweden.* McGill-Queen's University Press, Montreal.

Dahlerup, Drude (1986). *The New Women's Movement. Feminism and Political Power in Europe and the USA.* Sage. *The New Women's Movement.* Sage Publication.

Dahlerup, Drude & Gulli, Britta (1985). 'Women's Organizations in the Nordic Countries: Lack of Force or Counterforce', in Haavio-Mannila, Elina, Dahlerup, Drude, Eduards, Maud, Gudmundsdottir, Esther, Halsaa, Beatrice Hernes, Helga Maria, Hänninen-Salmelin, Eva, Sigmundsdottir, Bergthora, Sinkkonen, Sinka & Skard, Torild (eds.). *Unfinished Democracies. Women in Nordic Politics.* Oxford, Pergamon Press.

Drake, Jennifer & Heywood, Leslie (eds.) (1997). *Third Wave Agenda. Doing Feminist.* University of Minnesota Press.

Frank Goth, Anita & MacLean, Karen, Myong Petersen, Lene & Schelin, Katrina (eds.) (2000). *Nu er det nok – så er det sagt!* København, Rosinante.

Gustafsson, Gunnel, Eduards, Maud & Rönnblom, Malin (eds.) (1997). *Towards a New Democratic Order? Women's Organizing in Sweden in the 1990's.* Publica, Stockholm.

Holm, Adam, Bisgaard Munk, Timme, Thelle, Mikkel (eds.) (2000). *Hvordan mand?.* København, Tiderne skifter.

Kraul, Marie (ed.) (2000). *Fem@il.* København, Aschehoug.

Linder, Doris H. (2001). "Equality for Women. The Contribution of Scandinavian Women at the United Nations 1946-66", in *Scandinavian Studies, vol. 73 nr. 2.*

Lode, Veslemøy & évold, Camilla (eds.) (2000). *Feminisjon.* Oslo, Sosialistisk Opplysningsforbund.

Miller, Carol (1991). "Women in international relations? The Debate in inter-war Britain." In Grant, Rebecca & Newland, Kathleeen (eds). *Gender and international relations.* Open Milton Keynes University Press.

Miller, Carol (1994)."Geneva – The key to Equality: Inter-war Feminists and the League of Nations. " *Women's History Review*, vol. 3.

Naryan, Uma & Harding, Sandra (eds.) (2000). *Decentering the Center: Philosophy for a Multicultural, Postconial and Feminist World.* Indiana University Press.

Norrman Skugge, Linda, Olsson, Belinda & Zilg, Brita (1999). *Fittstim.* Bokförlaget DN.

Nussbaum, Martha (1999), *Sex and Social Justice.* Oxford University Press

Rimmen Nielsen, Hanne (2001). "Den hvide slavehandel. Bekæmpelsen af handel med kvinder 1900 –1950." In *Kvinder, Køn og Forskning* vol. 3.

Rupp, Laila (1997). *Worlds of Women, The Making of an International Women's Movement.* Princeton University Press.

Rönnblom, Malin (2002). *A Room of One's Own. Women's Organising Meets Established Politics.* Umeå University.

Saarinen, Aino, Römer Christensen, Hilda & Halsaa, Beatrice (2000) (eds.). *Women's Movement and Internationalisation: The "Third" Wave?* University of Oulu. 82/2000.

Sandnes, Cathrine, Nossum, Beate & Smith-Erichsen, Christina (eds.) (1999). *Matriark.* Oslo, Gyldendal

Silliman, Jael (1999). Expanding Civil Society: Shrinking Political Spaces – The case of women's Non governmental Organisations'. In *Social Politics,* spring edition. Oxford University Press.

Skov, Leonora Christina (2002). *De røde sko. Feminisme nu.* Tiderne Skifter. København.

Solheim, Hilde C. & Vaagland, Helle (eds.) (1999). *Råtekst,* Oslo, Aschehoug

Stoltz, Pauline (2000). *About Being (T)Here and Making a Difference – Black Women and the Paradox of Visibility.* Lund Political Studies 115. Lund: Department of Political Science.

Sørensen, Niels Ulrik (ed.) (2000). *Pikstormerne.* København, Informations Forlag.

von Braunmühl, Claudia (2002). "Mainstreaming gender – a critical revision", in Braig, Marianne & Wölte, Sonja. *Common Ground or Mutual Exclusion.* London, New York, Zed Books.

Wikander, Ulla (1994). "En utopisk Jämlikhet. Internationella kvinnokongresser 1878-1914" in Ulla Wikander & Ulla Manns *Det evigt kvinnliga. En historia om förändring.* (Stockholm/ 2001 Lund), Tidens Förlag.

Yuval-Davis, Nira (2000). "Ethnicity, Gender Relations and Multiculturalism." In Werbner, Pnina & Tariq Modood (eds). *Debating Cultural Hybridity. Multi-Cultural Identities and the Politics of Anti-Racism*. London and New Jersey, Zed Books.

Notes

1   Skov: (2002).
2   A selection of the flow of publications ranging from personal evidences to scholarly analyses affiliated with the third wave:
    Norway: Sandnes, Nossum & Smith-Erichsen (1999); Solheim & Vaagland (1999); Lode & évold (2000)
    Sverige: Norrman Skugge, Olsson & Zilg (1999)
    Iceland: Björnsdóttir, Sturludóttir & Hauksdóttir (2000)
    Denmark: Skov (2002); Kraul (2000); Frank Goth, MacLean, Myong Petersen & Schelin (2000)
    In Denmark young men have also participated in the launching of this new media wave, see Sørensen (2000); Holm, Bisgaard Munk & Thelle (2000)
    USA: Heywood & Drake (1997); and web-based manifests such as Tamara Straus: A manifesto for Third Wave Feminism; Krista Jacob: Engendering change: What's up with third wave feminsm. In Sexing the political. A Journal of Third Wave Feminists on Sexuality.
3   Saarinen, Römer Christensen & Halsaa (2000). Among the dissertations were: Chiara Bertone: Whose Needs? Women's organisations claims on Child Care in Italy and Denmark. FREJA, Aalborg University (2002), Stoltz (2000), Rönnblom: Women's Organising Meets Established Politics. Umeå University. (2002). Airi Markkanen: Ethnicity in the Finnish Romany Women's Life course. Joensuu University, (2003) Finland.
4   Briskin (1999). For differences in the Nordic profiles see Bergqvist *et al.* (1999). For research highlighting the resistance, see Gustafsson *et al.* (1997)
5   E.g. Dahlerup & Gulli (1985); Dahlerup (1985); Andreasen *et al.* (1991); Bergqvist *et al.* (1999)
6   Dahlerup and Stoltz in this volume
7   Laila Rupp (1997), Miller (1994)
8   Wikander (1994/2001); Rimmen Nielsen (2001)
9   Rupp (1997). 37
10 Miller (1991). 64
11 Rupp (1997). 139-140
12 Rupp (1997), Miller (1994), Christensen in this volume.
13 The contributions of Scandinavian women during this process is discussed by Linder (2001).
14 Linder (2001). 207
15 The role of the UN system is elaborated in Milwertz, Zhang, Halsaa, Kristmundsdottir, Krook, Christensen (all in this volume).
16 Silliman (1999).
17 Transversal politics, a model of political work named by Italian feminists that reflects anti-racist feminist analysis and practices. See Nira Yuval-Davis (2000)
18 Cf. Krook in this volume
19 Nussbaum (1999); Naryan & Harding (2000), Briskin (1999). See also review essay by Kathryn Trevenen: *Global Feminism and the "problem" of Culture*. www.*muse.jhuy.edu/journals/theory &_event/v005/5.1r_trevenen*. html.

20 Saarinen in this volume
21 Halsaa in this volume, also Bergman (1999)
22 Bergman (2000)
23 Halsaa and Zhang in this volume. The phrasing is from von Braunmühl (2002).

Part I

Construction and Deconstruction of Feminisms

CHAPTER 1

Contextualising and Contrasting Feminisms

Studying Women's Movements from a Cross-country Perspective

Solveig Bergman

Today, over thirty years since the resurgence of feminism, there is no doubt that the new women's movement has been one of the most important social movements in the post-World War II Western world. This movement has made a lasting impression on social, political and cultural life particularly in Europe and the United States. One result of this development has been an increasing scholarly interest in women's movements. However, relatively few attempts have been made to study these movements across national borders.[1] This is hardly surprising as such, since comparative studies face major theoretical, methodological and empirical difficulties. In this article I want to highlight some of these challenges on the basis of my experiences of a research project on the autonomous feminist movements in Finland and West Germany in the 1970s and 1980s.[2] I argue that a *contextual* and *contrastive* approach, where two (or more) case studies are used as frames of reference for each other, provides a fruitful methodological basis for a comparison of feminisms and women's movements in different political and cultural settings.

Irrespective of the focus being on a single movement or on two or more movements that are compared, certain methodological issues are common for all empirical studies of social movements. On the whole, such a study is a complicated task, as the movements are in a constant flux, changing in both structures and contents. The choice of the units to study is difficult, as movements often lack formal movement organisations and a movement is more than a sum of its organisations. Which period of time to study is another problem. Social movements experience ups and downs, expansion and stagnation. Their goals and strategies can change over time. Phases of self-reflection and outward going, spectacular actions take turns. The research methods used, the level of abstraction and the time-span of the analysis determine to a great extent which aspects of the movement are made visible. Therefore, no researcher can unambiguously explain or interpret the emergence and development of a movement. Moreover, there is reason to be sceptical of such generalising explanations. Different scholars bring up divergent results and analyses according to what material they choose to support their theoretical perspectives. As such, movement texts and narratives can always be viewed as representations or constructions.

Social Movements as Constructions

Against this background, it is understandable that constructivist and narrative approaches have become popular in movement scholarship.[3] It has, for example, been argued that a social movement is always a political construction: a reality produced in speech. "The movement exists, when it is *claimed* to exist and *believed* to exist".[4] From this viewpoint, the movement cannot be reduced to a simple "essence". A narrative can only claim to be a "thesis of the past". "Wie es eigentlich gewesen ist", is impossible to know, as Tapani Suominen[5] has phrased it. That is a question of interpretation by the researcher and/or the activists. Movement narratives focus on specifically chosen fragments from "reality". Different parts of the movement compete in defining and interpreting the movement. The movement can be seen as many narratives, which are all in a "move".[6]

I share the viewpoint of those who argue that knowledge is *partial, situated* and *constructed* rather than extracted from "social reality".[7] In this respect, I have received inspiration from post-structuralism and post-modernism. Thus, my research can be regarded as my particular narration or interpretation of two forms of Western feminism of the 1970s and 1980s. I have filtered the social "reality" through my theoretical framework and my particular positional starting points. In a way, I have produced my research object when choosing the material and methods. I have decided what information and material to gather, it has been my choice to decide how to analyse it and what aspects to focus upon.[8]

Yet, the interpretations are by no means arbitrary. The movements are not simply "imagined formations", produced by scholars in a textual form. A contextualisation is necessary, since relativism always lurks behind constructivism. It is not sufficient that merely scholars decide whether and when a social movement has existed or ceased to exist or which developmental phases it went through. The interpretations and conceptualisations of the actors are also needed. However, it is obvious that a selection has taken place also on behalf of the movements themselves; some phenomena are not reported upon, some groups may have left behind more material than others, etc. For these reasons, I do not believe that all movement narratives and texts have the same value or weight. Source criticism has to be maintained, although the interpretations of the sources may vary.

To reflect upon the relationship between the researcher and the researched phenomenon (or people) is always important in empirical sociology. In my view, it is valuable to possess own observations and experiences of feminist movements and to be able to use this knowledge for a scholarly study of feminism as a social movement. I am aware that a temporal and emotional distance to the research object – required by traditional social scientists – is hardly fulfilled in such a case. Yet I believe that closeness to the phenomenon studied can give several advantages and is often a prerequisite for a researcher who wishes to approach the movement and understand it. However, the familiarity and involvement have to be balanced with a critical and reflective distance not only to the movement, but also to oneself as a scholar. Naturally, when research focuses on societal and political phenomena that from a time perspective – or from an emotional point of view – are close to the researcher, one has to reflect on the existence of certain feelings, prejudices, strong opinions and pre-views, including one's own. It is therefore important to expose one's "everyday" knowledge and experiences for a critical introspection in order to reduce the risks of biased and hasty conclusions.

Comparisons in sociological and social movement research

Analyses encompassing more than one movement provide a more differentiated picture of recent or current feminisms than studies that are restricted to one national setting. Comparisons aim at confirming general features and patterns, but attempt also to make national variations visible. Through comparison, empirical phenomena that appear to be unified, such as the women's movement, can be reconstructed. Comparison is often a good means for developing and generating theory. Thereby, the validity in the interpretations that derive from studies of a single society can be either confirmed or challenged. In addition, cross-national or cross-cultural studies help to separate the impact and the effects of the women's movements from those social changes that would have taken place in society irrespective of the movements. Furthermore, such studies are crucial for the development of a stronger empirical basis for social movement research, which, in my view, has a tendency to be overly conceptual and theoretical. In sum, comparative work does not necessarily result in "better" knowledge than research limited to a single country, but it leads to a different kind of knowledge and, hopefully, to new research questions.

Since the 1980s, empirically oriented studies in social movement research have become more common.[9] Simultaneously, also social movement scholarship has witnessed a "methodological turn" with an increasing emphasis on qualitatively oriented research methods. For example, in-depth interviews, ethnography, textual and discourse analyses, as well as memory-work and life-history research are used to provide an understanding of the motivational, consciousness-related and discursive processes within the movement and among movement activists. These approaches throw light on the subjective side of social life, but can simultaneously offer tools to understand whole sets of social and discursive relationships and processes on both meso- and macro-levels. In recent scholarship, social movements have often been interpreted as social constructions. Thus, issues around collective identity, cognitive and cultural praxis as well as the symbols and rituals of the movements have increasingly come into focus.[10]

Although thinking in comparative terms is inherent in classical sociology (e.g., Durkheim, Weber), research that explicitly focuses on two or more objects of analysis (e.g., countries or states) has attracted renewed sociological interest only in recent decades. In particular, large-scale and standardised survey-based studies based on representative samples have become common. This kind of macro-sociological and quantitatively oriented comparison is normally conducted for a large number of countries. Technically such studies can be sophisticated and may provide a lot of empirical data at an aggregate level. Yet, methodological and theoretical matters are often of a secondary interest.[11] Comparative research seems to need a reorienting by means of the application of approaches and stimuli derived from qualitatively oriented research, including epistemological debates on science, scientific research and scientific "truth".[12]

Comparative studies based on qualitative methods have as yet been sparse, despite the general upsurge in such methods within the social sciences. One reason for this situation relates to the difficulties of combining a comparative or cross-national approach with a qualitatively oriented methodology. As qualitative methods do not aim at empirical generalisations and do not use traditional sampling methods, they do not meet strictly formulated conventional criteria for the representativeness of the data. Yet such criteria have traditionally been considered important in comparative research. On the whole, I believe that sociologists could gain inspiration from the way, for instance, historians and anthropologists have conducted cross-national comparisons that embrace whole societies by their use of synthesising and holistic approaches.

As such, cross-national comparisons may not constitute major or new methodological challenges for sociological research. The basic principles of the research strategies and methods commonly employed do not differ from general research methods. More problems arise at later stages in the research process, particularly with regard to the question of how to evaluate and interpret the similarities and differences in the countries being compared. The answer to this question depends upon the perspective and the analytical level used to view the countries concerned. The way in which research is framed influences both what is revealed and what is concealed.[13] Thus, the outcomes of a comparative study are affected by, *inter alia*, whether the emphasis is set on the differences or the similarities between the units that are compared.

For example, if the five Nordic countries are compared with the great variety of countries across the globe, it is obvious that they appear relatively alike at an aggregate and unified level and tend to constitute a cluster of their own. Examples of studies of this kind can be found within welfare state research and research on political systems as well as in research on gender equality. But, if another perspective is chosen for the research, the picture of a unified, homogenous Norden may change. A recent example of such a shift is provided by the authors of the book *Equal Democracies? Gender and Politics in the Nordic Countries*.[14] Here the focus is on inter-Nordic variations in political citizenship and mobilisation, the gender equality apparatus and the organisation of child care and family policies.

If the researcher compares units – for example, social movements – that are as similar as possible, she or he may hope to reduce the number of plausible explanations to any differences that are found. If, however, units that are as different as possible are chosen, the researcher may wish to differentiate between the "national logic" and the "inherent logic" of the movements.[15] Both of these strategies have their advantages and disadvantages. Which type of comparison is ultimately chosen, depends on the perspective chosen for the research. Some researchers think that every society is more or less unique and thus there would be little use in making comparisons, whereas others claim that all societies are amenable to comparison with the help of universalistic explanatory models.

As argued elsewhere in this volume,[16] the concept and metaphor of "waves" may not be appropriate for comparisons of women's movements across national borders, since the phases of development of these movements vary considerably, at least on a global scale. Moreover, the usage of this metaphor tends to direct our attention primarily to the expansive phases in the movement's trajectories. As a consequence, the more silent periods between the crests may receive too little attention. Yet, as Drude Dahlerup[17] argues, the notion of "waves" is as such in no conflict with the thesis of the historical *continuity* of feminism. Moreover, it also refers to *change* in respect of the movement's life-cycle. According to Dahlerup, there has been one continuous feminist movement since the latter part of the 19th century (in the West). In this period phases of expansion and stagnation, visibility and strength, have alternated. In other words, the movement is characterised by recurring waves, including both peaks and doldrums. Likewise, Ute Gerhard[18] talks about the "long waves" of the continuous international women's movement, but she also emphasises the need to reassess the more quiet periods in the history of feminism.

Feminism(s) and women's movements

One problem faced by comparative studies deals with the (non)equivalence of concepts, that is, whether the units or properties that are being compared in different countries or settings are *equivalent in their significance*. The question is whether the concepts and their operationalisation hold an equivalent meaning for the people, actors or participants in the countries concerned. Also, different years and time-intervals may have different meanings for the countries and the activities being compared. Establishing credible equivalence is difficult, since meaning is contextual. The missing equivalence of concepts can be a problem also for countries that resemble each other in several respects.[19]

The problem of translating a concept from one cultural context into another is particularly evident when the social phenomenon to be compared is as elusive as the *women's movement* or *feminism*. The understanding of such concepts varies across national and cultural boundaries. Even if there were a more or less shared collective identity *within* the movements as to what it means to "be a feminist", there may be different interpretations of the concept in the wider societies in question. As a consequence, the notions of feminism and women's movement have to be understood and interpreted within the context of the culture in which they are used.[20] Thus, in crossnational research in particular, "feminism" has to be approached flexibly, in terms set by the national, political and cultural contexts.

The definitions of a contested concept such as feminism depend on the circumstances and the outlook of those who make the definitions. Gisela Kaplan[21] has pointed out that although the term feminism came into use in some European countries in the 19th century, it has not been common everywhere. In some places it has had negative and pejorative connotations. Moreover, the definitions have varied over time and geographically. During the 19th century, the term was mostly used in respect of middle-class based liberal feminism. More recently, in the United States, feminism has often been used as a collective term for several orientations, that is, more or less as a synonym for the women's movement.[22] In several European countries, the definition making is complicated by the fact that many of those who are in favour of gender equality resist being labelled as "feminists".[23] In both Finland and West Germany, for instance, feminism was for a long time associated in the public mind with radical-feminists and was either seen as a synonym for "man-haters" or as a glorification of biological and cultural womanhood.

In my view, three characteristics tie different types of feminism together. Firstly, that gender is viewed as a primary, but not necessarily the only determining influence upon women's lives and as a way of structuring and organising society and cultural life. Secondly, that the existence of a gender-specific subordination or the systematic and institutionalised nature of discrimination against women is recognised. Finally, that the legitimacy of the present gender power order is questioned and collective organising is seen as a necessary strategy in order to break down the gendered distribution of power and resources. The parallels of the latter two elements to the definition used by e.g. Nancy Cott are obvious.[24] Yet my conceptualisation of feminism encompasses, more explicitly than Cott's, both definitions where women are seen as one social category or grouping, i.e. their commonalities are emphasised, and contexts where gender interacts with, for instance, class, ethnicity, "race" or sexual preference.[25] Similarly, both "feminism" and "women's movement" have often been used in all-embracing ways to encompass any and all activities and organisations that relate to "women" and the aim of improving women's life-situation, often including both equality- and difference oriented concepts of feminism. Other definitions have been narrower, restricting the concept to some factions of the movement, either on ideological or organisational-strategic grounds (e.g., radical feminism; equality feminism; autonomous feminism etc.).

I argue that irrespective of whether a broad or narrow concept is employed, it is difficult to confine the concept to well-defined empirical entities. Rather, the metaphor of a "movement" refers to a highly elusive social phenomenon or process that is in a continuous flux. I want to emphasise that the notion of a movement is rather an analytical than an empirical concept. The movement cannot be reduced to the sum of organised individuals, groups or organisations. The fluid and "diffuse" elements of the movement, like its cultural and discursive expressions, informal networks as well as all those individuals who carry the concerns of the movement into other settings, have to be included in the concept. Thus the movement is found in the discourses, identities and "politics of everyday resistance" of the participants, rather than in a set of particular organisations.[26] Such a conceptualisation of feminism includes all those forms of activity that contribute to the emergence of a new *collective identity* amongst women and a consciousness of the political relevance of gender.[27]

When the women's movement is not reduced to its organisational expressions, the continuity of feminism is perhaps easier to identify, not least in those countries where the women's rights organisations ceased to exist after their main goals (e.g., suffrage) had been achieved at the beginning of the last century. In Germany, the seizure of power by the Nazis in 1933 meant an end to the organised feminist movement and the political work for women's rights. Yet, as German feminist scholars argue, the women's movement did not enter the "doldrums" and stay there until the 1970s.[28] Although the period of 1933-49 resulted in a break with cultural and democratic traditions, many scholars are in the process of re-evaluating the "silent" post-war decades in the history of German feminism.[29] Likewise, a cultural-discursive analysis may show that Finnish feminism has been more vibrant than suggested by a traditional analysis of the movement's organisations. Thus, arguments about scarce movement activity in Finland have perhaps more to do with what scholars have focussed upon than with the movements themselves. Finnish feminism may have been vigorous in ways that scholars have not always recognised.[30]

Structural approaches in social movement research

Structural approaches have been popular in comparative movement research aiming at highlighting differences and variation in movement activity across national borders. For example, emphasis has been placed on the ways in which the movements are embedded in historical, socio-economic, political, cultural and discursive settings. These nation-specific features are considered to have an impact on the development of both the ideological visions and the political strategies of the movements. The popularity of such approaches is hardly surprising as such, since structural and macro-level analyses of social movements are undoubtedly easier to place into a traditional comparative framework than, for instance, constructivist approaches. Thus it has been common to estimate how powerful the consequences of a society's structural features are. Often the focus has been on the ways in which, for instance, political and socio-economic conditions, welfare state structures and society's gender order shape the relationship between women's movements and the state.[31]

The concept of *political opportunity structures*, as part of the political process approach within social movement research, is considered particularly useful and suitable for cross-national comparisons of the emergence and development of social movements.[32] This approach focuses on the interaction of social movements and institutionalised politics. Its starting point is that movements are shaped by the broader set of political opportunities and constraints unique to the national context in which they are embedded. This tradition contains both case studies of individual movements or protest cycles and cross-national studies of the same movement in different national contexts. Yet the conceptualisations of the "political opportunity structures" vary. Some scholars emphasise the structural and more static institutional aspects, while others focus on the more dynamic and conjunctural aspects such as public policy and political discourse.[33]

The approach based upon the concept of political opportunity structures has its limits. In particular, I wish to point out three problems. Firstly, this line of theorising fails to address all types and aspects of movement activity. It is primarily focussed on socio-political movements that target the state and view the formal political arena as the site of challenge. Thus, it may be less relevant for socio-cultural movements (or, the culturally oriented parts of a movement). Secondly, the movements are not only tied to the political culture of the country concerned and its set of nationally shaped political opportunity structures but they are also engaged in a *struggle to change these*. It is therefore important to combine an interactionist approach – including the movement's impact upon the polity – with a political opportunity approach. Thirdly, the notion of external opportunity structures has to be expanded to cover also *cultural* and *social opportunities*. Women's collective actions remain underplayed in social movement research, if this research fails to recognise the gendered power order and the significance of the welfare and gender political models for the collective mobilisation of women. Likewise, the cultural dimension in the range of external opportunities is important to take into account in an analysis of factors and contexts that facilitate or dampen the activities of feminist movements.[34]

Contextual(ised) and contrastive comparisons

In cross-national work the comparison can either be conducted over time or over space. Although the focus in my research was on recent or current societal and cultural specificities, including the gendered power structures that affect the shaping of feminism in West Germany and Finland, I attempted to some extent to combine a *spatial* and a *temporal* approach. In this way, I tried to identify both those variations in the movements that are tied to specific historical and cultural contexts and the more persistent or recurrent themes in feminism. Cross-time analyses have been important for that part of women's movement research where the *historical continuity* of women's collective protest and resistance has been emphasised. Obviously, feminist movements are not conditioned merely by present opportunities and constraints, but also by historically specific developments and social processes. In research emphasising the continuity of feminist protest, the post-war feminist struggle against patriarchal structures is not considered to be a "new" social phenomenon that is grounded in the structure of late capitalist societies. Therefore, the "new social movement approach", according to which feminist activity represents a qualitatively different conflict line in society and has grown out of the same ground as, for example, environmental and alternative life-style movements, has been challenged by feminists. Instead, they have focused upon important similarities between "old" and "new" feminism.[35]

In my research on Finnish and (West) German feminist movements, I treated the two case studies as *contextual* and *contrastive* frames of reference for each other.[36] There are obvious advantages in observing a country as an "outsider". Firstly, the distance makes it easier to see the general lines, and not merely the details. Secondly, as a consequence, one may see also one's "own" country with "foreign" eyes, at least partially. In fact, looking at both societies from the "outside in" makes it easier to understand possible national particularities. A comparison allows the mechanisms at work in each society to emerge more clearly, challenging what is often taken for granted.[37]

Feminists in Åbo, Finland, marching for peace. 1979. (Photo: Bror Rönnholm)

I regarded the movements in Finland and Germany as "strategic cases" with a particular interest for my theoretical aims. The Finnish case provides an example of a political project that has largely aimed at integration into state policies. In many ways, Finnish feminism has been linked to the existing politics of the welfare state. As a Nordic country, Finland has been considered to be open for feminist concerns and to have transformed them to "state feminism".[38] Yet the country seems to be less well known in international studies than the Scandinavian countries (Denmark, Norway and Sweden). Moreover, it has a political and social history that in many ways differs from its Nordic neighbours. By contrast, West Germany represents a case where substantial parts of the feminist movement defended a markedly separatist strategy of "autonomy" throughout the 1970s and a large part of the 1980s. Moreover, the relationship between the state and social movements has historically been strained.[39] As a result of the Anglo-American dominance in current social sciences, including feminist research, West German feminism is fairly unknown outside the German-speaking community.

Furthermore, I wanted partially to deconstruct the prevailing strong-rooted beliefs about "Finnish women's achieved equality" and "German women's subordination". Alongside with the other Nordic countries Finland is associated with the image of being a country that is in the forefront of gender equality, with strong, emancipated women, who were the first in Europe to gain the vote, women with a high degree of political participation and full-time employment. In many ways Finland is a Janus-faced country. I claim that although Finland has truly been a pioneer in many equality issues, it is also a country with deep-seated patriarchal and sexist structures and cultural patterns, perhaps more so than in the neighbouring Scandinavian countries.[40] Contrasting Finland with West Germany, another capitalist, industrialised country with a welfare state structure, but at the same time having a more active and radical feminist movement, is therefore a fruitful approach. Simultaneously I wanted to challenge the much cherished image of West German women being tied to the "three Ks" (*Kinder, Kirche, Küche*), and a gender order that in many ways prevents women's emancipation. Particularly in the 1980s, German feminism was an identifiable force in public life. Especially, there was a strong push towards promoting women's position in politics.[41]

Since the scope of my study was two case studies that were used to shed light on each other, their contextually defined differences were particularly highlighted. Similarly, since the focus in my research is on autonomous, grassroots oriented feminism and not on formal-hierarchical women's organisations, the differences between these two forms of feminism are easily polarised. I am aware of the fact that the outcomes of my study can be affected by these kinds of framing. The concept of a *political field* is one way of enlarging and complementing such an analysis.[42] I find that the division between social movements and political institutions is often too sharply drawn in social movement theorising. I use the notion of the "political field" in order to emphasise the movements' interaction with other forms of political organisations both within civil society and within the state system. Through this kind of concept, the specific organisational patterns and strategic decisions (e.g., whether to organise autonomously or not) of feminist movements can be examined within the context of the localised political field. In particular, in the Nordic countries there has been a continuous interplay between social movements and institutionalised political organisations. But, also in West Germany of the 1980s a similar development has been evident.

Cultural Diffusion

I find it crucial to include a discussion not only about the historical-cultural continuity of feminism, but also about cross-country similarities in present time. Next, I will therefore discuss the importance of the *cultural diffusion* of ideas and strategies across national borders.

The current emphasis in cross-national women's movement research appears to be on contextually defined differences and variety.[43] This is, to a large extent, the case also in my study. However, this approach is in clear contrast to earlier feminist thinking and scholarship, in which women's movements across national borders were largely considered to have common ideological goals, strategies, organisational forms and slogans.[44] Today, this kind of sense of commonality is challenged by, for instance, representatives of identity politics, difference feminism, black feminism, lesbian feminism as well as post-modern feminists.

Yet, an emphasis on variation and diversity easily leads us to overlook the striking affinities and parallels that exist between various forms of feminisms and women's movements across countries with respect to their discourses, strategies and ways of organising, action repertoires and trajectories. Certainly, these commonalities are partly due to the similar processes of social change and modernisation, but they are also a result of the *diffusion* of cultural ideas, innovations and social currents across national borders. Cultural diffusion often takes place within internationally shaped *protest waves* or *cycles*, often in combination with national stimuli. Social movement activists in different countries react simultaneously to a specific theme, a perceived social problem or grievance, with movement mobilisation as a result.

Social movements tend to borrow specific elements from similar groups and collectivities, and adapt such features to their specific situation and context. The "receiving" movements tend to transform the content from the "sending" movement, in other words, ideas are "adapted" rather than "adopted". The processes of diffusion take place through formal and informal links, for instance, through communication between movement organisations or individual activists or through indirect transfers of information that are filtered through mass media and literature.[45]

Obviously, the media channel has become increasingly important for social movements since the 1990s, especially through modern information technology and the Internet.

Feminist protest does not automatically flow from one country to another. Contextual factors seem to have an impact on the diffusion. Giugni[46] has suggested that cross-national diffusion occurs to the extent that the political opportunity structures are favourable to a movement's mobilisation. Movement activity is unlikely to spread to a country where the political opportunities are weak. In addition, certain organisational and cultural conditions have to be met. Cross-national diffusion in the social movement arena takes either the form of mutual involvement in the process or is a kind of "intentional cultural borrowing".[47] The latter form of diffusion can relate to factors of cultural dominance. For example, the United States had implications for several of the new social movements and the political discourses in Western Europe in the 1960s and 1970s. In fact, several features of the new feminism in Europe during its first phases may partly be associated to the ways in which these themes were articulated and established in the United States and framed in the media there.[48]

Although international diffusion processes provide one promising explanation for cross-country similarities between social movements, little theorising has hitherto been carried out on cultural diffusion within movement research.[49] Similarly, research on other forms of inter-movement links has, both within a national context and beyond it, been scarce. This theoretical gap is in contrast with empirical evidence on patterns of interaction and collective learning processes among social movements.[50] Conny Roggeband[51] has suggested that such similarities may be viewed as signs of the fact that there has been a global feminist movement operating, albeit with a variety of country-specific manifestations.[52]

Certainly, it is important to consider the growing permeability of the national borders and the impact of cross-national interaction on feminist organising. Large parts of movement cultures are to be seen as a result of cultural processes of communication that transcend national borders. As a result, it has become increasingly difficult to define "European", "Nordic", "German" or "Finnish" feminism in unified and clearly delineated terms. The question as to whether feminist theorising and political practice can be considered to have a "national" character, constitutes a major challenge to research on contemporary or recent women's movements. Is it plausible to identify feminisms according to national borders? More specifically, does feminism have national characteristics with respect to ideologies, strategies or political interaction? Or, does it have the character of a global movement, which is capable of shaping similarities with respect to the content and forms of the movements in different countries? Should "Finnish feminism" and "German feminism" preferably be viewed as discursive phenomena resulting from a historical and cultural construction?[53] Already when research questions are formulated, images of national differences (motivated or not) tend to be constructed or confirmed. On the other hand, it can hardly be denied that culturally specific features exist. At least they are, in their own right, efficient and powerful images. In sum, also my research (re)shapes contextually specific patterns and characteristics for the feminist movements in the two countries.

Towards transnational feminism?

Cross-country comparisons easily obscure diversities *within* the countries, such as regional differences. It is somewhat paradoxical that at the same time as feminist research increasingly focuses on diversity and variation or the local and the contextual, such features are easily disguised in comparative studies. I agree with Linda Briskin[54] that there is a tendency in comparative texts to produce "ideal types" in order to contrast and, for instance, to set up dichotomies between two countries.

Another potential paradox is worth noting. This concerns the argument that comparisons, by transcending the narrow scopes of the nation-states, contribute to diminishing the cultural differences and thereby strengthen the feelings of a uniform, homogeneous and global community. Yet comparative research, it is also argued, can be used to emphasise culturally unique features in individual countries. This trend has because of – or despite – internationalisation become more common in a world increasingly characterised by *glocalisation,* or a combination of the "global" and the "local".[55]

The social forces behind globalisation have contributed to the transformation of nation-states in the direction of both supra- and sub-national systems. As a consequence, it may become less relevant in future to view the nation-states as the primary or most "natural" units of comparison. Women's movements are in a process of developing networks and communities of interest across the international arena. Scholars are becoming increasingly aware of the international and transnational challenges and impact of social movements.[56] Processes of globalisation and internationalisation are transforming our cognitive map. Even when explicit or systematic comparisons across national borders are not carried out but the study is limited to domestic phenomena, a comparative approach is often, implicitly or tentatively, employed. Yet, whether it is possible to formulate general and universal categories that are not potentially exclusive is an open question. Social movement research, for example, has a tendency to consolidate Western and "white" hegemony. As shown by Pauline Stoltz[57] this is certainly true also for research on women's movements and feminisms.

References

Anttonen, Anneli (1997). *Feminismi ja sosiaalipolitiikka*, Tampere, Tampere University Press.

Basu, Amrita (ed.). (1995*). The Challenge of Local Feminisms: Women's Movements in Global Perspective*, Boulder, Westview Press.

Bergman, Solveig (1999). "Women in New Social Movements", Bergqvist, Christina et al. (eds.), *Equal Democracies? Gender and Politics in the Nordic Countries*, Oslo, Scandinavian University Press, p. 97-117.

Bergman, Solveig (2002). *The Politics of Feminism: Autonomous Feminist Movements in Finland and West Germany from the 1960s to the 1980s*, Åbo, Åbo Akademi University Press.

Bergqvist, Christina et al. (eds.). (1999*). Equal Democracies? Gender and Politics in the Nordic Countries*, Oslo, Scandinavian University Press.

Bertaux, Daniel (1990). "Oral history approaches to a international social movement". éyen, Else (ed*.), Comparative Methodology: Theory and Practice in International Social Research*, London, International Sociological Association & SAGE, p. 151-171.

Briskin, Linda & Eliasson, Mona (eds.). (1999*). Women's Organizing and Public Policy in Canada and Sweden*, Montreal, McGill-Queen's University Press.

Briskin, Linda (1999). "Mapping women's organizing in Sweden and Canada: Some thematic considerations". Briskin, Linda & Eliasson, Mona (eds.), *Women's Organizing and Public Policy in Canada and Sweden*. Montreal, McGill-Queen's University Press, p. 3-47.

Camauër, Leonor (2000). *Feminism, Citizenship and the Media: An Ethnographic Study of Identity Processes Within Four Women's Associations*. Department of Journalism, Media and Communication, Stockholm University.

Chamberlayne, Prue (1993). "Women and the state: Changes in roles and rights in France, West Germany, Italy and Britain, 1970-1990". Lewis, Jane (ed.): *Women and Social Policies in Europe: Work, Family and the State*. Aldershot, Edward Elgar, p.170-193.

Dackweiler, Regina (1995). *Ausgegrenzt und eingemeindet. Die neue Frauenbewegung im Blick der Sozialwissenschaften*, Münster, Verlag Westfälisches Dampfboot.

Dahlerup, Drude (2000). "Continuity and waves in the feminist movement". Saarinen, Aino, Rømer Christensen, Hilda & Halsaa, Beatrice (eds.), Women's Movement and Internationalisation: The "Third Wave"? Report from the Faculty of Education, University of Oulu, no. 82, p. 22-52.

della Porta, Donatella & Diani, Mario (1999). *Social Movements: An Introduction*, Oxford, Blackwell.

della Porta, Donatella & Rucht, Dieter (1995). Left-Libertarian Movements in Context: A Comparison of Italy and West Germany, 1965-1990. Jenkins, J. Craig & Klandermans, Bert (ed.): *The Politics of Social Protest: Comparative Perspectives on States and Social Movements*, London, UCL Press, p. 229-272.

Diani, Mario & Eyerman, Ron (eds.). (1992). *Studying Collective Action*, London, Sage.

Eyerman, Ron & Jamison, Andrew (1991). *Social Movements: A Cognitive Perspective*, Polity Press, Cambridge.

Ferree, Myra Marx (1987). "Equality and autonomy: Feminist politics in the United States and West Germany." Katzenstein, Mary Fainsod & Mueller, Carol McClurg (eds.), *The Women's Movements of the United States and Western Europe*, Philadelphia, Temple University Press, p. 172-195.

Ferree, Myra Marx (1990). "Gleichheit und Autonomie: Probleme feministicher Politik". Gerhard, Ute, Jansen, Mechtild, Maihofer, Andrea, Schmid, Pia & Schultz, Irmgard (eds.): *Differenz und Gleichheit: Menschenrechte haben (k)ein Geschlecht*, Frankfurt/M., Ulrike Helmer Verlag, p. 283-299.

Gerhard, Ute (1992). "Westdeutsche Frauenbewegung: Zwischen Autonomie und dem Recht auf Gleichheit". *Feministische Studien* no. 2, p. 35-55.

Gerhard, Ute (1999). *Atempause: Feminismus als demokratisches Projekt*, Frankfurt/M., Fischer Taschenbuch Verlag.

Giugni, Marco G. (1995). "The cross-national diffusion of protest". Kriesi, Hanspeter et al. (eds.), *New Social Movements in Western Europe: A Comparative Analysis*, London, UCL Press.

Hyvärinen, Matti (1994). *Viimeiset taistot*, Tampere, Vastapaino.

Jenson, Jane (1985). "Struggling for identity: The women's movement and the state in Western Europe", *West European Politics*, vol. 8, p. 5-18.

Johnstons, Hank & Klandermans, Bert (eds.). (1995). *Social Movements and Culture*, London, UCL Press.

Julkunen, Raija (1994). "Esipuhe: suomalainen takaisku?" Faludi, Susan: *Takaisku: Julistamaton sota naisia vastaan*, Helsinki, Kääntöpiiri [orig. Backlash: The Undeclared War Against Women], p. 7-21.

Julkunen, Raija (1997). "Naisruumiin oikeudet". Jokinen, Eeva (ed.): *Ruumiin siteet: Kirjoituksia eroista, järjestyksistä ja sukupuolesta*, Tampere, Vastapaino, p. 43-63.

Kaplan, Gisela (1992). *Contemporary Western Feminism*, London, UCL Press.

Kaplan, Gisela (1997). "Feminism and nationalism: The European case". West, Lois (ed.): *Feminist Nationalism*, London, Routledge, 3-40.

Katzenstein, Mary F. & Mueller, Carol M. (ed.) (1987). *The Women's Movements of the United States and Western Europe*. Philadelphia, Temple University Press.

Kriesi, Hanspeter, Koopmans, Ruud, Duyvendak, Jan Willem & Giugni, Marco. (1995). *New Social Movements in Western Europe: A Comparative Analysis*, London, UCL Press.

Lønnå, Elisabeth (2000). "Discussing waves in feminism". Saarinen, Aino, Rømer Christensen, Hilda & Halsaa, Beatrice: *Women's Movement and Internationalisation: The "Third Wave"?* Report from the Faculty of Education, University of Oulu, no. 82, p. 10-21.

Lovenduski, Joni (1997). "The integration of feminism into West European politics.". Rhodes, Martin, Heywood Paul & Wright, Vincent (eds.), *Developments in West European Politics*, London, Macmillan, p. 281-299.

Mansbridge, Jane (1995). "What is the feminist movement?" Ferree, Myra Marx & Martin, Patricia Yancey (eds.): *Feminist Organizations: Harvest of the New Women's Movement*, Philadelphia, Temple University Press, p. 27-34.

McAdam, Doug, McCarthy, John & Zald, Mayer N. (eds.) (1996): *Comparative Perspectives on Social Movements: Political Opportunities, Mobilizing Structures, and Cultural Framing*, Cambridge & New York, Cambridge University Press.

Melucci, Albert (1989*). Nomads of the Present: Social Movements and Individual Needs in Contemporary Society*, London, Century Hutchinson.

Morgan, Robyn (ed.). (1970*). Sisterhood is Global: The International Women's Movement Anthology*, New York, Anchor-Doubleday.

Mósesdóttir, Lilja (1999). "Breaking the boundaries: Women's encounter with the state". Christensen, Jens, Koistinen, Pertti & Kovalainen, Anne (eds*.): Working Europe: Reshaping European Employment Systems*, Aldershot, Ashgate, p. 97-135.

Offen, Karen (1988)."Defining feminism: A comparative historical approach". *Signs*, vol. 14, no. 1, p. 119-157.

éyen, Else (1990). "The imperfection of comparisons". éyen, Else (ed*.). Comparative Methodology: Theory and Practice in International Social Research*, London, International Sociological Association & SAGE, p. 1-18.

Ray, Raka (1998). "Women's movements and political fields: A comparison of two Indian cities". *Social Problems* 45:1, p. 21-36.

Robertson, Roland (1995). "Glocalisation: Time-space and homogeneity-heterogeneity". Featherstone, Mike, Lash, Scott and Robertson, Roland. *Global Modernities,* London, Sage, p. 25-42.

Roggeband, Conny (1996). *Is Sisterhood Global or Local? The Spread of Feminism Across Countries*. Paper presented to the Second European Conference on Social Movements, 2-5 October, Vittoria, Spain.

Rosenbeck, Bente (1998). "Nordic women's studies and gender research." von der Fehr, Drude, Jónasdóttir, Anna & Rosenbeck, Bente (eds.): *Is There a Nordic Feminism?* Cambridge, UCL Press, p. 344-357.

Rupp, Leila J. & Taylor, Verta (1991): "Women's culture and the continuity of the women's movement". Andreasen, Tayo et al. (eds.): *Moving On: New Perspectives on the Women's Movement*. Acta Jutlandica LXVII:1, Humanities series 66, Aarhus, Aarhus University Press, p. 68-89.

Scheuch, Erwin K. (1990). "The development of comparative research: Towards classical explanations". éyen, Else (ed.). *Comparative Methodology: Theory and Practice in International Social Research,* London*,* International Sociological Association & SAGE, p. 19-37.

Skocpol, Theda & Somers, Margaret (1980). "The uses of comparative history in macrosocial inquiry." *Comparative Studies in Society and History*: An International Quarterly, vol. 22, p. 174-195.

Snow, David A. & Benford, Robert B. (1999): "Alternative types of cross-national diffusion in the social movement arena". della Porta, Donatella, Kriesi, Hanspeter & Rucht, Dieter (eds.): *Social Movements in a Globalizing World*, London, Macmillan, p. 23-40.

Suominen, Tapani (1996). *"Verre enn Quislings hird": Metaforiska kamper i den offentliga debatten kring 1960- och 1970-talens student- och ungdomsradikalism i Norge, Finland och Västtyskland*. Unpublished doctoral thesis, University of Oslo.

Taylor, Verta & Whittier, Nancy (1995). "Analytical approaches to social movement culture: The culture of the women's movement". Johnston, Hank and Klandermans, Bert (eds.): *Social Movements and Culture*, London, UCL Press, p. 163-187.

Teune, Henry (1990). "Comparing countries: Lessons learned". Øyen, Else (ed.): *Comparative Methodology: Theory and Practice in International Social Research*, London, International Sociological Association & SAGE, p. 38-62.

Thörn, Håkan ((1997). *Modernitet, sociologi och sociala rörelser.* Monograph no. 62 from the Department of Sociology. Göteborg University: Göteborg.

Togeby, Lise. (1989). *Ens og forskellig. Graesrodsdeltagelse i Norden*, Politica, Aarhus.

Tyyskä, Vappu (1995). *The Politics of Caring and the Welfare State: The Impact of the Women's Movement on Child Care Policy in Canada and Finland, 1960-1990.* Annales Academiae Scientarium Fennicae: B: 277. Helsinki.

von Oerzen, Christine (1999): Women, Work and the State. Torstendahl, Rolf (ed.): *State Policy and Gender System in the Two German States and Sweden 1945-1989.* Opuscula Historica Upsaliensis 22. Department of History. University of Uppsala; Uppsala, p. 79-104.

Young, Stacey (1997*). Changing the Wor(l)ds: Discourse, Politics, and the Feminist Movement,* London, Routledge.

Notes

1 Recent studies with a comparative approach include, e.g., Kaplan (1992); Tyyskä (1995); Briskin & Eliasson (eds.,1999).
2 Bergman (2002).
3 E.g., Hyvärinen (1994); Suominen (1996); Thörn (1997); Camaüer (2000).
4 Hyvärinen (1994, 32, italics in original source).
5 Suominen (1996).
6 Hyvärinen (1994, 32); Suominen (1996, 18).
7 E.g., Camaüer (2000, 72).
8 Hyvärinen (1994, 40); Camaüer (2000, 72).
9 Diani & Eyerman (1992); McAdam et al., eds. (1996); della Porta & Diani (1999).
10 E.g., Melucci (1989); Eyerman & Jamison (1991); Johnston & Klandermans, eds., (1995); Taylor & Whittier (1995).
11 Scheuch (1990); éyen (1990).
12 Cf. Bertaux (1990).
13 Briskin (1999, 5).
14 Bergqvist et al., eds. (1999).
15 Katzenstein & Mueller (1987, 4); cf. Togeby (1989, 20).
16 Lønnå (in this volume).
17 Dahlerup (in this volume).
18 Gerhard (1999).
19 Teune (1990, 53f.).
20 Offen (1988); Lønnå (2000).
21 Kaplan (1997, 5).
22 Ferree (1987, 174).
23 Lovenduski (1997, 283).
24 Dahlerup and Lønnå (in this volume).

25 Bergman (2002, 19).
26 E.g., Mansbridge (1995); Young (1997).
27 Jenson (1985); Briskin (1999).
28 E.g., Gerhard (1999; cf. von Oerzen (1999).
29 For similar re-evaluations in the United States, see Rupp & Taylor (1991).
30 Bergman (1999).
31 E.g., Tyyskä (1995); Mosesdóttir (1999).
32 Kriesi et al., (1995); McAdam et al., eds. (1996); della Porta & Rucht (1995); see also Halsaa (in this volume).
33 Roggeband (1996, 3).
34 Bergman (2002).
35 Dahlerup (in this volume); Bergman (2002); Dackweiler (1995).
36 Cf. Skocpol & Somers (1980).
37 Suominen (1996, 14); Briskin (1999, 4).
38 E.g., Anttonen (1997); Bergman (2002).
39 E.g., Ferree (1987); Ferree (1990); Gerhard (1992).
40 Julkunen (1994); Julkunen (1997).
41 E.g., Chamberlayne (1993).
42 Ray (1998).
43 Kaplan (1992); Basu, ed. (1995).
44 The language of "sisterhood" and "feminist solidarity" was commonplace in the women's movement of the 1970s, especially among radical feminists (see, e.g., *Sisterhood is Global*, ed. by Robyn Morgan in 1984). Later, this emphasis on the global character of women's protest and resistance was challenged by the advocates of identity politics and the deconstruction of Woman/women.
45 Roggeband (1996).
46 Giugni (1995).
47 Snow & Benford (1999).
48 Thörn (1997).
49 See, however, della Porta & Rucht (1995); Giugni (1995).
50 See also Dahlerup and Krook (in this volume).
51 Roggeband (1996).
52 Bertaux (1990).
53 Rosenbeck (1998).
54 Briskin (1999, 8).
55 Robertson (1995); cf. Kristmundsdóttir (in this volume).
56 See Krook (in this volume).
57 See Stoltz (in this volume).

CHAPTER 2

Waves in the History of Feminism

Elisabeth Lønnå

The Wave as Image and Term

What is a wave? A force that lifts us up and lets us float, or, when it collapses, pulls us under and threatens to drown us. A wave can be topped with playful foam, breaking the light into exciting colors, or it can be heavy, gray and rolling. Waves subside, become fewer, till eventually the water is still. But, as everyone knows, in the great oceans there are always waves. No wonder the wave is a wonderful metaphor for developments in society, especially developments that touch us and let us see our lives as part of something bigger.

The Norwegian sociologist Harriet Holter wrote in the article "Words – Images – Women's Research" (Ord – bilder – kvinneforskning) that terms of language are meaningful when they can create images in our mind.[1] The word "wave" creates such an image. In her article Holter pointed out that from the beginnings of women's research in the 1970s there has been a close connection between the way an expression is used in everyday language and in politics and research. Some words, like "suppression" and "liberation" have been taken from everyday or political language and turned into terms that are used when studying society. They have been used and explored through research, then ploughed back into more general use loaded with more meaning than before. Other terms, like "sex roles" have been created through research, then adopted by the public. This process has connected women's research to women's lives, and made women able to use research results in their everyday or political lives. To make sense, words must create images, play on common associations and target something people think they have experienced or seen, Holter wrote. However, she also reminded us that words may change their content or stop being meaningful, either as everyday terms, as political terms or as scientific terms. They can function conservatively instead of innovatively; they can be "empirically hollowed out." They can be useful in a theoretical context without being part of general language. And sometimes they can hide more than they reveal.

The term "wave" has been used as a metaphor for developments in the feminist movement, both by those within the movement itself and by historians and sociologists studying that movement. It has never really been defined, and is still used in many different ways. This makes it a rather confusing term to apply when making comparative analyses. There is an even more serious objection against using the term, though. Thinking in terms of waves tends to let one focus on the tops and high-points of the history of the women's movement – without reflecting on the fact that the normal situation is what is going on in between such crests. When that is the case, it certainly is an expression that can hide more than it reveals. This means "wave" is a term that is not just imprecise and sometimes confusing, but may be misleading.

In this article, I want to discuss some of the problems that arise when using the term wave with regard to empirical, historical material. The basis for this discussion will be my own work on the history of *Norsk Kvinnesaksforening* (*The Norwegian Association for Women's Rights*) – a liberal, feminist organization. I will also draw upon Danish political scientist Drude Dahlerup's book *Rødstrømperne* (*The Redstockings*) – an analysis of the Danish Redstockings of the 1960s and 1970s. At the end of my article, I will briefly take up the question of the term wave as it is used in connection with feminisms of today and of the future.

How many waves?

The term wave has been used as an image describing developments in the feminist movement almost since the term feminism itself was coined in the 1880s.[2] Dutch authors Tjitske Akkerman and Siep Stuurman divide the modern history of European feminism into six major sub-periods, called waves, starting in the 1400s.[3] American Jo Freeman has pointed out that it was women involved in Women's Liberation who started calling themselves the second wave and that the reason for this was lack of historical insight. Though many had heard about the suffrage movement – which then became the first wave – they did not know much about the work that had been going on immediately before their time.[4]

Freeman believes that if one is to talk about waves at all, there must be at least three of them in the USA. Firstly, there was the movement to increase the rights of women, particularly the rights of married women for more independence from their husbands, as well as the right of all women to an education. In this perspective, the suffrage movement was really the *second* wave, nourished by the progressive movement. There was a flurry of activity during the 1890s, but the most active years for the women's movement were in the 1910s. So, according to Jo Freeman, if the second wave was the struggle for suffrage, then the women's movement in the 1960s and 1970s must be seen as the third wave of what she calls "conscious female activism" – not the second.[5]

Drude Dahlerup in *The Redstockings*, also employs three waves in her periodization: The first wave put women's rights on the political agenda in Denmark during the 1880s. This was connected to the battle for a more democratic leadership against a conservative government. The second wave rolled through during the period of 1907 to 1920 and was directly connected to the struggle for suffrage. Therefore, like Freeman, Dahlerup's third wave takes place in the 1960s and 1970s – and this is the theme of her book about the Redstockings.[6]

Although Dahlerup reckons with the same number of waves that Freeman does, she places them at different times. In other countries, these waves have to be placed at yet other times than in the USA and Denmark. In Norway, for example, the first wave can best be placed in the 1880s. But it is doubtful whether one can talk of a new wave stretching from the turn of the century until the victory of female suffrage in 1913. Probably it is better to talk about one wave that had a dip during the 1890s and then picked up again after 1900, with many of the same participants involved throughout. In any case, it had more or less ebbed out by 1914. From this perspective, there are also differences of "waves" within the Nordic countries.

These differences may not be important when one is working with women's history within each country, but they can become confusing and misleading when working with international questions – particularly when differences like these have not been perceived by all those taking part in a discussion. This is not a small matter of splitting hairs, and it does not concern only a small group of feminist historians. Feminist individuals, groups and organizations, even whole movements, have challenged gender roles and gender systems at least from the middle of the 19th century – some historians would contend much longer.[7] Gender is deeply imprinted on our thoughts and emotions and at the very core of our societies, providing the basis for what has been called the gender system.[8] The feminist challenges therefore necessarily have bearing on the fundamental structures of society. American historian Karen Offen, who has investigated three hundred years of European feminist history, writes:

> "This neglected – or forgotten – or (even worse) repressed history – which feminist scholars are now reclaiming – is central to understanding the political and intellectual history, as well as the social, economic and cultural history, of virtually every European society.[9]

Transcultural, comparative research into feminist movements and feminist critique will undoubtedly be more common – and more interesting – as results from national and regional research are made available in English. A comparative approach makes it all the more important to keep terms clear.

What counts as feminism?

A discussion of feminist women's movements will depend on how one defines the term feminism. Using a broad definition will provide different results than a narrow definition will. Is a women's movement to be counted as a feminist wave or part of such a wave if its aims are for instance temperance, political reform, the welfare of children or higher morality for men and women? These are aims that might not upset the structure of power between the sexes, or strengthen the position of women in society, or result in more equality between men and women. By excluding all such movements, however, one is excluding many issues that have been of interest to women, and which have engaged them and made them active. One also runs the risk of excluding movements that have actually functioned as vehicles for strengthening the position of women – even if this may not have been their primary or even explicit goal.

There are a number of definitions of feminism that make it possible to include such movements. One of the oldest and most well known of these is the term "social feminism", coined by William O'Neill in 1969. This includes in feminism groups of women who were mobilized in connection with the struggle for suffrage in America on a broad basis, including municipal civic reformers, settlement house residents and labour activists.[10] The social feminist position claimed a higher moral calling for women based on the differences between the sexes.[11] British Olive Banks brought into use the expression "welfare feminists", applying it for the kind of movement that was typical in Great Britain and the US after suffrage had been won. This composite term covers the notion of women activists working for welfare, but with a particular view to bettering the situation of women and children. In welfare feminism the traditional women's role was accepted. But, Olive Banks argues, it would be mistaken to think they were not feminist. They brought the needs of women and children to the forefront in an active and radical way.[12] Norwegian historian Ida Blom is among those who have used the term welfare feminism in her work.[13]

Another variant is Karen Offen's term "relational feminism".[14] In Offen's work, this stands for a feminism where the focus is not on the struggle for individual, gender neutral rights, but on the needs and rights of women as mothers nurturing children. Complementary gender roles are accepted.

It has been argued that with definitions as wide as these, the term feminism stands in danger of losing its meaning. It could cover all kinds of organized activity among women, even – if one stretches it to the breaking point – anti-feminist ones.[15] An example could be a reactionary movement like the Latin-American Marianismo, where women define themselves as superior to men on the basis of their motherhood.[16] Some writers prefer a narrower definition, weeding out organizations with social reform or more general aims, such as party politics, as primary goals. We find an example of a narrow definition in Richard Evans' 1977 book, *The Feminists: The Women's Emancipation Movement in Europe, America, and Australia, 1840-1920*. Here he defines feminism as "the doctrine of equal rights, for women, based on the theory of the equality of the sexes".[17] A Nordic example may be found in an article by Swedish historian Ulla Wikander in the book on labour legislation for women entitled *Protecting Women*. She defines feminism as "the organized demand for equality with men".[18] Definitions like this have been criticized for being too exclusive, making what Nancy Cott calls "hard-core feminism" the only true feminism.[19]

Ulla Wikander's definition works well in her article, where the point is separating different groups of organized women from one another, highlighting equal rights ideology. It might be more difficult to apply in a more general setting, however. For instance, it would leave out major trends and organizations during the 1960s and 1970s, where the aim was not primarily equality with men. How exclusive a definition may become when based only on the struggle for equal rights is illustrated by the fact that Richard Evans ended his book about the feminists in the year 1920, because in his view the epoch of feminism ended at that time. In the countries where women had gained the right to vote, feminist movements, in Evans' narrow sense of the term, weakened or were forbidden by law.

So what must one do? One must inform oneself about the content of different definitions, of course, weighing them against one another, being conscious that results will be different according to which one is being used. One can also try to find a definition which has the advantage of excluding organizations and ideologies that are negative or indifferent to women's rights as individuals or groups, while at the same time including more of those that have furthered the interests of women, even if they have not necessarily worked for equality. There are no perfect definitions in the end.

With a pragmatic basis like this as a point of departure, I have chosen a definition of feminism that I think is useful for the purpose of working with the question of waves in the history of feminism. This is Nancy Cott's "working definition", formulated by her as an answer to – among others – Karen Offen. This definition is compound, containing three main elements. The possibility for a separate discussion of each element makes the definition handy as a tool for analysis. The three elements are:

> "First, that feminism implies opposition against the gender hierarchy, where one gender is superior and the other inferior.
>
> Second, that feminism presupposes that women's condition is socially constructed, created by society – not given by nature or God.
>
> Third, that feminism implies the understanding that women constitute a social grouping, and it implies an identification on some level with 'the group called women'".[20]

Other writers who have used this definition in a Nordic context are Finnish historian Leena Laine in her work on women and sports,[21] Drude Dahlerup,[22] and the Danish editors of *Moving On*.[23] While mainly approving of Cott's definition, both Laine, Dahlerup and Andreasen et al. also raise some objections to it. The latter point out that only few women's movements will be able to live up to such a specific definition – i.e. it is too narrow. They therefore suggest that movements "are placed in a continuum according to the persuasiveness of the feminist impulses in the individual movement at different historical periods." One way to do this would be to use the definition with a generous spate of flexibility, and consider making use of other definitions when called for.

Drude Dahlerup objects to Cott's third point: That feminism implies the understanding that women constitute a social grouping, and that it implies identification on some level with "the group called women". Her first objection is that it excludes men – both female rights champions like John Stuart Mill and male members of *The Danish Women's Society* (*Dansk Kvindesamfund*). In Norway it would exclude male members of *The Norwegian Association for Women's Rights* (*Norsk Kvinnesaksforening*). I cannot see that this is a really significant argument against the third point. Why should not a man be able to identify with women? If one has a problem with that, one can simply say that men are pro-feminist, instead of using the term "feminist" and the problem is solved. Another objection Dahlerup makes is that not all women in the women's movement were talking about "we women", and therefore did not identify with women as such.

Here she touches on a really serious objection to Cott's definition. In what way do women constitute a social grouping, and what is actually "the group called women"? Both practical politics and research over the last decades have made it clear that it is problematic to see women as one group or even as a set of groups, because that means ignoring differences in class, ethnicity, sexuality and the way one perceives and lives out gender. Identifying with "the group called women" may even be in direct contradiction to another of Cott's points; presupposing that the category "women" is socially constructed. It might be argued that seeing women as a group would imply one-factor explanations for gender traits, i.e. nature/biology. Parts of my own material seem to confirm this tendency. On the other hand, it is hard to imagine anyone belonging to a women's movement without identifying with women. Without identification and some kind of common analysis of one's position in society, there simply would not be a movement or an organization with feminist or pro-woman aims. This apparent contradiction hinges on a serious feminist dilemma: the wish to be an individual and not to be essentialized as a woman or even "bunched up" with women as a category, while at the same time seeing the need for organizing – as a woman. Without claiming to solve this dilemma, I would suggest reformulating Cott's third point (on identification) to at least make it more flexible:

> Third, that feminism implies the understanding that the social conditions one is living under are dependent on gender, and an identification with one or more groups of women.

Dahlerup's own definition of feminism is the following: "an ideology whose goal it is to remove discrimination and disparagement of women and break down male dominance in society".[24]

This has the advantage of being shorter and simpler than Cott's definition – and my own modification of the same. It excludes reactionary movements, while offering the possibility of including reform organizations that, for instance, aim to strengthen the position of women. Dahlerup is moving in the same direction and has the same intent that Cott has, and this definition can be used together with Cott's.

Between the crests

A very problematic part of a division into waves is that it makes it difficult to perceive the often long periods between crests of activity. Such periods make up much of the history of feminism, and should be considered to be the normal condition during which women's movements have been quite passive, have had less vocal support and have been more or less invisible in the media. Feminists have felt that times were difficult, that there was a backlash, and that they were not able to recruit new supporters for the movement. These periods have not got much attention. Neither have they been included in studies of social or mass movements.

In spite of that, there have been groups or organizations that have worked intensely for their aims precisely during these downturns. A social movement needs a lot of publicity, but an efficient interest group can get much done without being dependent on public attention. It can be difficult work for the activists, but that does not mean there are no accomplishments. Even keeping up organizational structures during difficult times can be considered important, because it gives continuity to feminism and makes it possible to pass on traditions. New ideas and new norms may form that will gradually work their way into public life. When ideas and norms are new, it can be difficult to find support for them, but that does of course not mean that they are not important. In her article in this book, Cecilia Milwertz applies a definition of success in social movements borrowed from American Suzanne Staggenborg. Staggenborg defines success not only on the basis of short-term policy results, but also on the cultural consequences of the long-range process of the social movement in question. Such a definition – taking into account long-range, cultural success, could well give an impetus to more research interest in the quieter phases of the women's movement.[25]

Americans Leyla Rupp and Verta Taylor, who have been working with the long period between the struggle for suffrage and the movement in the 1960s and 1970s, see these years as a continuous flow of activity within the women's movement, rather than a break between two great waves.[26] They find no sharp breaks, but rather stages of "abeyance" and "mobilization". What happens when we take particular care to look into the stages of abeyance? Can we learn something different, something interesting from them?

In my own material, I find three periods which are very informative, though they have not been noticed much in spite of being important for the development of a more woman-friendly society. These are:

- The period from women gained suffrage in Norway till the middle of the 1930s,
- The last half of the 1930s and
- The period from the end of the Second World War till the middle of the 1960s.

I shall describe and characterize each of these periods making use for the most part of examples from my work in women's history. I will then use this local perspective as a point of departure for a more general discussion, applying Cott's and Dahlerup's definitions of feminism.

I suggest that the periods referred to above have been neglected for a number of reasons. Many activities have not been covered by the most common definitions of feminism. This is the case in much of the women's movements of the post suffrage period. Sometimes participants in movements did not succeed in attaining their goals. This of course applies to much work in women's organizations, but I think a striking example is the work done during the last half of the 1930s. The activists could belong to a small minority, an elite which managed to do a lot, but which had relatively narrow popular support. This applies to the post-World War II period.

From Women's Suffrage to the middle of the 1930s

The first period I'll look at is the time just after suffrage was won in Norway in 1913 until the middle of the 1930s. The outset of this period was marked by the outbreak of the First World War. Norway was neutral during the war, and Norwegian economy had a great upsurge as a result of this. For those who did not share in these riches, inflation and a lack of supplies led to hardship. Both working class and middle class women used much of their energy worrying about and providing for their families. After the war followed a series of economic crises, leading to large burdens of debt, bankruptcies and closing down of major industries, which in turn led to unemployment, loss of property and poverty for parts of the population. During this period of hardship and obvious social unjustice, many women turned their attention from equal rights to working for peace, welfare and social causes.

While economic trouble hit many families, Norway as a whole got richer, and Norwegian society underwent a process of modernization. An important part of this modernization was played by women, who eagerly threw themselves into rationalizing

Voters from Norway. (Courtesy of the Norwegian Association for Women's Rights.)

housework, making it more professional and preferably based on scientific knowledge. There was a lot of activity within a vast number of women's organizations, both middle and working class, almost all working with the aim of strengthening the housewife and creating better homes. The dominant view in these organizations was that this was in accordance both with women's position and with their nature and purpose in life. Women were fundamentally different from (and preferably superior to) men. This superiority was connected to their role as mothers and housewives.

But even if much of the work in women's organizations was focused on the individual home, there was a public side of this too, which mainly concentrated on creating better conditions for each home and therefore also for children. Women took part in public debates, speaking up for a society that cared for families and especially for children. Doing so, they took responsibility for and expressed themselves regarding economics and politics.

Equal rights organizations, which had been prominent in the period up to 1913, either disappeared, barely survived or redirected their efforts in the direction of the development of homes. However, this trend is not as clear as it might seem at first glance. There was still a good deal of work going on to attain the goal of strengthening individual women's rights. These efforts to promote equality used arguments that fit the times well because they emphasized "unique" female qualities. This was particularly true of those used by the women's trade union movement, like the Norwegian Association of Women Teachers and the Norwegian Nurse Association,[27] but also of the work done for the application of the newly won political rights.[28]

Vocational School in Domestic Economy 1901.
(Courtesy of the Norwegian Association for Women's Rights.)

Should this period be left out when summarizing the history of feminism in Norway? Again this depends on how one defines the term feminism. Let me apply Nancy Cott's definition in order to try to clarify this. The second point here – that feminism presupposes that women's condition is socially constructed, created by society – not given by nature or God – fits the 1920s poorly. Latent in the popular thought of "unique" female qualities lay the implication that those given qualities would have to be taken care of and developed. Whether they were created by God, evolution or had come into being some other way was not the issue. They existed in any case. This did not justify the position women had in society. But it reduced the opportunity to oppose that position, because it was exactly the most valued of these qualities which were the ones that led women to hold an inferior position; that is, those qualities that were connected with their roles as housewives provided for by husbands.

Does this mean that the first part of Cott's definition – that feminism implies opposition against the gender hierarchy, where one gender is superior and the other inferior – does not fit in the 1920s? It appears that way for some of the women in any case – for instance, for those in the housewives' associations. They cannot then be classified as feminist.

However, not all women's organizations and activities fall outside of Cott's three-part definition during this period. There were working women's organizations that were clearly critical to the male-dominated system. There were also women who strongly opposed male power within the home-focused organizations. It is worth noting that many of the participants in the home improving movement of the time called themselves feminists – they thought that by strengthening the homes they were strengthening the position of women. They also thought that establishing women in positions of power would create a better society.[29] This was also a period when Cott's (modified) third point can be seen very clearly. Identification with one or more groups of women was particularly strong, leading to an amazing abundance of organizations where women got together and worked for common aims. These are exactly the groups for which Olive Banks coined the term welfare feminists.

Are these to be excluded from the ranks of feminists? If so, one obviously has to bypass this as a dark valley between the high points of feminism. If not, one has to rethink the issue. Was there no true low point? Was it less deep than popularly thought?

Excluding women active during the period from about 1913 to the middle of the 1930s would be problematic. Many of them were, after all, intent on breaking male dominance. A movement which obviously had the intention of bettering women's life and strengthening their position would seem to disappear out of feminist history. It gives rise to some afterthought that with criteria like these we might be well on the way to excluding much of the feminism of the late 1980s and the 1990s, with its emphasis on women's culture, female qualities and the rationality of caring.

The Upturn at the middle of the 1930s

In Norway, as in the rest of Europe and the USA, the economy started improving after about 1934, giving rise to optimism and expectations for a better life. In the Nordic countries this optimism was strengthened by labour parties taking over government with programs involving the state in building up employment and welfare. By 1936 – 1937 things were improving markedly. Women, who had been pushed out of or to the edges of the labour market during the depression, were now starting to demand the right to work.

Just before the middle of the 1930s there was a new, strong interest in equality and women's rights, which resulted in a host of new organizations that seen together clearly form a social movement. Younger women went on the offensive forming Norwegian chapters of *Open Door* and *Working Women's Clubs (Yrkeskvinners Klubb)* – the latter quite large by Norwegian standards. The older Norwegian Association for Women's Rights also flourished once again on a platform of equal rights. Women within the Norwegian Labour Party and the Federation of Trade Unions also organized and spoke up for women's rights.

The trend was international, and women were reorganizing internationally. The organizations of the Union for Nordic Women's Rights picked up its work after many years of passivity, and the International Alliance of Women (IAW) also saw a surge of new activity. Women were able to look to one another across borders, getting together and picking up inspiration. This was definitely a case of the "international processes of learning" that Drude Dahlerup finds an important element both in the old feminist movement (before suffrage) and in the movement of the 1960s and 1970s.[30] At the same time, fascist suppression and expansion loomed over feminist efforts as a threatening shadow.

Participants in the radical, 1930s movement emphasized the right of women to an independent life outside of the family. Many wanted to combine family and employment, thus breaking out of the private sphere. There were demands for free abortion and for access to contraceptives. Voices were raised against the traditional view that women were higher moral beings. Some women demanded sexual rights, too, and there was a noticeably greater openness surrounding sexual issues. Thoughts that had been out of style but had solid roots in the previous century in the work of John Stuart Mill came to the fore again – the perception that both "femininity" and the position of women are cultural and social constructions that can and ought to be changed.[31]

This neatly fits Nancy Cott's second point in her definition of feminism: that the position of women be seen as created by society. Should the second half of the 1930s then be counted as the crest of a wave in feminist history? For my own part, I have written about the period between 1935 and 1940 as an important period both in Norway as well as in the Nordic countries and internationally. Work for equal rights was strengthened considerably by separate women's organizations standing in clear opposition to patriarchy.[32] This is close to "hard-core feminism" and with no problems at all fits into both Cott's and Dahlerup's definitions. Going to Sweden, Rene

Frangeur in her book *Yrkeskvinna eller makens tjänarinna? (Working Woman or Her Husband's Servant?)* shows how a strong movement of women from women's rights organizations, labour unions, professional women's organizations and political parties resisted efforts to keep women out of the labour market during the recession in the 1930s.[33] The movement was successful in that it managed to turn public opinion to the advantage of women in the labour market.

Why have historians – with the possible exception of the Swedes – given so little attention to this movement, which was both well organized and international? I think it stems from the fact that the participants at that time were not able to implement their ideas and proposals – again with the possible exception of the Swedes. The time was not right. Equal rights advocates were in disagreement with a large majority of women, who subscribed to what Swedish historian Yvonne Hirdman has aptly called "the housewife contract" – the accepted norm for gendered behavior, and the basis of the gender system in the Nordic countries during this time.[34] More importantly, the movement was never able to follow up its potential. It was cut short by fascism and the Second World War. After the war it had to start in part almost from scratch. Also, women had suffered a backlash regarding central issues like abortion and sex education. Further, in Norway at least, employment practices for women and the role of women in society in general had suffered a blow. For these reasons, the results of the women's movement in the second half of the 1930s were not nearly as great as they might have been. But this does not mean that this movement was not to have an effect in the long run – as a model for later activity, as an inspiration for new thoughts and as a starting point for recruiting a new generation of feminists, those who would fight for equal rights during the fifties. If one uses Staggenborg's processual thinking, taking in the long-range, cultural effects, the movement of the second part of the 1930s can very well be seen as a success.

From the second World War to the middle of the 1960s

After World War II feminism in Norway was first and foremost represented by The Norwegian Association for Women's Rights and The Working Women's Clubs. The other Nordic nations had similar organizations. The Norwegian Association for Women's Rights consisted of a small elite of well educated, motivated and capable women. Their ideological basis was resistance against the male breadwinner system. Thus they criticized and attacked the still prevailing housewife contract. Their political specialty was thorough and professional reports to the government, often followed up by lobbying. They concentrated their work on issues that had to do with education and employment. They achieved their goals with regard to several important issues during the period from 1945 through the 1950s. In 1959 the joint taxation system for husband and wife, which was very unfavourable for working women, was eliminated. In 1959, the principle of equal pay was adopted by parliament, the ILO Equal Pay Convention ratified and an Equal Pay Committee was set up. The Trade Union Federation and the Federation of Employers agreed to get rid of separate wage scales for men and women. This meant that an additional principle had been accepted – at least in theory, women and men were to be treated as individuals in the work place, not as representatives of their gender. At the same time, important goals were achieved in education. It was decided that boys and girls would have the same education in theoretical subjects.[35]

Together with practical political work like this, the Norwegian Association for Women's Rights was constantly working to influence public opinion. Starting in 1957, the Association incorporated into its ideology the new sociological, critical theory of gender roles worked out by Nordic sociologists, with Harriet Holter as a central figure. This was used as an instrument for drawing up a critique of the male breadwinner system. It also succeeded in getting quite a lot of attention in the media.

The victories from the 50s were consolidated in the 1960s. By the start of the decade equality was getting to be a generally accepted goal for society and women were on their way into education and jobs. By the end of the 1960s, the ideology of equality and the gender roles theory that had been advocated by a small but verbal group had become a part of established social policy.[36] Drude Dahlerup calls this time the "We are all human beings"- period. Separate women's organizations were discontinued in the name of equality. In Sweden the magazine "We Women" was renamed "We Humans".[37] Of course, modes of expression like this papered over serious discrimination towards women. Many feminists were very well aware of this and tried in different ways to better the situation by influencing public opinion and the law.

Continuity or discontinuity?

The young generation of the 1970s was critical of the "old" feminists, partly because their theoretical basis did not sufficiently take into consideration the particular situation and needs of women and partly because they were seen as being far too tactically cautious. After all, young people could clearly see that equality had not been established in practical politics. It is easy to contend that change came quicker when a new generation stopped being polite and reasonable, started saying things directly, and showed that they were angry and willing and able to break with good manners.

Looking back, however, it is important to point out their relationship to the preceding period. The feminists of the 1950s had laid the foundation for many of the opportunities which young women later had for education and employment. It is also reasonable to point out strong similarities between the women's movement of the 1970s and the feminism of earlier periods.

In *Redstockings*, Dahlerup emphasizes the novelty of what the new generation of feminists stood for. It is a central theoretical contention in her book that she sees "new thinking" as one of the most important foundations for social movements. She identifies the Redstocking organization as such a social movement, and succeeds in showing what is new: the radicalness, the strong sense of rebellion, the forms of action, the organization into basis-groups, the emphasis on consciousness raising.[38]

Another way to look at the movement of the 1970s would be to accentuate the continuity with the past. The New Feminists' style and working methods were new and different. They were much more aggressive. Overall ideology was different, more radical. Above all, they brought in the concept of consciousness rising through groups of women discussing their private lives and giving them a political context. But the demands for women were surprisingly similar: – the right and opportunity to have both a job and a family, – equal pay, – equal opportunity for and equal quality in education, – real opportunities for interesting work like men had, – day-care for children, – a fairer division of work in the homes, – full rights to abortion and contraceptives, – an end to discrimination of women in the media and public life, – an end to laws and regulations that hid women's individuality in marriage (the changing of names), – an end to women being classified according to civil status (Miss/Mrs.), – an end to commerce in women (prostitution, misuse of women in war and civic emergencies).[39]

These demands were basically about equality, which reflects the equal rights ideology of the feminists of the second part of the 1930s and of the period after World War II. It is the same ideology that the Nordic governments deferred to and which most old Redstockings now stand for, according to the results of a survey Drude Dahlerup presented in her book.[40]

When the radical, anti-capitalist vision receded in the 1980s, the concrete demands of women were what remained. Behind them is still a vision: that women should be able to live as individuals and be treated as such. This is the vision that has been at the foundation of the struggle for equal rights since the start of the feminist movements of the 19th century.

One sign of having reached a higher level of equality is that women now take part in political and employee organizations on a more equal footing with men, and have less of a need for separate organizations. Separate women's organizations typically lost members from the last half of the 1980s. This decline was more pronounced for them than it was for other types of organizations, and it is connected to the fact that women believed they now had more equal rights and opportunities.[41] Some of the demands for equality had been achieved and the individual's identification with women as a group weakened. In this way the women's movement lost members even though – or precisely because – it was seen as relatively successful.

To draw some historical parallels: In the period from 1913 to about 1935, when there was a strong group identity among women, there was an abundance of women's organizations in spite of limited opposition to the patriarchy.[42] In the 1960s, there was both a general agreement that the position of women was a result of developments in society and therefore could be changed, and widespread support for the thought that women were not to be subordinated as a gender. Identification with women as a group was weaker than earlier, however, and women did not feel the need for a separate organization that much. An effect of this was that feminist activity was rather low.[43] I think the same can be said about conditions today – in the postmodern, supposedly equal or genderless society. However, this does not mean that there is not a lot of feminist thinking and activity going on – as history has shown us, such activity is not only possible, but likely in the apparently quiet periods between the crests of the women's movement.

Conclusion

Feminist historians use the term "wave" in many different ways. This is because the material they are working with is different. In this article, I have tried to show some of the feminist organizations and movements that – for different reasons – have not been reckoned as part of the waves of feminism, based on materials from my own research. Other research will uncover different activities, different motivations and different reasons for arguing and organizing in the name of feminism. Thus, Leena Laine in her article in this book shows how the feminist movement within women's sports sometimes coincided with the classical high points of feminism, and sometimes occurred at other times, even during periods of low activity like the 1940s and 1950s.

Using the image of the wave to illustrate what one sees when delving into history can be quite effective. As a metaphor the wave is both strong and poetic. But employing it as the basis for a model or theory would be misleading. One major problem is that it must be applied in so many different ways that it does not give a good basis for comparing women's movements. Even more seriously, the wave concept can mask important historic events and activities. Feminist thinking and feminist activity may be overlooked because of not coinciding with an obvious crest of a wave. If one is also using a set definition that gives little room for nuances, this problem is enlarged.

This predicament, of course, becomes more acute the more international one's scope is. In this paper, I have written about Nordic countries, with the USA as a reference point. But difficulties would grow when studying countries – or continents – with greater cultural and economic differences between them. The same kind of problem arises when writing about feminist movements in multicultural societies – which today must be the case for most societies. As with all tools of ideological analysis, there is a real threat of arrogance on the part of those who make the definitions. That should give an extra impetus to being careful when setting up our models. As Pauline Stoltz emphasizes in her article in this book, focusing on waves may lead to focusing on the mainstream of political activists.[44] She takes as her point of departure black, migrant and refugee women, showing how they can be marginalized not only in politics, but also in research. Naming or defining can reinforce injusticies and inequalities, Stoltz points out.

Waves come in more or less regular intervals. History, on the other hand, does not work like that – every instance, every movement is unique. There is no regularity, nor are there any laws of history that makes it possible to predict the future on the basis of what has happened before. Believing in such laws would be equivalent to believing in destiny in history.[45] Searching for regular, repeating waves of feminism has been tried, for instance by Norwegian Else Wiestad, who found great "tidal waves" every 80 – 100 years when editing a book on European literary history, *De store hundreårsbølgene* [*The Great Hundred Years' Waves*].[46] Wiestad's periods are based on empirical findings, but not discussed in a theoretical perspective. Obvious questions are not asked. One major question would be: Why did these waves come exactly every hundred years? Was it accidental, or has destiny or some force of history made it so?

German Karl-Werner Brand tried to find wave patterns in several social movements during the 19th and 20th century. He shows how he ran into a great deal of problems constructing patterns – there were always exceptions, particular cases and waves that did not fit. All in all, he does not seem to find the results convincing. Brand also refers to several authors who have tried to establish cycles of a cultural climate that would be advantageous to social movements. The cycles vary from 30 to 50 to 60 and even 150 years, a disparity that does not inspire great confidence.[47]

Rejecting the concept of regular patterns in history also means that thinking about the future in terms of such waves would be misleading as a basis for continued, feminist activity. Waiting for or expecting a certain type of movement – for instance a powerful, united movement or a mass movement – is useless, since the future cannot be predicted on the basis of what happened before. It might even make it more difficult to perceive significant activity of a different kind.

In order to study history we need models and periodization. There has got to be some kind of system for mutual understanding and sorting out of trends and events. But using the concept of the wave as a basis for a historical model is not really fruitful. There can be no "wave theory", since the wave is not a scientific term, but a popular concept that has been adopted by researchers and writers in order to describe something that is perceived – i.e. a metaphor.

References

Andreasen, Tayo, & Anette Borchorst, Drude Dahlerup, Eva Lous, Hanne Rimmen Nielsen (ed.) (1991). *Moving On. New Perspectives on the Women's Movement*, Århus, *Acta Jutlandica* LXVII, Humanities Series 66.

Akkerman, Tjitske & Siep Stuurman (1998). *Perspectives on Feminist Political Thought in European History: From the Middle Ages to the Present*, London, Routledge.

Banks, Olive (1981). *Faces of Feminism. A Study of Feminism as a Social Movement*. Oxford, Martin Robertson.

Blom, Ida (1992). *Kvinder fra urtid til nutid. Fra 1500 til vore dage*, København, Politikens Forlag.

Brand, Karl-Werner (1990). "Cyclical Aspects of New Social Movements: Waves of Cultural Criticism and Mobilization Cycles of New Middle-Class Radicalism", Dalton, Russell J, Manfred Kuechler & Wilhelm Bürklin (ed.), *Challenging the political order*. Oxford, Polity Press p. 23-42.

Cott, Nancy (1987). *The Grounding of Modern Feminism*, New Haven, Yale University Press.

Cott, Nancy (1989). "What's in a name? The Limits of "Social Feminism"; or, Expanding the Vocabulary of Women's History", *The Journal of American History*, vol. 76, No 3.

Dahlerup, Drude (1998). *Rødstrømperne. Den danske Rødstrømpebevægelses udvikling, nytænkning og gennemslag 1970-1985,* København, Gyldendal

Dahlerup, Drude (2003). "Continuity and Waves in the Feminist Movement – a Challenge to Social Movement Theory." In this volume.

Evans, Richard (1979). *The Feminists: The Women's Emancipation Movement in Europe, America, and Australia, 1840-1920*. New York, Barnes and Noble.

Frangeur, Renée (1998). *Yrkeskvinna eller makens tjänarinna? Striden om yrkesrätten för gifta kvinnor i mellankrigstidens Sverige*. Lund, Arkiv förlag.

Freeman, Jo, (1996). Discussion e-mail to the H-Women list (Humanities-Women), May 31. www.jofreeman.com/feminism/waves.htm

Freeman, Jo, (1999). *A Room at a Time. How Women entered Party Politics*. Lanham, Rowman and Littlefield.

Hirdman, Yvonne (1994). "Genusanalys av välfärdsstaten: utmaning av dikotomierna". Fra kvinnehistorie til kjønnshistorie? Rapport III, Det 22. nordiske historikermøte, Oslo.

Hirdman, Yvonne (1998). *Genussystemet – Teoretiska funderingar kring kvinnors sociala underordning*. Maktutredningen, rapport 23, Uppsala.

Holter, Harriet (1987). "Ord – bilder – kvinneforskning", *Nytt om kvinneforskning* no. 4, p. 6-13.

Kristmundsdottir, Sigridur Duna (2003). "Deciphering the present: Women's movements and globalisation". In this volume.

Laine, Leena (2003). In this volume.

Lønnå, Elisabeth (1996). *Stolthet og kvinnekamp. Norsk kvinnesaksforenings historie fra 1913*, Oslo, Gyldendal.

Melby, Kari (1991). "Women's Ideology: Difference, Equality or a New Femininity. Women Teachers and Nurses in Norway 1912-1940". Andreasen, Borchorst et al.

Milwertz, Cecilia (2003). in this volume.

Offen, Karen (1988). "Defining Feminism – a comparative approach", *Signs* vol. 14, Nr. 1

Offen, Karen (2000). "Eruptions and Flows" – thoughts on Writing a Comparative History of European Feminisms, 1700-1950". Sogner and Hagemann (eds.) (2000).

O'Neill, William L. (1969). *Everyone was Brave: The Rise and Fall of Feminism in America*, Chicago: Quadrangle Books.

Popper, Karl (1957). *The Poverty of Historicism*. Routledge, London 1986. Routledge and Kegan 1957.

Raaum, Nina C. (ed.) (1995). *Kjønn og politikk*, Oslo, TANO.

Rupp, Leyla and Verta Taylor (1991). "Women's Culture and the Continuity of the Women's movement", Andreasen, Borchorst et al.

Scott, Joan W. (1986). "Gender: A Useful Category of Historical Analysis", *The American Historical Review,* 91:5 (Dec. 1986), pp. 1053-75.

Selle, Per and Bjarne éymyr (1995). "Det frivillige organisasjonssamfunnet i omforming: Vert kjønnsgapet borte?", Raaum, Nina C. (ed.).

Sogner, Sølvi and Gro Hagemann (eds.) (2000). *Women's Politics and Women in Politics. In Honour of Ida Blom*, Oslo, Cappelen.

Staggenborg, Suzanne (1995). "Can Feminist Organisations be Effective?", Ferree, Myra Marx & Patricia Yancey Martin (ed.), *Feminist Organizations*, Philadelphia, Temple University Press, pp. 339-443.

Stoltz, Pauline (2003). "Who are 'we' to tell?" In this volume.

Wiestad, Else (ed.) (1994). *De store hundreårsbølgene. Kjønnsdebatten gjennom 300 år. Tekstsamling med en problemhistorisk innledning av Else Wiestad*, Oslo, Emilia.

Notes

1   Holter (1987).
2   Offen (2000).
3   Akkerman and Stuurman (1998).
4   Freeman (1996).
5   Freeman (1999: 10f.).
6   Dahlerup (1998, chap. 3).
7   Offen (2000); Akkerman and Stuurman (1998).
8   Hirdman (1988).
9   Offen (2000, p. 281).
10   O'Neill (1969).
11   Cott (1989); Ryan (1992).
12   Banks (1981:3).
13   Blom (1992)
14   Offen (1988).
15   Andreasen, Borchorst et al. (1991, p. 9).
16   Kristmundsdottir (2003).
17   Evans (1977), p. 39.
18   Wikander (1995), p. 45.
19   Cott (1989), p. 825.
20   Cott (1987, p. 4).
21   Laine (2003).
22   Dahlerup (1998), vol. 1, p.120.
23   Andreasen, Borchorst et al. (1991): 9f..
24   Dahlerup (1998): vol.1, p.120.
25   Milwertz (2003); Staggenborg (1995).
26   Rupp and Taylor (1991).
27   Melby (1991).
28   Lønnå (1996), chap. 4.
29   Lønnå (1996), chap. 3.
30   Dahlerup (2003).
31   Lønnå (1996), chap. 7.
32   Lønnå (1996), chap. 8.
33   Frangeur (1998).
34   Hirdman (1994).
35   Lønnå (1996), chap.13.
36   Lønnå (1996), chap. 14.
37   Dahlerup (1998), chap. 3.
38   Dahlerup (1998), chap. 8.
39   Lønnå (1996), chap.16.
40   Dahlerup (1998), chap.16.
41   Selle and éymyr (1995).
42   Lønnå (1996), chap. 6
43   Lønnå (1996), chap. 15.
44   Stoltz (2003).
45   Popper (1957).
46   Wiestad (1994).
47   Brand (1990); Dahlerup (2003).

CHAPTER 3

Continuity and Waves in the Feminist Movement

– A Challenge to Social Movement Theory

Drude Dahlerup

> *"The feminist movement is like the sea:*
> *it comes in waves and cannot be stopped"*[1]

Introduction

It is common to regard the feminist movement as one long and continuous struggle for women's rights. Ever since the first feminist organizations arose in the second half of the 19th century, there have, it is argued, always been women who have joined together in a collective effort to better women's position and to challenge male supremacy. The rise and fall of feminist mobilization is usually described in terms of 'waves': the first wave of feminism, the second wave, and maybe the third. However, the theoretical foundation as well as the empirical base of this *continuity thesis* need to be clarified. [2]

Organizational as well as ideological continuity is at stake here. Contrary to the present preference for 'feminisms' rather than 'feminism', this article will be looking for the common core in feminism. I will argue that if we cannot identify a common core of feminism, then we cannot talk about one continuous feminist movement. Further, without a common core, feminism cannot be conceptualized as an 'ism', e.g. a political ideology in its own right, parallel to liberalism and Marxism, but only as a tendency within liberalism, Marxism or postmodernism (e.g. feminist liberalism rather than liberal feminism)

The claim that the feminist movement has existed for more than one hundred years challenges the argument put forward by New Social Movement theory, that the movements of the 1960s-1980s represent something fundamentally new in history, having no class base and expressing post-material values. How is it possible to see the rebellious new feminist movement in the 1960s-1980s as part of the expression of a whole new social order, as many researchers have done, if the feminist movement has existed for more than one hundred years?

In arguing for continuity, feminist movement research thus contributes to the critique and eventual demise of New Social Movement theory. Given the dominance of the 'newness' idea, however, a critical discussion of the NSM approach still seems highly relevant to me: Firstly, the recurring argument that we are witnessing a totally new era has become even more prevalent with the poststructuralist debate. That contemporary society represents something totally new seems in fact to be a recurring argument in history.

Secondly, for the feminist movement, this discussion underscores the need to clarify theoretically what constitutes the feminist movement and its cycles in history. The 'newness' discussion raises the fundamental question of what we mean by 'the feminist movement.' On what theoretical grounds can we speak of a long history of *the* feminist movement?

Three dimensions of continuity are discussed in the first part of this article. It is argued that it is possible to speak about one continuous feminist movement in terms of identity and ideology, even if organizational continuity is lacking. In the second part, the concept of waves in social movement theory is discussed. This discussion of continuity in the feminist movement challenges social movement theory, especially the New Social Movement theory. In the third and last part of the article a different perspective – the long tradition of 'emancipation movements' – will be presented. The methodological consequences for social movement research will then be discussed.

The empirical data used in this discussion derives from various studies of Western feminism, as well as from my own studies of the feminist movement in the Nordic countries and especially from my extensive study of the Danish Women's Liberation Movement 1970-85.[3]

Three dimensions of continuity

On what grounds do we speak of one continuous feminist movement spanning the last 100 years and more? Three criteria are discussed in the following: organizational continuity, shared identity over time and last but not least ideological continuity, that is, the question of a common core of all feminisms. It is the thesis of a common ideological framework, *feminism as an 'ism'*, that constitutes the widespread understanding of a long feminist history and of solidarity and sisterhood between feminist movements across borders and times.

Organizational continuity?

In the Nordic countries, the idea of a continuous feminist movement is unquestioned, as its continuity is taken to be common knowledge. This is due to the fact that, unlike in most other European countries, the original feminist organizations that fought for women's access to education, for the legal rights of married women, and later for suffrage, still exist in the Nordic countries, although at present at a low level of activity.

In this way, the notion of a long continuous feminist struggle is reinforced. Feminist magazines that are over one hundred years old are still being issued. In Denmark, the oldest feminist organization, *Dansk Kvindesamfund* (Danish Women's Society), founded in 1871, still exists, and has since 1885 issued the magazine *Kvinden og Samfundet* (Women and Society). The magazine claims to be the oldest feminist magazine in the world. In Sweden *Fredrika-Bremer-Förbundet* started in 1884, and its magazine, *Hertha* can be traced back to 1859, albeit under different names and issued by changing organizations (Manns 1997). The journal of the women's section of the Social Democratic party, *Morgonbris*, has been issued ever since 1904. Still active are also the Norwegian *Norsk Kvinnesaksforening* (The Norwegian Women's Rights' Association) from 1884, the Finnish *Unionen* from 1892, and the Icelandic *Kvénrettindafélag Islands*, which was established in 1907.

In many other countries in Eastern and Western Europe, as well as in the United States and other parts of the world, the most prominent feminist organizations were closed down after the vote was won. However, recent studies have revealed that in some countries, feminist organizations and groups continued their work and new groups emerged.[4] Studies in other countries might show the same pattern. The conclusion, however, is that a claim for the historical continuity of the feminist movement cannot rest on organizational continuity.

The metaphor of 'waves' has frequently been applied to the history of the feminist movement. The argument is that while the feminist movement has been very strong during certain historical periods, at other times in history feminists have engaged in more quiet, though persistent, work towards feminist goals.

In the following, I distinguish between two parts of the modern feminist movement: The more moderate and legislative oriented Women's Rights Movement, on the one hand, and the radical, leftist grass root Women's Liberation Movement, on the other. These two streams within the overall feminist movement have existed side by side during the last decades. The new radical, leftist Women's Liberation movement swept through all Western countries from the late 1960s through the 1970s and 1980s. Only in a few countries, first and foremost in the United States, did new and strong liberal feminist organizations emerge during the same period. The rebellious 'new' Women's Liberation type of feminism, however, faded away in the middle of the 1980s. Today, the more moderate Women's Rights feminism has again become the predominant type of feminism in most Western countries.[5]

Shared Identity over Time?

Shared identity is another aspect of the concept of continuity. Can we find evidence that women who worked in various feminist movements also *experienced* a sense of shared identity with a long historical chain of feminists themselves? Do feminists talk about the feminist movement in the singular? Interesting research projects are buried here.

My analysis of the Danish Women's Liberation movement 1970-85, which was called 'The Redstockings', shows that there was a clear sense of belonging to a historical feminist movement. But there was also disagreement. Feelings of dissent as well as of cooperation were directed at other feminist groupings of the same historical period. I have used specific policy issues like equal pay and abortion and events like March 8 and the women's festivals to trace patterns of cooperation and conflict in contemporary feminism in the 1970s-1980s. Which feminist groups joined forces in organizing the March 8 events in the 1970s and 1980s? The study shows cooperation as well as severe conflicts. The Danish Redstockings arose in opposition to the women's rights organization, *Dansk Kvindesamfund*, which they considered too cautious, too moderate and too bourgeois.[6]

It seems to be a fact that every new wave of feminist protest starts out from a sharp critique – not just of the male-dominated society, but also of previous and contemporary feminist organizations. In fact, my study also shows that in the beginning, many Redstockings were rather unaware of previous feminist movements. However, the history of feminism soon became part of the common knowledge of the new activists through their intense study and new interpretations of their feminist foremothers. Interestingly enough, the studies concentrated on the history of their grandmothers' or great-grandmothers' generation – women like Clara Zetkin, Alexandra Kollontai, Emma Goldman and other leftist feminists. Feminism in their mothers' generation was not as interesting for the young Redstockings.

The delegates of the Second Nordic Women's Conference in Copenhagen, June 1914. (Courtesy of the Women's History Archives, Denmark.)

A festival in the Woman's Liberation Movement in the 1970's. Is this the same movement as in 1914? Photo: Søren Sylvest. (Courtesy of the Women's History Archives, Denmark.)

Further studies are needed about this dimension of shared identity. But it seems to be a fact that the new feminist protest of the 1960s-1980s in the West identified itself as part of a long, continuous feminist movement. At the same time, the point of departure was a sharp critique of contemporary feminism and the activists' immediate predecessors, even if broad coalitions indeed were established on issues like equal pay, political empowerment of women, fighting violence against women, and abortion on demand.[7]

A common core of feminism?

The third aspect of continuity or discontinuity to be discussed here is the ideological aspect. Of the three dimensions, the question of ideological continuity is the most salient.

Today it is common to talk about 'feminisms' in the plural, indicating that there are many different types of feminism – which of course is true.[8] However, the task here is not to characterize different types of feminism within the long history of feminist ideas, such as classic liberal feminism, classic and modern Marxist feminism, utopian socialist feminism, modern equal opportunity feminism, modern socialist and/or radical feminism and poststructuralist feminism.[9] These various types of feminism are not our concern here.

Rather, the question is whether we can identify a common core of feminism. I see feminism as the ideology of the women's movement as well as that of certain individual writers. It is my claim *that if we cannot identify a common core of feminism, then feminism cannot be labelled an autonomous ideology, an ideology in itself.* In that case, feminism would be reduced to serving as a sub-ideology to other doctrines. Then we should speak of feminist liberalism and feminist socialism, instead of socialist or liberal feminism. Liberalism could be taken as a parallel example: Even if liberalism can be divided into several subcategories such as classic liberalism, social liberalism and neo-liberalism, a common core, 'liberalism', unites all tendencies.

Reading the 19th century feminists, it soon becomes clear that their ideas of women's and men's different biological constitutions are very far from contemporary feminist thinking about the social construction of gender. The goal of feminism has found is expression in concepts as different as equal opportunity, equality of result, different but equal, emancipation, liberation and many others. Is it the same movement? Is it the same ideology?

I will argue that it is possible to identify a core of feminism. The external boundaries are not discussed here, even if that is a delicate matter: Which organizations and authors should we select for scrutiny in search for a common core? Sometimes feminism is identified with the autonomous women's movement. A broader definition of the women's movement also includes women's sections or activities in political parties, trade unions, the peace movement and so on. Even housewife organizations may be included in the category women's movement.

In order to avoid arguing in circles – feminism is the ideology of those groups that have a feminist ideology! – I will define feminism theoretically. The basis of my reasoning is, however, an analysis of the ideas of the autonomous women's movements and the ideas of those who call themselves feminists or the equivalent in their own language.

It is not an easy task to define the common ideological core of feminism. A political ideology may be identified as a coherent system of normative and descriptive elements, including shared understandings of human nature, shared ideas of justice, property rights, equality and inequality, of the relation between state, market and civil society, as well as a shared vision for the future.

From the writings of those who call themselves feminists it soon becomes evident that no common utopian vision is spelled out, and that there is no such vision which could be the object of widespread consensus. Rather, we may speak of *partial visions*.[10]

A definition

In general, it is in fact easier to define feminism by what feminists are fighting against: Consequently, I define feminism as an ideology, which has as its basic goal to fight against male dominance, and against the discrimination and degradation of women and of the tasks predominantly performed by women.[11] Expressed in a more positive way, Imelda Whelehan, based partly on Judith Evans' book from 1986, states that all feminist positions are 'founded upon the belief that women suffer from systematic social injustices because of their sex and therefore any feminist is, at the very minimum, committed to some form of reappraisal of the position of women in society'.[12] So the core of feminism is the protest against male dominance, a dominance which implies the degradation of women. This implies that gender is seen as one of the most significant, if not the most significant, social cleavage.[13]

In an attempt to define feminism positively, in terms of the partial visions, I will point to fundamental feminist visions of autonomy and of equality. Feminism involves a vision of women as autonomous beings and of a relation between men and women based on equality. 'Autonomy' is here preferred to 'individualism', because individualism is so strongly associated with liberalism.[14] The concepts of autonomy and equality are as we all know defined differently by various feminisms, but it seems adequate to include the vision of autonomy and equality in a very broad sense in the definition of feminism. More research is, however, needed in this attempt to define a common core of feminism.

This combination of protest against male dominance and of positive partial visions of autonomy and equality is the defining characteristic of feminism, the common core. With this definition of feminism, it is possible to support the continuity thesis that a feminist movement has existed for more than 150 years.

Even if the *feminists* themselves often talk in terms of shared identity, see above, the question of the shared identity of *women*, of women as a group, nevertheless constitutes both the raison d'etre of the feminist movement – and its Achilles' heel.

The American historian, Nancy Cott, develops the definition further. Her definition, which explicitly is not tied to any historical period, has the following three components:

1. Opposition to sex hierarchy
2. Women's condition is socially constructed rather than predestined by God or nature.
3. Women are not only a biological sex but also a social grouping. Thus feminism implies some identification with 'the group called women'.[15]

Nancy Cott's first point runs parallel to the one about 'breaking male dominance'. The second point must obviously be a common idea of feminism. Otherwise any attempts to change women's position in society would be in vain. Also 19th century feminists revolted against traditional gender ideologies which defined women's proper position in society as exclusively predestined by biology and God. The third point is a very important, yet controversial, position, see also Elisabeth Lønnå's interesting discussion in this volume.

It may be questioned whether Nancy Cott's third point, some identification with women as a group, should be employed in the very definition of feminism. Firstly, it cannot be applied to individual male writers, who like John Stuart Mill or August Bebel stood up for women's rights against the 'Subjection of Women'. Some researchers have chosen to solve this problem by using the concept 'anti-sexist' men, thus reserving the term 'feminist' for women.[16]

Secondly, and more importantly, can women work for bettering women's position without identifying with women as a group? Did upper-class women, who in the name of the women's right movement organized education for servant girls, identify with those girls? Do working class women or ethnic minority women's groups, who work hard to change the position of women from their own kind, identify with all women? Can identification with women be partial, and still be labelled feminist? Can post-feminist women, who do not want to talk about women as a group at all, be labelled feminists? The fact that women do have multiple identities constitutes a barrier to achieving a common struggle undertaken by all women. Simone de Beauvoir stated that women are considered a group by society (women are so and so), but contrary to the 'proletariat', "women do not say "We""[17].

No doubt the construction of women as a collective subject (or several collective subjects) has been essential for all feminism. However, instead of going into endless discussions about whether this should be considered definitive of feminism or not, I suggest more empirical studies of women as a group should be undertaken: When in history has it been possible to form broad coalitions between many women's organizations and groups? What feminist issues have brought women together? Seen from this perspective, the split between women is the theoretical point of departure, while collective feminist actions become the object of empirical study.

The conclusion is that it seems possible to define a meaningful common core of feminism, a feminist ideology, even if history has witnessed many competing feminisms. Of the three discussed dimensions of continuity, the first, organizational continuity, could be found only in a few countries, among them the Nordic countries, but is not applied as an exclusive criterion for continuity. On the basis of the other two dimensions, a common core of feminist ideology and some degree of shared identity among feminists, it is concluded that it does makes sense to talk about a continuous feminist movement spanning the last 100 to 150 years.

Cycles and waves of protest

The continuity *and* change of the feminist movement is beautifully described in the epigram of this article: the feminist movement is like the sea, it comes in waves and cannot be stopped. Implicit in the wave metaphor is the concept that a feminist movement has existed all the time, but that its strength and visibility varies. But how should we understand the concept of wave in social movement studies?

I define social movement waves in terms of activities, mobilization and visibility. One might also add impact. During every new wave of the feminist movement, mobilization is running high, many new organizations are being created and a comprehensive debate concerning women's position makes it on to the public agenda. If successful, the movement contributes to changing the norms and values in society.

But also within each wave, a movement experiences ups and downs. A movement seems to have a life cycle: rise, peak and decline. Further, social movements seem to emerge in parallel waves, with many new movements rising at the same time. So many concepts of waves or cycles are involved.

'Cycles of protests' or 'protest waves' have long been subject of discussions by historians, sociologists, political scientists and many other scholars. One can identify at least three dimensions of this discussion:

1. Do individual movements have life cycles?
2. Do social movements come in waves, that is, do many new movements emerge at the same time in history?
3. Can we identify regularly recurring cycles?

The life cycle of individual movements

The feminist movement at large has had its cycles throughout history. The wave metaphor implies that although the feminist movement has existed continuously, it has had its ups and downs within that frame. Thus continuity as well as change prevails. Instead of 'rise and fall', the concepts of 'peaks' and 'doldrums' are preferable.

The feminist movement of the 1960s-1980s was therefore both new and old. It is common to characterize this movement as 'second wave' feminism or 'new' versus 'old' feminism.[18]

Other researchers have, however, identified three waves of feminism in their respective countries, and consequently the new feminist protest of the 1960s-1980s becomes 'third wave' feminism.[19] The argument is that the 19th century struggle for women's right to education and positions, as well as legal maturity for married women, constitutes the first wave, while the later campaign for suffrage around the turn of the century was the second. The two distinct waves were separated by a period of quieter feminist work. After the suffrage was won there again came a new period of more muted and dogged feminist activity.

It is disputed, however, whether the interwar period, during which a backlash against feminism emerged, should be labelled a silent period. Many new women's organizations, such as housewife associations and women's sections within the political parties, were formed in most Western countries during this very period. New issues like contraception and abortion reached the political agenda. In the same period, married women's right to hold jobs as for example teachers was questioned, because of the severely high unemployment of men during the economic crisis. Elisabeth Lønnå's rejection in this volume of the wave theory as such rests partly on her study of this interwar period. However, in my opinion this example does not falsify the thesis that the feminist movement has had its ups and downs in terms of activity, mobilization, visibility and impact. Rather, it shows the need for more empirical studies about women's organizations and their aims in various historical periods.

Within each wave, a movement also has its rise, peak and decline. Movements are fluid, as the American scholar Jo Freeman argues.[20] "All movements ebb and flow", Kuechler & Dalton write.[21] A social movement represents a protest against the established order, and the commitment of the participants is by definition a movement's main resource.[22] A social movement consists of many organizations and groups under a common ideological umbrella. These movement organizations and groups tend to have a *temporary* character. Some movements transform into a political party or an interest organization, in which case they by definition are no longer 'movements'. Others might turn into specialized institutions. Still others simply fade away.

While the rise of social movements has been a popular subject in social movement research, less interest has been paid to studies of movement *transformation and movement decline*. In my study of the Danish Redstocking movement I identify three stages of the movement:

Stage 1: 1970 to about 1974: The period of direct actions
Stage 2: about 1974-1980: The feminist counterculture flourishes
Stage 3: 1980 to about 1985: Specialization

Why and how did the movement change? Recent studies of the *transformation* of the feminist movement have preferred a resource mobilization perspective, see later.[23]

My own study of the development of the Redstocking movement challenges Claus Offe's three-stage model of social movement transition. According to Claus Offe, social movements tend to develop through three stages. From the take-off phase, over a phase of stagnation, to a third phase characterized by the 'attractions and temptations of institutionalization.[24] This model is based on the development of the environmental movement in Germany, which transformed itself into a political party. By contrast, the Redstocking movement in general resisted the 'temptations' of institutionalization. The final conclusion of my study is that the very ideology of the Redstockings, in which the flat group structure was an integrated part, prevented the institutionalization of the movement.[25] Only in Iceland did the Women's Liberation movement transform itself into a political party (1983-99).

Why did the new wave of the feminist movement decline? After the middle of the 1980s, the radical and leftist Women's Liberation type of feminism in my interpretation no longer existed as a collective force. Only smaller groups exist today. The sharp division between Women's Liberation feminism and the more moderate modern liberal and social democratic equal opportunity feminism has gradually disappeared in most Western countries.

From the Redstocking movement several specialized or even professional activities like gender studies, shelters for battered women and projects for unemployed women emerged.[26] My survey of 1,300 former Redstockings reveals that the lack of new recruits was one of the factors that led to the demise of the movement. The new specialized activities did not invite newcomers to join.[27] The change of political atmosphere and the decline of the New Left in general also contributed to this downturn, even if the feminist movement survived longer than most other new movements of the 1960s-1980s.

Do social movements come together in waves – and why?

In general, social movements do seem to emerge many at the same time. Also feminist mobilization has often started side by side with the emergence of other movements. In most Western countries – and this article is limited to those countries – the older feminist movements emerged in periods of general mobilization. In Scandinavia, the last part of the 19th century represented a period of general upheaval – the development of the labour movement, the agrarian movements, co-operative movements, new religious movements – and the feminist movement. Therefore, it makes sense to speak of general waves of protest. But what does this metaphor of general waves of protest signify?

Two of the major schools within social movement theory interpret this historical coincidence differently. *The New Social Movement school* with its structural focus, tries to explain the rise of the many new movements that emerged in the 1960s and 1970s by a *common cause:* the conflicts of post-industrial society.[28]

It is a central argument in New Social Movement theory, that the many new movements of the 1960s-70s in the Western countries represented something *qualitatively new:* representing post-material values, non-class based participation and a flat, anti-hierarchical structure. Contrary to the 'old' movements, the 'new' movements are not motivated by self-interest, but work for the common good.[29] The ecological movement, the feminist movement and the peace movement are not just new in a chronological sense, they are considered qualitatively different from 'older' movements. They represent a totally new historical period, created by (or the representatives of) new structural conflicts in society, New Social Movement theory argues.[30]

The feminist movement proves to be a critical case for New Social Movement theory. How is it possible to see the rebellious new feminist movement as part of the expression of a whole new social order, as many researchers do, when the feminist movement has existed for more than one hundred years? The peace movement of the 1980s does not seem to fit into the theory either, since peace movements emerged already in the 1890s, around World War 1, and again in the 1950s. This contradiction may explain why so few scholars have studied the feminist movement within a new social movement approach – it does not seem to fit!

'Resource Mobilization', another major school in social movement theory, takes a different point of departure. The main interest is not 'why', but 'how' movements emerge. Thus mobilization, strategy, organizations and social entrepreneurship become the focus. Studies of the importance of opportunity structures might be combined with the Resource Mobilization perspective.

The basis of Resource Mobilization theory is that social conflicts exist in all societies and at all times. Consequently, the existence of social conflicts cannot per se explain why new waves of movements occur. It thus becomes even more important to study when and how it becomes possible to mobilize sufficient resources for action.[31]

The Resource Mobilization approach has been used in several studies of the feminist movement, first in Jo Freeman's classic work on the new American feminist movements in the 1960s and 1970s, *The Politics of Women's Liberation* from 1975. Among newer books using a Resource Mobilization approach there is Barbara Ryan's book on the long history of the American women's movement, *Feminism and the Women's Movement,* 1992. From a Resource Mobilization perspective, Leila Rupp and Verta Taylor show in their book, *Survival in the Doldrums* from 1987, how the American feminist movement survived the period 1945 to the 1960s, when the general mood was anti-feminist. Myra Marx Ferree also makes use of this perspective.[32] In my own study of the Danish Women's Liberation Movement, 'The Redstockings', I combine a resource mobilization perspective with a social constructionist approach.[33]

However, the concept of waves and the theory of common causes behind such waves do have their limitations. Five points will briefly be discussed in the following, of which the three last ones are typical for the Resource Mobilization approach. First, *not all movements come as part of a common protest wave.* Throughout history, many movements have not followed such a pattern, and even within a specific period's 'movement family', some movements live much longer than others.

Second, the theory of common causes needs further discussion. Even if it seems obvious that there are some common structural roots underpinning a whole group of parallel movements, for instance the movements of the 1960s-1980s, *different movements are still reactions to different circumstances.* In this way, both the peace movement in the 1890s and the one in the 1980s emerged as reactions to current foreign policies, while other contemporary movements arose out of socio-economic conflicts. 'Feminism did not grow out of the left, feminism grew out of women's oppression', Petra de Vries writes, stressing this very point.[34]

Third, actual parallel emergence does not necessarily imply that common causes are involved at all, or are the most significant. Sidney Tarrow has pointed out that one group of protests may *pave the way for the next*, because the cost of protesting is lowered.[35]

Fourth, the study of the feminist movement shows a specific kind of link at the level of the actors: Feminist groups have often emerged because women who worked together with men for some common cause have experienced discrimination *because of their sex.* This happened to women in the abolition movement in 19th century United States, as well as to women in the New Left of the 1960s and early 1970s, who eventually refused to 'make tea for the revolution'. Here, the cost of participating rose for women, and consequently, these women went out and started their own feminist movements.

The fifth and last qualification to the theory of common causes, I have called *international processes of learning.*[36] Even the old feminist movement was very internationally oriented, and victories in one country were quickly reported to the other countries in a cross-country learning process. For the feminist movement of the 1960s-1980s, mass media coverage of feminist actions abroad gave lots of impetus, and activists from different countries often visited each other. Consequently, the common style, ideological similarities and the widespread use of the same consciousness-raising groups in most Western countries may not just be seen as a reaction to the same structural factors in each and every country. A lot of international learning took place in the rebellious new women's liberation movement of the 1960s-1980s. With the increase in international mass media coverage, this factor will no doubt grow in importance.

Can we identify regularly recurring cycles?

In his study of the cyclical aspect of new social movements, Karl-Werner Brand traces a picture of historical ups and downs since 1800 for as many movements as the feminist movement, the peace movement, the ecological movement and what he labels 'alternative movements'. He concludes that these movements seem to re-emerge in cycles of 40-50 years. The fist wave came around the 1840s, the second around the last turn of the century, while the third wave came in the 1960s-1970s. He tries to link these movement waves to the regular occurrence of economic waves, but finally rejects the connection.[37]

Many other scholars have also worked with theories of regularity in social movement waves. Harrington argues that the interval between waves of protest has decreased at the end of the 20th century, partly to be explained by the fact that the movements have become increasingly self-conscious and analytical of their own development.[38]

In my opinion, such theories of regularly reoccurring waves of protest lack any theoretical base. Why should waves of new movements return at regular intervals? Such a theory would imply that 30 years in the 19th century would be identical to 30 years in the 20th century. Why 30 years?

Only one researcher, the American feminist sociologist Alice Rossi, has come up with a theory of regular intervals that makes any sense. According to Rossi, the American feminist movement has developed in three waves, not just two: 1840-60, 1900-1920 and 1960 onward. The interval between these three waves corresponds to around 50 years or *two generations*. Not the daughters, but the granddaughters continue the feminist movement, according to Alice Rossi.[39]

This theory sounds specious. Along similar lines, a Swedish scholar, Helena Streifert has argued that the feminist movement more than any other movement experiences interruptions – instead of processes of collective learning from one generation to the next. The reason for this, Streifert argues, is that generational differences are greater among women than among men, because segregation by age is especially strong in women's lives.[40]

This thesis ought to be tested upon various countries. However, in the case of Denmark, such regular intervals cannot be found between the waves of the feminist movement, which I have identified as the 1880s, 1907-1920 and 1970-85.[41] Nevertheless, the generational conflicts have no doubt been important in the history of the movement, because of the crucial importance in feminism of changing identities. Not seldom were generational conflicts in the feminist movement played out around the dubious dichotomy between equality and difference.[42]

In this volume Elisabeth Lønnå argues that the variations found in the different scholars' periodication of the waves of the feminist movement are confusing and misleading when studying the movement internationally. However, such variations may in fact reflect differences in the actual historical development, rather than conceptual confusion.

Emancipation, anti-modernism and postmodernism

The continuous feminist movement contributes by its very existence to the critique of New Social Movement theory for being a-historical and for having exaggerated the 'newness' of the movements of the 1960s[43] to 1980s.[44] The changes in feminist ideology over time cannot meaningfully be captured under the label 'materialism versus post-materialism'. Further, the class base of both the old and the new women's movement has been identical: middle-class. [45]

Recently, the novelty theory of New Social Movement theory has been overhauled by postmodernist theory. Like the former, postmodernism is based on the idea that contemporary society, that is the late 1980s, the 1990s and on, is exceptionally new.

It is in fact amazing with what frequency scholars eagerly characterize their own time as extraordinary! Consequently, the critique of the assumption of the exceptional new-ness in New Social Movement theory remains highly relevant also today. In fact, this discussion touches upon our general understanding of history.

Karl-Werner Brand puts forward the interesting argument that social movements ever since the 19th century have been based on a critique of modernity. They represent a resistance against the modern project: industrialization, bureaucratization, political centralism and pluralism. In line with New Social Movement theory, Brand argues that the Western movements of 1960s to 1980s 'were borne by a revival of broad currents of modernization critique'.[46]

With the concept of *emancipation movements,* I want to stress a different under-standing of movement history. I see a long line of movements, which in spite of their differences have all been fighting for human rights, equal worth and individual auton-omy for an excluded group. They have struggled for the recognition of the members of their group as human beings of equal value. These movements have worked hard to obtain full citizenship – against discrimination, degradation and exclusion. In their work, they have all tried to construct their group as a political subject, as a group *für sich.*

Included in the family of 'emancipation movements' are the labour movement, agrarian movements, the civil rights movement and other minority movements, the feminist movement, and, in contemporary society, gay and lesbian emancipation movements. In the future, new protest movements of immigrants might be added to the list.

In spite of their obvious differences, they have all demanded that the classic liberal idea – that all human beings are born equal – come true. Therefore, they do not as Brand claims represent a protest against the ideas of the Enlightenment – the ideas of equality and freedom. On the contrary, they represent the demand that the promises of the French revolution and the American Declaration of Independence be fulfilled in reality, even if the belief in an unbroken line of progress has fainted. Whether the realization of this ideal can be obtained within contemporary social structure or whether it implies an overturn of the whole social order is, and has always been, a conten-tious issue for these emancipation movements. There have been numerous conflicts between these different movements, for instance between the labour movement and feminism. But history has also witnessed many processes of collective learning from one movement to the other.

If postmodernism implies a break with this struggle for emancipation, when it is urgently needed in most parts of the world, then we can really speak of 'newness'.

Conclusion: The new wave of an old movement

The metaphor of 'waves' implies continuity *and* change.The methodological conse-quence is that a *diachronous* as well as a *synchronous* perspective is needed when studying the feminist movement, because of its roots in the present as well as in the past. Even if the focus of this article is the feminist movement, the same methodology will probably also prove relevant for other movements with a long history.

The continuity argument does not imply that the same feminist organizations have existed during the last 150 years. Apart from the Nordic region this has only been the case in a few other countries. Within the overall ideological framework of feminism, the actual feminist agenda changes from generation to generation. The theoretical argument of continuity implies that since so many common features can be identified between the older and the newer feminist movements, it makes sense to maintain that the feminist movements that have emerged after the end of the 1960s are not a totally new phenomenon in history, but represent *the new wave of an old movement.*

Many more studies about the waves of the feminist movement are needed. No doubt, there is a connection between new feminist protests and the emergence of other movements in the same historical period – the synchronous perspective. But not all new waves of feminist protest occurred in parallel with other movements, and as in the 1980s, the life cycle of the feminist movement has not always followed that of other contemporary movements. Comparative studies between a selected number of countries would be fruitful.

Further, new waves of feminist mobilization should also be studied in their relation to – as inspired by and/or as a reaction to – previous feminist movements. This is the diachronous perspective. For all emancipation movements with a long history, this combined perspective seems relevant. For really 'new' movements the synchronous perspective is the most relevant.

Until now, feminist research has predominantly explained the rise of new waves of feminism, old or new, by theories of relative deprivation, and theories about the conflict between women's changing position in society and traditional norms and values. Often, historical changes in women's structural position have been the point of departure. Consequently, the rise of the first Women's Rights movement in the second half of the 19th century has been explained by theories of relative deprivation, that is by the increasing contradiction between the great opportunities that industrialization gave men of the educated class and the new middle class – compared to the lack of opportunities and lack of means of maintenance for women of the same classes. Women's experiences of discrimination in other movements and inspiration from other reform movements have also been added as explanatory factors.[47]

Along a similar line of reasoning, the rise of the feminist movement of the 1960s-1980s is often explained with reference to the contradiction between, on the one hand, women's new position in the labour market in the 1960s, the birth control pill and women's new educational opportunities and, on the other hand, traditional sex roles.[48]

We need further empirical investigation as a necessary background to developing theories about the rise of the different waves of the feminist movement. As it is now, explanations are apparently borrowed from one country study to the other. We need further investigation into the movement's relationship to other movements of the same wave. The flow of inspiration and ideas across borders also needs further attention. If a new movement takes after other contemporary movements or gets massive inspiration from abroad, then new feminist waves of protest cannot be explained solely by changes in women's structural position in that one society. We also need more research into the transformation and decline of feminist movements during various periods in history. In general, the study of the feminist movement needs a widened research agenda.

References

Bammer, Angelika (1991). *Partial visions. Feminism and utopianism in the 1970s.* New York and London. Routledge.

Batiot, Anne (1986). "Radical democracy and feminist discourse: The case of France". In Dahlerup, Drude (ed.). *The new women's movement. Feminism and political power in Europe and the USA.* Sage, 85-102.

Beauvoir, Simone de (1949/1961). *Le deuxiéme sexe.* Editions Gallimard. (English: Nature of the Second Sex. Square Books).

Brand, Karl-Werner (1990). "Cyclical aspects of new social movements: Waves of cultural criticism and mobilization cycles of the new middle-class radicalism". In Dalton & Kuechler (eds.): *Challenging the political order.* Polity Press, 23-42.

Brenner, Johanna (1996). "The best of times, the worst of times: Feminism in the United States". In Monica Threlfall (ed.): *Mapping the women's movement.* Verso, 17-72.

Bryson, Valerie (1992). *Feminist political theory.* Macmillan

Cott, Nancy F. (1987). *The grounding of modern feminism.* Yale University Press.

Dahlerup, Drude (1973). Socialisme og kvindefrigørelse i det 19. århundrede. Forlaget GMT.

Dahlerup, Drude (ed.) (1986). The new women's movement. Feminism and political power in Europe and the USA. London. Sage

Dahlerup, Drude (1993). "From movement protest to state feminism: the women's liberation movement and unemployment policy in Denmark". In NORA Nordic Journal of Women's Studies, Vol. 1, No 1, 4-20

Dahlerup, Drude (1998). Rødstrømperne. Den danske Rødstrømpebevægelses udvikling, nytænkning og gennemslag 1970-1985. Vol. I-II. København. Gyldendal.

Dahlerup, Drude (2000). "Continuity and Waves in the Feminist Movement – a Challenge to Social Movement Theory", in Aino Saarinen, Hilda Rømer Christensen & Beatrice Halsaa (eds.): *Women's Movement and Internationalisation: The "Third" Wave?* University of Oulu. 82/2000, 22-52.

Dahlerup, Drude (2001). "Ambivalenser och strategiska val. Om problem kring begreppen särart och jämlikhet i kvinnorörelsen och i feministisk teori", *Kvinnovetenskaplig tidskrift,* nr.1, 17-40.

Dahlerup, Drude & Gulli, Brita (1983). "Kvindeorganisationerne i Norden: Afmagt eller Modmagt? i Havio-Mannila, Elina et al.: *Det uferdige demokratiet. Kvinner i nordisk politikk.* Nordisk Ministerråd, 8-57.

Dalton, Russell J. and Kuechler, Manfred (eds.) (1990). *Challenging the political order. New social and political movements in western democracies.* Polity Press.

Dalton, Russell J., Kuechler, Manfred and Bürklin, Wilhelm (1990). "The Challenge of New Movements" in Dalton & Kuechler. *Challenging the political order. New social and political movements in western democracies.* Polity Press, 3-20.

della Porta, Donatella and Diani Mario (1999). *Social Movements. An Introduction.* Blackwell.

Evans, Judith (1986). *Feminism and Political Theory.* Sage.

Evans, Judith (1995). *Feminist theory today. An introduction to second-wave feminism.* Sage.

Evans, Richard (1977). *The feminists.* Croom Helm.

Ferree, Myra Marx and Hess, Beth B. (1985). *Controversy and coalition: The new feminist movement.* Twayne.

Ferree, Myra Marx and Martin, Patricia Yancey (eds.) (1995). *Feminist organizations. Harvest of the new women's movement.* Temple University Press.

Foweraker, Joe (1995). *Theorizing Social Movements.* Pluto Press.

Freeman, Jo (1973). The tyranny of structurelessness. In *Ms.* July.

Freeman, Jo (1975). *The politics of women's liberation.* Longman.

Freeman, Jo (ed.) (1983). *Social movements of the sixties and seventies.* Longman.

Gamson, William A. (1975, 1990). *The strategy of social protest.* The Dorsey Press (1st edition) and Wadsworth Publishing Company (2nd edition).

Gustafsson, Gunnel (ed.), Eduards, Maud and Rönnblom, Malin (1997). *Towards a new democratic order. Women's organizing in Sweden in the 1990s.* Publica.

Haug, Frigga (1988). Lehren aus den Frauenbewegungen in Westeuropa. In Frauenbewegung in der Welt. Ed. by Die Autonome Frauenredaktion. Vol. 1, 6-13.

Heywood, Andrew (1992). *Political Ideologies.* Macmillan.

Kaplan, Gisela (1992). *Contemporary Western European Feminism.* Allen & Unwin.

Kemp, Sandra & Squires, Judith (eds.) (1997). *Feminisms.* Oxford University Press.

Klandermans, P. Bert (1990). Linking the "old" and the "new". Movement networks in the Netherlands. Dalton and Kuechler: *Challenging the political order.* Polity Press, 122-136.

Kuechler, Manfred & Dalton, Russell J. (1990). "New Social Movements and the Political Order", Dalton & Kuechler (eds.). *Challenging the political order.* Polity Press, 277-300.

Larana, Enrique, Johnston, Hank and Gusfield, Joseph R. (eds.) (1994). *New social movements. From ideology to identity.* Temple University Press.

Lovenduski, Joni & Randall, Vicky (1993). *Contemporary Feminist Politics. Women and Power in Britain.* Oxford University Press.

Manns, Ulla (1997). *Den sanna frigörelsen. Fredrika-Bremer-förbundet 1884-1921.* Stockholm. Brutus Östlings Bokförlag.

McCarthy, John D. and Zald, Mayer N. (1977). Resource mobilization and social movements: A partial theory. In *American Journal of Sociology*, Vol. 82, no 6, 1212-1241.

McGlen, Nancy E. and O'Connor, Karen (1983). *Women's Rights.* Praeger.

Melucci, Alberto (1985). Symbolic challenge of contemporary movements. In *Social Research*, Vol. 52, no 4, 789-816.

Melucci, Alberto (1994). A strange kind of newness: What's "new" in new social movements? In Larana, Johnston and Gusfield: *New Social Movements.* Temple University Press. 101-130.

Offe, Claus (1990). "Reflections on the institutional self-transformation of movement politics: A tentative stage model". In Dalton, Russell J. and Kuechler, Manfred (eds.): *Challenging the political order*. Polity Press, 232-250.

Outshoorn, Joyce (1991). "A distaste of dirty hands: Gender and politics in second-wave feminism". In Tayo Andreasen et al. (eds.): *Moving On. New perspectives on the women's movement.* Aarhus University Press.

Rossi, Alice p. (1978). "Contemporary American feminism: In and out of the political main-stream". *International Symposium on the Research on Women's Organizations*. Stockholm. Fredrika-Bremer-Förbundet, 102-140

Rupp, Leila J. and Taylor, Verta (1987). *Survival in the Doldrums: The American Women's Rights Movement, 1945 to the 1960s.* Oxford University Press.

Ryan, Barbara (1992). *Feminism and the Women's Movement. Dynamics of change in social movement, ideology and activism.* Routledge.

Schenk, Herrad (1983). *Die feministische Herausforderung.* C.H. Beck.

Streijfert, Helena (1983). *Studier i den svenska kvinnorörelsen.* Sociologiska Institutionen, University of Gothenburg.

Tarrow, Sidney (1989). *Democracy and Disorder. Protest and Politics in Italy 1965-1975.* Clarendon Press.

Tarrow, Sidney (1994). *Power in movement. Social movements, collective action and politics.* Cambridge University Press.

Threlfall, Monica (ed.) (1996). *Mapping the Women's Movement.* Verso.

Tong, Rosemarie (1992). *Feminist Thought.* Routledge.

Touraine, Alain (1978). *La voix et le regard.* Editions du Seuil.

Vries, Petra de (1981). Feminism in the Netherlands. *Women's Studies International Quarterly.* Vol. 4, no. 4, 389-407.

Whelehan, Imelda (1995). *Modern Feminist Thought. From the second wave to 'postfeminism'.* Edinburgh University Press.

Zald, Mayer N. and Ash, Roberta (1966). "Social movement organizations: growth, decay and change". In *Social Forces*, vol. 44, March, 327-341.

Zetkin, Clara (1924/25). Erinnerungen an Lenin. In *Ausgewählte Reden und Schriften*, Dietz Verlag.Vol. 3, 89-160.

Notes

1   A quotation from a private letter from Dorthe Gjørup, member of a women's group in the Danish town of Skive, to Elin Appel, a feminist author and my mother, 26 August 1979.

2   Many thanks to Lenita Freidenvall, who has worked as research assistant on this article and to Alexandra Segerberg, who has worked with the language correction.

3   Dahlerup & Gulli (1983); Dahlerup (1986); Dahlerup (1998).

4   Rupp & Taylor (1987).

5   Freeman (1975); Dahlerup (1998).

6   Dahlerup (1998).

7   Schrenk (1983); Ferree & Hess (1985); Dahlerup (1986) and (1998); Rupp & Taylor (1987); Klandermanns (1990); Kaplan (1992); Lovenduski & Randall (1993); Threlfall (1996).

8   Kemp & Squires (1997).

9   Bryson (1992); Tong (1992); Evans (1995); Dahlerup (1973) and (1998); Whelehan (1995).

10 Bammer (1991).
11 Dahlerup (1986), p. 6.
12 Whelehan (1995), p. 25.
13 Heywood (1992).
14 Gertrud Bäumer, one of the liberal leaders of the autonomous German women's movement just after the turn of the previous century even expressed the view that feminism was a logical consequence of liberal ideas, and that even socialist ideas of women's emancipation rested on a hidden individualistic principle in socialism (Dahlerup 1973, p. 328).
15 Cott (1987), pp. 4-5.
16 Batiot 1(986).
17 Beauvoir (1961), p. 11.
18 Schenk (1983); Outshoorn (1991); Ryan (1992); Evans (1995); Brenner (1996).
19 Rossi (1978); McGlen & O'Connor (1983); Dahlerup (1986) and (1998).
20 Freeman (1983), p.4.
21 Kuechler & Dalton (1990), p. 284.
22 Dahlerup (1986), p. 9.
23 Rupp & Taylor (1987); Ryan (1992); Ferree & Martin (1995).
24 Offe (1990), p. 240.
25 Dahlerup (1998).
26 Dahlerup (1993).
27 Dahlerup (1998).
28 Touraine (1978).
29 Dalton, Kuechler and Bürklin (1990).
30 Offe (1985); Dalton & Kuechler (1990); Larana et al. (1994).
31 See Zald & Ash (1966); McCarthy & Zald (1977); Tarrow (1989); Gamson (1975) and (1990).
32 Ferree & Hess (1985); Ferree & Martin (1995).
33 Dahlerup (1998).
34 Vries, Petra de (1981), p. 391.
35 Tarrow (1994), p. 7.
36 Dahlerup (1998), vol. I, p. 162.
37 Brand (1990), p. 34.
38 In Freeman (1983), p. ix.
39 Rossi (1978).
40 Streifert (1983).
41 Dahlerup (1998).
42 Dahlerup (2001).
43 Foweraker (1995); Dahlerup (1998) and (2000); della Porta & Diani (1999)
44 Some scholars like Melucci have themselves later expressed some doubts about the NSM perspective, see Melucci (1994).
45 A more elaborated critique of the New Social Movement theory from a feminist perspective can be found in a previous version of this article, see Dahlerup (2000).
46 Brand (1990), p. 33.
47 Evans (1977); McGlen & O'Connor (1983).
48 Freeman (1975), Haug (1988); Threlfall (1996); Dahlerup (1998).

Part II

Sources of Activism

CHAPTER 4

No Bed of Roses?
Academic Feminism 1880 – 1980

Beatrice Halsaa

Introduction

When the feminist wave swept through Norway during the beginning of the 1970's, higher education was a major institutional foundation.[1] At first, ideas, activities and participants were basically the same inside and outside academia: Whether young feminists set to work as 'grass roots' activists or as students could hardly be kept apart. A process of differentiation soon begun, however, just before the crest of Norwegian feminism culminated in 1975. Feminist organisations and single-issue networks were established, such as the shelter movement and the women's studies movement, which sprang up simultaneously with the all-time high number of female students. Nurtured by a general climate of political optimism, the spirit of the student revolt and in particular by feminist visions, women and some men demanded a radically new scholarship. I claim that the modelling and introduction of women's studies and feminist research is one of the most impressive and enduring outcomes of the revived feminism of the 1970's.[2]

A sense of being part of something genuinely new was widespread among feminist students during the early 1970s. The jubilant feeling of constituting the very first generation of feminists in academia was not quite up to historical facts, however: There was a long tradition and continuity of feminist activism in academia, of which young feminists then were generally ignorant. The poor sense of history had obvious reasons: This history had never been focused, but the silencing and 'invisibilising' of women's lives were soon grasped by the reanimated feminist movement during the 1970s, and vigorously put on their political agenda. In fact, 'visibilising' became one of the most pressing feminist tasks. *Kvinnehistorie* – 'herstory' – was born, and some scholars began to unearth the histories even of academic women. A web of Nordic and international women's studies connections was soon established. Long-lasting ties between feminists inside and outside academia were uncovered, accentuating the political significance of education and the construction of knowledge.[3] Based on available research this article examines academic feminism as a social movement, focusing the shifting interplay between academic and non-academic feminism in Norway. The approach is both vertical and horizontal, comprising the history of academic feminism from women's struggle for access during the 1880s until the institutionalisation of women's studies in the 1970s. Norwegian academic feminism is incessantly discussed within a broader Nordic and international context, in accordance with a cross-border feminist perspective (see Heitlinger, this volume).

A Nordic context

Nordic feminist networks were important from the very beginning of the history of Norwegian academic feminism. The dissemination of ideas encouraged and legitimised feminist issues across the Nordic borders, and undoubtedly encouraged the process of institutionalising women's studies during the 1970's. Even the extended practical use of women's studies in policy formation in Norway is partly ascribed to Nordic co-operation.[4] The women's studies movements in 'the Nordic region' display some striking differences however, such as the beginning and type of local and national institutionalisation (see table 1). Also, the focus on research compared to curricula development and teaching has been quite different. The relationship between the new women's studies scholarship and the public gender equality institutions vary a great deal, and the attainments of governmental funding also varies considerably. Even the name of the field differs. During the 1970's Norway was regarded as a model country for women's studies, with a firm reputation for an efficient *national* institution[5] and a radical, feminist *research* profile. The substance of the field determined the Norwegian designation: kvinneforskning (women's research). This was in contrast to Sweden where teaching was encouraged by means of public funding of local forums and centres at the universities. Also, in Sweden the official term soon was established as 'jämställdhetsforskning' (gender equality research), in accordance with the term used by Swedish bureaucrats, and contrary to the women's studies community.[6] Generally Nordic differences in academic feminism are clearly related to national variations in the strength of the feminist movements and their interplay with the nation states.[7]

Although variations are noteworthy, I will focus on the significant similarities, as they are conceptualised in the well-established term *Nordic women's research*. Referring to more than just geography, the term indicates how certain material, cultural and political structures influence research processes and outcomes.[8] In spite of differences, it is my claim that 'the Nordic region' still reflects a cultural identity connected to the traditional Christian-protestant religion, to welfare systems strongly influenced by social democratic ideologies, and to political cultures nurturing negotiations and compromises. Historical periods of Swedish and Danish supremacy over Finland, Iceland and Norway never quite eradicated layers of social affinities between the Nordic countries.[9] Cultural, political and physical proximity have facilitated the diffusion of people, ideas and actions, including feminist ones. During the 20th century, a large number of Nordic political and cultural institutions were established to ease and stimulate practical co-operation. The field of gender equality and women's studies has been no exception. Feminists inside and outside academia have utilised these instruments skilfully to promote their cause.

Academic feminism as a social movement

My approach to the history of academic feminism is inspired by Social Movement Theory. Various efforts to bridge the gaps between three previously distinct perspectives on social movements – political opportunities, mobilizing structures and cultural framing – and to clarify the relationships between them, have been helpful.[10] In short, social movement theories provide one way to deal with a controversial question in feminist theory: women's agency.[11] Structuralists and poststructuralists have argued convincingly against individualistic approaches, but the challenge of dealing with agency still remains. Efforts have been made to carve out theoretical positions acknowledging material and discursive limitations without totally undermining agency, such as 'situated freedom', to accept the social and discursive construction of subjects while simultaneously allowing subjects to be constructed with potentials for criticism, resistance and alternative visions.[12] Social Movement Theory is another option for scholars wanting to approach the history of academic feminism without forgetting structural and cultural constraints focusing questions like these: How and when have academic feminists been able to take advantage of changing political structures? How have individual resources been mobilised into a social movement and movement organisations? What kinds of shared meanings and definitions have been constructed, and with what effects?

Social Movement Theory underlines the political embeddedness of knowledge and the importance of meaning-making politics, justifying a closer look at the role of intellectuals, such as academic feminists. I see them as constituting a social movement, a women's studies movement. A social movement is characterised by conscious and collective activities for change, which is exactly what academic feminism is about. The undeniably professional and institutionalised character of academic feminism growing out of the more hilarious 1970s, should not prevent us from applying a movement perspective. Feminist scholars themselves often refer to women's studies as a social movement; some even claim that it is '(…) one of the great intellectual movements of our century'.[13]

The movement designation has survived the 1970s for good reasons because academic feminism still contains fundamental movement characteristics: First of all, contemporary women's studies' practitioners' uphold feminism as a basic aspect of their professional identity. Feminist studies moves on within – various and shifting – feminist ideological frameworks, and even now encounters dubious and sometimes starkly hostile intellectual environments. Secondly, the production of feminist knowledge is a collective, conscious undertaking to effect social change, and not the result of lonely brains. Constructing new ways of understanding and challenging existing knowledge, norms and power structures within and outside higher education, academic feminism – the deliberate effort to disseminate new ideas and concepts to politicians, students and to the general public is about discursive politics. Thidly, personal motivation and resources, two vital movement hallmarks, have played a crucial role for the survival of the scolarship in the 1980s and 1990s, just as they did for the first generations of academic feminists in the 1880s.[14]

Let us now turn directly to the history of academic feminism, guided by the ideas and perspectives of Social Movement Theory, to see how it unfolded as a response to concrete problems and favourable occasions.

Struggle for access and 'survival'

When women in the Nordic region started their struggle for access to higher education during the 1870's, women's rights organisations were yet to come. On the one hand, the efforts of the individual pioneers obviously reflect changing social structures, on the other they also illustrate the endeavours of individual women to take advantage of the actual opportunity structure and to mobilise resources. Pioneers such as Cecilie Thoresen, the first Norwegian woman who consistently and successfully struggled for access, were well informed about the situation of her Nordic sisters and their various achievements (table 1). In spite of their privileged social standing, their university access and adventures of the pioneers were not a bed of roses. In general, powerful men in *academia* were either reluctant or bluntly against women's admission. For instance, the faculty of medicine at the University of Oslo argued against women's access by claiming that the education would be too much for women's nerveous system and health. She would loose her femininity, and she was too weak to practice medicine in the tough and rough Norwegian coast and rural districts.

On the other hand, liberal men in *politics* responded to women's demands by introducing the necessary bills in parliament. They pointed at the general advantages of better-educated labour in a period of economic transition. The increasing problem of providing for unmarried women who were no longer demanded as private labour, also counted in favour of women's rights. The legal propositions concerning women's access to higher education were accepted almost unanimously and without extensive debate in Norway. The reasons were partly inconsistent.[15] Some politicians expressed their genuine support for moderate claims for women's rights, while others refrained from explicitly rejecting them. In general they thought that just a very few, exceptional women would actually make practical use of the right to education, and therefore the issue was not one of priority.[16]

Favourable opportunity structures have to be underlined in order to understand women's access: Firstly, the deep technological, economic and demographic transformations of traditional agrarian societies opened new political opportunities. The first half of the 1880s was a period of unforeseen political turmoil in Norway. Constitutional conflicts completely dominated politics, and new political alignments were established. The liberal majority in parliament finally defeated the Swedish king and his conservative Norwegian council in 1884, and a parliamentary system was introduced. In this situation, women's demand for higher education was of minor importance compared to the major constitutional issues. At the same time, the explosive political situation had disclosed unique political alignments and a liberal majority in parliament. The political opposition was unable to mobilise sufficient support to reject moderate liberal bills for women's rights.

Secondly, constitutional civil rights such as freedom of speech, meeting and organising were conducive to efforts of collective protests. Women in Norway did not win universal suffrage until 1913, but fortunately there was no ban on voluntary organisations for women. In Norway, Cecilie Thoresen and five other women attending an

A-certificate course established a 'discussion club', *Skuld,* to promote women's cause in 1883. The first national political parties were established the next year, for men only. *Skuld* was transformed to a national organisation, *Norsk Kvindesaksforening, (The Norwegian Association for Women's Rights* NAWR), in 1884. Similar organisations were established in Denmark, Sweden and Finland, inspired by the same winds of change.[17] Organised feminism was the explicit response by women of flesh and blood to improve women's situation, with the enthusiastic participation of women in higher education.

Thirdly, women's access to higher education made new resources available to them. Although they were few, women made a difference because of their acute political awareness. They knew they were privileged, and they used their energy to improve other women's lives. They functioned as models for their successors, and they organized to promote the social and cultural interests of academic women. Similar initiatives in the Nordic region were stimulating, and close ties between the Nordic pioneers of higher education and the women's movement outside academia were evident from the very start.

Of course, the first wave of organised feminists in the Nordic region had nothing like women's studies to legitimise their claims. Instead, they had fiction and literary criticism to lean on, notably the feminist journal *Nylænde.*[18] Indeed, a feminist public had gradually been established within the Nordic region from the 1850s, with novels demonstrating women's hardships. The prompt translation of Mill's *On the Subjection of Women* (1869) into Nordic languages indicates the concern with women's issues. In fact, women's lack of freedom had become the very symbol of the critique of the traditional Nordic societies, and a range of gender issues therefore came front stage in a very lively political discourse. Novels such as Ibsen's *Et dukkehjem* (A Doll's House) and Bjørnson's *En handske* (A Glove) carved out new gender positions and profound changes in the discourse on sexuality. The flourishing of prostitution and sexually related diseases, as well as improved knowledge on female sexuality, strongly contributed to the political climate. A major topic was whether sexual abstention before marriage was advisable or not, and whether it applied for men as well as for women. The women's movement strongly opposed sexual liberation, liberal men were split between an abstentionist and a 'naturalist' standpoint, all of them provoking antifeminist arguments as well. During this genuinely *Nordic* controversy, called *sædelighetsfeiden*, feminist activists and writers travelled across the Nordic countries contributing to the political mobilisation and radicalisation of the public. The intensity of the discourse on sex and gender during the 1880s astonished continental Europe.

One step forward, two steps backward?

The liberal 1880s were succeeded by a decade of backlash against emancipatory ideas. Dilemmas also made a definite imprint on the professional careers of the first generations of women in academia. Husband and children soon absorbed the talented Cecilie Thoresen, for one. Generally women with higher education were facing multi-handicaps: The insufficient primary education in girl's schools warranted their exclusion from a range of university disciplines. Life at the edge of femininity made them vulnerable, and they were not granted the right to practice their academic skills in permanent posts as scholars or civil servants. Those who opted for a professional career anyway were expected to reject marriage and motherhood, the defining characteristics of womanhood. Complying with the prevailing social conventions concerning intellectual women was therefore no guarantee against discrimination and misogyny. One should not wonder, then, that women in academia felt a need to stick together as women. Fortunately some of them had the courage and resources to articulate their demands, to take advantage of their (relative to other women) privileged position and join forces in women's rights organisations and welfare organisations for academic women.[19] *Kvinnelige Studenters Klubb* (Female Students' Club) was set up in 1902. The leaders were involved in the struggle to improve motherhood, as well as in women's right to vote.

Two decades later, the Female Students' Club paved the way for a third and international generation of academic feminist organisations. *The International Federation of University Women* was founded in 1920 and national federations were immediately set up in the Nordic countries, reflecting the problems still facing academic women (Table 1). The Norwegian situation was said to be something 'between frugal and worrisome'.[20] Nordic co-operation was apparent in the *International Federation of University Women*, for instance in their successful efforts during the first congress to make it a truly international federation, instead of a federation for the winners of World War I. Locally, the Nordic branches of the federation were involved in practical matters like housing conditions for female students and foundations of fellowships and took part in the general public debate on women's issues.[21]

We do not know the extent of direct individual marginalisation and harassment these women suffered. In spite of obvious structural discrimination, some of them have described their relationship to male students and professors as 'excellent', thus diversifying the image of their lot. The high personal price obviously paid by some of the pioneers, established by feminist research, indicate a certain lack of distance and realism with respect to their own situation, such as the general construction of science and research as inconsistent with femininity. The dramatic decrease in the proportion of women with a university degree, from 15% during the first 25 years to 3% during the next 25 years, signifies how the influence of this misogynist discourse may have discouraged the succeeding generations of women in higher education.[22]

The dominant understanding of women and academic achievements as contradictions in terms has proved to be a tenacious discourse. Even so, Nordic women did not struggle in vain. For example, the civil service was gradually opened between 1911 and 1923 (Table 1). Formal rights are not equivalent to actual rights, however, as the ups and downs of women's access to paid work have demonstrated. The outright discrimination of married women during the 1920s and 1930s certainly did not prompt women to make strong bids for higher education. Their proportion of students increased very slowly, not to mention their proportion of scholars.[23] Almost a hundred years had to pass from women were admitted to higher education until their number equalled the number of male students. As we will see, when this happened women also made a breakthrough concerning the content of higher education. Up until then, university women had been marginalized both as subjects and objects of knowledge. During the 1950s however, the gendered content of research was challenged in the Nordic social sciences. Let us take a closer look.

Changing discourse: sex roles and feminism

Social science was not institutionalised in Norway until after 1945, with the independent *Institute for Social Research* (1950) playing an important role. Women's issues were not on the original social science research agenda, but Margarete Bonnevie – author and chairman of the *Women's Rights Association* – did her best to convince the new social scientists of their importance. Her efforts were strengthened by the short revival of Norwegian feminism in the wake of World War II, various initiatives by Nordic women to influence the United Nations; an optimistic belief in science as an instrument for democratic change; and last but not least the close connections between (a few) feminist scholars and activists outside academia. A radical shift in the Nordic gender discourse was to come, with a gradual shift from 'women's issues' to a more relational approach. Nordic sex role research played an important role, and so did the friendly relations between scholars, activists and the social democratic government.

In Norway, the sex role research was opposed to the hegemonic logical empiricism. Even though American structural-functionalism was very influential, sex role scholars were critical to the ideas of the sociologist Talcott Parsons, and consequently insisted on the social construction of gender. They differed from the harmonious perspectives of their American colleagues who thought sex role differentiation was beneficial for everyone. Instead, they used sex roles as a critical concept, and as an instrument for political change. While Parsons focused gender differences in reproduction, they focused the relation between production and reproduction, challenged the hegemonic understanding of the family as a harmonious unit, and highlighted the role of fathers. The Nordic sex role perspective introduced men as gender and had a forthright power aspect.[24]

A range of events outside academy also attracted interest in these issues. For instance in 1953 Åse Gruda Skard, a feminist, psychologist and scholar demanded the complete restructuring of the family, and recognition of 'fathers work', applying social science to underpin her arguments.[25] Then *UNESCO* picked out Norway as one of the countries in which to conduct a survey on the situation of women. A considerable mismatch between liberal sex role attitudes and traditional practices was disclosed, and 'the patriarchal features' of Norwegian society were thoroughly discussed in this radical study.[26] Even the *UN Commission on Women* was criticised in the study: "A society does not become more democratic simply because the same number of women as men take part in its dictatorship".

These events took place in the midst of a feminist backlash during the 1950's. The dominant discourse of women as housewives is well illustrated by a version of Ibsen's

Demonstration in front of University of Oslo.

A Dolls House set up in Sweden (1956), in which Nora does not leave her husband.[27] The backlash provoked responses, however, such as Myrdal and Klein's suggestions for a 'life phase strategy': Women should stay at home while their children were small, and enter the labour market when the children grew older.[28] Sex role scholars were invited to feminist organisations, and their arguments against biologically fixed sex differences fuelled a lively and influential new Nordic discourse on gender. According to Helga Stene, another activist and scholar, the sex role concept itself was introduced to the women's rights movement during a conference in Sweden in 1957. Even though the successful launching of the Russian *Sputnik* stole most of the media interest during the conference, the radical sex role perspectives attracted 'unbelievable interest from abroad'.[29] Shortly after, the *Norwegian Women's Rights Association* started using the term, in addition to underlining the importance of research for feminism.[30]

A second Swedish conference in 1959, on family and working life, also played a major role. A research network on sex roles was established between Norwegian, Swedish and Finnish scholars. Their book *Women's Lives and Work* soon became 'a Bible to knock on people's heads.'[31] The book was reprinted several times, and signalled a public breakthrough for the new social science approach. The Nordic discourse on sex was dramatically changed: Women's issues are no longer "just womens", they relate to the position of both genders. Sex roles mean that men's and women's roles are constructed, not innate: They are changeable.

The radical implications of this shift are related to the combined effects of the Nordic opportunity structure and the efforts made by feminists inside and outside academia. Ideologically, the sex role perspective broke new ground, and was gradually seen as matching the governing social democratic parties' quest for equality. Economically, it was a useful instrument in their efforts to meet new demands for labour. A number of policy documents throughout the 1960's, and the implementation of several *UN* and *ILO* declarations and conventions on women's rights clearly illustrate this point.[32] This means that sex role issues were being transformed to gender equality policies in the Nordic region before the outbreak of the 'new women's movement', with Sweden taking the lead.[33] A shift in the relationship between academic feminism and the women's movement took place when the sex role scholars constructed and disseminated their new theoretical perspectives. Until then, university feminists had contributed to women's knowledge in a personal and quite unsystematic way.[34] Now the very *contents* of scientific knowledge in some disciplines was finally becoming instrumental to feminism. Academic feminists went beyond focusing the discrimination of female scholars and addressed women as objects of research, challenging the actual substance of teaching and research.

The 1970s: spreading like wildfire

When feminist mobilisation exploded during the late 1960s and early 1970s, there was a concurrent increase in the number of female students. In Norway, there were 11 000 university students in 1961 and 33 000 in 1971, reflecting the importance of science in modern societies. The percentage of women went up from 25% in 1960, to 33% in 1971 and 50% in 1979. This shift from minority to (tiny) majority made a tremendous difference in the political climate. Now the very content of education and research could be challenged from within. The number of female students had made a difference, and the self-confident new feminist identity was reinforced by the general political optimism in Norway.

One of the leaders of the *Federation of University Women* expressed her hopes and anxieties this way in 1970: "Where do academic women want to position themselves in the future? The concept of the intellectual is changing. We live in a violent but also promising time of fermentation. Many young people are conscious about the barriers against women's full development. The young must take the initiative. The initiative is theirs.'[35]

How disappointed she must have been when the young feminists turned their back against established organisations. They even rejected the existing sex role theories. Preferring a fresh start, they spent their energy establishing new networks, concepts and theories. A different feminist discourse was born, criticising the means and ends of the old equality discourse. Very soon, demands for feminist studies were voiced. The new scholarship was eased by the parallel student revolt and the ensuing debate on epistemology in Norway, *positivismestriden* (the controversy of positivism). The innate connection between knowledge and interests was established, and the strong position of logical positivism was undermined.[36] In addition, feminist studies took advantage of a genuine Norwegian tradition for radical empirical action research, partly explaining why Norwegian women's studies got a Nordic reputation for empirical grounding of feminist theories. Sex role scholars like Harriet Holter and Berit Ås in Norway favoured the new feminist perspectives. They identified with the new women's research, and thus provided for continuity as well as some authority. The concern of sex role research with production and reproduction was continued, while the perspectives and focus on concepts like women's culture, responsible rationality and women's dignity represented new perspectives.

Few – if any – institutions of higher education were unaffected by the academic feminism during the 1970s. The new field of study challenged the traditional male-focused content of higher education, and brought forward an overwhelming amount of knowledge, from hard facts to contested perspectives. Also, it seriously questioned the very concepts of truth itself, of knowledge and objectivity. The explicit – although complex – relationship between feminist studies and the feminist movement strongly contributed to the keen interest in *fagkritikk* (criticism of curricula and epistemology). Feminist scholars expressed their intentions to use research and teaching as instruments for women's liberation. The struggle for intellectual space soon revealed systematic male prerogatives, and the feminist agenda demanded more 'space' to develop feminist scholarship, permanent positions for women in *academia*, and improved working conditions. Even though these demands are still relevant, courses dealing with women's or gender issues have been introduced at all universities, and there are some positions with a specific gender research or gender equality responsibility.

Feminist studies have been ridiculed and criticized, and there are confusing indications as to their present status. Rather than discussing their marginality or centrality, I want to focus on the very process of institutionalisation. The intellectual landscape has been reshaped, even though it may be fragile, and the question is: How could it happen? Theories of social movements suggest we take a closer look at resource mobilisation and opportunity structures.

Pressure and pleasure: academic feminism

The women's movement of the 1970's in the Nordic region started spontaneously, without any definite centre. The importance of higher education is obvious, however. In Norway the two most influential organisational events both started among the students.[37] Also, the movement ideas found fertile soil and quickly dispersed through a Nordic academic institution: *The Nordic Summer University*. During its session in 1971, students from the Danish feminist camp met feminists from the Swedish *Group 8,* and the *Norwegian Women's Campaign Against Membership in the European Community*. Spontaneously they set up informal feminist groups. These attracted large numbers of students, and a seminar next year prepared a formal Nordic Summer University study circle on 'The specific oppression of women under capitalism' in 1973. This time women from all Nordic university cities attended. The importance of creating space for theoretical discussions on feminism was demonstrated, and the summer university continued to stimulate Nordic feminist networks, research and curricula development.[38] The popularity of the Nordic Summer University feminist study circles has been accounted for by the impact of the feminist movement: The personal point of departure had made it legitimate to 'bring oneself' into academic discussions, miles away from the intellectual climate surrounding the pioneer generations.

Women's studies were quickly getting a foothold at the universities due to various Nordic events. The *Nordic Congress of Sociology* responded to the success of informal women's groups set up during its 1974 congress and established a new branch for women's research. This inspired a paramount event in Norwegian women's studies: The very first national, multidisciplinary women's research conference, took place in Bergen during the summer 1975. More than 70 feminists elaborated burning questions, and laid the ground for long-lasting friendships, networks and co-operation.[39] By then, Norwegian feminists had already set up courses at every sociological institution, and they were not the only ones. A multi-disciplinary *Sex role seminar* was set up at the University of Tromsø in 1973. At the Faculty of Law, University of Oslo, *Kvinnesaksgruppa* (*The Women's Rights Group*), had fervently taken advantage of the somewhat delayed student revolt at their faculty,[40] and set up '*Free Legal Advice for Women*' in 1974. The "flat" structure of the women's movement, and the combination of private and political matters attracted the energy of hundreds of students. The legal service accumulated an overwhelming amount of information, which motivated the Faculty's decision to establish *Women's law*, the first special discipline of its kind ever. The situation was paradoxical: Women were absent as staff and in the curricula but 'sex equality ideology' was widely accepted. Maybe some of the Faculty didn't quite understand the consequences of their decision, but others did and demonstrated the relative ease with which liberal men have responded to feminist demands given the right context. The strategic competence among activists to make the most of the opportunity structure should not be overlooked, either.

Feminist identities

The overlap between the new feminist movement of the 1970s and feminist studies is evident. The energy of this mixture partly explains the diffusion of feminist studies. What the young feminists did as students or as activists could hardly be separated, the feminist identity was shared. The urgent need for feminist theories to guide the elaboration of political strategies was quite adequately taken care of in higher education. Writing course papers, participating in seminars and during lectures and preparing for exams were all part of the feminist struggle. So were student protests against male-biased academic staff. Demands for relevant literature on women disclosed the non-existence of such material. Feminist curricula literally had to be written by the feminist students and the young teachers themselves. The literature scrutinised during political meetings and study circles were the same as that focused during academic seminars. The women's liberation aims were similar, the symbols, slogans, concepts and perspectives were similar inside and outside academic institutions. Pursuing feminism in higher education was as good and legitimate as any feminist activity. Everywhere, feminists were preoccupied in theoretical debates in order to solve strategic and practical dilemmas: What is the cause of the suppression of women? What is the ultimate aim of feminism, and how do we get there? Different and often conflicting opinions on how to promote women's liberation exposed various strands of feminism, and higher education was a major institutional setting for heated feminist debates. Thus, when feminist students vigorously criticised the curricula they were offered and pressed for changes, they were simultaneously involved in feminist politics.

There was next to no differentiation between the more intellectual and the more political language during those first formative years. Writing minor or major theses in feminist issues was seen as important contributions to the movement. The need for concrete information as well as theoretical perspectives was dramatic, and feminism in *academy* was an essential part of the general movement. There were few professors with any political or personal interests in women's issues, and the universities, polytechnics and colleges did not seriously define any institutional responsibilities to meet the demands from feminist students. Thus, the young students themselves had to fight for the curricula to be developed and offered as academic courses.

Offensive and defensive women's communities

The first feminist umbrella project financed by the Norwegian Research Council, the *Kvinners felleskap* (*Women's Community*), claimed that a discourse of comparison between groups is necessary to construct a common identity.[41] In addition a certain number of persons; a certain degree of similarity and nearness between them over time; and common experiences, available and competent leadership were claimed to be crucial factors. These elements neatly fit with women's situation in the 1970s: The blossoming gender equality / women's liberation discourses were both based on comparisons between men and women. Indeed, comparison was the kernel of the issue, whether one tried to prove or counter-prove discrimination and oppression. As for the other claims: The unforeseen increase of women in higher education implied more than "a certain number"; the social situation as female students made for similarities, spending their days on campus guaranteed closeness and common experiences. The system of higher education itself indicates that the time factor was fulfilled, and the presence of women who were willing and able to take leadership roles was obvious. The feminist ideals of "flat organisations" and circulation of tasks etc. during the formative years, probably meant a lot to motivate and train women in this respect.

The *Women's Community* project maintained that women's communities traditionally were defensive, focusing mutual assistance rather than political struggle, and prioritising the difficulties of 'others'. Women's rights organisations, however, were offensive and oppositional, based on the politics of making personal, daily life problems publicly known. With respect to academic women, their organisations up until the *International Federation of University Women* in the 1920's had been defensive, focusing social and cultural matters. For various reasons, the federation did not really attract academic feminists during the 1970s. At first they were part of the undifferentiated movement, and later on they preferred to set up new networks and institutions.[42] Norwegian academic feminists never set up a national feminist studies organisation, but inspired by Sweden and Denmark, several local *Fora for women's research* were active for some years.[43] On the other hand, Norwegian women's studies could lean on a national institution without the like in other Nordic countries: the *Secretariat for Women's Research*. The role of the secretariat in stimulating and consolidating feminist studies can hardly be overestimated.

Favourable political structures

The growth of feminist studies did not happen in a political vacuum, however. The political opportunity structure was extremely favourable in Norway during the 1970's: The recently discovered oil reserves in the North Sea had changed the economic expectations overnight, and counted for shifts in public policies to supply enough and relevant labour. This, of course, implicated a new and strategic role for women in paid work. In addition, there was a general political mobilisation concerning the 1972 referendum on Norwegian membership in the *European Economic Community*. The triumph of 'the political periphery' was not least due to the success of *Kvinner mot EEC* (Women against EEC). The Norwegian 'no' to membership sent waves of shock through the political establishment, forcing the Social Democrats to invent new political strategies after their painful defeat in 1972. A promise to propose a legal ban on the discrimination of women in 1973 was part of this response. The year before, Norway had established the *Sex Equality Council*,[44] following the *Equal Pay Council,* and a few years later there were femocrats in several positions in relevant ministries. The 1970's were also a breakthrough for women in politics. Both elements increased the number of allies with which academic feminists could co-operate. In addition to this, there were feminists in relevant positions inside the Norwegian research council who used their positions whenever they could.

Women's issues and gender equality were firmly set on the agenda, stimulated also by Nordic and international women's rights initiatives. The Nordic initiatives in the *UN Commission on Women* in 1972 to speed up the process of transforming the *Declaration on the Elimination of Discrimination against Women* to a compulsory convention, and the preparations for the *International Women's Year* in 1975 certainly aroused new interest in women's issues. Although the financial means of the Women's Year was nothing compared to other "years", academic feminists strategically took advantage of them: Feminists in academe were to gain from the Women's Year because of a series of seminars and meetings disseminating women's research to large and interested audiences (see Zhang in this volume on the UN and Chinese women's studies). Also, feminist scholars were well represented on the Norwegian Women's Year committee, and successfully connected their national work to their local contexts. For instance, a grant from the committee funded a position for a feminist scholar at the University of

Tromsø for one year, and their sex role seminar was institutionalised. The university also agreed to set up a gender equality committee, and to publish the first anthology in women's research from the northern parts of Norway.

Conclusion

The legitimisation of women's access to higher education as students was won during the 1880s. Their access to the positions and tasks they were prepared for took place during the 1910s. They organised nationally and internationally in the 1920s, but were up against feminist backlashes in the 20's and 50's, with World War II in between. The student and feminist revolts of the 1970s paved the way for more democratic academic institutions, and Norwegian academic feminists could voice their interests with pride and strength. The continuing deficit of female scholars in higher academic positions means, however, that the executive power is still very male-dominated. The ongoing demand in Norway for affirmative action for women in academic institutions has to be seen in this perspective.

Feminist scholars, men as well as women, challenged the content of research, from the 1950s. The breakthrough took place two decades later. The additive effects of several factors contribute to explain why feminist studies then spread like wildfire. I have highlighted these elements: The efforts of students and young scholars with unusual dedication to the feminist cause, the context of a strong feminist movement, the positive attitudes towards gender equality in the population generally, sympathetic political and administrative allies within the state at various levels, the structural need for labour, and international demands from the UN on governments to improve the conditions of women.

Table 1

	Access to A-level	Access to University	Access to Civil Service	Fed. of Univ. Women [45]	1st national Wom.Stud. Conference	1st national Wom.Stud Org.
Norway	1882	1884	1912	1920[46]	1975	[47]
Denmark	1875	1875	1921	1922	1978	1982[48]
Finland	1870	1901[49]	1916[50]	1922	1980	1988
Sweden	1870	1873	1923	1921	1978	1979[51]
Iceland[52]	1904	1911	1911	1928	1985	?

References

Albrektsen, Beatrice Halsaa & Else Skjønsberg (1975). *Referat fra kvinneforskningsseminaret på Fana 1975*, Oslo, unpublished.

Alenius, Marianne; Damsholt, Nanna & Bente Rosenbeck (1994). *Clios døtre gennem hundrede år*, København, Museum Tusculanums Forlag/ Københavns Universitet.

Arnfred, Signe & Karen Syberg (1974). *Kvindesituation og kvindebevægelse under kapitalismen*. København, Nordisk Sommeruniversitet.

Beckwith, Karen (2001). "Women's Movements at Century's End: Excavation and Advances in Political Science", *Annual Review of Political Science*, 4, p. 371-390.

Benhabib, Seyla; Butler, Judith; Cornell, Drucilla & Nancy Fraser (1998). *Feminist Contentions*. New York, Routledge.

Bergman, Solveig (1999)."A Bird's Eye on Women's Studies in the Nordic Countries", *News from Nikk* nr. 1, Oslo, Nordisk institutt for kvinne- og kjønnsforskning.

Bergman, Solveig (1999a). "Women in New Social Movements", Bergqvist et al. (eds.), *Equal Democracies? Gender and Politics in the Nordic Countries,* Oslo, Scandinavian University Press, 98-117.

Bergqvist, Christina; Borchorst, Anette; Christensen, Ann-Dorte; Ramstedt-Silén, Viveca; Raaum, Nina C. & Audur Styrkársðóttir (eds.) (1999). *Equal Democracies? Gender and politics in the Nordic countries*, Oslo/Stockholm, Scandinavian University Press / Nordic Council of Ministers.

Blom, Ida (1995). "… 'uden dog at overskride sin naturlige Begrænsning' – kvinner i Akademia 1882-1932", Lie, Suzanne Stiver & Maj Birgit Rørslett (eds.), *Alma Maters døtre,* Oslo, Pax, 19-32.

Boxer, Marilyn J. (1998). *When Women Ask the Questions,* Baltimore, John Hopkins University Press.

Dahlerup, Drude (1998). *Rødstrømperne. Den danske Rødstrømpebevægelses udvikling, nytænkning og gennemslag 1970-1985,* København, Gyldendal vol. I, II.

Dahlström, Edmund; Holter, Harriet; Brun-Gulbrandsen, Sverre & Per Olav Tiller (1962). *Kvinnors liv och arbete*, Stockholm, Studieförbundet Näringsliv och Samhälle.

Fehr, Drude v.d.; Jónasdóttir, Anna & Bente Rosenbeck (eds.) (1998). *Is there a Nordic feminism? Nordic feminist thought on culture and society,* London, UCL Press.

Florin, Christina & Bengt Nilsson (2000). *'Något som liknar en oblodig revolution…' Jämställdhetens politisering under 1960- och 70-talen,* Umeå, Umeå Universitet.

Fraser, Nancy (1997). "False Antithesis. A Response to Seyla Benhabib and Judith Butler", *Justice interruptus: Critical Reflections on the "Poststructuralist" Condition,* New York & London, Routledge, 207-223.

Graubard, Stephen R. (ed.) (1986). *Norden – the Passion for Equality,* Oslo, Norwegian University Press.

Grønseth, Erik (1955). *Kvinnen i samfunnsliv og politikk*, Oslo, Institutt for Sosiologi, Universitetet i Oslo.

Haavio-Mannila, Elina; Dahlerup, Drude; Eduards, Maud; Gudmundsóttir, Esther; Halsaa, Beatrice; Hernes, Helga Maria; Hänninen-Salmelin, Eva; Sigmundsdóttir, Bergthora; Sinkkonnen, Sirkka & Torild Skard (eds.) (1985). *Unfinished Democracy. Women in Nordic Politics*, Oxford, Pergamon Press.

Halsaa, Beatrice (2001a). "Finns det en nordisk feminism och en nordisk kvinno / genusforskning?", Frangeur, Rénee (ed.), *Gråt gärna – men forska,* Linköping, Linköping universitet, Forum för kvinnliga forskare och kvinnoforskning, 71-76.

Halsaa, Beatrice (2001b). "Kvinner og politikk i Norden – noen historiografiske refleksjoner", *Kvinder, køn og forskning,* 10, nr. 2, p. 20-33.

Holter, Harriet ed. (1982). *Kvinner i fellesskap*, Oslo, Universitetsforlaget.

Johnsen, Ingrid Sanness; Dahr, Eva Braathen; Krogsvig, Inki Steen, Reinton, Ingrid Evang & Thordis Støren (1970). *Kvinner i akademisk fellesskap. Norske Kvinnelige Akademikeres Landsforbund 1920-1970,* Oslo, Aschehoug.

Kalleberg, Annemor (1979). "Kvinnebevegelsen i Skandinavia i sosiologisk perspektiv", *Sosiologi i dag,* 2, p. 68-79.

Krogh, Jannik (1991). "Litteraturkritikk som politisk praksis", Åse Hiorth Lervik (ed.), *Den lange veien til parnasset,* Tromsø, Institutt for språk og litteratur, Universitetet i Tromsø, p. 31- 45.

Larsen, Jytte & Helena Wedborn (1993). "Nordic women's documentation centres", *NORA Nordic Journal of Women's Studies,* 2, nr. 1, p.125-130.

Lie, Suzanne Stiver & Maj Birgit Rørslett (eds.) (1995). *Alma Maters døtre,* Oslo, Pax.

Lønnå, Elisabeth (1996). *Stolthet og kvinnekamp. Norsk kvinnesaksforenings historie fra 1913,* Oslo, Gyldendal.

McAdam, Doug; McCarthy, John D. & Mayer N. Zald (1996). *Comparative Perspectives on Social Movements,* Cambridge, Cambridge University Press.

Myrdal, Alva & Viola Klein (1957). *Kvinnans två roller,* Stockholm, Tiden.

Moi, Toril (1998). "What is a women? Sex, gender and the body in feminist theory", Moi Toril, *What is a woman? And other Essays*, Oxford, Oxford University Press.

Ohlander, Ann-Sofie (1987). "En utomordentlig balansakt", *Historisk tidskrift,* 1, p.1-22.

Rosenbeck, Bente (1998). "Nordic women's studies and gender research", Fehr, Drude v. d.; Jónasdóttir, Anna G. & Bente Rosenbeck (eds.), *Is there a Nordic Feminism?,* London, UCL Press, p. 344-357.

Rønning, Anne Holden (1995). "Kvinner organiserer seg – 75 år med Norske Kvinnelige Akademikere", Suzanne p. Lie & Maj B. Rørslett (eds.), *Alma Maters døtre. Et århundre med kvinner i akademisk utdannelse.* Oslo, Pax, p. 117-128.

Rørslett, Maj Birgit & Suzanne Stiver Lie (1984). *På solsiden – kvinners kamp for kunnskap, hvor førte den hen?* Oslo, Cammermeyer.

Skard, Åse Gruda (1974): "Kvinnesak tredje akt", Kari Skjønsberg (ed.), *Mannssamfunnet midt imot,* Oslo: Gyldendal, 1974, p. 168-164.

Skjønsberg, Kari (1984). "Arkiv og dokumentasjon for kvinneforskning", *Synopsis,* 15, p. 183-184.

Sandlund, Maj-Britt (1968). *The status of women in Sweden: Report to the United Nations,* Sweden today, Stockholm, Swedish Institute.

Stene, Helga (1972). "Kjønnsroller i utdanningen: Norge, allmennskolen", *Könsroller och utbildning,* eds. Utskottet för utredning av frågan om könsrollerna i utbildningen, Nordiska Rådet, Nordisk udredningsserie nr. 6, Stockholm p. 164-176.

Notes

1 Higher education and Academia is used concurrently.
2 I use 'feminist studies', feminist scholarship', 'women's studies' and 'women's research' alternately, referring to research, curricula development, teaching and transmitting.
3 See Ohlander (1987); Blom (1995); Johnsen et al. (1970); Alenius et al. (1994); Lie & Rørslett (1995); Rønning (1995).
4 Bergman (1999).
5 NAVF's Sekretariat for kvinneforskning (the Norwegian Research Council's Secretariat for Women's Research)
6 During the 1990's the term 'gender studies' made its entry in Norway, often combined with 'women's studies', whereas 'genus' has become the public term in Sweden.
7 Kalleberg (1979); Haavio-Mannila et al. (1985); Rosenbeck (1998); Bergqvist et al. (1999).
8 Fehr et al. (1998), Bergman 1999.
9 Graubard (1986), Halsaa (2001).
10 Beckwith (2001); McAdam et al. (1996); Dahlerup (1998); Bergman and Krook in this volume.
11 Benhabib et al. (1998).
12 Siruated Freedom, see Moi (1998); Fraser (1997).
13 Boxer (1998) p. xvii.
14 Dahlerup (1998).
15 When unmarried women were granted legal status in 1863, the situation was similar: almost no debate in parliament.
16 The more radical and emancipatory claims, such as suffrage for women, were not smoothly accepted.
17 *The Danish Women's Society* in 1871; *The Fredrika-Bremer Association* in Sweden (1884) and *Suomen naisyhdistys* in Finland 1884 and Lønnå in this volume.
18 Krogh (1991).
19 For example, they established *Female Students Athlete Association*, *Female Students Ski Club, Female Students Song Association*.
20 Rønning (1995), my translation.
21 *IFUW* was involved in married women's right to employment, peace issues, and also focused the economic welfare of less privileged women at home and abroad.
22 Blom (1995)
23 In the period 1882-1932 5 % of women with an A-level completed a university degree, compared to 44% of men, Rørslett & Lie (1984).
24 Dahlstrøm (1962), Bergman (1999).
25 Skard (1974).
26 Grønseth (1955). Grønseth (male), was deeply inspired by the ideas of Bonnevie.
27 Lønnå (1996).
28 Myrdal & Klein (1957).
29 Stene (1972). The satellite was a shocking reminder of Soviet intellectual supremacy, and contributed to a closer look at women's situation in *academia* in the US, in order to save 'the intelligence reserve', Boxer (1998).
30 See Lønnå (1996) p.192
31 Dahlström et al. (1962), Florin & Nilsson (2000) p. 53.

32 Another consequence of the sex role debate was the founding of new feminist organisations like *Association 9* established in Finland in 1966 (Bergman 1999), and *Group 222* operating during the 1960s in Sweden (Florin 2000).

33 See Sandlund (1968), in which the Nordic sex role perspective is underlined.

34 Several 'pioneer' women at the universities had written women's histories, for example Kristine Bonnevie's 'Kvinderne ved universitetet', published in *Norske kvinner* (Norwegian Women) in 1914 (Ohlander 1987).

35 Johnsen et al. (1970), my translation.

36 This debate had in fact been going on in Norway since the 1950's.

37 *Nyfeministene* (1970) and *Kvinnefronten* (1972).

38 A major outcome was the book *Women's situation and the women's movement under capitalism* (Arnfred & Syberg 1974). This is probably the first Nordic feminist studies publication.

39 Albrektsen & Skjønsberg (1975).

40 The revolt of the law students started in 1973.

41 Holter (1982).

42 The membership has been fairly stable since the 1980s: app. 250-300 in Sweden, Norway and Denmark, lower in Iceland and a high record of 2500 in Finland.

43 A national organisation was set up in Norway in 2002.

44 This was the official English name until the 1990s, when 'sex' was substituted by 'gender'.

45 *National Federations of University Women*, affiliated with *IFUW*.

46 Rønning (1995).

47 A local Forum for women researchers and women's research was established in Oslo in 1985, but never really started. In Trondheim, however, the *Forum for women in research and planning* was successfully established in 1985, arranging several stimulating meetings.

48 1982: *Forum for kvindeforskning,* from 1990 *Forening for kvinde- og kønsforskning,* from 1999: *Association for Gender Studies*

49 Formal equal rights to enter the university. In fact, Finnish women had access since 1870 on dispensation. The first female doctor completed her education in 1878 http://www.helsinki.fi/akka-info/tiedenaiset/svenska/milstolpar.html

50 The right to teach at the university. In 1926 women gained the right to be appointed to office.

51 Local organisations.

52 Information from Sigríður Dúna Kristmundsdóttir.

CHAPTER 5

Religion as a Source of Activism

The YWCA in Global Perspectives

Hilda Rømer Christensen

The very subject of the YWCA – the *Young Women's Christian Association*, accentuates many of the challenges and issues at stake in recent intellectual debates on globalisation and postcolonialism. Accordingly my aim in the following is to address how a study of a presumably dull and middle of the road associations, that did not caught much public or intellectual attention throughout the 20th century – might be a splendid field for asking new questions and for the recasting of powerful key notions in Western thinking. Such as the dichotomised notions of religion and secularisation, of modernity and tradition, of centre and periphery, as well as for the troubling of fixed ideas of feminism and anti-feminism.

The YWCA represented an innovation in the landscape of Evangelical and missionary associations that flourished from the late 19th century. The YWCA – together with numerous other agencies and women's associations opened up new avenues for women at several levels: as a meaningful field of (leadership) activity for leisured class women, as a field for professional and waged association workers, and finally as a way of spending a meaningful spare time for adolescent and young women. The YWCA hostels became well-known icons for unfolding a variety of projects cultural, social and educational in many big cities in both the East and the West. Not least the travelling or migrating young women became a YWCA speciality and a focus of the work. The YWCA catered for both domestic migration and the flow of women from the country to the cities and in various ways the YWCA also took care of transnational female immigration.

In general the YWCA both nationally and internationally contributed very concretely to the modernisation of revivalist and missionary projects to also encompass women and their demands, for housing, financial independence and decent working conditions in a modern world.

The YWCA held a broad composition and succeeded to a considerable degree to attract women across social, racial and national boundaries. Due to spiritual commitments – the idea of "extension in all lands" and skilled organisation the YWCA was one of the few women's associations that successfully settled in metropolitan centres as well as in the socalled colonial peripheries. USA, together with Britain, Germany and the Nordic countries counted as impressive association countries in the Western world.

The striking issue of the YWCA is that the association has been able to survive and to mould itself into new challenges and new environments. During the 20th century the YWCA metamorphosed from a benevolent association started in the late 19th century environment of nationalism and colonialism into a modern and grassroots orientated women's NGO able to operate in a globalised and postcolonial world. Through this transformation the association also *decolonised* itself so to speak, and women from the developing countries became leaders at the top level. In terms of quantities it seems as if the YWCA is even culminating in the general wave of international feminism around the turn of the millennium. The YWCA by now caters for a worldwide membership of 25 million in around 100 countries. This compares to the first peak of YWCA organising in the mid 1930s where the membership culminated around 2 million from 23 countries; yet a considerable outreach compared to most women's associations at the time.

For a historical outlook, it is important to be aware of the fact that the YWCA cultures in the centres and in the so-called peripheries did not develop independently, but were deeply integrated. The aim of extending the work and reaching out profoundly influenced the entire agenda of the YWCAs both nationally and at the world's levels throughout the 20th century echoing the claim made by Edvard Said, that the historical experience of empire as a common one among both the colonizers and the colonized.

In the following I am going to unfold and to problematise what appears to be a story of successful integration and cooperation at the global level. Also I will focus on some implications of studying a religious based women's association in transnational and global perspectives. I am going to focus mainly on the first half of the 20th century, but several of the issues, conflicts and dilemmas that were addressed might still have relevance for current assessments of the YWCA as well as for the general assessment of social movements based on religion and spirituality.

Hegemonies and multiple voices

In recent theoretical debates regarding comparative methodology it has been discussed how to approach the study of social movements in a comparative or cross-national perspective. How are national features to be dealt with in cross-national analysis? How are the relationship between the national and the international or global scope to be handled?[1]

On one hand it is obvious that certain national features were determining the take-off of and profiles of the YWCA associations. National frameworks such as revivalist patterns, church structures, political cultures, and the overall level of industrialization and modernisation seem to have influenced the contested field of the way gender was perceived and the space of agency offered to women both in relation to revival enterprises and in relation to wider developments in society.

On the other hand also the so-called international processes of diffusion made substantial impact on the formation of the World's YWCA. Especially at the end of the 19th century where the "death of distance" embodied in improved infrastructures, modern travel technologies and the rising prosperity of revival communities facilitated religious encounters in many ways:

Either to meet face to face at the numerous meetings and conferences, or the growth in written communication and printed material. International diffusions, however, was not just an innocent exchange of ideas and practices. An interesting question is how diffusion was influenced and over-layered by geo-political power structures.

When the World's YWCA was launched at a meeting in London in 1894 the very name the *World's* YWCA was preferred to the word *international*, because the World's indicated overarching fellowship and not only the sum of national associations. The formation of a world's association had several roots and interrelated motivations. Here the lively cross-Atlantic revivalist diffusion of the late 19th century formed one branch of mental and spiritual motivation. The waves took off in the US and spread through gospel tours via Britain to the Continent and also to the Nordic countries, e.g. the Moodey and Sankey tours in Great Britain between 1874 and 1892. Here the American D.L. Moodey preached a simple message of salvation through God's love accompanied by Sankey's Solos. Several of the classic songs of the YWCA, such as *Onward Christian Soldiers* stem from this period. The Sankey and Moody spiritual modes made it fashionable to join revival sessions and the upcoming youth movement and became a melting pot for early networking and formation of evangelical communities.[2]

A more hard core motivation for the formation of the World's YWCA in 1894 was made up of an interest in reconciling competing expansionist interests of the YWCAs in Britain and the USA in particular.[3] This also connects the YWCA and its early enterprises to the larger colonial and imperial projects, where the moral and educational aims of the YWCA kind were appreciated as a necessity for humanizing and civilizing colonial subjects.[4]

By 1894 the two committees of the British YWCA responsible for the developing work in and outside Europe were transformed into two standing committees of the World's Committee for the European Continent, and for other continents respectively.[5] This partly reflected the power structure of the 1890s, and the British lead. But for the next decade the USA came to the fore and developed considerable work at destinations overseas. By the beginning of the 20th century, the world was mapped in a way that mirrored the lines of colonialism and spheres of interest of Britain and the USA. According to a kind of spiritual Monroe doctrine, South America was "given" by the World's YWCA to the United States, while India became the responsibility of Great Britain.[6] In the long run the balance of influence shifted towards the USA, not least due to the financial power. Here China makes up an illustrative example with the US catering for nearly half of the national budget in 1921.[7] The dominance of the British and American YWCAs was stressed by the national character of YWCA extension work and the relative lack of authority of the World's YWCA right up till after World War II.

The 1947 World's YWCA Council that was held in Hangchow in China marked a cross-road in terms of shifting the leadership from West to East. Here it was decided to channel all activities, economically as well as representative through the World YWCA headquarters in Geneva. Up till then the American YWCA had constantly catered for 90 overseas secretaries. The shift also reflected that this kind of American dominance would be regarded as a tool of neo-colonialism that was delegitimized by the new world order after World War II.[1]

Several of the grand old ladies of the Western YWCAs retired at this point and the World's executive Committee got a more global composition. Here several Asian women (from India and the Middle East in particular) came to play the role as mediators between the West and the rest in the following decades. At the turn of the 21st century Africa is the fastest growing YWCA continent and particularly during the 1990s African women have been integrated in world leadership.

Questions that were related to global issues cross-cut significant areas and issues of the work already in the first half of the 20th century. Forging new discussions and conflicts especially between the then dominant religious trends: with Lutherans from Germany, and the Nordic countries on the one hand and Anglo-American Evangelical communities on the other. Yet the interests of expanding the YWCA work in geographical terms displaced the YWCA outlooks and projects both in terms of social, racial and gender issues and also in spiritual and ecumenical respects. This again recasts the common assumption of the metropolis as the univocal centre of cultural production, while the periphery only develops derivative, imitative culture.[8] In many cases the so-called periphery took centre stage in relation to association strategies.

A striking example of productive and conflictual encounters was framed by the World's Committee meeting in Washington in 1924, the first time ever that a committee meeting was held outside Europe. The meeting was energized by the efforts put into new YWCA spheres in Eastern Europe and in the Orient. Here YWCA secretaries sponsored by British and American YWCAs pioneered new fields and work of the YWCA. This caused criticism and complaints of neglect from the Nordic YWCAs, perceived as dissenters in an Anglo-American Empire. A Nordic YWCA secretary lamented that

"At a World's Committee meeting which should point at work throughout the world there ought to be (the) same right for Anglo-Saxons and non Anglo-Saxons. In Washington most of the time was occupied by reports from the Anglo-Saxon workers, we non-Anglo-Saxons got as you know only five minutes to speak about the work in our countries, and I knew there were several who thought it was too little to do an America Touring for.

Of course the Anglo-Saxon part of the World's Committee takes more interest in hearing about the Anglo-Saxon work and about the work in the Orient – than about the work of the Lutheran countries, – and everybody who pays attention to the political development understands that the Anglo-Saxons must take the Orient into some consideration. But on the other hand it would be of importance if the Anglo-Saxon committee members knew a little about the work in the other countries. I have good reason to think that most of them know nothing about it."[9]

The American general secretary tried to settle the matter from the viewpoint of the World's YWCA."I think perhaps it has been a surprise for you to see what a very important place the Anglo Saxons have taken in the spread and development of the Y.W.C.A. work throughout the world. This has been true from the very beginning of its history, and was almost as marked at the World's Conference in Stockholm in 1914 as it has been at any time since, but since the war the beginnings in many countries have been made by the American Y.W.C.A. so that again and again it was Anglo-Saxons who represented and had to speak on behalf of their countries." In Washington this had been particularly true, because Americans represented many of the new YWCA countries in the Orient, Egypt, Syria, Turkey, Malaya and Italy.

The critic from the Nordic representative epitomised the religious poles of the World's association. While Germany and the Nordic YWCAs were strictly confessional and closely associated with the Evangelical churches, the Anglo-American YWCAs were marked by inter-confessionalism and by diverse commitments to a variety of evangelical state and free churches. The Nordic representative even claimed that Lutherans were perceived as *fundamentalists* as opposed to the more easy-going Anglo-American trend. Her claim was that especially the Americans were afraid of the Lutherans and referred to the Lutheran churches in the USA who disliked the YWCA and regarded them as too secularised and worldly. The general secretary in this respect tried to move the problem beyond the national YWCAs and their respective orientations. She stated that fundamentalists were to be found in every YWCA and that especially in the US they counteracted the dealing with pressing problems of the day.

She was probably right in this claim. Both Germany and Britain had gone through painful processes of disagreement along some of the same lines during and after World War I. Here the conflict resulted in the secession of several regional YWCAs, leaving especially the British YWCA with a strongly reduced membership, but also more dynamic.

The focus on the YWCA all in all implies a deconstruction of religion as a unified and stereotype concept and the co-existence of various expressions and strategies. Even though the conflicts were often profiled in national terms, the diversities and dichotomy of tradition and modernity as well as of spirituality and activism also traversed national contexts.

Global spirituality and its boundaries

At the YWCA World's Conference in Budapest in 1928, quite far-reaching changes were made in the YWCA Constitution both regarding the confessional basis and the organisational structures. The changes, aiming at enhancing greater diversity and internationalism and interdenominalism in the association, caused great controversies.

The question of church orientation had been painful already in the affiliation of the Lutheran associations in the beginning of the 20th Century. During the 1920s the Anglo-Americans pressed for the World's YWCA to adjust to ecumenical principles, meaning that the YWCAs were open to members from various branches of the Christian Churches. Here the openings of YWCA work in Southern and Eastern Europe and in Latin America made the question of how to deal with members of Orthodox and Roman Catholic convictions urgent.[10] The new Constitution from 1928 allowed Roman Catholics and Orthodox women as members, yet resulting in serious criticism from the sides of the Nordic Associations and from Germany. The step even caused the secession of the Finnish and the South African YWCAs.[11]

Roof-top scene at the YWCA National Training School at 600 Lexington Avenue, New York City 1915. The American YWCA sponsored students from Europe and became a framework for numerous transatlantic dialogues and diffusions.

The very processes of constructing and interpreting the Evangelical Basis and its boundaries were of great importance. The overall spiritual aim of the YWCA was spelled out in article III of the YWCA Constitution in 1898. The goal was to unite young women who accepted "The Lord Jesus Christ as their God and Saviour" and who desired "to associate their efforts for the extension of His Kingdom among all young women by such means as are in accordance with the Word of God."[12]

In the amended Constitution from 1930 and 1941, the outreach was made more explicit. Article III was extended by a chapter that pointed to the work for promotion of peace and better understanding between classes, nations and races "and that the obedience to the law of Christ will forge the extension of God's kingdom "in which the principles of justice, love, and the equal value of every human life shall apply to national and international as well as to personal relations".[13]

In spite of conflicting outlooks on the relationship between genuine spirituality and social and political interventions, it is obvious that the association was bound together by religious identity. In the basis of the association as well as in the general rhetoric one is struck by the passion for inner transcendence and reconciliation as a means of overcoming conflicts.

At the 4th World Conference in Berlin in 1910 attended by an impressive 850 representatives from 29 nations, the Japanese miss Micha Kaway forwarded greetings from 13,000 YWCA members in Asia and Africa. She also expressed what can be seen as the key raison d'être of the YWCA in the making of religious identity or world fellowship. In the speech she metaphorically referred to the racial elements of the relationship between East and Vest:

"Can you make a brown skin white? Can you make the spots of the leopard disappear?" she asked provocatively. And relaxed the dilemma in her answer: "In the outer circumstances the East will remain the East and the West will remain the West." But what united the many diversities was the God-created inner spirituality. "God," she said, "knows how to change us in sincere spirituality and to unite us all in one God-given Family. Whether East or West – we all belong to God's Family. We ought to reach out our hands in order to combat social and moral suffering and we shall let our lives be created from Heaven into one powerful harmony to the glory of God." The peaceful Japanese talk differed however from contemporary German YWCA rhetoric, marked by biblical and national tunes of militancy.

The creation of a common religious identity was successful in the sense that it headed off several crises caused by international political rivalry and conflicts, even though it was too weak to contest the outbreak of two world wars. But the common identities and the idea of an inner spirituality contributed to reconcile broken relations after the wars and also to a certain degree to moderate German dreams of revenge and expansion after World War I. The World's YWCA also tried to interfere when the German YWCA was forced to make "Anschluss" to the Nazi Jugend association, but in vain.[14]

When the headquarters of the World's YWCA was moved from London to the international capital of Geneva in 1930 it symbolised a new period of internationalism and interconfessionalism in the World's YWCA. It was substantiated in a more international composition of the World's executive and in the recognition of confessional and spiritual differences in the association. The executive committee was now to be composed according to democratic representative principles. A prominent Dutch woman, Cornelia M. Asch van Wijck, became the first non-Anglo-American president. She had a background in Dutch Calvinism and she was expected to bridge the gaps between the two most antagonised angles of the association, the Anglo-American trend and the continental Lutheran trend of the Nordic countries and Germany.[15]

It is interesting to note that the spiritual fellowship and the overarching religious identity of the YWCAs in the South Pacific were stronger than nationalism and the hostile relationships of national governments. Japanese and Chinese YWCAs maintained friendly relationships despite the 1937 Japanese invasion of China as well as the Japanese invasion of Korea in 1938 that made the Korean YWCA an affiliate of the Japanese association.

Again in Hangchow in 1947 the spiritual creed of the association was articulated as opposed to the materiality of war by Dr. Y. C. Tu, president of St. Johns University in Shanghai, who declared that the "issues of war are material, while the issues of peace are primarily spiritual." It was time to heal the wounds wrought by psychical strife, to bridge the spiritual barriers of race, religion, culture and ideology, so often the spiritual tensions of mistrust, suspicion and hatred, to restore the broken moral fibre of man, to re-establish man's faith in God and his destiny."[16]

The main outcome of the Hangchow meeting was the re-establishing of the YWCA as a world wide spiritual movement, a lay, ecumenical movement with a contribution to make in bringing together members of different Christian confessions. After 1945 the constitution was changed several times in order to encompass full membership of women of other (Christian) faiths – by 1955 they were made eligible for taking office in the associations.[17]

During the last decades of the 20th century it seems as if spiritual issues have lost momentum towards the social and political involvements and goals of the World YWCA. In 1979 five priorities were made at the World YWCA conference: Peace, Refugees and Migrants, Health, Human Rights and Energy and Environment, issues that clearly mirrored priorities of the UN and other transnational institutions aiming at progressive and human demands and change. Contrary to the first half of the 20th century, where conflicts were often spelled out over religious interpretations of how to handle the relationship between social and spiritual issues. Today the YWCA holds the position as a spiritually based NGO that has to compete with other – often younger and more fluent NGOs.

In a longitude perspective there is no doubt that this spiritual and moral emphasis has opened many doors for the YWCA in very different settings, politically and geo-graphically. Compared to openly political movements, as e.g. socialists and feminists contesting political regimes and openly demanding political rights from existing power systems. This might also be part of the explanation for the endurance and success of the YWCAs at the world level today.

Suffrage and beyond

At a principal level the Lutheran based associations stressed women as individuals and religion as a genderless force, while the Anglo-Americans stressed the gendered nature of the association and partly also of religion. Anglo-American associates were freer to handle religious rituals outside the churches, while the Lutheran associations relied heavily on professional interpretations made by (male) theologians. In this way the radicalism of Lutheranism in the assessment of personal evidence for God was modified. At the same time, however, the German YWCA became the framework of early careers of academic women theologians and later on for the relatively strong position of women in the Evangelical Churches in Germany.[18]

Even though the gender divided organisation of the YWCA were based on 19th century Victorian and religious values the YWCA gradually, and influenced by the suffrage mobilisation, developed a high consciousness of itself as a women's movement. At the world level several invitations from the men's YMCA to closer co-operation were openly responded to in terms of exchanges of ideas, problems and experiences. But the invitation was declined when it came to organisational unity. Not only single national mergers like the Norwegian in 1905 and lately of the Danish associations, but also the gender mixed *World's Student Christian Federation* challenged this pattern of gender divided work. The World's YWCA stressed women's need to obtain freedom and independence and acknowledged women as a minority group in many public arenas. Not least the opportunity to develop women's leadership abilities has been – and still is a driving force for maintaining a separate association.[19]

The impressive membership figures, which outnumbered most women's organisations, also women's rights associations at the time, can be illustrated by the following examples:

The British YWCA around 1902 already held 100,000 members. This compares to the political mobilisation and the 54,000 members of the *National Union of Women's Suffrage Societies* in 1913 on the one hand, and to the 237,000 members of the conservative and Anglican Church affiliated *Girls Friendly Society* on the other.[20] In the USA the YWCA held 212,000 members in 1910 that extended into 446,573 in 1937.[21] On the Continent Denmark and Germany counted as impressive YWCA countries. In Denmark the YWCA figured as the biggest women's association throughout the interwar years. In 1937 it held 33,687 members compared to the 10,000 members of the most prominent women's rights association, *Dansk Kvindesamfund*. In Germany the YWCA also grew immensely during the first decades of the 20th century. The membership extended from 92,000 in 1900 to 260,000 members at the peak in 1930 just before the Nazi take-over.[22]

Dependent on time and space, the relationship between the two trends of suffrage and confessional movements was sometimes conflictual and competitive, and sometimes marked by peaceful and complimentary co-existence. It is interesting that women of YWCA convictions did take part in the suffrage mobilisation and even formed their own suffrage associations, e.g. in Denmark and Sweden, while some of the tone-setting British YWCA women joined existing non-militant suffragist associations.[23]

The peak periods of the YWCA seem to be slightly displaced from the peaks and burn-outs of the first wave of suffrage movements. Moreover it seems as if the YWCA has operated with more continuity than most women's rights associations that were directly involved in suffrage mobilisation. While the national YWCAs in the big warfare countries and in Scandinavia survived, some of the women's suffrage associations went through organisational changes in the interwar years after suffrage victory, notably in the US and in Britain where membership declined and women's suffrage associations ceased or were re-organised.[24]

In relation to the debate of waves, of crests and abbeys of the women's movements, it occurs that the YWCAs had their peaks, in periods of pre- and post-suffrage mobilisation, making the YWCA a kind of reservoir of building up women's consciousness and gradually also in translating political influence into practical welfare and labour initiatives in the 1920s and 1930s. The YWCA became a framework for joined work at many levels: for networking and community-based organisation and for the development of social and industrial work in the wake of suffrage. Several of the first Women MPs in Britain were, even though they belonged to different political parties, close YWCA affiliates.[25]

In interwar China, marked by developments similar to the Western world, it is interesting to note how the YWCA developed into a kind of laboratory of exercise for women activists and cadres in the revolutionary communist movement. The Chinese association was founded in 1890 and had its heyday during the 1910s, where city-work thrived together with student work. The Chinese YWCA got a stronghold in industrial work in the big Chinese cities, while Chinese students gradually replaced foreign – mainly American secretaries.

But it is also thought-provoking that during the 1920s, when the Communist party gained momentum, the YWCA became subject of Communist criticism and accused of Western imperialism, remote Christianity and old-fashioned gender ideals. Nevertheless the Chinese YWCA managed to survive as a respected association. Not least due to the development of an outstanding educational programme that met the needs of working women, the association managed to balance and bridge – and manipulate the gaps between Christianity, Communism and women's organising.[26] As such the Chinese YWCA offers a good example of how American dominated interventions were absorbed and moulded into local interests. A fact that also reveals the complexity and (perhaps) unintended results of cultural imperialism at work.

The integration of the YWCA in political and public affairs in the 1920s had different implications. The role of the American YWCA broadened and became close to an institution that catered broadly for the welfare of young women in all life aspects at work and during leisure time. The British YWCA on the other hand went through a painful period of conflict and successive reductions in membership due to the new and more liberal outlook obtained by the leadership during World War I.

In Germany the goal-orientated involvement in state affairs during the 1920s not least in the area of moral and youth education went hand in hand with a youth mobilisation, built on authoritative aesthetics, emotions and hopes for a new national-religious awakening. How was the co-operation among religious associations that were marked by such profound differences possible? Here again the primary emphasis on spiritual dimensions may be the explanation why the World's YWCA succeeded in playing the role as a melting pot aimed at negotiating the different views and emphases of the national associations.

Chinese YWCA poster aimed at reminding of the factory worker, who has to work 12-hour shifts at night.

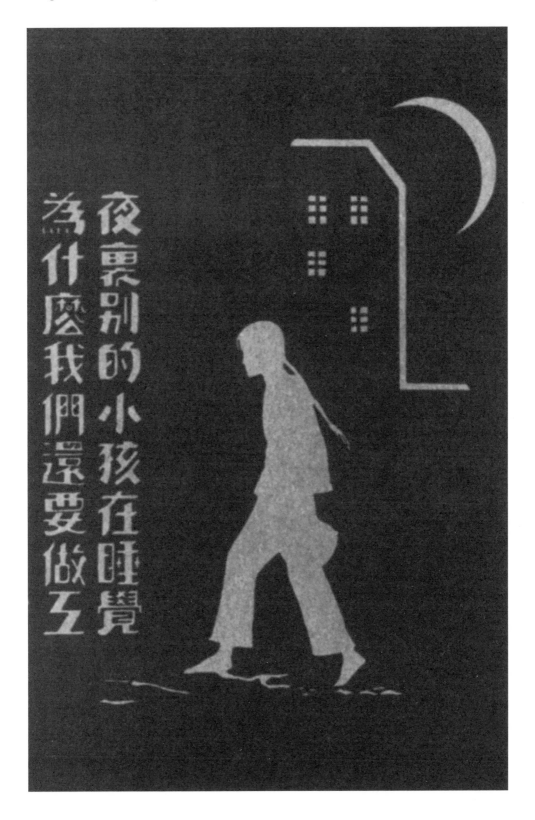

International networking: peace and disarmament

The stress on the YWCA as a women's organisation also implied the YWCA co-operation with other tone-setting women's associations at the international level. With the
end of World War I, and the formation of the League of Nations in 1919, new possibilities for the international women's associations were opened. The international
scene in Geneva created a unique place where international women's associations
pioneered their aspirations and pushed for change in the field of foreign policy and
international relations to also include social issues and peace as well as the quest for
gender equality.

Despite the provision in 1919 that all League of Nation positions would be open
equally to women and men the status achieved by women soon turned out to be very
disappointing.[27] Yet motivating closer co-operation between a handful of international
women's association, formalised in 1925 through the creation of the *Joint Standing
Committee of Women's International Organisations.*

The collaborating associations were labelled as the "Principal" and the "Chief"
women's organisations by the inviting organisation the *International Women's Council.*[28]

When it was discussed to confine the committee to strictly *feminist* societies, it
is striking that the representative of the World's YWCA disliked the term feminist
and corrected the rhetoric. The YWCA asked "for representation not as feminist
but as a matter of principle because we believed that women had a certain contribution to make on many of the subjects before the league commissions."[29] This
mirrored the internal competition among the women's international associations
and their different outlooks. Here the *woman* approach of the YWCA was more
in line with the outlook of the League and of the *International Labour Organisation,* ILO, than the radical feminist approaches that stressed universal equality
and citizenship.[30]

Through the creation of the *Liaison Committee of the International Women's
Organisations* in 1931, this collaboration was formalised even further, and came to
incorporate co-ordinated actions towards the League of Nations. An off-shoot of this
was the creation of a special disarmament committee in 1931, *The Disarmament Committee of the Women's International Organisations.* The committee held a broad composition of 14 international women's associations, including also Jewish and working
class women as well as the old and more radical *Women's International League for
Peace and Freedom.*[31] It is interesting that the Disarmament Committee was chaired
by the dynamic YWCA secretary Mary Dingman, who undoubtedly influenced the
profile of the committee in avoiding radical stances and in the ability to link with high
politics and big business. The committee turned out to be immensely efficient both
regarding top level networking and regarding initiatives at the rank and file level such
as collection of disarmament petitions and in the creation of spectacular activities to
the up-coming Disarmament Conference to be held under the aegis of the League of
Nations in 1932.

The women's Disarmament Committee carried on after 1935 under the name of the *Peace and Disarmament Committee of the Women's International Organisations*, when it even became known as the Dingman Committee, but not without criticism. The *Women's International League for Peace and Freedom* gradually found that the Dingman Committee did not function as a collaborative committee for independent organisations, which was the original idea.[32] Besides the success of the committee was suspended by the steadily shrinking role of the League in the maintaining of collective security. During the 1930s disagreements among the great Powers weakened the League's ability to resolve major disputes. And most of them began to rearm.

Equal rights or the status of women

The focus of networking among international women's associations gradually shifted. From an initially narrow focus on the appointment of women to international agencies and posts, the perspective expanded during the 1930s to include equal rights for men and women in a wider sense. Catalysts of this development were the *Open Door International* and *Equal Rights International*. Their entry on the international scene led to a revitalisation of the agendas in Geneva, but also caused antagonistic conflicts between the proponents of equality on the one hand, and of supporters of gender-difference on the other. The disagreements crystallised around the issue of protective labour legislation for women, and culminated in the debate around a general resolution on equality, the *Treaty of Equality*.[33] Within the international women's organisations, this treaty provoked a debate for and against special protective legislation for women that spelled out different notions of equal rights both within and across international women's associations. Some supported the demand for consequent equal rights legislation, while others thought that equal rights had broader implications. One of the members of the Peace League said that she could not "accept the interpretation which makes equal rights imply identity of law as regards men and women".[34]

In spite of different opinions both the *International Council of Women* and the *Women's International League for Peace and Freedom* acceded to the equal rights treaty.

While the World's YWCA sided unanimously with those who supported special legislation for women, and collaborated closely in this field with the ILO, which right from the very beginning in 1919 had initiated special legislation,[35] the World's YWCA found it particularly important to maintain these agreements in countries with weak welfare and labour legislation, as well as in relation to women in industry. As a substitute for the treaty method the YWCA initiated knowledge-based and bureaucratic strategies and in 1934 the World's YWCA commissioned a study of women in industry and in the professions, as well as in local communities, in the church and at home.

In 1935 the international women's associations requested that issues such as the status of women and the equal rights treaty were put on the agenda at the General Assembly of the League of Nations. While the treaty was turned down, the general inquiry into the status of women was carried. A request that was made made by *World's YWCA* and the *International Federation of Business and Professional Women* and the World's YWCA agreed with more moderate forces, in desiring a gradual implementation of equal rights. In the following years a study was completed to which both governments and women's organisations contributed. The World's YWCA focused its energy on the economic aspects of the status of women, in collaboration with the international federations of university and of business and professional women. In the words of the World's YWCA: "Because of our various categories of members which include students, business and professional and industrial women, we felt we had a special concern in this phase of the study and were the best equipped to work in this field."[36] Several other international women's organisations focused on civic and political aspects of the enquiry. A focus that reflected and produced the various political interests and informal division of labour among the tone setting women's associations.

Again in 1937 a range of international women's organisations pushed for the passage of an international convention on equal rights. While the World's YWCA maintained their earlier reservation they instead exhorted the League of Nations to commission an analysis of the results of the *Status of Women Enquiry*. The initiative yielded a resolution that pointed optimistically to the gradual implementation of equal rights legislation and suggested the preparation of a three-year study of women's legal status. World War II however delayed the results.

When preparations for the United Nations were under way in 1945, a sub-commission was appointed on the *Status of Women* under the *Economic and Social Council*. Here a handful of women, who had been active in the League, were pushing for new initiatives. As a result equality and women's issues were included at strategic and institutional levels: The principle of equality between men and women was made explicit in the new *United Nations Charter* from 1948 and a permanent *Commission on Women* was launched.

As concerns the initiatives during the 1930s, the role of the World's YWCA was to assist in the adoption of the principle that the status of women was not merely a national but an international matter. At the same time the World's YWCA also participated in the foundation of the gradual and moderate principle on this matter. Instead the association favoured reconciling and moderate initiatives that also maintained and bridged the relationship between women's international associations and International institutions, such as the League and ILO. It even looks as if the World's YWCA made it possible for the various initiatives actually to be implemented. It did so by virtue of its prominent status in the efforts for peace and social rights.

Conclusions and research perspectives

In a longitudinal historical perspective the YWCA has been marked by more continuity than most women's rights and women's liberation movements. And the YWCA seems to have operated at the outskirts of feminist radicalism and waves, making the YWCA a reservoir for consciousness building and for the maintaining of practical community based projects. Another outstanding feature of the YWCAs consisted in their roles as laboratories for the creation of cross cultural and multiethnic communities. Both in relation to the forging of contacts between different confessions and religions as well as a locus for widening agency and opportunities of women at the grass roots levels in ethnic and non-Western communities.

The YWCA innovated social Christianity in the affiliation of Christian goals and social needs, and in this way the YWCA acted as a buffer and translator between the otherwise dominant social movements of the 20th century: With the polyphony of Liberal, Socialist/Labour and women's rights/feminist movements as the most significant. All in all the YWCA approach indicates a context of real *politics* and of practice rather than of theories and utopias. In certain senses the YWCA can be seen as a pragmatic interpreter and practitioner of several of the ideas of feminism and of socialism at the time. The very dynamic of the YWCA in a broad field of issues related to women workers derived from the coping with changing conditions of women during the 20th century and in the social field the YWCA was more dynamic than the parallel YMCA associations for men. Even though the YWCAs mostly clung to the idea of maternalism, the YWCA projects supported and widened women's opportunities in a much wider range.

A question for future research is to investigate closer the role of the YWCA today in post-communist and post-colonial settings where the YWCA still seems to attract women by the millions. At the world level the Association today claims to cater for more members than ever before in its long history. In that sense the YWCA might form an interesting and overlooked part of the new third wave of women's movements at the dawn of the 21st century.[37]

Religious movements like the YWCA confronted individuals with religious thoughts and choices, a fact that is challenging the idea of secularisation of Western societies as something that does away with religion as such. Rather secularisation might be regarded as a process through which religious issues became transformed from the agenda of society to the personal or individual level, meaning that the wider culture, knowledge and world views were secularised, while religion and Christianity were imposed as personal matters.[38]

Through such processes that seem to be crucial elements in the formation of modern societies, religion and Christianity became issues of consideration and choice, rather than something given and unreflected. Here the YWCA together with other religious movements performed the double aim of confronting young women with personal religious reflections and also to maintain, modernise and extend Christian values and morals at both open and hidden stages in society at large.

Last but not least remains the question of how to assess the YWCA in the framework of social movements. Does the YWCA as an old and historical movement qualify at all as a social movement? The answer of course is dependent on the definitions. If one subscribes to a broad idea of social movements understood as a web of organisations, aiming at collective, organised agency and at reforming society in a comprehensive sense, the YWCA clearly does count.[39] A more narrow definition has been spelled out, by restricting the label of social movements to the so-called emancipation movements. I.e. the ones that have fought for human rights, equal worth and individual autonomy for an excluded group. A position that tends to reduce a social movement to the progressive political elements and to the question of citizenship, but leaving untouched issues affiliated with history, tradition and spirituality that might be important for the self-understanding and as a mobilising resource.[40] My suggestion is to move beyond this kind of opposition and to relate the multiple ideas and activities of the YWCA to a broad continuum of women's movements and of feminisms where anti-feminism forms one pole and radical feminism another pole.

Here I find the suggestions made by the British sociologist Anthony Giddens useful in assessing the YWCA. Giddens links the concept of *emancipatory politics* to movements aiming at emancipating "others", and points to the Labour movement and liberal-democratic movements of the 19th and 20th centuries as classic examples, while the idea of *life politics* marks a new way of political activity. This includes a politics of self-actualisation that is focused on the self and on ethical choices.

For a closer look, I find that the YWCAs count as a social movement in either understanding. The YWCAs formed a type of movement that operated in the space between classical emancipatory politics and life politics. The YWCAs at certain points participated in the discursive formation and in the grounding of women's rights and emancipation. At the same time the YWCA, forged by its religious commitments, continuously performed the task of putting ethical and moral questions to the fore, both at the personal, national and global levels. This approach might apply to the entire cluster of feminist movements and contribute to recasting future research perspectives.

References

Bergman, Solveig (1999). "Studying Women's Movements in a Cross National Perspective: Dilemmas and Potentials." In Saarinen, Aino, Christensen, Hilda Rømer, Halsaa, Beatrice (eds.), (2000). *Women's Movements and Internationalisation*. Reports from the Faculty of Education. University of Oulu. 82/2000.

Boyd, Nancy (1986). *Emissaries. The Overseas Work of the American YWCA 1895-1970.* New York. The Women's Press.

Christensen, Hilda Rømer (1995). *Mellem Backfische og pæne piger. Køn og Kultur i KFUK 1883-1940*. København. Museum Tusculanums forlag.

Christensen, Hilda Rømer (1996). „Geschlecht und Kultur in dem Evangelischen Verband für die weibliche Jugend Deutschlands 1893-1940" (unpublished paper)

Christensen, Hilda Rømer (1999)."Aspirations for Peace and Equality. The World's YWCA 1894-1940". Saarinen, Aino, Christensen, Hilda Rømer, Halsaa, Beatrice (eds.), (2000). *Women's Movements and Internationalisation*. Oulu University.

Christensen, Hilda Rømer (2002). "Deviants of an Empire? Encounters between the Nordic and the World's YWCA 1900-1940." (unpublished paper)

Cott, Nancy (1987). *The Grounding of Modern Feminism.* Newhaven and London, Yale University Press.

Dahlerup, Drude (1998). *Rødstrømperne: Den danske Rødstrømpebevægelses udvikling, nytænkning og gennemslag 1970-1985.* Bd.1-2. København. Gyldendal.

Drucker, Alison R. (1979). The Role of the YWCA in the development of the Chinese Women's Movement 1890-1927. *Social Service Review.* Sept.

Eyerman, Ron (1996). "Sociala rörelsers kulturella praxis." *Sociologisk Forskning* 1.

Gerhard, Ute (1992). *Unerhört. Die Geschichte der deutschen Frauenbewegung.* Reinbek bei Hamburg. Rowolt.

Giddens, Anthony (1991). *The Consequences of Modernity.* London. Polity Press

Gundelach, Peter (1988). *Sociale bevægelser og samfundsændringer.* Aarhus. Politica.

Harrison, Brian (1987). *Prudent Revolutionaries. Portraits of British Feminists between the Wars.* Oxford. Clarendon Press.

Huber, Mary Taylor, Lutkehaus, Nancy C. (1999). "Introduction: Gendered Missions at Home and Abroad." Huber, Mary Taylor, Lutkehaus, Nancy, C. (eds.) *Gendered Missions. Women and Men in Misisonary Discourse and Practice.* Ann Arbor. University of Michigan Press.

Johnson-Odim, Cheryl and Strobel, Margaret (eds.) (1992). *Expanding the Boundaries of Women's History. Essays on Women in the Third World.* Bloomington and Indianapolis. Indiana University Press.

Law, Cheryl (1997). *Suffrage and Power. The Women's Movement 1918-28.* London.

Mayor, Stephen (1997). *The Churches and the Labour Movement.* London. Independent Press.

Miller, Carol (1994). "Geneva – The key to Equality: Inter-war Feminists and the League of Nations." *Women's History Review,* vol. 3.

Miller, Carol (1991). "Women in International Relations. The Debate in Inter-war Britain." Grant, Rebecca and Newland, Kathleen. (eds.). *Gender and International Relations.* Milton Keynes. Open University Press.

Olesen, Elith (1996). *De frigjorte og trællefolket. Amerikansk-engelsk indflydelse på dansk kirkeliv omkring år 1900.* København. Anis.

Pugh, Martin (1992). *Women and the Women's Movement in Britain 1914-1959.* London. Macmillan.

Anna Rice (1947). *A History of the World's Young Women's Christian Association.* New York, The Women's Press.

Rupp, Laila (1997). *Worlds of Women. The Making of an International Women's Movement.* Princeton University Press.

Sanders, Hanne (1995). *Bondevækkelse og sekularisering. En protestantisk folkelig kultur i Danmark og Sverige 1820-1850.* Stockholm. Studier i Stads- och kommunhistoria 12. Stads- och kommunhistoriska Instituttet. Historiska Institutionen, Stockholms Universitet.

Seymour-Jones, Carole (1994). *Journey of Faith. The History of The World YWCA 1945-1994.* London. Allison and Busby.

Stibbe, Matthew (2002). "Anti-Feminism, Nationalism and the German Right, 1914-1920: A Reappraisal." *German History,* vol. 2, no. 2.

Veer, Peter van der (2001). *Imperial Encounters. Religion and Modernity India and Britain.* Princeton University Press.

Notes

1 This approach is inspired by Bergman (1999) and Bergman in this volume. Recent comparative studies tend to blur the distinctions, see e.g. Helmuth Gruber and Pamela Graves: *Women and socialism, Socialism and Women. Europe between the two World Wars*. Berghan Books. New York and Oxford 1998, Ida Blom, Karen Hageman and Catherine Hall (eds.) *Gendered Nations. Nationalisms and Gender Order in the long Nineteenth century*. Berg, Oxford and New York. 2000.

2 The later influential Norwegian moral reformer Marie Michelet attended the Sankey and Moodey Mission in London. in the mid-1880s. The formation of the KMA – Women Missionary Workers in Sweden and in Denmark was directly influenced by Jessie Penn-Lewis, who also spent time in Germany. Both trends influenced the activism of women in the YWCAs. The diffusion happened in spite of Lutheran reluctance. See Olesen (1996) 355-361.

3 In 1891 it was reported from India, by the prominent UK YWCA leader, Emily Kinnaird, that 2-3 different YWCAs were being started in new countries on lines mirroring the home country/ nationality of the YWCA worker, rather than the country they operated in. Rice (1947), 49-50.

4 See Huber and Lutkehaus (1999), 10.

5 Rice 1947, p. 111-112.

6 Boyd (1986), 31.

7 In 1921 the US supplied 14,700 dollars in a total budget of 33,550, Drucker (1979)

8 Veer (2001)

9 18.9. 1924 Letter to Miss Niven from Ingibjörg Olafson, Archives of the World's Young Women's Christian Association, Geneva.

10 E.g. Brazil 1920, Chile 1921, Bolivia 1930, Czechoslovakia 1919, Estonia 1920, Romania 1919, Bulgaria 1922.

11 The conflict is elaborated in Christensen (2002)

12 Rice (1947), 271.

13 Rice (1947), 276.

14 Christensen (1996)

15 Germany did not play a very significant role during the inter-war years due to interior problems both financially and politically. Criticism of the Versailles Treaty and of Anglo-American dominance was headed off by a generous gift from the British YWCA that rescued the German YWCA from bankruptcy.

16 Seymour-Jones (1994), 41.

17 By 1955 the World's YWCA became the World YWCA that stressed the global and co-operating scope.

18 E.g. Anna Paulsen, who became Director of the German YWCA *Seminar für Kirchlichen Frauendienst* in 1926.

19 Rice (1947), p. 142-143. In 2001 other priorities of the World YWCA are advocacy of Social and Economic Justice and People Centred Development, see: *WWW.world YWCA*. And Musimbi Kanoyoro: YWCA, where the W matters. Paper, YWCA/YMCA of Denmark, May 18-19, 2000. (unpublished)

20 Numbers extracted from Harrison (1987).

21 All 1937 numbers from "Notes from Geneva". In *Blue Triangle Gazette*, Oct. and Nov. 1937. For Denmark see Christensen (1995).

22 See *Fürsorge für die weibliche Jugend* nr. 7, July 1910 and Stibbe (2002).

23 Law (1997) and Christensen (1995), 92ff.

24 E.g. the *British National Union of Women's Suffrage Societies* in 1919 broadened into the national *Union of Societies for Equal Citizenship* while another branch developed into the *Women's Employment Federation* in 1934. One branch of the NUWS survived as the *Fawcett Society*. See Harrison (1987) 4-5 and Pugh (1992), 43 ff.

25 This applies to the Conservative Lady Nancy Astor and Lady Artholl as well as to the labour MPs Marg. Bondfield, Mary Phillipson and Edith Picton-Turbervill. Here the British YWCA functioned as a framework for networking among the female elite and for the formation of cross-political initiatives and lobbying. On the Continent the YWCA affiliates only involved themselves in politics along strictly conservative lines. E.g. the Danish Gerda Mundt, member of the Danish Parliament for the Conservative Party and the German Paula Müller Ortfried, chair of the DEF and member of the German parliament for the conservative party *Deutsch Nationale Volkspartei* during the entire Weimar Republic.

26 Drucker (1979) and Honig (1992). It is worth to note that some of the most progressive and forward-looking American secretaries spent some time in China, e.g. Agatha Harrison and Mary Dingman, the latter to become prominent in the interwar peace work in Geneva. See also Zhang in this volume.

27 Miller (1991), 65.

28 The committee consisted of the following organisations: *The World's Women's Christian Temperance Union, The International Council of Women, The World's Young Women's Christian Association, The International Council of Nurses, The International Alliance of Women for Suffrage and Equal Citizenship, The Women's International League for Peace and Freedom, The World's Union of Women for International Concord,* and *The International Federation of University Women*. The charmed circle did not include other confessions or labour women.

29 8.7.1925 Letter to Ruth Rose from Charlotte T. Niven. Archives of the *World's Young Women's Christian Association,* Geneva.

30 The radical branch embodied by the *American National Women's Party* and the controversial chairwoman, Alice Poul.

31 Including the *League of Jewish Women* and the *International co-operative Guild of Women.*

32 The Peace and Disarmament Committee and the International Women's Peace League apparently competed for the honour of the Nobel Prize. The Peace and Disarmament committee was nominated for the Nobel Peace Prize and was granted financial support by the Nobel committee, while the Peace League and its chair Jane Addams won a shared Nobel Prize 1932. Rupp (1997), 42-43, 221.

33 The purpose of the *Equal Rights Treaty* was to initiate equal rights legislation from above, and the countries who signed the treaty were to work towards equal rights or gender-neutral legislation. The Equal Rights Treaty was introduced by a Conference of American States in 1933, where it was signed by a handful of Latin and South American countries: Cuba, Ecuador, Paraguay and Uruguay.

34 Rupp (1997), 145, Miller (1994), 26, 230.

35 E.g. the *Night Work Convention* and the *Childbirth Convention,* both of 1919.

36 Miller (1994), 27.

37 Cf. Interview with Musimbi Kanyoro, General Secretary, World YWCA, July 2001 and Musimbi Kanyoro: YWCA, where the W Matters. Paper, YWCA/YMCA of Denmark, May 18-19, 2000 (unpublished)

38 For an elaborated debate of secularisation see Sanders (1995), 16ff.
39 Gundelach (1988), 24. The broad definition acknowledges both progressive and regressive elements **within** social movements as well as social movements with different political ends.
40 Eg. Dahlerup (1998). For a cultural approach, see Eyerman 1996).

CHAPTER 6

Women's Movements in Sport: National and International Issues

Leena Laine

The issue of this chapter is women's organisations, solutions and strategies in sport from the end of the 19th century to the 1950s. In focus are the Nordic countries with outlooks to Europe and the USA. When defining women's activities in the sports movement(s) I have taken into account (1) independent, autonomous movements and (2) women's activities in joint organisations – more or less organised by women/ feminist groups there. Besides I am going to deal with the complicated relationship of sporting women to international co-operation in two concrete cases: women in athletics and women in skiing.

My purpose here is to present and analyse the way different women's movements developed in the context of modern sport.[1] Here the ideas of difference and equality have been central.[2] In the framework of women's sports movements this becomes visible in two distinct tendencies. On the one hand we find the women's gymnastics associations, marked by the idea of gender difference, as a strategy to obtain inde- pendence and self-definition. On the other hand women were engaged in competitive sports, whose focus was on the idea of equal rights, and the right for women to take part in the exercise of sports on an equal footing with men. Both tendencies were to be found in the gender-mixed organisations, and from time to time in separate women's organisations.

It is hard to find another social area, compared with the sports movement, where the male control has been as effective and powerful. Women's opportunities were limited and I am going to demonstrate that women's goals could easily differ radically from each other, and even become contradictory and turn against each other.

Women's activities and movements in sport challenge the periodisation of the women's movements and the idea of certain tidal waves.[3] The idea of two or perhaps three waves or crests of high activity in the women's rights movements are under- mined from the perspective of the women's sports movements. Elisabeth Lønnå, in her analysis of women's movements in Norway in this volume, finds hidden activity crests during the 1920s and 1930s and again during the 1950s. This complies with the activity crests in the Nordic women's sports movements.

Historical outlines and perspectives

In the Nordic countries the earliest forms of physical education consisted in gym- nastics education in girl's schools or private gymnastics exercises. Since the 1850s gymnastics was organised in very rare private women's gymnastics clubs, or, as in

Norway, in women's sections of men's gymnastics clubs.[4] With the growing popular movements and the women's liberation movement at the end of the 19th century, special women's gymnastics clubs and even gymnastics associations were founded. Gymnastics was then connected with middle class leisure activities: walking, riding, dancing and different ball games – which formed part of women's self-expression, joy and emancipation. Women also took part in local or national competitions in rowing, skiing and athletics. On the international level they participated mostly in figure skating (since the 1880s) and in the Olympic Games between 1900 – 1920 in golf, tennis, archery, figure skating and swimming. The activities were strongest in countries like the USA with a crest from 1911 to 1917. Also in Germany and in the Nordic countries women's sport activities were growing.[5]

I am going to focus on the decades between 1920 and 1940 because they were clearly marked by two strategically different activities. On one hand there was a take-off for the women's gymnastics movements that challenged the (male) competitive model of sports. At the same time women made their way into competitive sports, e.g. through the formation of the *International Women's Sports Federation*. In addition, the workers' sports movement represented yet another field of pioneering women's parciticipation and integration: Here women were present in both gymnastics and in competitive sports.

Women's gymnastics. The making of a mass movement

At the end of the 19th century especially, physical educators, consisting of middle and upper class women, in many countries rejected the emerging competitive sports that was severely criticised in society at large. In opposition to the male dominance in the emerging field of sports, these women developed separate women's physical cultures. This often took the shape of educational gymnastics (callisthenics in USA) and of non-competitive sports. They founded women's gymnastics clubs, and even federations with alternative physical education programmes.[6] The development of physical activities 'suitable' for girls and women often implied the strategical *feminisation* of certain areas of sport.

Educational gymnastics in the form of mass gymnastics became a special women's issue and developed into a women's major activity in the Nordic area in the 1930s. In Norway, Sweden and Denmark women worked in federations led by men. Gradually, and at the latest after the Second World War, women reached a majority in membership. In Finland the landscape of associations in the field multiplied. Here women's gymnastics was organised in women's clubs from the 1870s and a national federation was founded in 1896. In 1921 the national federation was split into three different branches according to language and class. During the 1930s women's gymnastics developed into a mass movement that counted almost 100 000 members in the late 1940s.

From a generational point of view the first generation of gymnastics women (1870s-1910's) was political, emancipated and involved in the fight for national struggle for independence against Russia. The year 1906 also brought Finnish women the vote. The second generation of Finnish women who were active in the gymnastics movement during the 1920s and 1930s, were more conformist and emphasised motherhood and femininity. At the same time they forcefully defended women's independent organisations against male intrusion.[7]

In the Nordic countries, England, Germany and especially in North America the organised female physical educators and their organisations were working along the same lines and with the same aims. Professional physical educators played a major role in what developed into a major movement in women's physical culture between the world wars.[8] The women's gymnastics movement aimed at enhancing health, as well as physical and social skills. At the same time they also included social politics and education in their activities. In general they stressed moderation and ignored competitions. They mainly operated at local or national levels. One exception here was a small Nordic *Association for Women's Gymnastics*, founded in 1922. The goal was to initiate a gymnastics method especially for women and to challenge the wide-spread Swedish gymnastics system, developed and controlled by male authorities.

Another international association, organised along somehow different lines and goals, was the *Women's League of Health and Beauty*. Launched in Britain in 1930, its goal was to develop a body culture that nurtured the 'natural' woman's body as opposed to the aggressive and mechanised modern sports. The organisation developed into a mass sports association at the global level, and in 1939 it held a membership in Britain alone of 166 000.[9]

In general the women in non-competitive sports and in gymnastics acted at the local or national levels. International co-operation was restricted to the elaboration of common standards in leadership education, and in scientific conferences and international festivals. An international federation for modern gymnastics (*League Internationale Gymnastique Moderne*), established in Germany in 1952, has continued to promote this kind of co-operation.

Women in competitive sports and in the Olympic Games

The sports movement is the largest popular movement in the Nordic countries today. Since its formative stage, in the latter half of the 19th century, it has been strongly affiliated with the national frameworks that in many cases were formed in parallel with the sports movement.

In the logic of the national state, men's physical exercise was of importance for the purpose of national defence. Women's physical exercise was connected with reproduction: the patriotic duty of the female members of the state was to give birth to healthy strong new citizens – soldiers and mothers of the future.[10] This has laid the foundation and framework for the field of international competition where national celebrations have been based exclusively on men's achievements.

The *International Olympic Committee* (IOC) was founded in 1894, and the modern Olympic Games were organised for the first time in 1896. Special federations were founded to control the emerging competitive sports in their respective areas, nationally and internationally. It has even been argued that the Olympic movement was launched as a reaction towards the emerging modern femininity and was meant as a site for male domination, freed from modern gender struggles.[11]

After World War I the rise of *women's competitive sport* became a fact in most countries. This happened in parallel with the mobilisation of male sports. At the organisational level both national and international organisations went through a period of stabilisation, a process that resulted in the restriction of women's activities. Women's entrances were barred or at least strongly opposed, particularly in sports of national importance or sports deeply rooted in national male culture. The sexualisation of the female body also became an issue in this period. Below I am going to focus on two examples where women's organisations/activities were launched due to gender conflicts.

During those first decades of emerging modern sport, a gendered mapping of sports became evident, which also included a hierarchical segregation of men's and women's sports. Sports, where aesthetics and beauty of performance are central (like figure skating) were transformed into 'feminine', *'women's sports'*, while sports emphasising strength (athletics) and physical contact between the competitors (boxing and wrestling), were labelled as 'masculine' or *'male sports'*. The segregation was based on the biological construction of two different sexes, 'men' and 'women' that were seen as compensating each other.[12] The 'compensatory' women's sports won earlier acceptance e.g. in the frame of Olympic games. Sports signifying and representing the masculinity in different cultures stayed an area for men only – and women's events in these sports in the Olympic Games or other important international meetings were rejected.

It is interesting that this manifest gender hierarchy in the international sports movement was challenged by the workers' sports federations in the inter-war years. In the Communist *Red Sport International* (RSI, 1921) women competed on all levels. *The Red Sport International* was rooted in the Soviet Union, where women's participation in all kinds of sports was seen as a tool to further women's social emancipation.[13] The *Socialist Worker Sports International* (SWSI, 1920) founded a women's committee in 1929, when a program for promoting women's sport, the first in world history, was also accepted. It is striking that the Finnish *Worker's Sports Federation* (1919) functioned as a pioneer in terms of women's organisational work: The federation established a women's secretary and a journal, and women's committees were founded at all levels from the beginning. All the work was directed by women themselves. At the international level women's events were included in the socialist Winter and Summer Olympics from 1925 till 1937 that were organised by SWSI. In the late 1930s the activities of both internationals was halted by fascism.[14]

After World War II, particularly in the Nordic countries, women for the first time widely challenged the power exercised by the leading male sports organisations, and women's sports spread successfully. At an international level, e.g. the European Championships, most sports were opened for women. In the Olympic Games, female sports stars were celebrated, and during the 1940s, women's sports evoked great attention and interest in the international media. Women's participation was partly motivated by

Winter games in Eastern Finland, Wiborg, 1910. Winners of the women's 3 kilometers event, the youngest of them only 13 years. The first prize was a silver brooch. (Suomen Urheilulehti 1910 no 4/5.)

the attraction to sport itself, but was also from time to time motivated by the interest in promoting women's rights.

During the late 1940s and early 50s the Nordic countries pioneered the foundation of women's committees in the central sports organisations in Norway, Finland and Sweden. Danish women did not claim women's committees arguing that they had been represented at central levels since 1921.[15] Committees organised competitions and mass sporting events for women, arranged seminars and educated female administrators, coaches, referees etc., and fought for publicity in (sports) journals. During the late 1940s and 50s women's committees obtained quite a large autonomy concerning women's interests in sport, excluding, however, control of resources and top level competitions.

Co-operation between the Nordic countries was also established. But the Central Federations led by men rejected the launching of a permanent Nordic committee in 1956. Such a committee was regarded as unnecessary and expensive.[16]

The positive developments did not, however, change the basic power relations in sport: the number of women in leading positions in the federations or as sports officials, coaches etc. was not growing significantly. In Norway the advancement of women declined in the 1940s, with the 'rationalisation' of the central organisation. In Finland and in Sweden efforts to improve women's conditions in sports vanished during the 1960s.

The Nordic committee period made up a new stage in striving for the recognition of women in sports. During the same period women and women's position in the mainstream sports organisations were made an issue and the committees furthered the co-operation among women.

The International Women's Sports Federation and women's athletics

For those women active in competitive sports – international by nature and structure – an unlimited participation was substantial. Thus the struggle for full rights was an organising element, and even a base for international co-operation among active woman athletes.

In order to make space in the international field of sport women had two choices: Either to co-operate with men in joint organisations or to found their own (independent) organisations. The former alternative called for a wide acceptance of women and women's performances at the national level. Neither was the latter an easy choice in the regulated and male-controlled sports system. In the following I am going to present the implications of the only independent international women's organisation in the history of competitive sports: *The International Women's Sports Federation* that operated in the 1920s and 1930s.

In 1917, during World War I, Alice Milliat, who was later to become a famous sports leader, founded a sports association for women in France. Already in1921, the first international women's athletic meeting was held in Monte Carlo, an event that facilitated contacts between athlete women. This event inspired Milliat to launch the *Fédération Sportive Féminine Internationale (FSFI*, the Women's International Sports Federation) in Paris autumn 1921. The founding members were representatives from France, Great Britain, USA, Czecho-Slovakia, Italy and Spain. In the following years national women's federations and women's committees in athletic federations grew in number and affiliated the international organisation. The FSFI petitioned the International Olympic Committee to include women's athletics in the Olympic programme. When this was turned down the separate *Women's Olympics* were launched. They took place every fourth year and with national representation. The first games were held in Paris in 1922. Only athletic events, 11 in number, were included in the programme that in terms of public attention was successful in attracting 20 000 spectators.[17]

The International *Amateur Athletics Federation* (IAAF) was the leading body in the international athletics, which controlled this sport also as regards Olympic Games. Now IAAF saw its authority threatened by the success of FSFI. Negotiations between the two organisations resulted in the inclusion of five women's athletic events in the Olympics' program, the first time as an experiment in 1928. On a basis of reciprocity the International *Women's Sports Federation* consented to change the title of the Women's Olympic Games to *Women's World Games.* [18]

At the Nordic level FSFI also influenced activities and initiated new legitimacy. The newly founded Swedish women's sports association hosted the Second Women's World Games in Gothenburg in 1926. Women's athletics in Sweden had a fervent male advocate, Rector Einar Lilie from Gothenburg, who was also a board member of the Swedish Athletics Federation. Inspired by FSFI activities, he proposed a motion in 1925 to the Swedish Athletics Federation to set up a women's division. The federation, however, preferred a separate women's association, which was set up in 1925. The Women's World Games in 1926 was a huge public success, again. After that the Swedish Athletics Federation willingly founded a women's committee and the women's own association was dissolved.[19]

The inclusion of women's events to the Olympic program in 1928 awoke an enormous debate and opposition among the male sports leaders and in the public. It is striking that the inclusion came as a shock in Finland, where women's national championships in athletics had been abolished just a few years previously. In both Finland and Sweden the arguments were based on rigid ideas about gender: the Olympic athletic arena was an exclusive male domain that would loose its dignity if women were to appear. In the media all kinds of arguments for and against the participation of women in athletic competitions were applied. Women were as divided as men on the issue. Both gymnastic leaders and medical authorities presented crude portrayals of the potential damage athletics could cause to women – or to the female body: transformation into men, loss of maternal will.[20] The debate gives evidence of the harsh tune of the inter-war gender debate.

The success of the International Women's Sports Federation influenced the agendas of the International Olympic Committee and the IAAF. When women were promised a full Olympic programme the powerful FSFI, with affiliated members from 30 countries, agreed to halt its activity during the late 1930s. Women's World Games were staged twice more, in Prague in 1930 and in London in 1934. Promises to introduce the full athletic program for women in the Olympic Games were still not kept. The compromise resulted in only the merge of International Women's Sports Federation with the International Amateur Athletic Federation.[21]

The co-operation and compromises with IAAF caused heated debates at the meetings of the International Women's Sports Federation. President Alice Milliat saw the limited Olympic program as an underestimation of women. Some FSFI organisations were afraid that parents would not allow their daughters to participate in the same competitions as men, some did not accept men's control over women – and some men did not want to control.[22] Finally some women groups saw the international federation as more than merely a "substitute organisation": they regarded women's co-operation and autonomy as significant also for future intervention.

In 1928, the powerful English Women's Athletic Association boycotted the Olympic Games in protest, and in 1932 alternative women's games were organised during the Olympic Games in Los Angeles. The ranks of FSFI were splitting.[23]

It is interesting here that female gymnastics leaders e.g. in Finland and in the USA were against women's participation in the Olympics. They feared that men would invade women's territory through competitive sports and undermine their federations.

The motives behind the founding of the International Women's Sports Federation lay in the male dominated system and the ignorant attitudes towards women's athletics. FSFI's strategy, as women's version of the male model, was to show and assure the public that women were capable of the same things as men, and many male sports leaders were in favour. At the same time the success of this international federation illustrates the enormous potential of women's autonomous organisations, even if they were only in existence for a limited time.[24]

Women in Nordic skiing: negotiating the space

Long distance (Nordic) skiing makes up another striking example of women who fought for acceptance in the problematic joint organisations and in the complicated context of sport, nation and gender. Skiing was developed as the Norwegian national sport during the national mobilisation and fight for Norwegian independence around the turn of the 20th century. When Norway was made independent of Sweden in 1905, skiing was even emphasised in Sweden as bearer of the national male heritage. In Finland, skiing was overshadowed by athletics and the male world success in the field (Paavo Nurmi etc.), and was profiled as a (second) national sport first during the late 1920s.

The top international competitions such as the Winter Olympics, which were started in 1924, and the World Championships in skiing, held for the first time in 1926, included events in Nordic skiing and ski jump, but only for men. In around 1936-37 alpine skiing was opened for men and for women as well. But women's events in Nordic skiing were not included in the Winter Olympics or the World Championships until the early 1950s.[25] It is striking that women's access was barred for a long time due to the particular identification of national pride and masculinity that made especially the Norwegian Skiing Federation an ardent opponent of women in the discipline of Nordic skiing. This was true in spite of long-held traditions in the Nordic countries for women's competitions in winter sports.

When competitions in Nordic skiing were introduced at end of the 1870s women participated under the same conditions as men in both Norway, Finland and Sweden. In Finland women participated in the National Championships from 1911, and in Sweden from 1916, while the so-called *Nordic Games* opened up international competitions for women in 1909. In Norway women stayed outside the national championships till 1954. Here women's sports clubs or women's political societies had organised local competitions in downhill, ski jump and also in long distance skiing since the end of the 19th century. While women's skiing competitions were winning full public acceptance in Sweden and Finland, the attitude in Norway was less permissive. Here the early activities were criticised in the media due to women's unsuitable clothing and to various health issues.[26]

In several cases the permissive attitude in both Finland and Sweden changed during the 1920s, due to growing international change, competition between nations as well as changed gender perceptions.

In Sweden, in the beginning of the 1920s, when the prominent "Vasa Competition" was launched, women were excluded. It was argued that the presence of women would turn the male game into a "circus". Later in the 1920s, women's participation in the Nordic Games and in the Swedish championships was aggressively criticised by some sports leaders and in the press. At the same time the different disciplines in skiing were gendered. It was pointed out that even long distance skiing was too heavy a sport for women and subsequently slalom was recommended as more suitable for them. In 1937 the new trends translated into introduction of Swedish Championships in women's slalom.

In Finland internationalisation of skiing had consequences for the participation of women. In the mid-1930s the most important ski event, called the *Games of Salpaus-selkä*, made an international breakthrough. Also here internationalisation implied that the women's event was dropped from the programme.[27]

At the beginning of the 1930s women's skiing was developing into a popular women's sport in Norway, outside of the ski federation. Even ski jumping became a favourite activity among young women. It was a field that enabled them to become sports stars, and even participate in competitions abroad. In 1931 Norwegian women demanded that the national ski federation include women's long distance skiing and ski jumping in its programme. It is interesting that only alpine skiing was accepted. According to Gerd von der Lippe this sport was not of national significance, and consequently it was *suitable* for women, and did not challenge male pride.[28]

The restrictions were also due to (men's) confrontations at the international level. Since the 1920s two different winter sports cultures, the Nordic and the Central European, were competing and striving for international hegemony. In this situation, women were excluded and even marginalised. The workers' sports movement, again, made up a challenge to this kind of attitude and its restrictions based on national and masculine pride. The Workers' Winter Olympics thus included women's long distance skiing in 1925, 1931 and 1937 when alpine skiing was also included. Both the Finnish and Norwegian women participated in these Olympics and competed on the national level.[29]

In 1946, the *Women's Committee for Alpine Sports* was founded in the International Ski Federation. At the Nordic level women in Sweden and in Finland successfully started committee work in the national ski federations aimed at counteracting the restrictions on women's Nordic skiing. In 1948 these organisations suggested the inclusion of a women's event in the Olympics and in the World Championships programme. A lot of propaganda for the proposal was disseminated around Europe by Swedish and Finnish federations, women activists and leaders.

Only Norway stood out and denied the inclusion of women in national competitive activities. During the 1940s "style skiing" was introduced in Norway as a compensatory way of including women in Nordic skiing. Here male officials controlled the style

by hiding behind the trees near the ski track. Nevertheless Norway had the honour of organising the historic first women's long distance skiing event in the Winter Olympics in Oslo 1952. Finally women's national championships in skiing was launched in Norway in 1954.[30] At the international level a special committee for women's Nordic skiing was not founded until 1965 in the international ski federation.

Also in relation to women in skiing we can speak of certain moves and crests that resemble the sports movements among women in general. The visible moves or activity crests in this field seem to be the beginning of the 20th century, again in the 1930s and finally in the late 1940s. It is also interesting to note how skiing, especially in the case of Norway, became a highly gendered field due to the intersection of skiing and the fight for national independence. Also the field of skiing makes evident how the fight for hegemony at the international level has marginalised women's activity and the willingness to include women.

Women's movements in Sport: Challenging and displacing the waves

Women's activities and movements in sport challenge the common way of periodising activity waves which locates the first wave around suffrage campaigns in the 1880s and again between 1907-1920, and the second wave around the events of the 1960s.[31] This approach conceals the unique activity crest in the women's sports movements between 1920 and 1940, and the crest after World War II. In her analysis of women's movements in Norway historian Elisabeth Lønnå also outlines a different picture and locates activity crests in the 1920s, 1930s and again in the 1950s. This fits into the periodisation of Swedish, Finnish and Norwegian women's movements in sport and might also reveal the interchange and parallel between the two branches of associations.[32] The multifaceted women's movements in sport challenge restricted notion of waves. In total they form "a continuous flow of activity", even between the suggested crests.

As in the women's rights movements, the women's movements in sport seemed to have diverging, even conflicting strategies too. Here it is important to bring into the discussion the context, the social values and goals, asking what kinds of change (in sport) these movements were striving for.

Participating in sports activities meant self-expression, health and joy. When this right was restricted, sporting activities became a political movement. While adapting to a larger social programme for bettering women's lives, the women's gymnastics

A "modern sportswoman" Halina Konopacka, Poland, throwing discus at the "Second International Ladies' Games". The new title of the games originated in Gothenburg, Sweden, 1926. (Riksföreningen för Gymnastikens Främjande årsbok 1938, Göteborg 1938, p.155)

movements achieved continuity. Conversely, movements within competitive sports that concentrated exclusively on women's rights in sport reoccurred in shorter periods. One explanation for the breaks is the connection between crests and the *generations* of women with whom the activities increase and then decline.

The modern national and international sports community was built according to and conforming to the male norm, the feminine body being the exception. This is one reason why women could not gain access to the high level competitive sports. The meaning (significance) of sport has been committed to male achievements, and has been represented as male power in society. This point of view challenges and undermines the core concept of *sportification* developed in the field of sports research which sees sport as marked by socially neutral developments.[33] Male researchers were thus producing a gender blind theory which made them unable to see the gendered, exclusive nature of modern sport.

During the expansion of modern sport women held an active role in the movement, as demonstrated in examples from Europe and the Nordic countries. It seems as if systematic restriction of women and their activities in sport began in the 1920s, in national states where competitive sport was a part of establishing the new gender order. At the same time women's activities both in separate and joint organisations succeeded gradually in influencing the issues of the top international associations such as the International Olympic Committee and the International Amateur Athletics Federation.

It is hard to reach a final conclusion relating to women's movements in sports because of their multiple expressions and emphases, and the complicated context of modern sports. In the Nordic countries, the site of what is today appreciated as the ideal countries of equality – women's opportunities in the period up till World War II were not largely better than in many other western countries. There were significant differences in terms of gender distribution of rights and in terms of the social distribution. In general middle class and upper class women and students initiated the movements. But also the workers' sports movement acted as a pioneering framework. The early suffragists definitely played a role as inspiration for the emergence of physical activities for women. And later, when the suffragist movement vanished, the women in sports and gymnastics helped waving the flag for women's rights.

References

Annerstedt, Claes (1984). Kvinnoidrottens utveckling i Sverige, Malmö, Liber förlag.

Bornholdt, Kerstin (2001). *Frauensport in Norwegen. Analysen zu einer medizinisch geführten Diskussion in der 1930'er Jahren*. Magisterarbeit, Humboldt-Universität zu Berlin, Philosophische Fakultät II, Nordeuropa-Institut, Berlin den 14. Juli 2001. (unpublished).

Cahn, Susan K. (1995). *Coming on strong. Gender and Sexuality in Twentieth-Century Women's Sport*, USA, Harvard University Press.

Fenner, Antje (1999), "The First German Fräuleinwunder. Early Development of Women's Athletics in Germany", Trangbaek, Else/ Krüger, Arnd (Eds.), *Gender and Sport from European Perspectives*, Copenhagen, CESH, 97-112.

Fletcher, Sheila (1984). *Women First. The Female Tradition in English Physical Education 1880-1980.* London & Dover, New Hampshire, Athlone Press.

Goksøyr, Matti (1994). "Winter Sports and the Creation of a Norwegian National Identity at the Turn of the 19th Century", Matti Goksøyr, Gerd von der Lippe and Kristen Mo (Eds.), *Winter Games – Warm Traditions. Selected Papers from the 2. International ISHPES Seminar, Lillehammer.* The Norwegian Society for Sports History-ISHPES.

Guttmann, Allen (1991). *Women's Sports. A History*, New York, Columbia University Press.

Hargreaves, Jennifer (1994). *Sporting Females. Critical Issues in the History and Sociology of Women's Sports*, London and New York, Routledge.

International Encyclopedia of Women and Sports, (2001), Volume 2. New York, Macmillan Reference.

Howell, Reet (Ed.). (1982). *Her Story in Sport. A Historical Anthology of Women in Sports.* New York, Leisure Press.

Jallinoja, Riitta (1983). *Suomalaisen naisasialiikkeen taistelukaudet* [The struggle periods of the Finnish feminist movement], Juva, WSOY.

Krüger, Arnd and Riordan, James (Eds.) (1996). *The History of Worker Sport*, Champaign, IL., Human Kinetics.

Kryger Pedersen, Inge (2001). "Den olympiske sport er ikke blot et spejl af samfundet", Jørn Hansen, Thomas Skovgaard (Eds.). *Idraettens Mangfoldighed Idraettens Graenser?* Idraetshistorisk årbok 2000, 16. årgang, Odense, Universitetsforlag, p. 103-119.

Laine, Leena (1984). *Vapaaehtoisten järjestöjen kehitys ruumiinkulttuurin alueella Suomessa v. 1856- 1917,I-II,* [The Development of the Voluntary Organisations in the Physical Culture in Finland 1856-1917 I-II], Liikuntatieteellisen Seuran julkaisuja No 93A-93B, Helsinki.

Laine, Leena (1989). "The 'Nature' of Woman – the 'Nature' of Man: The Effects of Gender Images on Organizing Sports in Finland in the 1920s and 1930s", Marjo Raivio (Ed.), *Proceedings of the Jyväskylä Congress on "Movement and Sport in Women's life"*, Volume 1, Reports of Physical Culture and Health 66, University of Jyväskylä, p. 120-137.

Laine, Leena (1998). "How to Cross Borders – Women and Sports Organisations in the Nordic Countries", – *The International Journal of the History of Sport Vol.* 15, No.1 (April), London, Frank Cass, p. 194-205.

Laine, Leena (2000a). "Jämlik idrott – ett brutet löfte", Bo G. Nilsson (Ed.), *"Idrottens själ". Fataburen 2000. Nordiska Museets och Skansens årsbok 2000*, Stockholm, Nordiska Museet, p. 54 -74.

Laine, Leena (2000b). *Työväen urheiluliikkeen naiset* [Women in the Worker Sports Movement], Helsinki, Otava.

Laine, Leena (2001). "What Happened to the Early Queens of Sport? Problematizing the Discontinuity and Breaks in Women's Sport", Jürgen Buschmann/Gertrud Pfister (Hrsg.), *Sport und Sozialer Wandel*, ISHPES- Studies Vol. 8. St Augustin, Academia Verlag, p. 42-53.

Laine, Leena (2002). "Naishiihdon pitkä matka olympialajiksi" [The Long Journey of Women's Skiing to Olympic Sports], Heikki Roiko-Jokela and Esa Sironen (Eds.), *Lajien synty. Suomen urheiluhistoriallisen seuran vuosikirja 2001-2002*, Jyväskylä, Atena Kustannus Oy, p. 121-138.

Laine, Leena (Manuscript 2003). In Search of Women's Alternatives in Sport: Women's Movements in the Finnish and Swedish Sports Culture.

Laine, Leena & Sarje, Aino (2002). *Suomalaisen naisvoimistelun maailmat* [The Worlds of the Finnish Women's Gymnastics], Helsinki, Naisvoimistelun Tuki.

Laqueur, Thomas (1994). *Om könens uppkomst. Hur kroppen blev kvinnlig och manlig.* Stockholm, Brutus Östlings Bokförlag Symposion.

Löwdin, Inga (1994). "Tillbakablick på skidornas damlängdlöpning som tävlingssport 1880-1965", *Svenska Idrottshistoriska förenings årskrift*, Helsingborg, p. 41-59.

Olofsson, Eva (1989). *Har kvinnorna en sportslig chans? Den svenska idrottsrörelsen och kvinnorna under 1900-talet*, Pedagogiska institutionen, Umeå universitet.

Pfister, Gertrud (1994). "Demands, Realities and Ambivalences – Women in the Proletarian Sports Movement in Germany (1893-1933)". *Women in Sport and Physical Activity Journal*, Vol. 3, No. 2, Fall 1994, p. 39-68.

Pfister, Gertrud (1999). "Physical Education – From Male Domain to a Female Profession. The Controversy over Women as Physical Educators in Germany", Trangbaek, Krüger.

Arnd (eds.), *Gender and Sport from European Perspectives*, Copenhagen, CESH, p. 69-82.

Pfister, Gertrud (2000). "Die Frauenweltspiele und die Beteiligung von Frauen an Olympischen Spielen", Behendt, M. Steins, G. (eds.). *Sport(geschichte). Berichte und Materialen, Sporthistorische Blätter 7/8*, p. 157-171.

Riordan, Jim (1996). "Worker Sport within a Worker State: the Soviet Union", Krüger, Arnd and Riordan, James (Eds.), *The History of Worker Sport*, Champaign, IL, Human Kinetics, p. 43-65.

Rosenbeck, Bente (1994). "Politik, videnskap och kön", *Det 22. Nordiske historikermöte, Oslo, 13-18 August 1994. Rapport III. Fra kvinnehistorie til kjönnshistorie?*, Oslo, p. 33-46.

Trangbaek, Else (2001). "Kvindeidraettens pionerer og den moderne kvinde", Jorn Hansen, Thomas Skovgaard (Eds.). *Idraettens Mangfoldighed Idraettens Graenser?* Idraetshistorisk årbok 2000,16. årgang, Odense Universitetsforlag, p.75-84.

Webster, F.A.M. (1930). *Athletics of To-day for Women. History, Development & Training.* London and New York, Frederick Warne & Co., Ltd.

von der Lippe, Gerd (1989). "Kvinneutvalg – organisering av kvinners 'särintresser' i idretten", *Nytt om kvinneforskning*, 13. årgang, nr. 4, Oslo, p. 34-44.

von der Lippe, Gerd (1997). *Endring og motstand mot endring av feminiteter och maskuliniteter i idrett og kroppskultur i Norge: 1890-1950.* Norges Idrettshögskole, Institutt for samfunnsvitenskaplige fag. (unpublished).

Notes

1   In this text *"sport"* means the system together: organisations, activities and ideology; sometimes one form of activity (like swimming). *"Sports"* means the practical activities in common. *Physical culture (and sport)* is the larger context for physical activities. The empirical material for the article is contained in my yet unpublished manuscript for a dissertation, if other sources have not been shown. See Laine (2003, manuscript).

2   As demonstrated by e.g. Elisabeth Lønnå and Irina Yukina in this volume.

3   The wave concepts are being discussed in Dahlerup and Lønnå in this volume. Dahlerup sug-

gests three waves in the case of Denmark. Also in Finland three crests have been defined: 1884 -1908, 1966-70 and 1973ff by Finnish sociologist Riitta Jallinoja (1983) (p. 9-13, 248).

4 von der Lippe (1997), p.190; Trangbaek (2001).

5 See e.g. Laine (1984), Laine (1998); Laine (2001); von der Lippe (1997), Annerstedt (1984); Cahn (1995); Pfister (1999); Fenner (1999); Fletcher (1984).

6 See e.g. Howell (1982), Chapter IV; Fletcher (1984); Laine (1984); Laine (1998).

7 Laine (manuscript); Laine & Sarje (2002).

8 Laine (1998); Olofsson (1989); Trangbaek (2001); Pfister (1999); Howell (1982); Fletcher (1984); Hargreaves (1994).

9 Laine & Sarje (2002). The work laid on Finnish Elli Björkstén and her method; Hargreaves (1994), p. 134 -136.

10 See e.g. Laine (1984); Goksøyr (1994); Rosenbeck (1994). See also Kristmundsdottir in this volume.

11 Kryger Pedersen (2001).

12 Laqueur (1994) speaks of two genders' system, based on two sexes' biology, which is a more precise way to define a gender system, as a heterosexual order, a basic element for the modern sports culture.

13 Riordan (1989), p. 50. About Germany: see Pfister (1994); Finland (Laine 2000b).

14 After the war a new co-operative organisation was founded, a women's committee being set up first in 2000. Laine (2000b); Krüger & Riordan (Eds.) (1989), Appendix A; Hargreaves (1994), p.140-141; Pfister (1994).

15 von der Lippe (1989); Olofsson (1989); Laine (manuscript).

16 Laine (1998); von der Lippe (1989).

17 Webster (1930), p. 32-33; Pfister (2000); Guttmann (1991), p. 167

18 Webster (1930), p. 98-100; Pfister (2000); Guttmann (1991), p. 168.

19 Laine (2000 a).

20 Laine (1989); USA: see Cahn (1994), Chapter 3.

21 Webster (1930), p. 101-107; Pfister (2000); Hargreaves (1994), p. 213-214; Guttman (1991), p.170-171.

22 Webster (ibid.); Pfister 2000.

23 Hargreaves (1994), p. 214-215; see also Pfister (2000).

24 In 1949 a new international federation was founded, the *International Association of Physical Education and Sport for Girls and Women* (IASPEGW). It is an interest organisation that nowadays works in all continents. Its roots lay in women's co-operation in athletics in the 1920's-1930's. *International Encyclopedia of Women and Sports*, Volume 2, p. 575-576.

25 See Laine (2002).

26 Annerstedt (1984); von der Lippe (1997), p. 197-202; Löwdin (1994); Laine (2001); Laine (2002).

27 Laine (2002); Löwdin (1994).

28 von der Lippe (1997), p. 203.

29 Goksöyr (1994); Laine (2002).

30 Von der Lippe (1989), p. 203; Laine (2002); Löwdin (1994).

31 Dahlerup in this volume; Lönnå in this volume.

32 Lønnå in this volume.

33 See e.g. von der Lippe (1997), p. 14 -17.

CHAPTER 7

Contested Ideological Issues of Early Russian Feminism

Irina Yukina

The ideas of early Russian Feminism are quite unknown both in Russia and elsewhere. This article is one of the first attempts to highlight its main trends, elaborating the lives and ideas of two prominent feminists – Maria Pokrovskaya and Olga Shapir. They illustrate two different strands of 19th century feminism in Russia. The tricky problems and disagreements they were confronting are still a challenge to feminist theory and practice: how to settle the sources of oppression and the understanding of gender as equal or different. Before presenting the two ideological forerunners of Russian feminism, however, the article presents a historiography of social movements research in Russia and also outline the theoretical perspectives applied on the study of the early feminist movement.

Social movement research in Russia – forgetting women

The history of the first, second and later waves of the feminist movements has not yet been thoroughly investigated in Russian social and human sciences. The sociology of social movements as a research subject was established in Russia during the time of *perestroika* (1985- early 1990's), when social movement activities once again became possible after a long historical period of virtual non-existence during the Soviet state (1917-1989). The gap in movement activities was due to the fact that any nongovernmental, independent social activity was punished quite hard. Hence the trade unions, the youth and the women's movements from the late 1920s to the second half of the 1980s cannot be identified as genuine social movements. The movements were in fact governmental, since they were initiated by the State and guided by the Communist Party. They were in no way allowed to formulate their own ideology and policy, or to determine their own activities.

The development of scientific research on social movements was also virtually non-existent, primarily because the research subject itself was missing. Ideological issues also played their role, however, because the development of social movements' studies would have implied a challenge to the hegemonic Marxist theory, which was the only recognised theoretical foundation for social studies of any kind. Theoretical approaches apart from Marxist ones were labelled as an anti–Soviet activity with all ensuing complications. Russian scholars had practically no opportunity to get acquainted with Western achievements in sociological studies of social movements.

It was only in the late 1980's that social movement studies were initiated in sociology. The prioritised subject of these analyses was the movements of the 1980s – the period of the emerging democracy in Russia. The first publications were of a rather popular character due to the lack of research methodology and traditions.

The Russian methodology of social movement studies was developed gradually through the revaluation an analysis of Western theoretical approaches and of the empirical results of various Russian studies. Sociological reassessments of various Russian social movements from the periods before the 1980s were yet to come.

Of course, social movements of the past had been studied by Russian historians before the 1980s. However, these studies were based on Marxist ideology and devoted exclusively to the workers' and trade union movements. The women's movements were less lucky to attract academic interest. Firstly, this movement did not fit into the rigid class structure of the Soviet society. Secondly, the problems of gender inequality and gender confrontation were defined as insignificant from a Marxist point of view, or understood as already solved problems. Due to the hegemonic position of Marxist theory among the Soviet historians, the women's movement did not enjoy popularity as a research subject. Thus, very few historical studies of the Russian women's movement of the first wave were accomplished during the Soviet period.

Before proceeding further into the topic of the article, I should clarify my notions of the women's and feminist movements. My understanding of the women's movement is quite broad: It includes all kinds of collective activities by women in the interests of women as a social group.[1] My notion of the feminist movement is more narrow, referring to women's collective activities based on a common *ideology* which explains and criticises society from women's point of view. The feminist ideology shapes the strategy of the feminist movement, and hereby also creates new resources for the movement.

According to these definitions, the women's movement in Russia began at the end of the 1850's when the first women's organisations appeared. The first wave of feminism began some decades later, at the end of the 19th century when feminist ideologies were first outlined in Russia. The crest of the first wave took place at the beginning of the 20th century, in 1905, when the first all-Russian political women's organisation appeared, the Union of Women's Equality (*Souz Ravnopraviaj Zhenshin*). The organisation fought for full civil rights for women, including political rights.[2] Thus, the first wave of the Russian feminist movement was characterised – as in the West – by women's struggle for the right to vote (the second half of 19th century to the early 20th century). The second wave in Russia, the New Feminism or Women's Liberation, started during the *perestroika*.[3]

Studies of the women's movements in the Russian historical science were initiated at the same time as in the West, i.e. during the 1970s and 1980s. The main focus of these studies were women's efforts to establish institutions of higher education for women, the activity of various women's organisations such as Russian Women Mutual-Philanthropic Society (*Russkoe Zhenskoe Vzaimno Blagotvoritelnoe Obshestvo*) or Women's Publishing Co-operative (*Zhnskaja Izdatelskaja Artel*) and the participation of women in protest actions, such as revolutionary events.[4] The feminist movement as such was not studied at all in Russia, while the feminist movement was a popular research subject among Western feminist historians.[5] The political discourse described feminism negatively as a bourgeois phenomenon in Russia, which made it impossible to carry out any unbiased research.

Unfortunately, the tendency to reject feminism as a relevant research topic still exists. The modern, or second wave Russian feminist movement, which began at the time of *perestroika* and which I have identified as the second wave of Russian feminism, has not yet attracted the interest of the Academic community.

To do justice to this allegation, it should be noted that pre-revolutionary scholars also often ignored feminism as a theory, an ideology and a style of life preferred by hundreds of Russian women. The opinion that feminism was not typical for Russia was quite widespread among the historians and sociologists of the Slavophil direction even at the end of the 19th century.[6] They asserted that Russia had its own specific (non-western) way and possibilities of development. One of the well-known leaders of the Slavophil direction in Russian philosophy, Nikolai Strakhov, published a critical review on Mill's book "The Subjection of Women".[7] During the 1870s Mill's book was very popular among educated Russian women; it was even called 'the women's Bible'. Such popularity caused alarm among the conservative political activists (professors, journalists and bureaucracy) and some of them tried to challenge Mill's ideas in order to diminish the significance of his work. In 1882, Strakhov devoted a whole chapter of his monograph "The Struggle with West in our Literature" to the criticism of Mill's position.[8] He described Mill's arguments in favour of women's equality as "fluffy declarations of an accomplished Englishman" and he asserted that in Mill's treatment of the "women's issue" there was not a single original Russian feature.

Revolutionary activists also contributed to the discrediting of Russian feminism. One of them was the well-known Alexandra Kollontai. It was she who introduced the term *bourgeois feminism* into the political discourse. For her this concept was intended to make women turn away from feminism. In her anti-feminist speeches Kollontai stressed the privileged social background of Russian feminists and opposed them to the less favourable conditions of women of the proletariat. Kollontai initiated various political measures in order to strengthen her influence over working women. She feared the increasing role of feminists and their attempts to include female workers into women's organisations. Kollontai appealed to women from the proletariat to boycott such organisations. In contrast to the Western celebrations of Kollontai as a prominent feminist activist and writer, she has been acknowledged as a Communist Party activist in the Soviet Union, where her anti-feminist activities have been studied and recognised as an asset.[9] That is why modern studies of Kollontai's views are investigated along with her activities. These studies have revealed a biased and incorrect evaluation of Russian feminism in the works of Kollontai.[10]

Consequently, Soviet historiography has established a tradition according to which various social movements of women in Russia were categorised as women's movements, and never as feminist. This was done although the women's movements in Russia and in the West were more or less identical concerning their goals, ideology and types of organisations from the end of the 19th century through the beginning of the 20th century. They even interacted with each other to quite an extent. In the West these movements were classified as feminist, while Soviet historians described them differently as women's movements. The intellectual sources of the Russian feminist movement and its channels of information were never investigated and included in the scientific publications. For this reason even modern Russian reference books neglect such significant feminist actions as *The First All-Russian Women's Congress* in 1908, and the demonstration in Petrograd in support of equal suffrage in 1917, attracting forty thousand women.[11] The books do not even mention the fact that Russian women were granted the right to vote in September 1917.[12] The activities and roles of the feminist organisations in Russia in the struggle for equal voting rights were not studied either, and neither the scientific nor political effects of feminism have been scrutinised. Consequently, it is not surprising that many Russian historians tend to define the Russian feminist movement as weak and not original. They believe it to be based on ideas borrowed from the West. Only recently has Russian feminism become a subject of serious research interest.

Theoretical approaches and the importance of ideology

In my studies of the first wave of Russian women's and feminist movements I have applied various theoretical approaches adopted in Anglo-American sociological studies of social movements. The analysis of historical movements by means of sociological approaches allows the revelation of a whole set of issues previously ignored by Russian historians.

My focus has been the outlining of various attitudes to some of the controversial problems confronting the Russian women's movements. Concepts and models from two different theories are used: theories of resource mobilisation and theories of collective behaviour.[13]

The theory of resource mobilisation allows one to identify the different types of movement resources used by women's organisations in order to achieve their goals. This approach embraces the mechanisms of movement development, the channels of movement influence and the methods of recruiting new participants. Theories of collective behaviour and relative deprivation are useful in order not to underestimate ideology as a movement' resource, and to avoid insufficient attention to the reasons for individual participation.[14]

The use of theories and conceptual systems from different paradigms seems justified, firstly because no single theoretical approach or paradigm fully represents a complex social phenomenon. This has rather to be accomplished through a combination of theories and key concepts. Secondly, such an approach allows one to apply the principle of the mutual complementarity of different paradigms. This permits the scholar to use different and sometimes opposite methods for the description of one and the same phenomenon, eventually contributing to a more complicated and complete picture of the past.[15]

As for the ideology of a social movement I maintain that it consolidates dissatisfaction, encourages actions and thus determines the very existence of the movement. In short: Ideology is extremely important for the development of any social movement. It is instrumental in helping the activists to evaluate their situation, to assert the meaning of social change and to give people motivations to engage. On the one hand, it helps to create and shape the general culture of the movement itself. On the other, it promotes the development of explanatory theories for the interpretation of the existing reality, description of the future and creation of the resources and strategies of the movement. In other words, an ideology generally performs two functions – one explanatory and one unifying. The first mobilises ideas, the second mobilises people.

Early feminist ideologies in Russia

I believe that ideology is the most distinguishing feature of a social movement. It is the ideology that serves as a watershed between a feminist movement and any other women's social activity in the interests of a certain social group, usually defined as a women's movement. The ideologies of the first women's organisations in Russia, during the 1860s, were not really outlined. During the first decades the identification of women's problems and the methods for solving them were still vague and based on intuition. The necessity for developing a consistent and explicit ideology was yet to be recognised. We can say that no feminist ideology existed before the 1890s. However, I believe that the key factor of a feminist movement is the existence of oppositional consciousnesses based on coherent ideas that are shared by the movement participants. The ideology of a movement together with the emergent norms and values constitute the collective identity of its participants. An ideology which expresses doubts regarding the justice of the existing gender system identifies the gender system as the foundation of a patriarchal society, outlines activities aimed at changing the gender roles and gender relations, and to abolish the patriarchal society, is a symbol of feminism as a theory, practice and way of life.

Feminism can be defined as a social movement based on an ideology which criticises the existing gender system and describes the necessary collective actions whose final aim is to change the present gender relations and gender roles in the society and to destroy the patriarchal society itself.

The purpose of early Russian feminist ideology was to reveal the reasons for gender inequality and injustice and to define ways of solving these problems. During the 1890s the gender system of the Russian society was openly and resolutely criticised for the first time in the works of feminist writers. The feminist writers also identified many sources of gender inequality, and suggested various ways of resolving the problems.

The major problem confronting the pre-revolutionary Russian feminist movement at the beginning of the 20th century was the grave social inequalities. The feminists approached this issue by discussing the basic mechanisms of social hierarchy in the Russian society: Class and gender inequalities were outstanding, but which was the primary? In answering this question feminists differed from all political voices by focussing gender as a primary category. Neither the representatives of liberal ideology, nor the social democrats defined gender inequality as the basic social contradiction.

There was, however, no unity among the feminists themselves concerning the relative importance of class and gender. Enthusiasm for left-wing ideas was widespread among feminists, and many feminists made an effort to combine class and gender explanations in their theories and strategies. But they all, without exception, stood on the suffragist platform during the 1890s: They demanded universal suffrage for all categories of women (peasants, working-class women, etc.).[16] The second important problem the Russian feminists set out to solve was the fundamental feminist dilemma between gender *similarity* and gender differences. Is full equality between men and women possible, they asked. If it is possible, how can it be achieved? If it is not possible, should feminists rather try to achieve equality in opportunities while recognising underlying gender differences?

Different answers to the tricky questions of the relationship between gender and class and between similarity and differences characterised the various ideological strands of Russian pre-revolutionary feminism. They also differed concerning tactics and strategies.

During the Soviet period, 1917-1989, the political discourse changed dramatically, and questions concerning the basis of social hierarchy and social inequality were not discussed. A class ideology based on Marxism dominated completely as the one and only official, public ideology. This ideology alone was taken to explain all problems related to social inequality. Feminist issues were totally removed from the official political agenda. It was assumed that gender problems would be solved through women's participation in the production sphere, according to Marxist ideology.

Feminist ideas in the crisis epoch at the beginning of the 20th century had, however, given birth to a variety of theories and practices influenced by the constant critical pressure from the liberal and radical ideologies of the time. It should be noted that the various directions of Russian feminism during the first wave shared the basic ideas that women should be independent and sovereign, that women should resist male dominance and unite in order to promote common *female* interests. The foremost practical goal of Russian feminism was to achieve the right to vote for all women, disregarding class and social strata differences. This basic feminist idea united them in their various collective activities. Supporting each other's actions was their rule and principle.[17] In addition to focusing the same questions and sharing some basic ideas, the leading figures of Russian feminism, as I shall discuss later, also had a similar way of living: All of them were professionally active women. They earned their living by their professional activities, and were also materially independent women. The Russian feminists asserted that feminism was not just an ideology and the activities of feminist organisations with the collective subject women. Feminism was also a way of life.

The two most prominent feminists who will be discussed in the following chapters were no exception. One of them was a medical doctor, the other one was a popular writer. They were deeply involved in elaborating feminist ideas, in somewhat different directions based on their attitudes to the issues of class/gender and equality/distinction. There were two distinct strands in this early, first wave of Russian feminism, expressed in the lives and writings of Maria Pokrovskaya and Olga Shapir.

The feminism "of men's rights" by Maria Pokrovskaya

One of the main strands of Russian feminism can be defined by the words of the leader of the Womens Progressive Party Maria Pokrovskaya (b. 1852 – the year of her death is unknown) as the *feminism of men's rights*.

Maria Pokrovskaya was not only a doctor, she was also the organiser and chairman of the *Women's Progressive Party* (1906-1918) and the *Women's Party Club* (1906-1918) and editor and owner of the journal Zhensky Vestnik, the *Women's Herald* (1904-1917). She entered the women's movement in the late 1880's upon her return to St. Petersburg after several years of work as a *zemsky* doctor in a provincial town.[18] Pokrovskaya immediately perceived that the movement was undergoing a deep crisis. She was alarmed by the fact that all the collective and individual activities and efforts of the women's movement were aimed at the very same goals as 10-15 years ago, without accomplishing any significant results. Prokovskaya considered the role of women's organisations in charity work and in education and their ambitions to establish new work places for women within the sphere of traditional women's employment to be quite outdated. She assessed charity and its ideology as patches on an old dress. Pokrovskaya believed that the women's movement needed new ideas,

Maria Prokoskaya

new types of organisations and new activities. For her the most progressive idea was that of promoting sexual restraint.

Feminism was understood by Maria Pokrovskaya in the same way as it was understood by the majority of the activists of the women's movement, ascending from the ideas of Mary Wollstonecraft (1792), Harriet Taylor (1856) and John Stuart Mill (1870), the emancipation of women was both in the interests of women themselves and of society as a whole.

However, like many of her female contemporaries who participated in the women's movement, Prokovskaya shared the idea that the "full emancipation" of women was possible only within a different social order. In this respect she supported the widespread socialist ideas and tendencies of her time. Pokrovskaya never quite explained what she meant by *full emancipation.* But she called women to take action, and not to wait patiently for the right time to come, "when socialism is established and is able to liberate them of slavery".[19]

In Pokrovskaya's view, male dominance was based on the existing social hierarchy. She blamed men for all the injustices and imperfections of the world: "The experience of many thousand years has shown that male dominance is unable to give mankind what it craves for – enlightenment, happiness, justice, equality, brotherhood, freedom and material wealth."[20]

Men's dominance, men's rights and men's freedom were regarded by her as the very instruments of the suppression of women: "... man, using his superiority, strives to arrange everything the way he wants, guided by his own ideas of communal well, often egoistic and one-sided... They (women), wishing to make their life better, are fighting male dominance...".[21]

A particular feature of Pokrovskaya's doctrine was her elaboration of a way to solve the basic social contradictions between men and women, described as two different gender communities.

Separate women's communities

Pokrovskaya advanced the idea of a women's community existing beyond all class differences and based on gender only. She believed in women's uniform purposes and common values on the one side, and on an internal hierarchy in such a community on the other. She stressed the special responsibility of women to "initiate a new social construction". In the language of the beginning of the 20th century, this meant a process of democratic changes in society. She also perceived that there was a direct link between solving the problems of the oppression of women and the progress of human civilisation as such.

In Pokrovskaya's elaborations of the internal hierarchy in her proposed female community, she assigned the responsibility for women of the deprived and uneducated classes to educated women. The relations within such a female community were described by her as *help to sisters* or *sisterhood* (*sestrinstvo*). The term sisterhood seems to have been introduced into the Russian language at this particular time – at the beginning of the 20th century.

Pokrovskaya used the Marxist terminology to describe women's status in the society. She classified educated middle-class women as the *educated proletariat*. Women of lower classes Pokrovskaya named as the *uneducated proletariat*. To her, gender was the main explanation of the exploitation of women, while class was a less important distinction and explanation. Therefore, according to Maria Pokrovskaya, the women's movement was a non-class notion in the traditional sense of the word. The movement should rather be seen as struggling for the interests of *the class of women*. She defined the Code of Laws of the Russian Empire as an illustrating example of the discrimination of women by the political regime.

The goals of the women's movement were expressed by Pokrovskaya in the combined rhetoric of liberal ideas and concepts of gender struggle that is feminist liberalism: "the main objective for them (women) is aspiration to struggle for liberation from slavery imposed by men".[22]

Pokrovskaya actively used the term *feminism* trying to remove all its negative connotations. She also introduced the terms *diffident feminism* (stydlivyi feminizm) and *diffident feminists* to describe the situation in which women take advantage of the ideas and strategies of feminism while denying their adherence to the ideas.[23]

As many other feminists, she thought the main strategy for the movement in order to achieve its goals to be political activity through separate women's organisations. She believed that political parties were not interested in solving women's problems; so women themselves were to solve their problems through specific women's organisations. Pokrovskaya did not support women's participation in the existing political parties, stating that in such parties women worked not for their own freedom but for that of men. For this very reason, she established and officially registered the *Women's Progressive Party* (Zhenskaya Progressivnaya Partiya), consciously creating a precedent for a party built on a gender basis. According to Pokrovskaya, the Progressive Party allowed women to be involved in political struggle and to influence the political situation.

Maria Pokrovskaya was sure that the unification of the *educated proletariat* with the *uneducated proletariat* and peasant women was the only strategy that would succeed in obtaining civil rights for women. The *educated proletariat* could introduce knowledge and organisational experience into the women's union and act as its "brain and soul", and the *uneducated proletariat* could be its "hands". It is interesting to note that she referred to Finland as a model case: She believed that the strategy of non-class co-operation between women for the attainment of voting rights had been successfully implemented in 1906 in Finland.

Her active involvement in social activities, she had been publishing her journal for 13 years, and her attempts to act on a wider political arena made her conclude that obtaining legal rights by women would not automatically bring them equal civil rights. She "revealed" the problem of the double sexual standards regarding women and men and wrote in her journal: "Men are the masters and women are their slaves. That is why the first are free to do whatever they want, and they get off with it. And for the second, everything is forbidden and they are never pardoned".[24]

She came to the conclusion that women's lives were more restricted than men's lives because of the conventional traditions. What was not explicitly forbidden for women by the law was often not accepted by the society. Consequently, Pokrovskaya concluded that "(…) in order to allow women to freely develop their individual abilities, it would not be enough to liberate them from all legislative restrictions, it would be necessary to grant them all men's rights".[25]

In other words, she identified men's rights as the genuinely human rights. This was her reaction to the existing gender gap between the actual social opportunities and ways of personal self-fulfilment. Hence the tactic goals for the women's movement were defined by Pokrovskaya as the removal of all barriers restricting women's chances to fulfil the *human* ideal. Those barriers were characterised as formal as well as informal. In order to abolish the barriers, in her opinion, the women's movement should promote equal standards and stimulate equal expectations and norms of behaviour for both genders.

As a way of fighting anti-female ideas, stereotypes and physical resistance from men in the professional sphere, she suggested that the women's movement should:

- outline and reassess anti-female stereotypes and myths, trying to find new meanings for them.
- establish a community of women, in order to create a new spirit of solidarity and corporativeness.[26]

Prostitution and 'chastity communities'

Another problem attracting Prokovskaya's attention as a doctor and a feminist was related to prostitution. The phenomenon of prostitution was for her the quintessence of men's dominance over women. She saw prostitutes as the main victims of gender and class antagonisms in society. Her approach to this problem was getting more and more radical as the movement progressed as a political movement. In her writings, men were described as a united anti-female community with no class distinctions, paralleling her way of describing the community of women.

She suggested equal sexual ethics for women and men as a way of solving the problem of prostitution. Chastity before marriage was proclaimed as the genuine means to realise her slogan: gender equality. Thus, she was in favour of creating "chastity communities", similar to the English *White Ribbon* organisations whose members took the oath to keep abstinence for 25, 30, 40 or even more years. She also insisted on medical examination of the brothel's customers. She defined men as consumers of prostitution, and put forward ideas of men's responsibility for the degradation of prostitutes.

Pokrovskaya considered such sexual innovations as effective strategies to promote her ideas of gender equality. From today's point of view, we may conclude that she tried, if not to abolish men's control of female sexuality, to establish the same social control over men's sexuality as women's.

Pokrovskaya's activities encouraged public discussions of gender equality and issues concerning women's and men's rights. She introduced to the public her idea that society solves its sexual problems at the expense of women, a social group with no rights. Thus she confronted the penitential attitudes towards prostitutes that were widespread among Russian intelligentsia. Consequently, in the 1880s-1890s the fate of the Russian prostitutes became the subject of heated debates.

Pokrovskaya was known for her strict principles, pretensions and nonconformity. She opposed the widespread opinion that women were inferior to men, that their problems were less important and that women's work had insignificant public value. She wrote: "The problem of labour here in Russia concerns several million, probably 5 or 6, but the problem of women affects 60 millions. What is more important – to improve the circumstances of 5 or 60 millions? The answer is obvious. But we see how much attention the Russian intelligentsia pays to the problem of labour and how little concern is given to the problem of women. In the opinion of the intelligentsia, the question of labour will soon be resolved, but the problem of women depends on the improvement of the situation in general".[27]

Her feminism was stimulated by the emergence of a new, strong public belief in the virtues of mankind: pacifism, compassion and non-violent behaviour. These virtues justified arguments in favour of human reforms by implementing mild, legal methods. Pokrovskaya believed in this optimistic spirit. She was convinced that women' entry into politics would restrain the display of force and aggression.

Pokrovskaya's feminism was a feminist alternative to the new theory of a non-violent development of mankind. Her suggestions for doing away with gender stratification was not to do it by eliminating men's rights and privileges, but rather through the eradication of differences between the genders.

Prokovskayas feminist ideology "of men's rights" was basically an example of early liberal feminist ideology in Russia. It was characterised by the basic aspects of a suffragist platform combined with the recognition of gender similarities. However, Pokrovskaya's feminism also contained rudiments of radical feminism. This was revealed in her descriptions of society as based on two biological categories alien to each other, her suggestions for establishing separate female communities, and in her demands for social control of male sexuality.

"Equality with Difference". The feminist ideas of Olga Shapir

The second distinct strand of early Russian feminism is found in the life and works of Olga Shapir (1850-1916). She is known for her study of the problem gender *similarity – difference* and most of all for her development of the concept of *difference*. Olga Shapir was a popular writer, an active participant in the women's movement, vice-president of the *Russian Women's Philanthropic Society* (1895-1918) and one of the organisers of the *First All–Russia Women's Congress*, a meeting which took place in St. Petersburg in 1908. Her works criticised the understanding of the first wave of liberal feminism whose primary feature was a commitment to the idea of *equality* and *similarity* between women and men.

Olga Shapir criticised the androcentric approach of identifying *the genuinely human* with *the masculine*. She did so in spite of the fact that a majority of her female colleagues in the movement thought these were equivalent since in reality 'the human' belonged to men. She maintained that the troubles and misfortunes of mankind were caused by male dominance. She considered male dominance to be a slip in the development of human civilisation, an error which had global consequences. The results of this erratic course of history were deformations in the development of *female capabilities*.[28] She also stressed, however, that "(…) although female spiritual power was never free to develop in a normal way (…), the free masculine power also took a one-sided course. This is another result of the broken equilibrium."[29]

Olga Shapir doubted that the methods of masculine self-fulfilment and masculine values could be applied to women. She also warned women that the "blind following in men's footsteps would demand similar qualities from women. (…) Will we be able to find such qualities for everything? Will we be able to develop them in ourselves, and do we want to do so?", she questioned her female colleagues on the platform of the First Women's Congress.[30]

The ideological sources of her feminism were the same as those of the other Russian feminists: She regarded feminism as the theory and practice of women's emancipation, for the benefit of the general public as well as for women's personal interests.

The most outstanding element of Shapir's feminism however, was the analysis of the mechanisms of women's oppression. Gender inequality was regarded as the general source of social inequality: "Social oppression has developed from sexual oppression",[31] "Lack of women's rights is the primary source of any inequality."[32] Inequality occurs because men, "(…) being solely in charge of the fortunes of the world (…), established their own laws everywhere, their own ideas, customs and tastes to ensure their dominance". She came to the conclusion that for this very reason "we have only the culture of power (…). This is a culture based on gender and labour oppression".[33]

Shapir paid special attention to the study of the sources of women's oppression. She saw the fundamental source of oppression in the "special qualities of women's gender", that is in biology. She wrote: "the equality in the exact meaning of this concept may be found in the functions of organisms created in a different way". In her opinion, the oppression of women was produced through the channels and structures of traditional culture. A *culture of power* supported the dominance of men through customs, public opinions and laws.[34] She described such mechanisms of women's oppression as love, motherhood, control of female sexuality, economic and psychological dependence of women upon men.[35]

According to Shapir, the mechanisms of oppression were thoroughly established and integrated in women's identities. Thus, women's emancipation could not be achieved through the fulfilment of suffragist demands only, i.e. through the attainment of political rights.[36]

A women's movement for her was a necessary and civilised way of addressing women's problems. Collective actions should involve not only political activity, but also focus on the development of women's consciousness: "Women have to face a double goal in their great struggle. They need all the efforts of their will, brain and labour to make progress on their way to real achievements; but progress in spiritual emancipation requires even *more conscious efforts…*"[37]

She maintained that equality could only be attained through the conscious understanding of gender differences. She proclaimed the slogan *equality with differences* which became the cornerstone for the activity of one of the directions of Russian feminism.

Her expectations concerning the feminist movement presupposed the emergence of emancipated women who could change the direction of human evolution towards its humanisation: "The future will show what enlightened, spiritually liberated women with equal rights can offer to mankind."[38]

From today's point of view, Shapir's feminism can be regarded as ordinary liberal feminism. However, at the beginning of the 20th century her ideas were a theoretical break-through for a different feminism. Shapir was trying to overcome the constraints of the concept of gender *similarity*, which in her time was shared by wide masses of women. She was the first one in Russia to put forward the idea of *equality with differences,* a concept which was developed further by the second wave of feminism during the 1960's. But in the key components of her theory, Olga Shapir also included elements of radical feminism. Consequently, she based her theoretical strategy on the concept of *differences*. She declared that it was necessary for women to accept their individuality, including sexuality, conscious motherhood and estrangement from the *power of gender.*

Shapir's feminism appeared as an alternative theory of cultural evolution based on changes in gender stratification through the recognition of gender differences and the development of the entire legal and factual equality.

Concluding remarks

The ideologies of Pokrovskaya and Shapir have both had great influence on the women's movement in Russia. Accordingly, the first wave of Russian feminism contributed to the reformatory direction in the liberation movement of Russia. Their ideas on gender equality and difference carry insights that still attract wide attention. The hard questions of the oppression of women continue to puzzle us, and the perspectives of the two early Russian feminists are refreshing and deserve further attention. Studies of the feminist movement in Russia have just begun, based to a large extent on theories developed among western scholars. Hopefully, the Russian studies will contribute not just to a broader understanding of the history of Russia, but also enrich the theoretical approach to the studies of social movements.

References

Dahlerup, Drude (1986) "Introduction", Drude Dahlerup (ed.), The New Women's Movement. Feminism and Political Power in Europe and in the USA. London, Sage.

Dahlerup, Drude (2000) "Continuity and Waves in the Feminist Movement – a Challenge to Social Movement Theory", Aino Saarinen, Hilda Römer Christensen, Beatrice Halsaa (eds.), *Women's Movement and Internationalisation: the "Third Waves"?* Oulu Yliopistopaino.

Edmondson, Linda H. (1984). *Feminism in Russia, 1900-1917,* Stanford, Stanford University Press.

Engel, Alpern Barbara (1986). Mothers and Daughters: Women of the Intelligentsia in Nineteenth–Century Russia, Cambridge.

Gamson, William & Meyer, David (1996) "Framing Political Opportunity", David McAdam, (ed.), Comparative Perspectives on Social Movements: Political Opportunities, Mobilizing Structures and Cultural Framings, Cambridge University Press.

Goldberg (Rutchild), Rochelle (1976). *The Russian Women Movement,* University of Rochester.

Grishina, Zoya (1977) *Women's Organizations in Russia. 1905 – February, March 1917,* PhD dissertation in History. Moscow.

Grishina, Zoya (1982) "Movement for Equal Rights for Women During the First Russian Revolution", Herald of Moscow University. Issue 8, *History,* No 2.

Grishina, Zoya (1984) "Women's Higher Education in Pre–revolutionary Russia", Herald of Moscow University. Issue 8, *History,* No 1.

Lønnå, Elizabeth (2000) "A Division Into Waves", Saarinen, Aino; Christensen, Hilda Rømer; Halsaa, Beatrice (eds.), *Women's Movement and Internationalisation: the "Third Waves"?* Oulu Yliopistopaino.

MacCarthy, John D. & Zald, Mayer N. (1977) "Resource Mobilization and Social Movement: A Partial Theory", *American Journal of Sociology,* Vol. 82.

Mill, John Stuart. (1870) *The Subjection of Women,* London.

Mironov, Boris (1999). *Social History of Russia: Empire Period (18th – beginning of 20th century),* Vol. 1-2, St. Petersburg, D. Bulanin.

Obershall, Arthur (1973) *Social Conflict and Social Movement,* New York.

Pavluchenko, Eleonora. (1986) *Women in Russian Liberation Movement: from Maria Volkonskaya to Vera Figner,* Moscow.

Pokrovskaya, Maria I. (1904). "Preface", *Women's Herald,* No 1, p. 1-2.

Pokrovskaya, Maria I. (1904). "Women's Question – a Toy", *Women's Herald,* No 4, p. 2-4.

Pokrovskaya, Maria I. (1904). "Women and War", *Women's Herald,* No 12, p. 98-100.

Pokrovskaya, Maria I. (1905). "Goals of the First Russian Women's Congress", *Women's Herald,* No 1, p. 1-3.

Pokrovskaya, Maria I. (1905). "The Necessity of Women's Work for Russia", *Women's Herald,* No 2, p. 35-38.

Pokrovskaya, Maria I. (1905). "Feminism", *Women's Herald,* No 5, p. 129-132.

Pokrovskaya, Maria I. (1906). "Women's Meeting", *Women's Herald,* No 5, p.153-155.

Repina, Larina P. (1998). New Historical Science and Social History, Moscow, Russian Academy of Sciences.

Rutchild, Rochelle (2002). "The Return of the Women's History: Gender, Class and Feminism", Elena Gapova, Almira Usmanova, Andrea Peto (eds.), *Gender Histories in Eastern Europe.* Minsk.

Robson A.P. & Robson J.M. (eds.) *Sexual Equality: Writing by J.S. Mill and Harriet Taylor, and Helen Taylor,* (1994). Toronto.

Serditova, Svetlana (1959) *The Bolsheviks in the Fight for Women's Proletarian Masses,* Moscow.

Shapir, Olga A. (1908). "Women's Congress. Impressions and Results", *Russian Gazette,* No 295, December 20, p. 2-3.

Shapir, Olga A. (1909). "Ideals of the Future", *Papers of the First All-Russia Women's Congress,* St. Petersburg, Russian Women's Philanthropic Society, p. 895-898.

Shapir, Olga A. (1916). "Women's Inequality", *Stock-exchange Gazette,* No. 162, July 16, p. 2-3.

Smelser, Norton. (1963) *Theory of Collective Behaviour,* New York.

Stites, Richard. (1978). *Women's Liberation Movement in Russia,* Princeton, NJ: Princeton University Press.

Strakhov, Nikolai. (1870) *Women's Question,* St. Petersburg.

Strakhov, Nikolai. (1882) *Struggle with West in Our Literature,* St. Petersburg.

Tilly, Charles. (1978) *From Mobilization to Revolution,* Englewood Cliffs.

Tishkin, Gregori. (1983) "Women's Question and Governmental Policy 1860-1870", *Problems of Russian History in the 19-20th centuries.* Leningrad.

Tishkin, Gregori. (1984) *Women's Question in Russia in the 50s–60s of the 19th century,* Leningrad.

Turner, Richard. (1981) "Collective Behaviour and Resource Mobilization as Approaches to Social Movements: Issues and Continuities", *Research in Social Movements, Conflicts and Change.* Vol. 4.

Tuttle, Lisa. (1986). *Encyclopaedia of Feminism,* London, Longman Group Limited.

Wollstonecraft, Mary. (1992) "For Protection Women's Rights", Miriam Schneir, ed. *Feminism: The Essential Historical Writings.* Moscow.

Notes

1   See also Drude Dahlerup's interesting discussion on the construction of women as a collective subject in the present volume.
2   Up to 1905, men as well did not have the right to vote; the first Russian Parliament was instituted only in 1906.
3   Lønnå (2000), Dahlerup (1986), (2000).
4   Grishina (1977), Tishkin (1984), Pavluchenko (1986).
5   Rutchild (1976), Stites (1978), Edmondson (1984), Engel (1986).
6   The Slavophil direction is a social and political direction the adherents of which claimed that Russia should follow its own way, i.e. go back to the ideals of the Russia before Peter the Great, to Orthodoxy, and should not accept "Western" ways of social life.
7   Strakhov (1870).
8   Strakhov (1882).
9   Serditova (1959).
10 Rutchild (2002).
11 Mironov (1999).
12 The official regulations regarding elections were adopted by the Provisional (liberal bourgeois) Government on 20th July, 1917 and took effect on 11th September, 1917.
13 MacCarthy & Zald (1977), Obershall (1973), Tilly (1978), Gamson & Meyer *et al.* (1996).
14 Smelser (1963), Turner et al. (1981).
15 Repina, (1998).
16 The universal suffrage for men was introduced in Russia in 1905.
17 See Drude Dahlerup's discussion on the common core of feminism and Elisabeth Lønnå's discussion on social groups.
18 A doctor hired by a local municipal department – *Zemstvo*. It was a low-status and the lowest-paid position for doctors in the Russian Empire.
19 Pokrovskaya (1906) p. 154
20 Pokrovskaya (1905a) p. 2.
21 Pokrovskaya (1904a) p. 2.
22 Pokrovskaya (1905a) p. 1.
23 Pokrovskaya (1906) p. 155.
24 Pokrovskaya (1905b) p. 36
25 Pokrovskaya (1904b) p. 99.
26 Pokrovskaya (1904a) p. 22.
27 Pokrovskaya (1905c) p. 130.
28 Shapir (1909) p. 896.
29 Shapir (1909) p. 897.
30 Shapir (1909) p. 898.
31 Shapir (1916) p. 2.
32 Shapir (1916) p. 3.
33 Shapir (1909) p. 897.
34 Shapir (1909) p. 896.
35 Shapir (1909) p. 896.
36 Shapir (1909) p. 896.
37 Shapir (1909) p. 898.
38 Shapir (1909) p. 897.

CHAPTER 8

Contrasting Discourses of Gender-Equality

Local Women's Groups Facing Established Politics

Malin Rönnblom

Women's movement in Sweden – rural examples

In 1995, the UN named Sweden as the most gender equal country in the world. Since then, the Swedish government has used this as a strategy to promote Sweden in different contexts – not least in connection with the Swedish Presidency of the European Union during the spring of 2001. While, at the beginning of the 1990s, the focus concerning issues of gender equality was directed towards women, at the beginning of the new century, the focus in the Swedish (official) context has shifted towards men. This is in many ways related to the institutionalised strategy of gender mainstreaming that was accepted by the Swedish government in 1996, in connection with the International Conference on Women in Beijing, 1995.

At the same time, during the 1990s, Swedish women were organising more widely than ever – both when it comes to form and content.[1] Women's organizing in Sweden is characterized by diversity, ranging from the women's political associations and the Fredrika Bremer Society, with roots in the latter part of the 19th century, to the women's houses and outward oriented manifestations of the 1970s. The 1990s were characterised by 'Women Can' fairs, centres for women's studies and different forms of women's networks.[2] Another, less known, part of the Swedish women's movement is rural women's groups – especially in the Northern parts of the country – and it is this latter form of women's organising which is put in the centre of attention in this chapter.

Interest in the importance of territoriality is the main reasons why I chose to study women's groups in three municipalities in the northern part of Sweden. The women's groups highlighted in this chapter are *Qulan* in Kiruna, *Robertsforsvinden* in Robertsfors and *Q i Berg* (a group that after a while became seven village-based women's groups in the municipality of Berg). An important reason for choosing these groups was that they all had an overarching goal of improving women's situation and position in their local communities, and were all initiated at the end of the 1980s. During 1996,

1997 and 1998 I conducted interviews in the three municipalities, both with activists (women active in women's groups) and local politicians. The interviews were both focusing the women's groups as such – goals, activities and forms of organising – and the views of activists and politicians concerning women's organising, the possibilities for women to get influence in local politics and the issue of gender-equality.[3]

The goals of the groups were widely defined. Instead of focusing on just one theme or question, they wanted to make their local community a better place for women to live. There were also ambitions to gather "all women" in these fairly small municipalities and to work on several different issues, depending on the needs and demands of the women in the community. The form of organisation was non-hierarchical, or in "networks", something that was perceived as important for the activists. When asked why they chose to engage in a women's group instead of, for example, a political party, one recurring statement in the interviews was that ordinary politics is organised in a hierarchical way and this form of organisation was perceived as non-democratic.

Gradually, all of the groups established some form of more "tight" organisation, with a chairwoman and a board. This was largely in response to demands imposed by different state actors when the women's groups tried to get public funding for their projects. In line with this organisational change, the groups have also gradually been formed around a "core group" of activists, and these activists are the ones interviewed in this study. The active women could generally be described as white, middle or sometimes, working class, often between 35 and 55 years old, married or divorced with children.

The activities arranged by the three women's groups have embraced a wide range of themes – from consciousness raising and making demands on the local politicians, to arranging courses in managing and marketing an own business. When trying to identify some themes to describe the activities of the groups, I think it is possible to discern education and labour market as themes common to all of the groups. Supporting women in more general terms, creating meeting-places and making women more active in their local community have also constituted an overarching theme in the work of the women's groups.[4]

From my interviews with local politicians, it is clear that their information on and interest in women's organising in their community are quite low. Women's groups are seen by some politicians as something necessary in connection with the problem of women leaving the community. Almost all of the politicians consider that women ought to organise together with men – but some see women's engagement in a women's group as "a first step to real political activity". As I will show in the following sections on views of gender-equality, the statement "It's ok as long as it's not too much" also occurs frequently when the politicians are talking about women's organising. Too much separate organising could, in their view, result in conflicts between women and men – something that is not perceived as positive. Women's organising seems to be all right as long as it does not really challenge ordinary forms of organisation and politics. In my view, the results of the interviews with the politicians on their views of women's organising illustrate the argument developed by the Swedish political scientist Maud

Eduards – women's separate organising is to be seen as a potential threat to established forms of politics.[5]

In sum, these three women's groups described could not be defined as radical in terms of putting forward women's interests opposite to the interests of men, i.e. they do not formulate their demands in terms of power relations between women and men. In spite of this quite reformist approach, the groups meet resistance from local politicians, from having difficulties in getting economic and moral support to more advanced ruling techniques like making fun of their commitment or making their demands invisible.[6] This resistance from local politics, in connection to the relations between women and men is central in a feminist approach and made me interested in studying women's organisation as a way of scrutinising established forms of politics.

Studies of women's movements as a way of deconstructing "normal politics"

In this chapter, I have chosen to focus one part of the empirical material from the three municipalities, and the choice is based on the assumption that a study of women's organising is also a study of the construction of politics. My aim here is to focus on the limits of established politics and democracy by analysing how feminist activists and local politicians respectively argue how gender equality should be defined.[7] In this way, studying women's organising is seen as a strategy to analyse "normal politics" and "normal democracy".[8]

I have chosen to define women's organizing as an expression of resistance against the existing power order between women and men. I.e. women's organising means a potential challenge to the political order in that it goes against the underlying norms and rules that constitute the basis for established politics.[9] In this way, women's groups are not determined by their common experiences, but by their commitment. This will, of course, be different for different women, depending on where they are and who they are, which in turn is determined by gender and by the fact that the gender power order is a contextual process grounded in change.[10] Against that background, I would like instead to emphasize women's collective practices as a point of departure for a definition of the women's movement. This argument goes in line with the way of defining the women's movement put forward by Solveig Bergman in her chapter in this book, i.e. as action and discourse.[11]

According to Eduards, the fact that women organize as a *group* also means that men are forced to see themselves as a group instead of as free individuals.[12] Women's organizing as a group may also demand the emergence of a new way of regarding politics. When women act as a collective, without regard for the demands placed on them to be gender neutral individuals, it becomes clear that the political order on which normal politics is based is actually founded on the exclusion of gendered, non-normal politics. It is important to remember that this means that established politics is built on conflicts of interest between men and that men have the privilege of being regarded as a heterogeneous group. The great challenge then becomes to come to see women as a heterogeneous group.

To study gender power relations is not an easy task, and of course there are several different approaches to use in order to achieve such an analysis. I have chosen to use this question as starting point in my analysis: *How do power relationships between women and men in local, specific contexts manifest themselves when women attempt to increase their influence?* In order to find an answer to this question, the relationship between established politics and women's groups' attempts to achieve change is put in focus. The geographical space of the rural, as well as politics and women's possibilities to act, should be looked upon as central aspects of this analysis. Neither rural nor politics are seen as fixed terms. Instead, the focus is on the construction of these in the analysis of the local gender power orders.

In my attempt to analyse the values of activists and politicians on the issue of gender equality, I have chosen Carol Bacchi's "What's the problem?" approach.[13] In this approach, it is the way of constructing problems – or how problems are represented – that is focused in the analysis, not "the problem" as such. The latter is always something that is defined, constructed, by someone. From a "What's the problem?" approach questions like: What do views on politics and democracy mean in relation to the subordination of women? How is the dominant perspective established? What is left outside? are put. The point is to always question phenomena that are defined as natural or self-evident, or, in other words, to deconstruct dominating discourses.

My definition of gender lies in line with this approach, and starts from Teresa de Laureti's discussion of "technologies of gender", which means that gender is not embedded in the body as something originally essential.[14] Instead, gender is continuously produced and this production of gender is to a large extent infused with power in the form of discursive disciplinary practices. Regarding gender as constructed does not necessarily imply that this construction is based on something that is permanently biological. Gender is instead seen as constructed and produced in negotiations. This does not mean that gender does not exist in historically specific and cultural situations. It is precisely in such situations that it is possible to study gender and power.

The same approach is used when defining politics. By shifting the focus from the institutionalised political order, which we have become accustomed to, other forms of political activity become visible. Politics need no longer consist only of an established institutionalised structure or a mechanism for allocating values. Instead, the definition of politics can be broadened and defined as an activity, a complicated pattern of women's and men's daily and collective actions.[15] By using a more overarching term, I want to highlight the fact that all spaces can become political through people's collective actions. In this way, women's organising is clearly defined as a form of political action. Accepting this definition of politics is not the same thing as perceiving politics as everything – as feminist researchers are sometimes criticised for doing. Instead, what I am arguing here is that everything is possible to *politize*.

Before presenting how the activists and politicians perceive and discuss gender-equality, I will contextualise the analysis by discussing the relationship between gender and rurality, and between rural women's organising and the state.

Gender and rurality

At least since the 1960s, but also in earlier periods, the problem of people leaving northern Sweden, particularly the inland areas, has been an important political issue. In the 1980s, this discussion also started to include the fact that women move more often than men – and especially that in contrast to young men they tend not to return after some years. When discussing the problem of falling population in these parts of the country and in particular, reasons to explain why women do not want to stay in the rural communities, the local men were often portrayed as riding snowmobiles and going hunting or fishing.[16] The cultural geographer Gunnel Forsberg claims that this is in part a scurrilous portrait of the rural districts which aims at emphasising the benefits of the urban in relation to the rural.[17] In her own words:

> "The countryside, or sparsely populated areas, is/are defined with the population centre as a starting-point. Without densely populated areas it would be irrelevant to talk about sparsely populated areas."[18]

The picture of women in rural areas that we meet in the national media, if we meet any at all, is often one of the 'traditional' woman – in line with the picture of the "traditional man" illustrated above. Her interests are cooking or handiwork, or perhaps she has her own business. We seldom get the message that this business provides a profit or creates jobs, that is, is regarded as important. You could say that there exists a myth about rural women. In this myth, the rural woman upholds the picture of the traditional woman. One reason for this is that rural areas are regarded as more patriarchal/traditional than urban areas and, therefore, rural women are regarded as "more oppressed" than urban women. In the discussions connected with Sweden's entry into the European Union, women in rural northern Sweden were often regarded as striving backwards, incapable of absorbing the 'true' information that the cities' and the markets' urban representatives advocated. In line with Gunnel Forsberg's argument, this way of presenting urban women as modern and equal with men is produced in relation to a construction of rural women as backwards and subordinated, i.e. modernity is constructed in relation to the traditional or not modern.[19] In addition to this, if not scrutinised, the hierarchical relationship between urban and rural also tends to create a dichotomy between urban and rural women.

In the modern project, the city has always stood for development and innovation while the countryside has stood for backwards striving and small-mindedness. Even though one could say, roughly, that we are leaving the modern industrial society and entering the so-called post-modern information society, I think that these values and ideas live on. The notion that rural areas can offer other opportunities, which in turn make other strategies for change useful, is not part of the logic.[20] Against this background, I argue that a gender power order, or gender-power relationships, may manifest themselves differently in rural areas, but I would like to leave the question of the level of oppression unanswered.[21] In other words, I emphasise the importance of illuminating the relationship between gender and a territorial dimension when analysing the subordination of women as a group in society.

On basis of the interviews made with activist women, I would argue that one major territorial impact to their organisation is that they organise as women because they *have to*. In other words, there is *a discourse of necessity* established in these rural communities. In contrast to urban forms of organising, these women not "only" organise in order to struggle for gender-equality. They also organise because they want to live in these rural territories.[22]

Rural women's movement and the state in Sweden

Since the end of the 1980's, several municipalities in northern Sweden have funded various so-called women's projects, with the aim of getting women both to remain in, and to return to, the local community. Sometimes the initiative has come from a group of women, using the "opportunity window" that was opened when the local politicians realised that they had to do something in order to stop the women leaving the community. This was the case with the three women's groups discussed in this chapter. In other cases, the local politicians and/or civil servants initiated a women's project, which then often aimed at organising women in some kind of network.[23]

As mentioned, the active women themselves established all the three women's groups that I have studied. At the same time, they fairly soon applied for funding for their activities, mainly from local or regional authorities. Their applications have been motivated by the fact that women do not enjoy living in the community and therefore, to a greater extent than men, choose to leave. Local politicians have accepted this as a reason for giving money to the projects. In other words, the awarding of public funding has not been motivated by any explicit gender-equality reasons – for example, to increase the influence of women in the local community. Instead, the interest of the politicians has been to solve the problem of women leaving (and no connection has been made between those two arguments). You could say that this relationship shows some form of glide or drift between women's organising and state projects that in my view illustrates a quite close connection between this form of women's organising and different actors in the Swedish state, i.e. established politics.

One important aspect in this context is the possibility of getting regional (state) funding and later funding from the structural funds of the European Union. In the middle of the 1990's, you could also say that rural women's organising was partly institutionalised in the Swedish state through the establishment of Resource Centres for Women. The aim of these resource centres was to support and improve the living conditions of women, especially in rural and sparsely populated areas. The establishment of the centres was a result of mainly femocrats, but also politicians, researchers and activists, lobbying for more funding for women's issues and projects.[24] In my view, this made the work and activism of women's groups both easier and harder at the same time. On the one hand, it was easier to get some funding, and to get in contact and network with other groups. On the other, the women's groups had to adjust to different rules and demands concerning forms of organisation and so on.

The resource centres were established on three levels, national, regional and local, with the main focus put on the regional level. The county administrative boards were commissioned by the Government to establish the regional resource centres for women, although they did not get any extra funding for this assignment. In my view, the resource centres for women could be described and interpreted in different ways. On the one hand, they could be seen as a state initiative supporting women, especially in rural areas – based on women's own organising. On the other, they could be considered as a similar organisation to the county administrative boards, i.e. simply a part of the formal administrative system, only with less funding and resources. While the latter interpretation may seem to be an exaggeration, I see this as a way of focusing on the centres as an established form of politics, instead of talking about them in terms of support for women – and in this way also constructing women as "needing" and the state as "giving". Further, the goals of the resource centres were quite as overarching as the goals of authorities such as the county administrative boards – to support and improve citizens' living conditions.

Added to this is the special priority that the resource centres were to give to women living in rural areas which also strengthens the picture of rural women as being in need of more support than urban women. Again, the problem was put on (rural) women, and not on the political establishment – not least by the terminology used – *resource* centres connote women as being in need of extra resources, because they are not getting what the so-called democratic citizenship gives to men. To be in need of support is double edged – of course it is positive that women's situations in rural areas are receiving attention, but as the same time it also means reproducing rural women as more in need, more subordinated.[25] Similar contradictions, or paradoxes, are discussed both in Alena Heitlingers' but especially in Natalia Khodyrevas' chapter in this volume, although their focus is on more transnational processes. But the issue of funding and the risks of cooptation are similar.

In this section, my ambition has been to illustrate the close connections between the (rural) women's movement in Sweden and established forms of politics. I believe that these connections also illustrate the importance of studying the relationships between the views and values of gender-equality between activists and local politicians.

Interpretations of gender-equality

Gender-equality, or "jämställdhet" in Swedish, is a commonly used word in the Swedish debate on the positions of women and men in society. In fact, Sweden seems to be the only country in the world with a separate term that concerns the equality between women and men – maybe with the exception of Norway. One fundamental problem with how the concept of gender-equality is used, for example in official documents, is that this visionary word is used to signify a problem. Gender-equality, like democracy, carries a positive connotation, i.e. no one can be against gender-equality. Gender-equality is also a gender-neutral concept in the sense that it does not tell us anything about discrimination of women.

I have chosen to study what "gender-equality" means for the activists of the women's groups and the local politicians in order to analyse how these different actors produce gender. As I see it, this form of analysis can be regarded as a strategy to understand the limits of established politics and democracy in relation to gender, and also to understand why women's organising meets resistance from established forms of politics. To study the activists' views on gender-equality could also be seen as a way of understanding why these women have chosen to join a women's group – what are they making resistance against? In other words, my analysis of activists' and politicians' values of gender-equality should be seen as a way of saying something about the limits of women's agency in today's Swedish society.

The next section focuses on the values and views of the politicians concerning gender-equality. After that, I describe and comment on how the activists understand this theme or problem. I end the chapter by discussing what the views presented on gender-equality could mean in terms of women's freedom of action.

"Gender-equality is all right, as long as it's not taking over ..."

Everybody should have the same opportunities in society, regardless of sex. This view sums up how the politicians define gender-equality. Women's and men's equal opportunities to influence their own lives are looked upon as important. You could say that the vision of every individual's free choice is seen as a key to gender-equality. Gender-equality is also often connected to a question of numbers; a gender-equal society is seen as a society where there are the same number of women and men in different societal spheres. Some politicians frame this in terms of minority and majority, something that, from my perspective, turns "the problem of gender-equality" into a problem connected to majorities and minorities. In places where women are a minority, they are subordinated – and in places where men are a minority they are subordinated.

All the politicians also agree that Sweden is not a gender-equal society – yet. Some of them think that "we are almost there", while others believe that there is a long way left to go before reaching "full" gender-equality. Gender-equality is also discussed in terms of relativity, something we can have more or less of, and Sweden is often compared with other countries that are seen as "worse". Differences in wages between women and men, and the lack of female leaders, especially in the private sector, are put forward by the politicians as examples illustrating that Sweden has not reached a state of "full" gender-equality. As these examples suggest, the arena of paid work and employment is often the place in society where the politicians locate questions concerning gender-equality. For example, the gender-segregated labour market is regarded as a problem connected with old-fashioned traditions, traditions that are perceived as still very much alive, although the politicians consider that society has changed a great deal. In Kiruna, an old mining community, the politicians often refer to the mine as a traditional male workplace – a fact that is also seen as explaining why Kiruna is still, to a large extent, dominated by men and male interests.

Most politicians see a gender-integrated labour market as a positive goal. If this were to be achieved, they believe it would then be possible to take the capacities and experiences of both women and men into account. Again, the positions of women and men in society are looked upon as complementary. With regard to the choice of profession, most politicians mention the importance of taking in more women in traditional male occupations – as pilots or executives. The need for men to choose to a greater extent traditional female professions such as nursing or preschool teaching is seldom mentioned in the interviews. Overall, strategies to break the gender-segregated labour market are often discussed in terms of "the need for women to take action", or sometimes "the need for women to let men in". In other words, women are, in these interviews, often made responsible for the changes required.

The family, and frequently the politicians' own private situations, are also used when discussing the values of gender-equality. Also here, the free choice of the individual is seen as a key factor when working for gender-equality. However, the politicians do not focus on the need to change women's roles in the home to the same extent as in the labour market. None of the politicians suggest that women ought to repair the car or chop firewood as a strategy to make the housework "more gender-equal". Several of the politicians point out that traditional gender-roles still affect what women and men do in the family, but that this will change gradually as the younger generations form families. At the same time, all the politicians argue that there are differences between women and men that are impossible to change, i.e. differences that are biologically determined. The fact that women give birth is seen as a "natural" explanation of some of the household work divisions.

The way in which the politicians reason on difference and sameness is often contradictory. In a gender-equal society, women and men ought to have the same opportunities – but at the same time several politicians point out the importance of difference between women and men, and that this difference must be preserved in a gender-equal society. In the interviews, I put considerable effort into discussing what the politicians mean when they talk about difference. It seems as if they are quite used to stating that there are differences between the sexes, but have difficulties in explaining what these differences consist of. "We must accept the differences", is one common way of putting it. Differences between women and men are presented as something positive, something worthwhile maintaining. If these differences are not taken into account when working with gender-equality, some politicians argue that there is a risk of "too much" gender equality. In other words, gender-equality is connected to sameness, not difference.

As I mentioned earlier, when trying to explain why women and men are different, the politicians present these differences as biological and natural. Women have children, not men, is the most common example in the interviews. So-called natural differences are, in other words, connected to what *women* are made, or born, to do. The connections with childbirth, and sex-segregated work in the family, also combine sex-differences with a prevailing heterosexual, or heteronormative, discourse.

One of my conclusions concerning the politicians' views on gender-equality is that they seem to interpret the free choice of the individual differently depending on which arena in society is in focus. In the labour market, it is seen as important that women and men are working with the same things; this makes the labour market more complete. When it comes to the family and household work, the "natural differences" between women and men are looked upon as "natural reasons" for a division of work and responsibilities. You could say that these are two ways of discussing the same phenomenon; the importance of difference, natural and biological difference. In both the labour market and the family, women and men are ascribed different abilities. In the labour market, this means that the work will be done in a more complete way if both women and men carry it out. In the family, this means that women and men should have responsibility for different tasks. To sum up, the issue of gender-equality is discussed in complementary terms, not in terms of influence or subordination. The problem is not perceived in terms of women's subordination and men's superior positions, but instead that women and men must be given the opportunities to complement each other.

My conclusion concerning the impact of the politicians' values on gender-equality is that these values exclude an interpretation of gender-equality in terms of power and the subordination of women. Instead, a gender-equality discourse based on "natural differences" and complementary positions is constructed. Some of the politicians talk of differences between women and men in terms of differences in social conditions, but a large majority points out natural differences, difference in "being". Gender-equality is constructed in complementary terms, and the goal is to give two different sorts of individuals the same opportunities – mainly by making them work together in the same jobs.

When the politicians discuss gender-equality, they try to to a large extent to "defend" women's nature. From the starting-point of women having children (and without reflecting on the fact that not all women can or would like to have children), the politicians are producing femininity. As the Swedish sociologist Carin Holmberg puts it; "What women and men *do* becomes what women and men *are*."[26] By making something natural, it becomes possible to question why our society is constructed in the way it is. It is a strategy of avoiding a discussion in which gender and power are put in relation to each other. Making parts of society the result of natural differences is also a way of de-politicising and, in this case, placing questions of gender in a private, non-political sphere.

One important ingredient in the politicians' talk about differences between the sexes is the connection between difference and women. There are women who are seen as different – in relation to whom is seldom articulated, i.e. men are not defined in relationship to their biology in the same way as women. *Not* being able to give birth is not given as an example of natural, male difference. The possibility for women to, for example, work in traditional male occupations, and still retain their "femininity" is often mentioned as an example of good gender-equality work. The opposite, that men should be able to do traditional female work without losing their "natural masculinity", is never given as an example. In this way, men and masculinity are made so self-evident that there is no need for definitions. In other words, the normal is implicitly constructed through defining the not normal. Women are, as de Beauvoir says, defined as the Other.

"There's a long way to go ..."

When I started analysing the activist interviews, I soon realised that there were few visions, or pictures, of what a gender-equal society should look like. Few of the activists expressed their visions more than in terms of equal value, equal distribution of money and influence in society. This approach to gender-equality differs a great deal from the way in which the politicians presented their views. To a large extent, all of the interviewed politicians gave more or less detailed descriptions of what they wanted a gender-equal society to look like. Among the activists, the prevailing way of discussing gender-equality was in terms of absence, the lack of equality. In relation to the politicians' views, it was quite clear that for the activists, gender-equality is something essential in society, and that they see their own organisation as a necessary step in order to reach this goal. For the politicians, gender-equality was a question of low priority that mostly concerned private relations between women and men.

In the interviews, most activists focused on issues concerning the home, care, family and children when discussing (the lack of) gender-equality. The situation of women in the so-called private sphere was put forward as central in relation to the conditions and opportunities for women when, for example, competing with men for influential positions. In short, women are not seen as having as much time and own space as men. Some of the activists argued that men are favoured at women's expense, while others spoke about the adjustment of women to traditional gender roles. A couple of activists also mentioned men's sexualised violence towards women as an example of how men control women.

None of the activists thought that household work is divided equally between women and men. Still today, it is women who generally carry the main responsibility for home and children, although some of the activists suggest that some changes are going on in younger generations. Several of the activists pointed out that a gender-equal household does not have to be the same thing as women and men doing the same things. Some division of tasks is seen in positive terms, and often commented in relation to differences in interests and skills between individuals – not necessarily connected to sex/gender.

In conclusion, there is a common view among the activists that women's overall responsibility for the household limits their freedom of action. However, there are differing opinions among the activists as to whether women are better equipped for housework than men. One of the women interviewed considered that the traditional views of women's and men's biological differences are used in order to maintain the household as the domain of women. The fact that women give birth to children is, in other words, seen as way of also making the care of children and housework into something "natural" for women to do. Another activist argued that "boys are allowed to be boys" while girls are confronted with gender related demands that constrain their freedom of action. In this line of argument it becomes clear that "being a boy" is the same thing as not having to adjust to gender limitations. Boys could just "be", while girls have to live up to demands connected to both traditional femininity and more gender-equal inspired demands. In other words, girls have to be both "the same and different" at the same time. In this way, this activist means that the demands of change are placed on girls and women.

Some of the activists, like almost all the politicians, argued that there are biological differences that affect what women and men are best suited to do in society. Contrary to the politicians, these activists do not connect this with opinions that women are better suited for some jobs, and men for others. Their main point is that it is natural for women to take greater responsibility for the children, and that this means that it is important that this "caring-work" is given a higher status in society. A couple of activists also expressed views that women are "better" than men, meaning that if women were able to influence society in an higher degree, we would get a better (more friendly, more peaceful) society.

To sum up, the activists do not stress the connection between gender-equality and biological difference in the same way as the politicians. Instead, there is a focus on experiences of injustice when discussing issues of gender-equality.

A constantly recurring argument when the activists are discussing gender-equality is the stress on women's adjustment. In their view, one significant example of the way which society is not gender-equal is that women adjust all the time, in different public situations and to their own husbands. When talking about different contexts, from women's position in the labour market and in politics, to their position in the family, the activists comment on women's lack of free agency (freedom of action) – both in practical and more abstract ways. One argument is that although women carry the main responsibility for the household, they do not have the same amount of influence on family decisions. Another example of the adjustment of women is that this is something that girls are socialised into from early years. The upbringing of girls includes less freedom of action in school; an example that is brought up in several of the interviews. Also in this context, the activists think that girls have to fight for their rights while boys "just get what they want and need, as something self-evident". Because they have to be explicit about needs and demands, it could seem as if girls get more than boys.

In conclusion, several of the activists think that women are brought up to be passive and not demand their own freedom of action. This image of "a real women" is perceived as being nurtured in the media, where young women often are described as passive and irrational. Some activists point to the fact that men in today's society take a lot for granted and in this way get a greater freedom of action, but that this freedom of action is built on women's adjustment to men. One activist takes her own family life as an example: "When I have an evening appointment I have to inform my husband several days in advance. When he's doing something he just lets me know right before he leaves home."

Pictures of discrimination

The picture of gender-equality that appears in the interviews with the activists is that the freedom of action for women in today's Swedish society is limited – above all in a more abstract way. The formal opportunities for women to for example choose education or profession have to a large extent increased during the last twenty years. At the same time, the activists point out, women still limit themselves in their choices, and adjust and adapt to traditional views of femininity. In my interpretation, this means that women's formal possibilities for free choices in life are limited by a subtle gender-power-order – a narrow discourse when it comes to making so-called free choices.

As a result of the activists focusing on "inequality", or discrimination, when discussing gender-equality, gender becomes to a large extent a question of social construction instead of natural or biological differences. The demand that women should have rights and opportunities to influence both their own lives and society are not motivated in terms of women's biological difference. As I have shown earlier, there are differing views of gender differences among the activists. However, what they have in common – something that also distinguishes their views from the views of the politicians – is that they do not put questions of gender difference and sameness in the centre of the discussion on gender-equality. Another difference, compared with the politicians' views on gender-equality, is that the activists place the problems concerning gender-equality primarily in the so-called private sphere. While the politicians mainly meant that gender-equality – if it is a political problem – is something that concerns the labour market, the activists focus on the impact of family life on women's possibilities of freedom of action in society as a whole.

A dominating discourse of gender-equality – and an outlook epilogue

As I stated earlier in this chapter, the women's groups I have studied consist of women who mainly regard their organising as necessary if they are to survive in their local territory. In other words, few of these women were, or are, driven by some kind of feminist ideological force when deciding to join or form a women's group. Concerning their goals, the activists often talk in terms of making society better for women, and children and men, in their local community. In relation to other forms of women's organising, for example shelters for battered women, anarchy feminists and centres for women studies, these groups cannot be characterised as radical or, at least in an explicit way, as a challenge to, for example, the established political institutions. Why then do they meet resistance from local politicians?

Through my empirical review of the values of gender-equality among both activists and politicians I have hopefully given one set of answers to that question – namely the importance of differences in problem formulation concerning gender-equality, and how this is connected with views on the definition of gender. What these women's groups do, both in their organising practices and when the activists present their views on gender-equality in the interviews, are to argue that a main problem in society is that women are subordinated. In other words, they connect questions of gender with different forms of injustice in society, and in this way they *make* gender, i.e. gender becomes socially constructed. By doing this, they question the discourse of gender-equality presented by the local politicians, a discourse built around a perception of gender as biological and natural, with no connections to power-relations in society. In conclusion, this means that definitions of both gender and gender-equality are crucial to the possibilities for women to increase their freedom of action in society.

As a way of summing up my analysis – and also to put the question of gender equality into a broader context, I have briefly studied both Swedish national policies for gender equality, and the policy of the European Union. My focus has been how the problem is framed in some central policy documents, and the most striking result in relation to the material that has been presented in this chapter is the use of expressions like gender power and discrimination of women. For example, in a short summary from DG5 on Equal Opportunities for Women and Men, Current position and outlook, it is stated:

"Equality between women and men is a fundamental principle of democracy. However, in actual fact sex-based discrimination continues to exist. Hence, women are more likely to be unemployed than men. There are more likely to hold contingent jobs and make up the bulk of part time workers."[27]

In this citation, the expression "sex-based discrimination" is used when describing the problem that work for gender equality is directed towards. In another EU document concerning a forthcoming strategy for gender equality, the problem is presented with expressions like "structural sex-discrimination that among other things is illuminated by the under-representation of women or violence against women".[28] One interpretation is that in the way that "the problem of gender equality" is framed in these documents, there is a possibility to look upon this problem as a problem that concerns power, gender-power.

On the Swedish, national level, it is also possible to find expressions that frame the problem in terms of gender power. When the Swedish government writes about the politics of gender-equality for the new century, this is stated in the introduction:

"Gender-Equality is about justice and the distribution of economical and political power. It is about democracy, about the equal value of women and men. It is about breaking the structure in society that is still prevailing, and which every day tells us that: men are the norm and women are the exception, men are superior and women are subordinated, that men have great power and women have little."[29]

Of course, when going through these documents on gender-equality, both from the European Union and from the Swedish government, it is possible to find expressions that connect the problem of gender-equality with the same principles as in my own interview material, for example gender difference and complementarity. However, it is interesting to notice that these statements cited frame the problem of gender equality in power terms. This opens up a possibility to contradict the established political discourse on gender-equality found in my material, without going outside established forms of politics. It is also possible to discern a contradiction between European Union and national rethorics on gender-equality, and the local established discourses that in my view could be interpreted as a Swedish gender-equality practice. In my view, this illustrate how complex the field of gender-equality is, and that this complexity would be far more interesting for Sweden to "export" than the success-story that most of the time is presented – at least if the purpose is to work against structural discrimination of women. This contradiction also highlights the importance of regional and local studies when trying to elaborate our understanding of the relationships between gender and power.

References

Bacchi, Carol Lee (1999). *Women, Policy and Politics. The Construction of Policy Problems*, London, Thousand Oaks, New Delhi, Sage.

Eduards, Maud (1992). "Against the Rules of the Game. On the Importance of Women's Collective Actions", *Rethinking Change. Current Swedish Feminist Research*, HSFR. Uppsala, Swedish Science Press.

Eduards, Maud (1993). "Politiken förkroppsligad", von Sydow, Björn, Wallin, Gunnar och Wittrock, Björn (ed.), *Politikens väsen. Idéer och institutioner i den moderna staten*, Kristianstad, Tidens förlag.

Eduards, Maud (1995). "En allvarsam lek med ord", *SOU 1995: 110*, Stockholm, Publica.

Eduards, Maud (1997). "The Women's Shelter Movement", Gustafsson, Gunnel (ed.), *Towards a New Democratic Order? Women's Organizing in Sweden in the 1990's*, Stockholm, Publica.

Eduards, Maud (2002). *Förbjuden handling. Om kvinnors organisering och feministisk teori*, Stockholm, Liber.

Elman, Amy (1996). *Sexual Subordination and State Intervention. Comparing Sweden and the United States*, Providence, Oxford, Berghahn Books.

Forsberg, Gunnel (1996a). "Rum med utsikt – modulationer på ett grundtema". *Kvinnovetenskaplig tidskrift* nr. 2.

Forsberg, Gunnel (1996b). Är landsbygden en kvinnofälla? Papper presented at the seminar *Kvinnor och män i dialog om regionernas framtid*, Östersund 2-4 oktober, Nationellt resurscentrum för kvinnor, NUTEK.

Friberg, Tora (1993). *Den andra sidan myntet. Om regionalpolitikens enögdhet*, Östersund, Glesbygdsverket.

Holmberg, Carin (1996). *Det kallas manshat: en bok om feminism*, Göteborg, Anamma förlag.

de Lauretis, Teresa (1989). *Technologies of Gender: Essays on Theory, Film, and Fiction*, Basingstoke, Macmillan.

Ljung, Margareta (1995). *Lyft jorden mot himlen: växande i kvinnogrupper och kvinnliga nätverk*, Stockholm, Carlsson.

Mansbridge, Jane (1995). "What is the feminist movement?", Marx Ferre, Myra & Yancey Martin, Patricia. *Feminist Organizations. Harvest of the New Women's Movement*, Philadelphia, Temple University Press.

Massey, Doreen (1994). *Space, Place and Gender*, Cambridge and Oxford, Polity Press.

Meddelande från kommissionen till rådet, europaparlamentet, ekonomiska och sociala kommittén och regionalkommittén. På väg mot en ramstrategi för jämställdhet (2002-2005). 2000/0143 (CNS).

Månsson, Hans (1993). *Framtidens vägvisare*, Östersund, Glesbygdsverket.

Pateman, Carole (1988). *The Sexual Contract*, Stanford, Stanford University Press.

Regeringens skrivelse om jämställdheten inför 2000-talet, 1999/2000:24.

Rönnblom, Malin (2002). *Ett eget rum? Kvinnors organisering möter etablerad politik*. Statsvetenskapliga institutionen, Umeå universitet, Doctoral dissertation.

Rönnblom, Malin (1997). "Local Women's Projects", Gustafsson, Gunnel (ed.) *Towards a New Democratic Order? Women's Organizing in Sweden in the 1990's*, Stockholm, Publica.

Scott, Joan (1988). *Gender and the Politics of History*, New York, Columbia University Press.

Ås, Berit (1982). *Kvinnor tillsammans: handbok i frigörelse*. Stockholm, Gidlund.

Notes

1 Eduards et al. (1997).

2 See for example Eduards et al. (1997) and Ljung (1995).

3 The total amount of interviews conducted in relation to the project were around eighty persons, with a majority of activists. Fifty-five of them were used for the analysis presented in this chapter. For a more elaborated discussion concerning the interviews, see Rönnblom (2002).

4 In this very short description of the three women's groups studied, I have chosen not to make any distinctions between the three. Of course, there are differences in development, focus and organisation, and for a more thorough exposition of the groups see Rönnblom (2002) and (1997).

5 Eduards (2002).

6 See Ås (1982).

7 In my dissertation, the same material is also used for analysing negotiations about politics – where politics should take place and which activities that should be considered as political. See Rönnblom (2002).

8 See Eduards (2002).

9 Eduards (1992); Eduards (1993).

10 de Lauretis (1987).

11 I do not make a distinction between women's movement and feminist movement. The main reason for this is my focus on women's separate organisation as a method or a strategy to scrutinise established or traditional forms of politics, which means that I emphasise what happens when women organise together, without men. Often activities that in some situations could be defined as reproducing a traditional gender order could in other situations, or places, be defined

as a challenge. In Jane Mansbridge's words: "What distinguishes feminist movements from movements by and for women is that feminist movements are to end male domination. The line between feminist and women's movements is not completely clear. Movements by and for women, including antifeminist movements, may in the long run help end male domination by, among other things, promoting women's political conciousness" (Mansbridge, 1995) page 33. This argument connects to what Elisabeth Lønnå writes in her chapter in this book on the risks of making some forms of the feminist movement invisible when describing this movement in terms of "waves".

12 Eduards (1997).

13 Bacchi (1999).

14 de Lauretis (1987).

15 Eduards (1993).

16 Månsson (1993).

17 Forsberg (1996b).

18 (Forsberg, 1996b: 3, my translation)

19 Forsberg (1996a).

20 In my approach, the rural is constructed in relation to the urban, which for example means that although the municipality of Kiruna has 25 000 inhabitants, it could be defined as rural in relation to its peripheral location, in the very far North with 350 kilometres to the nearest city.

21 The relationship between the urban and the rural is in this chapter used as a the theoretical framework in order to situate my study of rural women's group. Of course this relationship could also have been studied empirically, for example through a comparison between women's organising in both rural and urban spaces.

22 Of course there are other examples of women organising for necessity, or in other words for survival, for example the many "take back the night" demonstrations that have been occurring in many cities in different countries in the western world. From my perspective, these forms of women's organising also highlight the importance of an analysis that includes a territorial dimension, or in other words, puts focus on dimensions of space and place, see for example Massey (1994).

23 See also Rönnblom (1997).

24 Friberg (1993).

25 This could also be seen as an example of what Joan Scott calls the feminist paradox. To name some form of injustice or power order is also, at the same time, reproducing the same (Scott, 1988).

26 Holmberg (1996) p. 27.

27 Http://europa.eu.int/scadplus/leg/en/cha/c00006.htm. printed 2001-10-10.

28 Meddelande från kommissionen till rådet, europaparlamentet, ekonomiska och sociala kommittén och regionalkommittén. På väg mot en ramstrategi för jämställdhet (2002-2005) p. 3.

29 Regeringens skrivelse om jämställdheten inför 2000-talet, 1999/2000:24, p. 5.

Part III

International Fora and Transnational Networks

CHAPTER 9

Unintended Consequences of Hosting a Women's Conference: Beijing and Beyond

Naihua Zhang

In 1995, China hosted the United Nation's Fourth World Conference on Women and its concurrent unofficial Forum of Non-Governmental Organizations (NGO) amidst great international controversy.* The controversy started right after China was granted to host the event with the debate over whether China "deserved" this honour, and went straight through the whole preparation and conference phrase. The aims and accomplishments of China related to the Fourth World Conference on Women have been debated ever since.[1]

The present work attempts to explore the impact of the UN Conference and NGO Forum on China (thereafter referred to together as the Conference, unless specified otherwise), with a specific focus on its effect on the Chinese women and the women's movement. This is a shift away from the previous coverage by the global media and the comments of some western feminists who tend to focus their attention exclusively on the Chinese government. Undoubtedly, the act of the Chinese government pertaining to the Conference was a major source of controversy.[2] However, such exclusive focus on the government ignored the fact that this Conference was about women and it portrayed Chinese women as passive victims of an authoritarian state. Not only were Chinese women's agency and their organized effort to strive for equality ignored in the debate, many observers were also unaware of the fact that there was an emerging women's movement in China prior to the Conference. As a result, the general attitude in the media and of some Western feminists, towards the Conference, was generally negative, and their assessments of the effect of the Conference on the Chinese women's movement were reserved.[3]

In this chapter, besides focusing on Chinese women themselves, I am going to consider the Conference not as a single event but rather as a series of events adding up to a process which includes the pre-stage of preparation beginning in 1992 and the aftermath. I am also going to look at the Conference in its social and historical con-

---

* Special thanks to Esther Ngan-ling Chow and Beth Hess for their support and constructive suggestions on an earlier draft of this paper, to John McKay and Anthony Guneratne for their helpful review and editorial assistance, and to Hilda Rømer Christensen and Beatrice Halsaa for their thoughtful comments and final editing of this paper. I am grateful also to Aino Saarinen and others at the Women's Movement and Internationalization Network seminar. They inspired me with their activism in the women's movements and their vision of the feminist future.

text, to demonstrate how it took place at a time when the emerging Chinese women's movement was reaching out for inspiration while China's hosting of the Conference provided the opportunity for Chinese women to contact the outside world. Subsequently, the Conference became the seminal event that marked China's integration into the international women's movement. The effect of the impact of the Conference on Chinese women is thus examined in terms of the interaction and interplay between local and global feminisms and the consequences of such an exchange.

This chapter is divided into three parts: 1) an overview of Chinese women's connection to the outside world, 2) an outline of the changing political and social context for the women's movement, 3) a discussion of the expansion and dispersion of the women's movement. It concludes with my observation of the interplay between the local and the global as well as the domestic and international interplay.

Chinese women's connection to the outside world: an overview

To fully appreciate the significance of China's hosting the Conference, a brief review of the history of the international influence on China under the leadership of the Chinese Communist Party (CCP) is necessary. Western feminist ideas were first advocated and appropriated by male reformers of the mid-1890s. Among the first works translated into Chinese, many from their Japanese translations, were John Stuart Mill's "On liberty" and "Subjection of Women" and Herbert Spencer's "The Right of Women." Humanist liberal ideas of women's rights as "natural rights," "rights of human beings" became the underlying theme for reformers who attacked foot binding and campaigned for women's formal education as an important measure for national strengthening. Various other feminist ideologies from the West, including anarchist, socialist and Marxist ideas on social change, were subsequently introduced and circulated widely during China's May Fourth era (1915-1925). Women's emancipation was presented as the key to changing and modernizing China, and feminist agitation and activism reached its peak in the early 1920s.[4] When the Chinese Communist Party was founded in 1921, some of its founding members were inspired by western liberal feminist ideas of sexual equality.[5] But early feminism fell victim to the ideological conflicts within the international women's movement and the exigencies of political and class struggle in China. It began to carry a negative meaning and was characterized as a "bourgeois" women's movement inspired by Western cultural ideals. The CCP mainly followed an orthodox Marxist class-based approach to the woman question.[6]

Organizationally, after the establishment of the People's Republic of China in 1949, Chinese women's main international connection was with socialist oriented Women's International Democratic Federation through the All-China Women's Federation, a national women's organization established with the support of the party and the state. At a time when China was not a member of the UN, such a contact, though mediated through the state, was an important channel for Chinese women to connect to the outside world. Ideological conflicts with the former Soviet Union in early 1960s led to China's withdrawal from its active participation in Women's International

Democratic Federation's activities, culminating in the isolation imposed during the Cultural Revolution of 1966-1976. Limited participation in events organized by the United Nations resumed, following China's return to the UN in 1971 as a member state, especially after China became a member of the UN Commission on the Status of Women in 1974. However, China did not officially endorse all the themes of the UN Decade for Women – Equality, Development, and Peace – until 1980[7], after China introduced economic reforms and opened itself to the rest of the world in 1979. China was represented at the first three UN World Conferences on Women in 1975, 1980 and 1985 by an official delegation, whose primary concern at the official conference was foreign policy related issues. They did not engage themselves in the gender-focused debates that had marked the women's organized activities at the international arena since the 1970s. China did not have any formal participation in the NGO Forums attending the conferences, except the NGO Forum at the Nairobi Conference in 1985. Inspired by the warm atmosphere there, the official delegation joined the Forum with an ad hoc panel describing the progress Chinese women had made in China.

Things were quite different for the 95 Conference. For the first time China fully participated in both the official conference and the NGO Forum. More than 5000 Chinese women and 55 Chinese organizations were involved. China sponsored 47 panels and workshops[8] as well as part-taking in the pre-Conference planning and preparatory activities and other major international conferences. At the official UN Conference in 1995, the Chinese government focused on gender rather than on foreign policy issues in its formal presentation, and gave full endorsement to the Beijing Platform for Action without any reservation. The occasion marked China's full engagement with the international women's movement.

One factor that did not receive adequate attention from the overseas observers at the Conference was that China's hosting of the Conference was not a governmental action alone. By the mid-1980s, an urban-based women's movement had emerged in China, characterized by the rise of women's consciousness about themselves as women, their organized activities to combat the old and new problems women faced, and most important, by the development of women's organizations and women's studies.[9] The Women's Federation was taking a stronger stance in representing and promoting women's interest in a more open political and social atmosphere during China's reform era. In addition, a new type of women's organizations appeared. These were spontaneous organizations established by women, quite independently of the state. The new organizations were generally formed by intellectual and professional women from inside as well as outside the Women's Federation, engaging in research on women and in projects promoting women's interests or providing services. They represented independent types of associations and thinking in China, and the new women's studies had become an important arena for creating new discourses on women.

By the 1990s this movement was reaching outside China for inspiration and for organizational connections. The activists had found a new term, "NGO", to refer to their organizations.[10] They were among the first groups in China to receive foreign funding and to attend various Conference-related activities. They were also among the first to have direct contact with their counterparts outside China and to expand the scope of their organizing activities. Generally, they felt greatly empowered.[11] In this way, China's hosting of the Conference provided much-needed opportunities and resources for the women's movement and for its connection to the international women's movement. Chinese activist women also played a vital role, though often constrained, in shaping the organization and the outcome of the 95 Conference, putting pressure for change on the government – from below and from within.

Today, looking back seven years at the Conference, there is no doubt that it has had a big impact on Chinese women and the women's movement in China. I will focus on the two most prominent aspects: 1) its effect on the changing political and social context in which the women's movement is carried out, and 2) its effect on the Chinese women's movement itself.

Changing political and social contexts for the women's movement: domestic and international

First, women's issues received a "status lift" on the national agenda and received more publicity and resources and reiterated commitment from the government starting from the pre-Conference stage.[12] One example of a major effort made before the conference was the production of two important state documents: 'China's Country Report on the Implementation of the Nairobi Forward Looking Strategies for the Advancement of Women' and 'Chinese Women's Development Program: 1995-2000'. Unlike the typical "achievement reports" usually made in China, the Country Report was framed according to the categories and critical issues of the Nairobi Forward Looking Strategies. The report identified China's weaker areas in implementing the Nairobi Strategies and outlining goals for action. These goals were further elaborated in the Chinese Women's Development Program, the first state program ever made specifically for women, whose development had been treated previously only as part of the general social development scheme. As a consequence, this led all provincial governments and many municipal governments to develop their own programs on women's development as well as initiating institutional mechanism to measure and monitor the implementation of the Program. At the 95 Conference, the Chinese President Jiang Zemin stated in his welcoming speech to participants of the official Conference that equality between men and women was "a fundamental state policy for promoting social development." This wording for the first time put gender equality in the same category as other "crucial state matters" such as family planning, the protection of land and environmental questions.

These reiterated public commitments, even when they are only found at the symbolic level, were important for women. This is especially true in present-day China where the emphasis on economic growth and efficiency tends to override concerns for social equality, and where the rising neo-liberalism in China calls for women to sacrifice themselves for the "modernization" of the nation. Furthermore, these public com-

Demonstration against imperialism at the 4th World Conference on Women Beijing 1995. (Courtesy of the Women's History Archives, Denmark.)

mitments stand in sheer contrast to what is happening in the former socialist countries and the new states in East and Central Europe. In these countries the state policies on women are discredited with the collapse of the Communist Party rule and the political climate on gender issues is taking a distinctly regressive character.[13] The unique situation in China has to be understood, in part, as the result of the interplay between international and local politics due to China's hosting of the 95 UN Conference. Chinese women have wasted no time in utilizing the elevated status and to challenge any measures that run counter to the spirit of this "fundamental state policy". They use the Women's Development Program as a mechanism to evaluate women's situation and to put forward demands for the needed resources to fulfill specific goals.

Secondly, the ideas and agenda of the international women's movement, in the form of the UN documents, became a new source in shaping the official Chinese gender rhetoric and policy agenda. As mentioned earlier, major pre-conference documents were formulated on the basis of the Nairobi Forward Looking Strategies for the Advancement of Women. The current Chinese Women's Development Program: 2001-2005 was framed according to the Beijing Platform for Action, with special attention to the 12 critical areas of concern specified in the Beijing Platform for Action.[14] As a result, issues that were previously not part of the focus of the state policy have now entered public discussion, often formulated using the language and ideas of the international documents. Examples are issues such as women's health, violence against women, domestic violence, and girl children. Thus, ideas from the international women's movement became normalized in China, in effect pressuring the government to make them official from above. Sometimes, a concept is quickly taken over by the government or by other organizations (such as the Women's Federation) and included in the official rhetoric in order to show that China is on track with international "norms", even at the risk of distorting the concept, as in the case of gender.[15] A concept can also be adopted and appropriated differently to suit a specific need or occasion, as in the case of the concept of NGO.[16] International institutions, however, do lend legitimacy to certain values, norms, and ideas and allow for a more open attitude towards such ideas. This provides a better environment for feminist scholars and activists and thus for further engagement with these ideas. Chinese women are making conscious efforts to use the UN leverage to mainstream feminist ideas and agendas. The rapid success of the women's movement against domestic violence, for example, illustrates how fast domestic violence has become an important issue which can be found on many national and local agendas in China today.[17]

Third, China's hosting of the UN World Conference in 1995 resulted in China's greater openness to outside influences and facilitated China's contact with the international women's movement. The process related to the conference has widened the door for incoming ideas as well as for various foundations and organizations. It has also provided opportunities for individual women and groups of women to be in direct contact with their counterparts outside China. Such direct non-official exchange amongst women at this scale was unprecedented in the post-1949 era. These changes put the Chinese women in a unique situation with regard to domestic politics in China. Of the three major mass groups under the direct control of the Chinese Communist Party through their respective mass organizations: youth, workers and women, only women have formed independent organizations and had this kind of direct contact with international organizations.

Another sign and result of this opening up and increased external influences is the large amount of foreign funding coming into China, at the time when the dwindling of funding is confronting NGOs in many other places of the world. The Ford Foundation is a leading source of funding for projects concerning women. Its funding and conceptual framework led to the development of a new research area in China: women's reproductive health.[18] Another fast growing research area initiated by outside funding is women and development. The sources of funding and the academic connections established in the process of research have had an important bearing on numerous projects. Women's Studies in China, for example, is strongly influenced by American feminist scholarship, while the field of women and development, due to the active involvement of organizations such as Oxfam, is more influenced by European approaches.

China's independently organized women's groups are sustained mainly by funding from outside of China; even the All-China Women's Federation receives most of its funding from outside. Foreign funding inevitably draws researchers and activists to particular issues and concerns that were initially externally defined, which furthermore shapes the agendas and perspectives of the funded groups. The foreign ideas and organizations coming to China are very diverse. The ultra-conservative religious groups from the United States collaborating with some Chinese women's groups and even government agencies in advocating chastity education and opposing safe sex education as the means to avoiding HIV/AIDS[19] is one case reflecting the complexity and variation of the external influences coming into China. A consequence of China's eagerness to "connect to the international rails" after decades of isolation is that makes China less critical and more vulnerable to global impact.

Expansion and disperse of the women's movement: opportunities and challenges

For the Chinese women's movement, the 1995 Conference provided stimulation, inspiration and new energy and resources; it had a direct, powerful, and long lasting impact on those who were actively involved in it, and it spurred progress in the Chinese women's movement. The following discussion will touch on two aspects affected most by the Conference: women's studies and women's organizations.

Women's studies in China emerged in the mid-1980s and have followed a path somewhat different from its counterparts in other parts of the world. While universities in Norway and other Nordic countries provided the fertile ground for the development of both the women's movement and women's studies with their activists consisting mainly of young students[20], women's studies in China were pushed by female intellectuals[21] in their 30s and older. This generation, who grew up in the Mao era, had believed that they were "liberated" but became aware of gender inequality brought into the open with economic reform. They therefore found their space and voice in a more liberal political atmosphere coming with the reform and opening up of the country. They came from mainly two institutional settings: 1) the all-China Women's Federation that began setting up research units within its own system in 1983 and then coordinated establishment of various research associations bringing interested scholars and professional women together to study issues concerning women, and 2) the academy – the first women's studies group was formed in 1985 in Zhengchou University; women from universities and research institutions were also the core members for research oriented women's organizations outside university campuses. The two groups operated in different institutional settings, with differences in source of funding and theoretical orientation and research focus, but there is also a great diversity within each group and commonality and cooperation between the two.

The 95 Conference helped open up space for women's studies and expand the scope and depth of the studies. Organizationally, the preparation for the Conference started from the second half of 1993 spurred establishment of 18 women's studies centers in Chinese universities in two years' time, a big addition to the initial 4 women's studies centers that were formed before. By the end of 1999, another 13 women's studies centers had joined the rank thereafter.[22] Women's studies centers also found their ways into 9 provincial academies of social sciences around and after the Conference.[23] At end of 1999, the Chinese Women's Association was founded, with the coordination of Women's Studies Institute of the All- China Women's Federation, gathering many research organizations and individuals together into this national association. It has since organized national conferences on Chinese women's participation in politics, to celebrate the five-year anniversary of the 95 Conference, and on the impact of mass media on women.

A growing number of women's studies centers have been established and younger scholars are now joining rank which is making the field more diverse. The 95 Conference and the Beijing Platform for Action also inspired scholars to take up new research topics such as women and health, domestic violence against women, women and the environment, women and the media, and women and human rights. New perspectives are also applied to the study of established research areas, such as women's employment, and women and economic development.[24] The adoption of gender analyses is the most significant development. Gender analyses first got the attention of scholars at a workshop held in Tianjin in 1993. The 95 Conference brought gender further into the attention of both the public and the academia, stimulating discussion and debate that have influenced both domestic gender politics and academic research. In China, gender is still a highly contested concept. It is used in a variety of ways and scholars differ in their view of its meaning and application, in terms of its relation to Western feminist theory and to Marxist perspectives on women, and especially its application to China.[25] Nonetheless, it has become a powerful analytical tool and a critical perspective for a large number of scholars, and it has resulted in some highly regarded scholarly work.[26] With its spread and prevalence, misunderstanding and misuse of the concept is also increasing. Sometimes it is used uncritically as a statistical indicator referring to women, and sometimes it replaces the term "men and women" because it sounds more neutral and apolitical. The way it is translated into Chinese has complicated the situation further.[27]

Another recent development in women's studies is discipline building and curriculum development. Some researchers think that women's studies have moved to focus more on "doing projects" – a concern for the practical problems women face and in response to funding agencies. These people want to refocus on "discipline building" – to bring together disciplinary scholarship, from both within and outside China, together in order to build China's Funuxue (womenology, liberally, to emphasize its nature as an academic discipline, as opposes to Funu yanjiu, which means women's studies, a term used in a more general sense). They want to compile textbooks for women's studies courses in universities, and to spread this scholarship to college students. Gender is a central organizing theoretical concept in their research. Since this effort began in 1999, there has been much interaction with feminist ideas outside China, in particular, with direct exchange with scholars from the United States being built into their projects. The first three disciplines they focus on are history, sociology, and education. Last year, efforts in engendering literature also began. However, they also expressed concern over the great variation among growing women's studies centers and programs, over the attempts to shape women's studies as a venue to disperse dogmatic official, traditional or essentialized notions about women.[28]

Women and development is a whole new area of study that was driven by attention to the theme of development brought by the 95 Conference, the introduction of development studies and the inflow of government and foreign funding for development projects, especially related to poverty alleviation. Introduction of feminist scholarship on women and development has led the way in critically examining issues concerning modernization and development, and scholars working in this field spearheaded a new research topic in China: women and ethnicity/ethnic minority.[29] This is also the field that is experiencing rising neo-liberalism and modernization discourses, coming down from the state development programs and brought in by various externally funded development projects.

The spreading and growth of projects have become the most prominent phenomenon in this field. This is the area where the impact of globalization on China's economy and community is most evident. Incoming money and development projects have made poor, remote provinces such as Yunnan and mountainous areas in Shannxi – the most unlikely places – highly connected to the globalization process. In the word of an activist, development projects in Yunnan are "so many that we cannot handle them all." The concept of gender, while hotly debated in cities, is also spreading quickly in some rural areas, through gender training classes popularized by development projects. Inspired by the Gender and Development (GAD) approach in development, several women's groups and networks are organized named after GAD. Gender training, Participatory Rural Assessment, and other methods used in projects are hailed by some activists as effective tools for doing all kinds of organizing work. Some local Women's Federation cadres who are involved in local development activities commented that from doing development projects they have learned new ways to carry out their work on women. Some Women's Federation branches are also carrying out development projects, conducting their own micro-credit programs among women, which in turn are also used to promote family planning.[30] The growth of development studies and practice also produced a number of NGOs, not necessarily all women's NGOs. A group of "professional experts" in doing development projects has already formed in China.[31]

The impact of the 95 Conference on Chinese women's organizations has also been profound. It brought a surge in women's organizations. The Conference lent legitimacy to independently organized women's groups and helped the ACWF maximize its resources and organizational network as well as increase its influence on the decision-making bodies.[32] The number of activists in the women's movement has grown a lot, as shown in their ability to mobilize resources, to deploy new groups around new projects rapidly, to network extensively, and to expand their repertoire of working methods.

This is evident in the growth in women's networks as they reach out to gather strength and share information and resources. Among the newly established networks are networks around GAD, women and the media, and domestic violence. Some groups have turned inward to their own organizational development, for sustainability, for

Women in Black. Demonstrating against violence at the 4th World Conference on Women. Beijing 1995. (Courtesy of the Women's History Archives, Denmark.)

democratization, or to determine their future development. Several more established groups are moving toward the direction of professionalization.[33]

There are now signs of specialization and dispersion in the activities of women's groups – an indication of maturity and peaking of the women's movements, moving towards a phase of more steady development. Of the women activists and scholars who were previously engaged in similar organizational activities under the banner of women's studies, some are now focusing more exclusively on academic work on campus, while some are engaged more in "doing projects" and work on intervention. Some scholars argue that such differentiation in research focus and the return to campus is needed for the further development of women's studies,[34] others are concerned that this would result in less attention given to practical issues which women face in their lives. They are afraid that the attempt to consciously separate the two activities and portray "doing projects" as only empirical in nature and inferior to work in the ivory tower will hinder, rather than enhance, the producing of knowledge and theories.[35]

In any case, there are more people involved in organizing activities on diverse topics. Beside the continued coalition between women from both inside and outside the Women's Federation forming groups to work on specific projects, differences remain in emphasis and approaches between the two types of organizations. The independently organized groups work on various issues, targeting marginal groups to serving their individual needs and interests. They are quick in taking up new issues and they focus on issue-specific intervention and pragmatic strategies, as in the case of domestic violence, women and development, migration women workers and prostitutes etc. The Women's Federation, on the other hand, focuses more on political representation and advocacy, utilizing their resources, including mass media (of the 123 women's newspapers and magazines, the ACWF system run 48 of them) to influence public debate on women's issues, with a special focus on impacting legislation and laws and utilizing their connection to women in rural villages and urban neighborhoods to affect more women at the grassroots level.[36] Its research and practical work focus more on issues with nation-wide implications, such as its role in designing and assisting the 2000 National Survey on Status of Women in China and its recent success in blocking "staged employment". This means that women working before marriage but staying home after giving birth to a child as a way to reduce labour redundancy were barred from entering the state's 10th Five-year plan as an employment policy.[37] The Women's Federation also played a crucial role in the formation of the new marriage law enacted in 2001. It is a typical belief among some Western and in particular American feminists that independently organized women's groups represent the genuine, autonomous women's movement in China while the institutionalized Women's Federation does not. My research shows that in the context of the women's movement in contemporary China, both forces are crucial for its progress. And their encounter with the 95 Conference has brought changes to both.

Conclusion

This paper demonstrates that China's hosting of the 95 Conference was a seminal event marking China's incorporation into the international women's movement. The Conference had a tremendous impact on the Chinese women's movement, both on the environment in which it operates and on the movement itself. My conclusion focuses on my observation of the interplay between local and global feminisms examined through the Chinese experience.

China's case gives testimony to the development of feminisms at both local and global level and illuminates the scholarly debate over global and local feminisms.[38] At the local level, a Chinese women's movement wave had already risen prior to the Conference. The fact that this movement was not induced by influence from the West but was indigenous in its origin and with its own particular characteristics and concerns was a determining factor affecting the nature and dynamics of the local/global exchange. Yet, equally important was what was happening at the global level. By the time China hosted the Conference, the international women's movement had overcome major hurdles that had sharply divided its participants from the North and the South. The international women's movement had reached consensus on some major issues concerning all the women of the world, as shown in shared vocabulary, strategies and objectives of the movement outlined in the Nairobi Forward Looking Strategies for the Advancement of Women. The success of feminist organizing both within and outside the UN system also resulted in feminist ideas being mainstreamed into UN documents and thus creating international norms that would effect the behaviour of its member states, pressuring them to confirm from above. The United Nation's NGO Forum and the emerging transnational networks provided a meeting place and channels for Chinese women to join hands in pursuing their common agenda. These were signs of emerging elements of global feminisms and provided the very favorable condition and context to allow the international/local movements to connect.

However, China's experience also showed that the exchange between the Chinese and international women's movements was far from being equal, as it was very often one-sided and dominated by Western (read American) feminism. International feminism is not inclusive, international or global enough to reflect the voices and experiences of Chinese women. Key concepts such as feminism, NGO, and human rights developed in the Western context and experience brought new inspiration and perspective to China and challenged the official ideology and approach to the woman question. Yet, when it is presented as a supranational, universal truth and a model of movement to be followed everywhere, it risks marginalizing Chinese women in the international women's movement, because the specific route and characteristics of the Chinese women's movement developed under the Chinese conditions do not measure up to the autonomous, independent, bottom-up Western model of the women's movement. This resulted in some people raising the question of whether the movement was feminist of nature and whether there are "real" NGOs in China. China's long lasting isolation from the international women's movement also made it hard for Chinese women's groups to get into the transnational networks.

In any case, China's hosting of the Conference opened the door to external forces and influences which bring to China both opportunities and challenges. Some scholars use "internationalization vs. indiginization" to describe the pushes and pulls the Chinese women's movement and women's studies are facing – by the proponents or opponents of internationalization respectively.[39] My research finds a more complicated picture in Chinese women's interaction with the outside world than this binary model suggests. I see the two not as separate trends moving toward opposite directions, but as one process, with effort going into both directions intertwined and engaging with each other. The point is that since the 95 Conference, it is no longer possible to talk about women's needs and interests in purely local terms. None of the people at the forefront of the Chinese women's movement, including those who call for "indigenous research" (bentu yanjiu), meaning research without any outside influence[40], are operating only at the local/domestic level and they have all had and benefited from contact with international feminism. What is defined as indigenous or international is negotiated by all on both sides, through the conscious positioning of themselves and appropriating concepts and resources at both levels, and through active interplay of local and international feminisms. Since around the 95 Conference, external influences have inevitably become the "third force," in addition to women's push from above, with the institution, and from below, in shaping domestic gender politics and the dynamics of the women's movement, fundamentally altering the context and the way the movement is carried out. This is perhaps the biggest impact.

In sum, the impact of China's hosting of the 95 Conference on the women's movement was far-reaching and profound for Chinese society and for the women's movement, more than just "creating ripples."[41] Such consequences were definitely not intended and anticipated by the Chinese government who bid to host the event in 1991 to help itself break the sanction imposed for its bloody suppression of the students' movement in 1989. The longer-term effect of this event and its outcomes for both China and the international women's movement are yet to be seen.

References

Basu, Amerita (1995). The Challenge of Local Feminisms: Women's Movements in Global Perspective. Boulder: Westview Press

Bunch, Charlotte (1985). Global Feminism: Going beyond boundaries, *Sojourner*, 10, no.8, p. 13.

Chen, Martha Alter (1995). "Engendering World Conferences: The International Women's Movement and the United Nations", *Third World Quarterly,* 16, no. 3, p. 477-493.

Cockburn, Cynthia (2000). "The women's Movement: Boundary-crossing on terrains of conflict", Robin Cohen and Shirin M. Rai (ed.) *Global Social Movement*, London and New Brunswick, NJ: The Athlone Press, p. 46-61.

Du Fangqin (2000). "Yunming yu shiming: gaoxiao funü yanjiu zhongxin de licheng he qianjin" (opportunities and mission: path and prospects of women's studies centers in universities), *Funu Yanjiu* (*women's studies*), no. 3, p. 16-20.

Gilmartin, Christina (1995). *Engendering the Chinese Revolution: Radical Women, Communist Politics and Mass Movement in the 1920s,* Berkeley. University of California Press.

Howell, Jude (1997). "Post-Beijing Reflections: Creating Ripples, But Not Waves in China", *Women's Studies International Forum*, 20, no.2, p. 235-252.

Hsiung, Ping-chun & Yuk-lin Renita Wong (1998). "*Jie Gui* –Connecting the Tracks: Chinese Women's Activism Surrounding the 1995 World Conference on Women in Beijing", *Gender and History*, 10, no. 3, p. 470-497.

Jiang, Yongping (2001). Shiji zhijiao guanyu jieduan jiuye, funü huijia de dataolun (Great debate over stage employment, women back home at the turn of the century *Funü Yanjiu luncong (Collection of women's studies)*, no. 2, p. 23-28.

Judd, Ellen (2002). *The Chinese Women's Movement: Between State and Market,* Stanford, California: Stanford University Press.

Kang, Ling (1996). "'Zhongguo funü fazhan gangyao' chansheng de shidai Beijing, zhuyao neirong ji zhongda yiyi" (historical context for formulating 'Program for Development of Chinese Women', its main content and significance *Fuyin baokan ziliao: iunu yanjiu (reprinted materials from printed Media: Researches on women)*, no. 4, p. 17-19.

Li, Huiying (1999). "The Dissemination and Study of Gender Consciousness in Mainland China", paper presented at the conference "Reevaluation and Repositioning: Gender, Women's Agency and Development in China at the Threshold of the New Century," Boston, March 10-11, 1999.

Li, Suwen (1975). "Geguo funü yao zhengqu jiefang bixu jinxing fan di fan zhi fan ba douzheng" (to win liberation women of all countries must carry out the struggle against imperialism, colonialism and hegaminism), *Renmin Ribao (People's Daily)*, June 24, p.5.

Li, Xiaojiang (2000). "50 nian, women zou dao le naili? – Zhongguo funü jiefang yu fazhan licheng huigu (Fifty years, where have we gone? --looking Back onto the Process of the Liberation and Development of Chinese Women*)", Funü yanjiu (women's movement), no. 2, p. 58-64.

Li, Xiaojiang (2001). "Youli yu bianyuan yu zhuliu zhijian" (in between margin and the center), *Zhongguo nuxing wenhua (Chinese women's culture),* no. 1, p. 42-54.

Liu, Bohong (1999). "95 shijie funü dahui he zhongguo funü yanjiu" (95 World Conference on Women and Chinese women's studies), *Fuyin baokan ziliao: iunu yanjiu (reprinted materials from printed Media: Researches on women,* no. 2, p. 13-18.

Milwertz, Cecilia (2001). *Beijing Women Organizing for Change: the Formation of a Social Movement Wave.*

Moghadam, Valentine M. (1996). "Feminist Networks North and South: DAWN, WIDE and WLUML", *The Journal of International Communication,* 3, no.1, p.111-126.

Molyneux, Maxine (1996). "Women's Rights and the International Context in the Post-Communist States", Monica Threlfall (ed.) *Mapping the Women's Movement: Feminist Politics and Social Transformation in the North,* London and New York: Verso, p. 232-259.

Morgan, Robin (1996). The NGO Forum: Good News and Bad, *Women's Studies Quarterly*, 24, no.1-2, p. 46-53.

Peng Peiyun (2001). Speech at the *All-China Women Federation's* National Meeting on Federation's work on Education, *Zhongguo fuyun* (Chinese Women's Movement), no. 9, p. 4-8.

Rupp, Leila J. (1997). *Worlds of Women: The Making of An International Women's Movement,* Princeton, New Jersey: Princeton University Press.

Smith, Bonnie G. (ed.) (2001). *Global Feminisms since 1945.* NY: Routledge.

Smith, Jackie (2000). "Social Movements, International Institutions and Local empowerment", Kendall Stiles (ed.) *Global Institutions and Local Empowerment: Competing Theoretical Perspectives,* New York: St.Martin's Press, p. 65-84.

Spakowski, Nicola (2000). "The Internationalization of China's Women's Studies," *Berliner China-Hefte,* 20, p. 79-100.

Stienstra, Deborah (2000). "Making Global Connections among Women, 1970-99 ", Robin Cohen & Shirin M. Rai (eds.) *Global Social Movement*, London & New Brunswick, NJ: the Athlone Press, p. 62-82.

Wang, Zheng (1997). "Maoism, Feminism, and the UN Conference on Women: Women's Studies Research in Contemporary China", *Journal of Women's History*, 8, no. 4, p. 126-143.

Wong, Yuenling (red) (1995). *Reflections and Resonance: Stories of Chinese Women Involved in International Preparatory Activities for the 1995 NGO Forum on Women.* Beijing, Ford Foundation.

Xu, Wu, Xu Ping, Bao Xiaolan, Gao Xioalxian (eds.) (2000). *Shehui Xingbie fenxi:Pinkun yu nongcun fashan (Gender analysis: Poverty and Rural Development)*, Chengdu: Sichuan People's Press.

Yi, Ying (2000). Dangdai zhongguo funü yanjiu zuzhi chutan (primary review of women's studies organizations in modern China*), Funü Yanjiu luncong (Collection of women's studies),* 2000, 2: 34-38.

Yin, Yungong (1994).*"wei shixian 'guojia baogoa' queli de gexian mubian er nuli fendou"* (*strive to achieve the goals set in the 'State Report'*), *Zhong guo fu yun (Chinese Women's Movement)*, 12, p.13-14.

Zhang, Naihua (2001). "Searching for 'Authentic' NGOs: the NGO Discourse and Women's Organizations in China," Ping-Chun Hsiung, Maria Jaschok, & Cecilia Milwertz (eds.) *Chinese Women Organizing: Cadres, Feminists, Muslims, Queers.* Oxford, England: Berg Publishers.

Zhang, Naihua & Wu Xu (1995). "Discovering the Positive Within the Negative: The Women's Movement in a Changing China", Amrita Basu (ed.) *The Challenge of Local Feminisms: Women's Movements in Global Perspective.* Boulder, San Francisco, Oxford: Westview Press, p. 25-57.

Notes

1 For discussion of the debate, see Hsiung and Wong 1998; for controversy over whether the state supported All China Women's Federation was legitimate to attend the NGO forum, see Zhang, 2001.

2 For example, the attitudes of the government toward the conference kept shifting, from an early embrace to the opportunity to hold the event to subsequent paranoia and tightened control, which reached its height during the conference, and finally to claiming the victory of holding a successful international conference afterwards. Wang, 1997.

3 See Morgan, 1996, for her observation of the Conference; and Howell, 1997, for her post-conference evaluation of the event. An exception in their positive evaluation of the Conference was Hsiung and Wong, 1998.

4 See Lu and Zheng, 1990.

5 Gilmartin, 1995.

6 See the discussion of Marxism and feminism in Yukina's chapter in this volume

7 For China's position on a separate women's movement and the issue of peace, see the speech given by the head of the Chinese delegation to the Mexico Conference in 1975 (Li, 1975); for the Chinese government's support for the UN Decade for Women and its themes, see report on Deng Yingchao's statement, People's Daily, May 15, 1980:1.

8 Liu, 1999.

9 Zhang and Xu, 1995.

10 NGO is an abbreviation for Non Governemntal Organizations.

11 For their personal stories and experiences with the 95'Conference, see Wong, 1995.

12 Even though many of the actions were taken by the government intended to demonstrate China's commitment to women's affairs and its "superior" record, as openly admitted by those involved in the formulation of the two pre-Conference documents. See Yin, 1994; Kang, 1996.

13 Molyneux, 1996.

14 They are areas that need to be addressed to overcome discrimination and inequality experienced by women, including poverty, education and training, health care, violence against women, armed conflict, economic structure and polices, political participation and decision making, mechanisms to promote the advancement of women, human rights, media, environment, and female children.

15 Impressed by the prevalence and prominence of "gender" in the 95' documents, a All-China Women's Federation leader proposed "mainstreaming the gender perspective in decision mak-

ing." Soon after, its chairwoman further stated that "Marxist view on women analyzes women's problem from a gender perspective. Its essence is equality between men and women." See Li, 1999. The Women's Federation leader later discovered the inaccuracy of this statement. Unable to resolve the relationship between 'gender perspective" and the official "Marxist view on women," the Women's Federation dropped "mainstreaming gender perspective in decision making" from the official documents of the Federation's national conference in 1998. Towards the end of 2001, the Women's Federation chairwoman openly acknowledged that gender as a "perspective", a "method of analysis" should be critically employed in the study of women's conditions and position in China while Marxist theories on women should remain the foundation for theorizing women's issues in China. See Peng, 2001.

16   See Zhang, 2001.

17   See Cecilia Milwertz's discussion in this book on domestic violence in China.

18   For more on the role of the Beijing Ford Foundation and influence of international feminism, see Spakowaski, 2000. The implications of foreign funding is discussed also in Hetlinger and Rönnblom in this volume.

19   Milwertz, 2001.

20   See Beatrice Halsaa's chapter in this volume.

21   This term is used in China to describe women of higher education who work as professionals – professors, researchers, writers, journalists, artists, and so on.

22   See Du, 2000.

23   See Yi, 2000.

24   Liu, 1999.

25   Last summer, a scholar wrote to Chinese Women's News, against incorporating the gender perspective in the Chinese official theoretical framework on women's issues, arguing that it is ahistorical, anti-man and would hinder emancipation of women and mankind (from my interview, Beijing, summer, 2001)

26   liu, 1999.

27   For example, it is translated either into xinbei (similar to Chinese word sex) or to she-hui xingbei (social sex) – emphasizing its social construction. While the latter is a better and more critically minded translation and is taking hold in academia and the women's media, it can perpetuate the dichotomy of sex and gender as concepts in opposition, each occupying a separate, either biological or social, realm. Now "gender equality " – the most popular phrase in the international women's movement is being used more in China. I am afraid that its literal translation – either as "sex equality" or "social sex equality" now appearing in the media and in official documents is doing a disservice to the banner of the Chinese women's movement that has been expressed since the beginning of the 20th century as nan nu pingdeng (equality between men and women).

28   From my interview in China, summer, 2001.

29   See Xu et al., 2000, and their forthcoming book based on a workshop on Ethnicity and Community Development held in Guiyang, China, 2001.

30   I credit Lihua Wang for this observation. She is now doing research on this topic. Also see Ellen Judd, 2002, who dubbed the indigenous 'two studies, two competitions' campaign initiated by the Women's Federation to help rural women be competitive in rural economy through literacy and technical training "GAD with Chinese characteristics." (s.33)

31   Information in this paragraph is from my interview in China, summer and winter, 2001, unless specified otherwise.

32   Yi, 2000.

33 Among them, the Shaanxi Women's Theories, Marriage and Family Research Society and Rural Women knowing All magazine in Beijing.
34 Li, 2001.
35 From my interview in China, summer 2001.
36 For more discussion of the All- China Women's Federation, see Zhang, 2001, and for its work among rural women since 1989, see Judd, 2001.
37 Jiang 2001.
38 While sharing a consensus acknowledging the amazing expansion of the women's movements at both the global and local levels since the UN Decade for Women, some scholars emphasize the coming of age of the global women's movement Bunch (1985), Moghadam (1996), Chen (1995), Rupp (1997), Stienstra (2000), while others stress the diverse, dynamic women's movements with local origins, characteristics and concerns Basu (1995), Smith, J. (2000), Smith, B. (2001), Cockburn (2000).
39 Spakowski, (2000).
40 Li (2000) p. 62f, cited from Spakowski (2000), p. 94.
41 Howell (1997).

CHAPTER 10

Cross-border Connections of Czech Women's Groups:

The Role of Foreign Funding*

Alena Heitlinger

The main goal of this article is to explore the nature of cross-border links involving women and feminism in post-communist Czech Republic. The article highlights local and transnational women's networks and organizations to which Czech women activists belong, documents sources of funding for Czech women's projects, and evaluates the impact of foreign funding and cross-border networking on the legitimacy, empowerment, and survival/viability of local women's groups. It concludes with an assessment of the ways in which sponsorship by foreign organizations has increased the capacity of women's groups for both local and transnational networking, and for domestic political influence.

Conceptualising cross-border feminisms

Various authors have defined cross-border feminisms differently, but they all start from the premise that local feminisms vary across time and space, that feminist ideas and practices cross national borders, and that the transnational diffusion of the political and academic discourses of feminism is a constitutive dimension of globalization, involving networking, co-operation, and transfer of resources among women and women's movements worldwide.[1] The main limitations of this literature are its neglect of history, its preoccupation with the North-South (or 'Western' – 'Third World') axis at the expense of post-communist countries in East Central Europe, and its lack of attention to the significance of international funding for local and global feminist movements.

Contrary to the popular wisdom created by some of the writings on the globalizing world economy, cross-border links involving women and feminism are not only a late twentieth century phenomenon. For example, Czech feminism in the Habsburg

*   Research for this article was carried out with the financial assistance of a grant from the Social Science and Humanities Research Council of Canada (No. 410-98-0225). I would also like to thank my research assistant Mirek Vodrazka for his invaluable contribution to the research project, and to members of the WMI Network for their helpful comments on an earlier draft of this article.

Monarchy[2] was deeply embedded in transnational feminist organizations and personal networks.[3] Cross-border connections between various women's organizations within Latin America can also be traced to the nineteenth century, as can Latin American memberships in a number of international women's organizations.[4] Similar developments occurred in Asia and in what we now call the Middle East.[5]

Cross-border feminist networks represent three distinct forms of feminism: international, transnational, and global. Moghadam[6] defines international feminism as synonymous with international women's organizations such as the Women's International League for Peace, The International Young Women's Christian Association, or the International Federation of Business and Professional Women. In existence for several decades and in some cases for over 100 years, most of these organizations have local branches or other forms of federative links to women's movements and organizations in various countries, including the Czech Republic. Moghadam[7] makes clear that "*international* is not the same as *transnational*, which suggests a conscious crossing of national boundaries and superseding of national orientation." In turn, she defines *global feminism* as "the discourse and movement of women aimed at advancing the status of women through greater access to resources, legal measures to effect gender equality and the self-empowerment of women within national boundaries but through transnational forms of organizing and mobilizing".[8]

Thus, then as now, international and global feminisms have entailed flows not simply of ideas, but also of money, organizational forms, and power relations. Making funds available for bringing women from poorer countries to attend conferences in the West, translating and reproducing locally pamphlets and documents produced by activists in the U.S. and Western Europe, setting up local branches, and organizing national tours by foreign activists are practices of some historical standing.[9] Moreover, the historical and cross-national record also suggests that local and cross-border feminisms can be equated not only with oppositional political practice, but also with numerous class-based projects. These include the various middle-class dominated suffragist movements and the socialist feminisms of the Second International or the Third Communist International (Comintern).[10]

According to Moghadam, global feminism "is predicated upon the notion that notwithstanding cultural, class and ideological differences among the women of the world, there is a commonality in the forms of women's disadvantage and the forms of women's organizations worldwide." Thus, in her view, "feminist groups and women's organizations remain rooted in national or local issues, but their vocabulary, strategies and objectives have much in common with each other and have taken on an increasingly supra-national form".[11]

Czech women's groups and cross-border feminisms

Although feminism has a strong negative connotation in the Czech Republic, there is a nascent, grassroots women's movement which has emerged in wake of the November 1989 Velvet Revolution. The movement functions as a loose and fluctuating network of thirty or so women's groups, which have self-organized around a wide spectrum of "single issues" such as education, consulting, human rights, art, religion, violence against women, environmental pollution, prostitution, lesbianism, single motherhood, and women's entrepreneurship. Some additional groups have formed as women's sections of political parties or local branches of international women's organizations. Functioning as clubs, professional associations, social service and educational organizations, foundations, and public advocacy groups, the women's groups cooperate on all kinds of issues, and increasingly form a vibrant but highly vulnerable women's movement.[12]

The groups are quite diverse, small, and mainly Prague-based.[13] For the most part, they fall under the rubric of what Jenkins calls *"professional movement organizations*[14]*,* which are staff-driven, derive their resources from institutions and isolated constituencies, and 'speak for' rather than organize their official beneficiaries". The only group with a mass membership base and a national profile is the successor to the communist Czech Union of Women (CUW). Its main focus is on rural areas and small towns, and its leader, Zdenka Hajná, has been quite effective politically. However, Prague, as the country's capital and the largest city, is where lobbying and attempts to influence state policy take place, so the location of the majority of the women's groups there is hardly surprising.

There are some genuine political advantages for professional movement organizations in remaining small and diverse. As the spokesperson of one of the leading women's groups, ProFem, explained to Poole in an interview,

> we believe that we would not gain anything from merging with other groups because we are not an organisation based on membership. If we were an organisation that has members, then we could merge to one big organisation. But in the situation when we don't have a lot of members, we would be a small organisation. But when it comes to political lobbying we can co-operate and work together. And when we are not one organisation trying to influence the government, but four or five, we have more influence. So if the organisations that exist today were one big organisation, we would not be stronger. We would still be a small organisation, and only one.[15]

Another advantage, pointed out by Moghadam, is that "the smaller the group, the more opportunities members have to get to know other people well and establish close ties with them".[16] Among the Czech women activists, the ties have varied from close friendships to mere acquaintance or secondary relationships. Notwithstanding some personal animosities and conflicts, the personal ties have been key to both domestic and transnational networking and coalition building.[17]

As in post-communist Russia[18], most of the Czech women's groups were inspired by and formed networks with similar groups abroad only after the fall of communism. The Czech Union of Women, founded in 1967, is the only women's organization that was established prior to the Velvet Revolution.[19] The federative international networks to which some of the Czech groups belong include the IYWCA, United Rural Women of the World (Czech Union of Women), European Ecumenical Women's Forum (Eunika), and the Watch Union of Catholic Women's Organizations (Union of Catholic Women). Groups belonging to looser transnational networks include Gender Studies Centre and ProFem (FAS, the Network of Central and East European Women's Projects linked with the German Frauen-Anstiftung foundation); LaStrada (member of a Dutch- and EU-financed transnational network dedicated to the prevention of trafficking in women, which also operates in Poland, the Ukraine, Bulgaria, the Netherlands and, to a more limited extent, Russia[20]; Bliss without Risk (which focuses on the needs of sex workers); GAIA (part of a transnational ecofeminist network); and the Association of Women Entrepreneurs and Managers (which has links to several transnational business women's networks). The Social Democratic Women group is active in a Norwegian-sponsored transnational project called "Women Can", whose goal is to offer training to women interested in democratic political activity. Social Democratic Women also belong to the supra-national European Union Network of Equal Opportunities. Most groups belong to more than one network, thus creating many points of intersection, which are conducive to coalition building and mutual cooperation.

As Poole has pointed out, the European Union has been particularly important for framing issues of women's equality, networking, and accessing foreign funding.[21] The existence of EU women's networks, directives, declarations, and programmes have enhanced Czech women's groups' legitimacy, and helped in their selection of political priorities. As Barbel Butterwech, the German-born and Czech-speaking leader of LaStrada has pointed out in an interview,

> in the field of women's issues the EU have declarations where the issue of trafficking in women is mentioned. So, I believe that using the Czech application for the EU is our big chance to get Czech politicians to listen to us. My colleagues from Poland are thinking the same, and they tell us that the Polish State attitudes have changed because of their application for membership in the EU. I think that when the Czech Republic became an official candidate… the ministries began to invite us to different commissions, they became more eager to get information from us, and they even financed some small projects for us. So, I think that the attitudes towards us have changed since the Czech Republic became an official member candidate. The EU, on the other hand, is pressuring the Czech Republic to take women's issues more seriously. Now the government needs information from us. For us political work is more fun than it used to be, and this kind of work is starting to get very interesting.[22]

The capacity of a social movement to form successful transnational coalitions is often key to its success, especially in situations when domestic structures initially inhibit its activities. Cross-border contacts between movements with overlapping agendas can therefore empower social movements which are domestically weak, thus enabling those movements to have a greater impact on societal transformation than might otherwise be the case.[23] Transnational networking can facilitate the introduction of new terminology, political strategies, organizational forms, and sources of funding. As Sperling has argued for Russia, "not only have terms like "gender" permeated Russian women's activists vocabularies, but, as the movement increasingly tries to affect the policy process, a new series of terms has been borrowed to express activities and ideas that were largely absent from the Soviet political scene – because the NGO sector too was absent – terms like 'advocacy' and 'lobbying' (lobbirovanie). Similarly, the presence of foreign granting organizations has brought terms like 'granty', 'fandraising', and 'treining' into common movement parlance."[24]

The tendency in Anglo-American feminist literature has been to regard international and global feminist practices as a form of domination by Western feminists, who generally have superior financial resources and a more developed feminist theory and political practice.[25]

However, for those at the receiving end, these connections often have different meanings, since they can bring resources and create valuable autonomous political spaces which otherwise would not exist. Thus the Prague Gender Studies Centre owes its existence not only to its founder, Jirina Siklová, but also to the discursive and financial assistance from the U.S.-based Network of East-West Women, and the German feminist foundation Frauen-Anstiftung.[26]

Fiscal ressources

Since transnational and global feminisms involve not just flows of ideas and people, but also of money, political opportunities, organizational structures, and power relations, it is important to document the sources of funding of local women's groups, and analyze the impact of the type of funding received on the legitimacy, scope, and viability of these groups. Since the post-communist transition to a market economy, democracy and civil society is occurring in a global context, the nation state is not necessarily the only or even the optimal focus of feminist political efforts. In fact, throughout the 1990s, Western governments, multilateral organizations, and private individuals and foundations have been in the forefront in encouraging the development of civil society in post-communist states, mainly through the funding of non-governmental voluntary associations.[27] The director of the Civil Society Development Foundation, funded by the European Union's PHARE program for Central Europe, estimated that half of the funds for Czech non-profit non-governmental organizations (NGOs) had come from foreign sources.[28]

The dependency of women's groups on foreign funding has been much greater. Busheikin's and Potocková's guide to funding opportunities for women's projects in the Czech non-profit sector lists thirty international and only five Czech sources.[29] While the Czech sources are limited to state funding through the ministries of culture, the environment, work and social affairs, health, and education and youth, the international funds are much more diverse. They include several programs funded by the European Union, assistance projects funded by various Western governments, grants provided by foundations sponsored by German political parties (such as Frauen-Anstiftung/Heinrich Böll-Stiftung sponsored by the Green Party), and aid from private foundations such as the Ford Foundation or the Open Society Fund sponsored by the financier George Soros. The guide also lists eight international women's organizations and networks providing nonmaterial assistance. The publication of the guide was itself sponsored by a foreign source, the German feminist foundation Frauen-Anstiftung.

All Czech women's groups have severe financing problems, with the possible exception of the mass-based CUW. As a successor to the communist Czech Union of Women, CUW did not have to start building its infrastructure from scratch. The Union has also been quite successful in attracting multiple project funding from both domestic and foreign sources. CUW's communist legacy and its better material resources have been deeply resented by most of the other groups. They typically either receive no funding at all (i.e. they are run entirely by dedicated volunteers), or their funding is quite precarious, consisting of special project money rather than unrestricted operating grants. As we noted, most of the Czech groups are volunteer or paid staff-driven professional movement organizations with few members, which operate on the basis of organizational patronage and clientism. The women's NGOs are typically funded with grants for specific small-scale projects from national and especially foreign organizations. Failure to secure such patronage, and excessive reliance on a handful of dedicated individual volunteers, have led in varying degrees to personal burn-out, restriction of the number and the scope of activities undertaken, and in several cases, institutional collapse. Success in obtaining and keeping a grant has often resulted in 'mainstreaming' and adjustment of discourse. For example, Barbel Butterwech from LaStrada (a group working against trafficking in women) stated in an interview, that "if we were not completely dependent on our donors, we would certainly be more radical, in the sense that we would stress more the situation of women rather than talk generally about criminality."[30]

Foreign funding

The EU PHARE program, designed to support the development of a post-communist civil society, has been of particular significance for Czech women's groups. For example, Zdenka Hajná, the previously mentioned leader of the Czech Union of Women, has acknowledged in an interview that obtaining a grant from the EU PHARE democracy project was very helpful in building up CUW. She also acknowledged that once CUW "was entered into the data base of the European Union as a participant in the project PHARE democracy, then automatically the Union would receive an invitation to apply for all sorts of projects."[31] However, as a large bureaucratic organization, the EU mode of operation tends to favour organizations which are already privileged in terms of personnel and fiscal resources. As is well known, preparing a grant application for every project requires specific writing and organizational skills, and is an extremely time- and labour-consuming process. The EU is also notorious for taking its time to transfer money for projects it has approved. What this means is that many activities have to be financed from other sources before the grant finally arrives, which again privileges already established groups.[32]

Thus not all experiences with EU funding have been positive. As the highly experienced Jana Outratová, the founder of the International Women's Network (IWN), who during 1968-1989 lived in exile in Canada, stated in an interview,

> the rules for accessing [grants] though PHARE or the EU are unclear and impossible to understand, and I am now convinced that this is deliberate. I am not that daft that after a two years' effort I am still in the dark. In fact, I have now given up and I will try to get funds from local entrepreneurs, because I will not waste my youth on filling application forms which turn out to be a waste of time. I even paid my own way to attend a seminar in Vienna called "Women Managers European Union Project." After spending two days at the seminar, we were all agape, and told the lecturer, 'Excuse us, we don't understand, the rules are not clear to us'. His answer was that 'Yes, you are right, the rules are not clear, and I have no idea when they will be clear, because [EU officials] are re-working them, and the rules will be ready when they are ready.' I am regularly phoning Brussels to ask them when they will send me the rules governing applications for EU projects, and their answer always is 'next month'. [33, 34]

Outratová found applying for funds provided by the Canadian government much easier, since in her experience, the Canadian granting agencies tend "not to play any silly games. They want concrete work and concrete results, and writing that grant application won't take too much time at all." Donor agencies with established local branches, such as *Open Society Fund Praha (OPFP)* make the grant application process somewhat easier, but the funds are earmarked for highly specialized, small-scale, one-time projects. For example, OPFPs advertisement of its "Gender" grant program cites the following eligible activities as examples of activities on gender issues OPSFP is interested in funding: public seminars, courses, round tables and so on, publication of new textbooks, and staging art exhibits.[35]

Only two organizations – Gender Studies Centre and ProFem – have had foreign operational funding. As noted, the Gender Studies Centre was started in 1991 in her apartment by the well known Charter 77 dissident Jirina Siklová. Discursive and one-time financial assistance came initially from the U.S.-based Network of East-West Women. A more stable operational funding was in 1992 secured by Alexandra (Saša) Marie Lienau from the German feminist foundation Frauen-Anstiftung (FAS), where she was then employed.[36] While helpful and crucial for the Centre's survival, this financing has not been without its problems. As a rule, Western and supra-national granting agencies have provided funds for NGOs rather than for universities and academic programs, and this has presented particular difficulties for the Gender Studies Centre. Although the Centre has an excellent library, it cannot hire academics and offer credit courses. All it has been able to do academically is to run an annual series of popular lectures on variety of topics, both by local speakers and by visitors from abroad. Moreover, as a Western-funded institution, the Centre can offer what by local standards is a generous speaker's fee, thus creating tensions caused by the wide discrepancy between what the Centre and what local universities can pay. Yet the positive role of the Prague Gender Studies Centre is undisputable, given that the NGO organizational form was the only way in which Western funds could be tapped and utilized.

ProFem, with its revealing sub-title – Central European Consultation Centre for Women's projects – was founded in November 1993 by the already mentioned Saša Lienau within the framework of Frauen-Anstiftung. By 1993, FAS was financially supporting several women's projects in the Czech Republic, Slovakia, Russia and Poland, and was increasingly worried about the lack of proper management and fiscal accountability. Since the informal character of the groups was creating problems for FAS in its relations with the German state, something had to be done. Hence came the idea to establish a feminist consultancy organization for all post-communist countries in Europe to advise women "how to manage an organization, how to form its structure, what form the organization should choose (association, foundation, etc.) and also to offer psychological counselling".[37] To this end, during the past decade ProFem has organized 'open houses', seminars and courses focusing on various forms of self-help including self-employment, self-defense, fundraising for women's projects, and women's involvement in politics. ProFem soon became formally independent of FAS, and assumed a character of a FAS-supported project.[38]

In the early post-communist period, the German Green Party was quite eager to support grass roots women's organizations in post-communist East Central Europe, and both FAS and the groups it supported had lots of independence. The relationship between FAS and its partner-organizations was non-hierarchical and democratic, allowing for an open debate about the politics of funding, and thus meeting all of the criteria Moghadam identified as characterizing global feminism.[39] As Engert described it, FAS "reached a level of cooperation in which the partners do not simply act as representatives of their organization at home, but as participants in joint network, where projects are planned and realized cooperatively, with a division of labour between different countries. This means not just projects of the projects, but also a common concern for the management and the politics of the whole net".[40] However, such genuinely feminist forms of collaboration and funding will be much harder to secure in the future, since the Green Party is now less interested in funding feminist NGOs, and more interested in "supporting political parties. The Green Party wants women's organisations to co-operate with environmental groups in founding a political party".[41] FAS no longer exists: in 1998 the three separate foundations that used to operate under the Green Party were merged into one, the Heinrich-Böll-Stiftung. The latter no longer supports ProFem with operational funding. Thus it is by no means certain that ProFem will survive, though it certainly cannot be yet written off. ProFem has been active in collaborative projects concerning violence against women, for which there is some local funding, and Saša has been trying to transform ProFem into a feminist legal advisory clinic she would like to call "Advocats for Women".[42]

It is clear that without foreign funding, most of the Czech women's groups would be considerably weaker, and many would cease to exist. The success of foreign sponsorship of Czech women's groups in the early post-communist period demonstrates that even small amounts of money can make a huge difference to a social movement, by providing resources for books, journals and conferences, and for an office with telephone, fax, computer, and paid staff. Such resources are critical to all social movements aiming to mobilize and gain political voice. However, as most of the foreign funding has been limited to special project grants, and is in any case declining, in order to keep operating, Czech women's groups have been forced to seek multiple grants, and increasingly rely on domestic sources of support.

Domestic funding

Women's groups offering services under the rubrics of arts and culture, the environment, employment and social affairs, health, and education have been able to access some state project funding through the ministries, municipalities, and grant-giving NGOs operating in these areas. The groups which have been able to fund some of their activities in this way include Bliss without Risk (for work in health education, especially AIDS), Czech Union of Women (for running a training school for 16-19 years old girls in the city of Brno and summer camps for children with family problems), YWCA (for after-school activities), and GAIA (for several ecological initiatives). The Association of Women Entrepreneurs and Managers obtained a one-time project grant from the Ministry of Trade and Industry, while the Democratic Alternative and the Movement for Women's Equal Rights in the Czech Republic were granted funds for specific translation projects by the Ministry of Foreign Affairs. However, state grants often come with various strings attached, including the prohibition to use them for paying salaries.[43]

Czech post-socialist governments have not been eager to fund women's groups (or NGOs in general), though this has begun to change in recent years as a result of pressure from the European Union. In 1998, after the fall of the second Klaus government, the interim Tošovský government set up seven government committees with the mandate to fund NGOs operating in areas such as health, education, human rights, and environmental protection. The revenue for these NGOs' grants was supposed to come from the proceeds of privatization of state assets, but these have been well below expectation and are quite insufficient. Moreover, since there is no local foundation for women's projects[44], women's groups could not receive any of these project grants directly as women's groups. They could apply for them only as service providers in the eligible areas, where they had to compete with more established non-women's groups.

As Fric and Goulli have argued, the Czech state allocation of NGO grants has favoured organizations which have eschewed public advocacy, or which were in existence already during the communist era (such as the trade unions or various professional associations).[45] Such organizations were able to establish relatively good working relations with the state, since they addressed "routine problems, the solutions of which did not bring them into conflict with the government or the ministries. "In contrast, "new organizations (founded after 1989) had to first establish relations with state agencies, and by their naming of new problems, criticism of current government approaches to social problems, and non-traditional methods of solving them, upset the routine of public administration… State officials were not familiar with such situations, and were not used to negotiating with various interest groups and organizations. Even today government officials tend to act from a position of a monopolistic supplier of social services." Moreover, whatever state funding was received was limited to one-time as opposed to meeting recurring annual expenses.[46] Thus due to the severe underfunding and institutional structures working against women's groups, the Czech state NGO initiative has been a failure for women's projects. Instead of creating a viable alternative to foreign funding, it has prolonged the 'agony of dying'.

The history of the group Bliss without Risk (BWR) – an advocacy group for prostitutes founded by sociologist and amateur theatre director Dr. Hana Malinová – is a case in point. Established in 1992 after Hana attended, in the fall of 1991, in Frankfurt am Main, Germany, the first European Congress of Prostitutes, BWR's activities have been focused on an innovative and highly successful club house/health clinic located in the centre of Prague, where sex workers could relax and receive anonymous medical check-up for sexually transmitted diseases (STD). Another initiative has been an ambulance serving as a mobile ambulatory laboratory for STD testing. Initially without any financial resources, BWR was supported for the first nine months of its existence with very little money out of Dr. Malinová's architect husband's earnings. However, Hana's networking at a conference entitled "AIDS and WE" brought some funding, initially from a Czech-Slovak-Swiss Health Association and later from the EU PHARE program, the Czech Olga Havlová's foundation (which specializes in health issues), and for office/club house renovation from Prague municipal housing agency.[47] BWR also received a one-time project grant from the Czech Ministry of Health, but like many other NGO grants, that grant could not cover Dr. Malinová's salary. Thus, when re-interviewed in May 2001, Dr. Malinová was unemployed and lived on social assistance, and BWR ceased to operate. BWR has been unable to attract sufficient domestic funding despite the undeniable success of the project, the important social service BWR has provided for the sex workers and in AIDS prevention, and a favourable Czech TV coverage, such as the special 2-part documentary on BRW which was broadcast by Czech TV on May 18 and 25, 2001.[48]

Groups which are affiliated with domestic political parties or religious organizations, such as Social Democratic Women or the Union of Catholic women, have been able to access some operational funding from their parent organizations. However, such funds also come with strings attached, since the affiliated women's group typically loses some of its political independence. Moreover, the fiscal crisis of the Social Democratic Party in the late 1990s demonstrates the vulnerability of such funding. The drastic cuts the Social Democrats were forced to make were passed down to the women's group, with the result that Social Democratic Women now have the same problems with financing as all the other Czech women's groups.[49] Groups involved in class-based projects such as the Association of Women Entrepreneurs and Managers or the International Women's Network have obtained some funding from corporate sponsorship, but this option is obviously not open to groups engaged in more opposi-tional activities, or to groups serving marginalized and stigmatized client groups such as prostitutes.

Relying on revenues from membership fees is also not a viable fundraising strat-egy, because of the small size of the Czech women's groups, the interrupted tradition of philanthropy (during the communist era), and the poverty and stigmatization of some of the clients the groups serve. However, several groups – the Czech Union of Women, YWCA, Prague Mothers, Social Democratic Women, the Association of Women Entrepreneurs and Managers (AWEM), GAIA, Forum of Women, and the Clubs of Christian Women – collect membership dues, and more groups might do so in the future, especially if institutional sponsorship continues to decline.

Conclusion

More than a decade has passed since communism collapsed in Czechoslovakia. During that time, the climate of political pluralism has taken root (evidenced, among other things, in the peaceful break-up of Czechoslovakia in 1993), and Czech women activ-ists have acquired an impressive range of political and organizational skills. They have learned how to self-organize, work with very limited funds, write grant applications to domestic and foreign agencies, how to manage an NGO, and how to take advantage of windows of political opportunity, such as the Czech Republic's becoming an official candidate for membership in the European Union. They have also learned the kinds of issues on which they can agree and cooperate. Thus, the main conclusion to draw is that transnational networking and foreign funding have given Czech women greater political voice, and empowered them in their struggle for equality, social justice, and the building of a democratic civil society. What has not been achieved is Czech state recognition of the importance of women's NGOs. Such recognition, in the form of some on-going operational funding, might come too late to ensure the survival of many of the women's groups currently operating in the Czech Republic.

References

Alexander, Jacqui M. & Chandra Talpade Mohanty (ed.) (1997). *Feminist Genealogies, Colo-nial Legacies, Democratic Futures,* New York, Routledge.

Basu, Amrita (ed.) (1995). *The Challenge of Local Feminisms. Women's Movements in Global Perspective,* Boulder, Co.,Westview Press.

Busheikin, Laura (1993). "Is Sisterhood Really Global? Western Feminism in Eastern Europe", p. Trnka, with L. Busheikin (eds.) *Bodies of Bread and Butter: Reconfiguring Women's Lives in the Post-Communist Czech Republic,* Prague, Gender Studies Centre), p. 69-76. Reprinted in Tanya Renne (ed.) (1997). *Ana's Land. Sisterhood in Eastern Europe,* Boulder, Co.,Westview Press, p. 12-25.

Busheikin, Laura & Dana Potocková (1996). *Kabelky plný prachu. Pruvodce fondy pro zenské projekty v neziskovém sektoru,* Praha, ProFem.

Chilton, Patricia (1995). "Mechanics of Change: Social Movements, Transnational Coalitions, and the Transformation Processes in Eastern Europe", Thomas Risse-Kappen (ed.), *Bringing Transnational Relations Back In: Non-State Actors, Domestic Structures and International Institutions*, Cambridge, Cambridge University Press, p. 189-226.

David-Fox, Katherine (1991). "Czech Feminists and Nationalism in the Late Habsburg Monarchy: 'The First in Austria'", *Journal of Women's History*, 3. Fall, nr. 2, p. 26-45.

Engert, Steffi (1995). "The Network of Central and Eastern European Women's Projects Linked with the FAS", Aspekt collective (eds.) *Prelude. New Women's Initiatives in Contemporary Central and Eastern Europe and Turkey.* Hamburg/Bratislava, Frauen-Anstiftung, p. 78-80.

Fric, Pavol & Goulli, Rochdi (2001). *Neziskovy sektor v Ceske republice,* Praha, Eurolex Bohemia.

Grewal, Inderpal & Caren Kaplan (eds.) (1994). *Scattered Hegemonies: Postmodernity and Transnational Feminist Practices,* St. Paul, University of Minnesota.

Hauserová, Eva (ed.) (1994). *Altos and sopranos (a pocket handbook of women's organizations),* Prague, Gender Studies Centre.

Heitlinger, Alena (1996). "Framing Feminism in Postcommunist Czech Republic", *Communist and Post-Communist Studies,* 29. March, nr. 1, p. 77-93.

Heitlinger, Alena (1999). "Introduction", Alena Heitlinger (ed.) *Émigré Feminism: Transnational Perspectives*, Toronto, University of Toronto Press, p. 3-16.

Iggers, Wilma A. (1995). *Women of Prague. Ethnic Diversity and Social Change from the Eighteenth Century to the Present*, Providence, R.I./Oxford, U.K., Berghahn Books.

Jayawardena, Kumari (1986). *Feminism and Nationalism in the Third World,* London, Zed Books.

Jenkins, Craig J. (1998). "Channeling Social Protest: Foundation Patronage of Contemporary Social Movements", Walter P. Powell & Elisabeth p. Clements (eds.) *Private Action and the Public Good* (New Haven and London: Yale University Press), p. 206-216.

Lienau, Marie (1995) "Profem (Central European Consultation Centre for Women's Projects)", Aspekt collective (eds). *Prelude. New Women's Initiatives in Contemporary Central and Eastern Europe and Turkey,* Hamburg/Bratislava, Frauen-Anstiftung, p. 24-25.

Mani, Lata (1990). "Multiple Mediations: Feminist Scholarship in the Age of Multinational Reception", *Feminist Review*, 35. Summer, p. 24-41.

Mies, Maria & Vandana Shiva (1993). *Ecofeminism*, London, Zed Books; Halifax, Fernwood Publications.

Miles, Angela (1996). *Integrative Feminisms. Building Global Visions, 1960s – 1990s,* New York, Routledge.

Moghadam, Valentine (1996). "Feminist Networks North and South. DAWN, WIDE and WLUML", *The Journal of International Communication*, 3. nr. 1, p. 111-126.

Moghadam, Valentine (2000). "Transnational Feminist Networks. Collective Action in an Era of Globalization", *International Sociology*, 15. March, nr. 1, p. 57-85.

Mohanty, Chandra Talpade, Ann Russo & Lourdes Torres (eds.) (1991*) Third World Women and the Politics of Feminism*, Bloomington, Indiana University Press.

Molyneux, Maxine (1998). "Analysing Women's Movements", Cecile Jackson & Ruth Pearson (eds.) *Feminist Visions of Development. Gender Analysis and Policy*, London, Routledge, p. 65-88.

Olson, David M. (1997). "Democratization and Political Participation: the Experience of the Czech Republic", Karen Dawisha and Bruce Parrott (eds.) *The Consolidation of Democracy in East-Central Europe,* Cambridge, Cambridge University Press, p. 150-196.

Peterson, Spike V. & Anne Sisson Runyan (1993). *Global Gender Issues,* Boulder, Co., Westview Press.

Pettman, Jan Jindy (1996). *Worlding Women. A Feminist International Politics,* Sydney, Allen & Unwin; New York, Routledge.

Poole, Sonja (2000). *The Emergence of a Women's Movement in the Czech Republic: Opportunities, Mobilising Structures and Framing.* An unpublished MA thesis, Department of Administration and Organisation Science, University of Bergen, Norway.

Saxonberg, Steven (2001). "In the Shadow of Amicable Gender Relations", Helena Flam (ed.) *Pink, Purple, Green: Women's Religious, Environmental, and Gay/Lesbian Movements in Central Europe Today,* Boulder, East European Monographs.

Schild, Veronica (1999). "Transnational Links in the Making of Latin American Feminisms: a View from the Margins", Alena Heitlinger (ed.) *Émigré Feminism: Transnational Perspectives,* Toronto, University of Toronto Press, p. 67-94.

Snitow, Ann (1997). "Appendix: A Postscript to Laura Busheikin", Tanya Renne (ed.) *Ana's Land. Sisterhood in Eastern Europe,* Boulder, Co., Westview Press, p. 238-239.

Sperling, Valerie (1999*). Organizing Women in Contemporary Russia. Engendering Transition,* Cambridge, Cambridge University Press.

True, Jacqueline (1997). "Victimisation or Democratisation? Czech Women's Organising Potential in a Globalising Political Economy", *Statsvetenskaplig Tidskrift,* vol. 100, nr. 1 p. 47-62.

True, Jacqui (1999). "Antipodean Feminisms", Alena Heitlinger (ed.) *Émigré Feminism: Transnational Perspectives,* Toronto, University of Toronto Press, p. 267-293.

Notes

1 Mani (1990); Mohanty et al. (1991); Mies and Shiva (1993); Peterson and Runyan (1993); Grewal and Kaplan (1994); Basu (1995); Miles (1996); Moghadam (1996); Moghadam (2000); Pettman (1996); Alexander and Mohanty (1997); Schild (1999).

2 Although the Czechs date their national history to the Great Moravian state in the ninth century, the modern Czech national identity was formed only in the nineteenth century, during the process of national 'awakening'. The Czechs lost their independence in 1620, when Czech Protestant nobles were defeated by Austria in the Battle of White Mountain, the first battle of the Thirty Years War. The next two and a half centuries of Czech history, generally referred to in Czech textbooks as the 'Period of Darkness', were marked by re-Catholicization and Germanization. The Czech national 'awakening' began to gather momentum in the 1830s. Czech nationalists focused their efforts initially on the rehabilitation of the Czech language – but, as the movement expanded, the predominantly cultural definition of the Czech national identity gradually gave way to a more political conception, and to demands for political sovereignty. Thus the history of Czech feminism, and of some of its transnational links, is closely connected with the history of the Czech national movement. For example, the first Czech women's organization of significance – Prague's American Ladies Club – was founded in 1865 by an influential Czech male nationalist and philanthropist, who was forced to flee to America after the failure of

the 1848 revolutions. Vojta Naprstek spent the next ten years in Milwaukee, where he became interested in American feminism. Several years after his return to Prague, Naprstek began to invite prominent Czech 'ladies' of Prague to lectures by eminent speakers on 'women's topics' which he organized for them in the reading room of his house. He also made available to them his extensive library and a technical museum devoted to objects useful to women's work. The guest speakers included the future president of the First Czechoslovak Republic (1918-1939), Thomas Garriegue Masaryk. Another transnational link was provided by the American-born wife of Masaryk, Charlotte Garrigue, who in 1890 translated into Czech John Stuart Mill's *On the Subjection of Women*. She is also known to have strongly influenced Masaryk's feminist ideas on 'the woman question.' Czech feminists also belonged to an international women suffragists' alliance, and in 1913 hosted in Prague a contingent of delegates from ten countries en route to the International Suffrage Alliance in Budapest. For more details, see David-Fox (1991) p. 28-30; Iggers (1995), p. 17-19.

3   David-Fox (1991).

4   Schild (1999).

5   Jayawardena (1986), p. 17.

6   Moghadam (2000), p. 60.

7   Moghadam (2000), p. 60-61

8   Moghadam (2000), p. 62.

9   Heitlinger (1999), p. 8-9.

10 Heitlinger (1999), p. 10.

11 Moghadam (2000), p. 61-62.

12 As Molyneux (1998), p. 68, points out, "there are contrasting views as to what a women's movement is. On the one hand, there are clearly identifiable women's movements that, like those which mobilised to demand female suffrage, have a leadership, a membership, a broader following and a political programme. On the other hand, there are more diffuse forms of political activity which can also qualify as a movement, as distinct from other forms of women's solidarity such as those based on networks, clubs or groups. The definitional boundaries are complicated by the fact that networks or clubs sometimes develop into or form part of social movements." Moghadam (1996), p. 124-5, suggests that the "network form of a feminist organisation may be the most suited to transnational organising, mobilising, policy-oriented research and advocacy that also includes non-hierarchical and democratic objectives. It may also be the most effective form of feminist organising and mobilising in an era of globalisation." For literature on Czech women's movements, see Busheikin (1993); Hauserová (1994); Heitlinger (1996); True (1997); True (1999); Poole (2000); Saxonberg (2001).

13 Most of the data on Czech women's groups presented in this article are derived from interviews conducted during 1998-2001 by Mirek Vodrázka and myself with spokespersons of 28 women's groups. Vodrázka initially contacted officials of all of the 32 women's groups listed in Hauserová's (1994) guide to Czech women's initiatives. However, he soon found out (by trying to make a telephone or written contact) that the guide contained several defunct or non-functioning groups, such as the women's committee of PEN or L-klub Lambda. On the other hand, he also learned through informal networking about some groups which were not included in the guide, such as Eunika, Baaba, and Inkodnito. He also contacted the Union of Roma Women, but he soon learned that it is not clear who actually represents the group. Its first leader, Alzbeta Miková, was part of the first migration/refugee wave to the U.K. in 1996. Her successor, Ms. Ferkova, agreed to an interview for our project, but when Mirek Vodrázka made another attempt to contact her in the summer of 1999, he was told that Ms. Ferkova was currently in the U.K., and that she may, or may not, return to Prague, depending on her assess-

ment of the situation Czech (and Slovak) Romas face in the U.K. Additional interview data cited in this article are derived from Poole (2000) and Saxonberg (2001).

14 Jenkins (1998), p. 208

15 Poole (2000), p. 133

16 Moghadam (1996), p. 112

17 Interview with Laura Busheikin, July 23, 1998

18 See Sperling (1999), p. 220-254; Saarinen, in this volume; and Khodyreva, in this volume.

19 Groups such as the YWCA or the Clubs of Christian Women have a longer history than the Czech Union of Women, since they operated during the interwar period. When they re-established themselves in the wake of the Velvet Revolution, they were consciously re-claiming Czech pre-communist democratic tradition of civil society.

20 The impact of EU-sponsored networks and organizations involved in combating trafficking in women is not limited to EU members and official candidate members. For example, as Natalya Khodyreva points out in her chapter in this volume, the St. Petersburg Crisis Centre prepared in 2000 a report for the European Parliament on the trafficking situation in Russia, even though Russia is currently not an official candidate. In 1999, the St. Petersburg Crisis Centre participated in the meetings of experts in Warsaw devoted to the third anniversary of the La Strada project. Later that year, with the support of the Miramed Institute and "La Strada-Ukraine", the St. Petersburg organization joined the International Coalition Angel, an umbrella organization against trafficking from Russia, USA and NSI countries. See also Aino Saarinen in this volume, who discusses functional, 'glocal' links in "networks which are building bridges between actors combating prostitution and trafficking both in the countries of origin and of arrival far away from each other, within one continent, for example, in NW Russia and central Europe, and even across the continents, in the Asian Third World countries and Western Europe."

21 Poole (2000), p. 162-3.

22 Quoted in Poole (2000), p. 112.

23 Chilton (1995).

24 Sperling (1999), p. 245.

25 However, as Cecilia Milwertz points out in this volume, not all ideas and organizational structures flow unidirectionally from Euro-North American women's movements. "Not only were many young women in Europe and North America fascinated by images of the liberated, socialist Chinese woman. Moreover, consciousness raising – the sharing of personal experience, used as a means to shift the locus of problems from the personal to the political, which was an integral part of Euro-North American women's movements, was inspired by the Chinese practices of 'speaking bitterness'".

26 Busheikin (1993); Snitow (1997); Interviews with J. Siklová, February 2, 1999, and with A.M. Lienau, May 4, 2000.

27 For example, most of the crisis centres set up in the Russian Barents during the last part of the 1990s were funded by agencies from the Nordic countries, some West European countries, and the U.S. In fact, four nation states and several overlapping multinational institutions such as the UN, Council of Europe, the EU, NCM and the BEAR– the Barents Euro-Arctic administration – currently operate in the Barents region, forcing local women's movements to adopt complex, multi-layered and multi–tiered strategies for their political efforts (Saarinen, this volume).

28 Olson (1997), p. 161

29 Busheikin's and Potocková (1996).

30 Interview with Barbel Butterwech, June 9, 1999

31 Interview with Zdenka Hajná, August 17, 1999

32 Interview with A.M. Lieanau, May 24, 2001.

33　Interview with Jana Outratová, July 22, 1999.

34　The European Union is, of course, not the only funding agency which small women's groups find it difficult to work with. For example, Natalia Khodyreva describes in this volume the failure of the St. Petersburg Crisis Centre to obtain any funding in 1997 from the American agencies UNISEF and the Ford foundation. She is also critical of USAID, which insisted on funding only one Russian project on domestic violence, thus encouraging competition rather than co-operation between St. Petersburg and Moscow crisis centres. Khodyreva found the funding criteria of some private US foundations and agencies from 'middle' European countries "more flexible, more sensitive to regional interests, and [thus] more effective."

35　*Prague Post*, 23.9.-1.10.2000.

36　Saša Lienau spent the post-1968 'normalization' period in exile in West Germany, where she became politically active in the Green Party and the feminist movement. That involvement taught her valuable political skills in agenda setting, building coalitions, lobbying, writing grant applications, and generally accessing financial resources and courting support. Saša has been able to put those skills to good use both in ProFem, and in the broader Czech feminist milieu. Interview with A.M. Lienau, May 4, 2000.

37　Hauserová (1994), p. 86-87.

38　Lienau (1995), p. 24-25; Interview with A.M. Lienau, May 4, 2000.

39　Moghadam (2000), p. 6.

40　Engert (1995), p. 78.

41　Quoted in Poole (2000), p. 126.

42　Interview with A.M. Lienau, May 24, 2001

43　Interview with YWA's director, Jirina Kozderková, August 16, 1999.

44　Lienau thinks that the failure to establish a foundation for the women's non-profit sector has been a real political mistake, which will be detrimental to the Czech women's movement for years to come. In her experience, Czech ministries do not take individual women's groups very seriously, since it is bureaucratically much easier for the government to allocate money by sector, and to single umbrella organizations and foundations. Moreover, because of shortage of funds, most of the money allocated for NGOs by the Tošovský's government initiative went only to these broad umbrella NGO foundations. Because women do not have such a foundation, their projects received hardly any funds. Interview with A.M. Lienau, May 24, 2001.

45　Fric and Goulli (2001), p. 95-97.

46　Saxonberg (2001).

47　Interview with Dr. Malinová, September 8, 1999.

48　However, as Milwertz demonstrates in this volume in her study of Jinglun Family Centre and Women's Research Institute, some apparent 'failures' are actually 'successes' of a sort, by contributing new ideas, cultural practices and organizational forms to later collective action.

49　Poole (2000), p. 125.

CHAPTER 11

Promoting Gender-balanced Decision-making:

The Role of International Fora and Transnational Networks

Mona Lena Krook

Introduction

Recent years have witnessed an explosion of interest in questions of women's political representation. In the late 1980s and early 1990s, academics, activists, and politicians around the world increasingly set out to study and to document women's under-representation in politics, and subsequently, to reflect over and to propose concrete measures to bring more women into political office. With their attention focused on national level developments, however, few observers have noted this common cross-national trend in mobilizing for gender-balanced representation. Even fewer have paid attention to the role that international level activity has played in identifying political decision-making as an area critical to overcoming gender-based inequalities. A closer look at the genealogy of campaigns to increase women's political representation, however, suggests that all these developments are fundamentally linked, as activism at the international and transnational levels has produced studies, declarations, and actions that have served as a point of support for women nationally who demand the equal sharing of decision-making power.

The emergence of campaigns around this issue marks a distinct break from earlier trends both in feminist organizing and in academic work on women in politics. In the 1960s and 1970s many feminists were skeptical about participation in conventional politics, preferring instead to engage in extra-parliamentary activities, but in the 1980s some slowly reversed this stance as they began to focus increasingly on women's exclusion from the public arena as a major reason why women's status had not sig-nificantly improved, despite numerous formal legal advances.[1] In a complementary way, research on women and politics has long concentrated on why women are *not* more involved in electoral politics, rather than how and why they are – or could be. Standard explanations list a sturdy configuration of barriers to women's full political participation: *individual level factors* like socialization into prescribed gender roles, situational constraints related to motherhood and occupational opportunities, and levels of education and labour force participation, and *national level factors* like electoral systems, and recruitment practices of political parties. New thinking in activist circles, however, has suggested moving away from the old emphasis on social structural factors that cannot be replicated easily in new national contexts – for example, proportional representation electoral systems, the cultural standing of women, and women's participation in the labour force – towards the proposal of gender quotas or targets as the best strategy for quickly increasing women's representation, as well as one that might be applied in a variety of political settings.

International organizations and transnational networks have played a crucial role in effecting this shift in focus. Scholarly studies documenting international and transnational influences on national campaigns for gender-balanced representation, however, are virtually non-existent; when such effects are mentioned, they are typically remarks made only in passing. Recent work on transnational advocacy networks and the role of norms in international politics, however, suggests a framework for characterizing these campaigns and for understanding their potential effects on domestic politics. In the sections which follow, I assess the resources and the limitations in focusing on the international and the transnational dimensions of campaigns for 'gender-balanced decision-making,' which I use here as a more general term encompassing demands both for quotas for women in politics and for parity democracy.[2] I begin by defining international institutions and transnational networks and then outlining the ways that they interact within international fora to provide opportunities and resources for scholars, activists, and politicians to politicize new issues through the exchange of information. I next present a genealogy of international and transnational efforts to target 'decision-making' as an area vital to promoting substantive equality between women and men. In this initial analysis, I focus on the United Nations (UN), the Inter-Parliamentary Union (IPU), the Council of Europe (COE), and the European Union (EU) as international fora in which transnational networks of scholars, activists, and politicians interact with institution officials to develop new ideas and strategies for gender equality.[3] I emphasize that this is a preliminary mapping and that the connections I draw are necessarily partial: more studies will be required to trace the concrete connections between work at the international, transnational, and national levels to show how these different arenas interact to define issues and to spread new definitions and understandings. In the final section, I conclude that international institutions and transnational networks can play a potentially crucial role in establishing underrepresentation as a *political problem amenable to political solutions*. Ultimately, however, national level actors will have to adapt this insight to domestic conditions to take initiatives to recruit more women.

International institutions, transnational networks, and the politics of information

International institutions and transnational networks offer a number of potential tools for domestic activists who may or may not lack the resources to wage effective campaigns at the national level. Joined often by scholars and politicians, activists reach out beyond their borders to *exchange information*: they share their own experiences, both successful and unsuccessful, in promoting change on a certain issue, and they seek to learn from the experiences of others. By this process of exchange, tactics which appear to be particularly effective or the countries where they are undertaken frequently become recipes or models for action. Although assuming one paradigm will work everywhere is misguided, awareness of activities beyond home can help activists innovate in the arguments and the strategies they employ, as well as in the goals they endeavour to attain. Nonetheless, generating change domestically requires that activists consider carefully the conditions or circumstances under which they mobilize, because "[c]ampaigns are processes of issue construction constrained by the action context in which they are to be carried out."[4]

In contrast to states and domestic social movements, which relate to one another in conflict,[5] international institutions and transnational networks coexist more or less peacefully.[6] Indeed, "[r]ather than being the antipodes of transnational contention, international institutions offer resources, opportunities, and incentives for the formation of actors in transnational politics."[7] When states create international institutions to serve their collective interest and to monitor each other's behaviour, they create a space – an *international forum* – for the discussion of issues of common concern. While initially controlled by governments, this international space may take on a life of its own such that its inputs and outputs are no longer the sum of its parts, but something altogether different. This transformation occurs as scholars, activists, and politicians come together – encouraged by officers of international institutions seeking legitimacy and information to validate and to facilitate their own work[8] – to share ideas hitherto confined to academic circles or to personal struggles. International fora, therefore, are often the sites of the introduction and the promotion of new political concepts, like 'parity democracy' and 'mainstreaming.' International institutions give flesh to these issues by presenting opportunities for networking via their meetings, conferences, workshops, and publications, as well as by creating new bodies and agencies to specialize in these questions. They lend veracity to claims for change by financing the collection of statistics and passing international legislation, albeit non-binding, which together identify the issue as one of concern and call upon states to take steps to alter the *status quo*. Finally, international institutions often provide for follow-ups on conferences, studies, and legislation which keep the issue on the agenda, or at least prevent it from disappearing completely. Analyses of initial statistical studies, for example, may spark further investigation into the reasons behind women's low level of representation, while reviews of existing legislation may lead officials to refocus their efforts or to refine their recommendations to improve the likelihood of success in changing the current situation.

Transnational networks, for their part, operate within international fora and may include a wide configuration of groups working at the local, regional, and global level. They are often the ones introducing new terms into global discourse, as well as the ones generating and sharing the information that informs international policy docu-

4th World Conference on Women Beijing 1995. (Photo: Kirstine Theilgaard.)

ments. Their most important contribution, however, may comprise their efforts to frame issues across borders: precisely because they seek to unify actors from very different backgrounds, they are highly sensitive to cross-national variations in the meaning and the interpretation of different social concerns. While they are not always successful – indeed, often they are not – they foster the emergence of competing explanations and solutions to various problems, laying bare the possibilities for bridging (or not bridging) gaps in understanding. Their concern to gain cross-cultural resonance often compels them to innovate continually, developing new concepts and strategies that would not have been possible solely at the national level. Transnational networks may take three forms: *transnational social movements*, "socially mobilized groups with constituents in at least two states, engaged in sustained contentious interaction with powerholders in at least one state other than their own, or against an international institution, or a multinational economic actor"[9]; *international non-governmental organizations*, "organizations that operate independently of governments, are composed of members from two or more countries, and are organized to advance their members' international goals and provide services to citizens of other states through routine transactions with states, private actors, and international institutions"[10]; and *transnational advocacy networks*, "those relevant actors working internationally on an issue, who are bound together by shared values, a common discourse, and dense exchanges of information and services."[11]

While a step removed from grassroots organizing, transnational advocacy networks can lend domestic movements support via the slightly different tactics and resources they can employ, precisely because they operate outside and across national borders. Keck and Sikkink categorize these tactics as: *information politics*, the ability to quickly and credibly generate political usable information and move it to where it will have the most impact; *symbolic politics*, the ability to call upon symbols, actions, or stories that make sense of a situation for an audience that is frequently far away; *leverage politics*, the ability to call upon powerful actors to affect a situation where weaker members of a network are unlikely to have influence; and *accountability politics*, the effort to hold powerful actors to their previously stated policies or principles.[12] Campaigns to increase women's presence in politics draw primarily on information and account-ability tactics. To transform information into a political tool, international institutions and transnational networks devote considerable energy to producing and distributing statistics on the low percentages of women in national, regional, and local politics and to organizing conferences and networks through which women activists and politicians can exchange tips on strategies to bring in more women. They put the accountability process into motion by pressuring governments and other actors to sign international documents to express some sort of minimal rhetorical commitment to the goal of increasing women's political representation. Although such moves appear to entail only cosmetic change, since governments and other powerful actors often change their positions on issues hoping to diffuse or to divert public attention, network activists can try to make such statements into opportunities for accountability politics: once a government has publicly committed itself to a principle, networks can use those posi-tions, and their command of information, to expose the distance between discourse and practice. Still, they must transform ideas into norms: while ideas are about cognitive commitments, norms make behavioural claims on individuals.[13] Further, they must remain aware that the process of creating and institutionalizing new norms may be quite different from the process of adhering to norms that have already been widely accepted.

United Nations

The international institution perhaps most closely identified with the development and the diffusion of women's rights worldwide is the UN: "[a]lthough the international women's movement began at the grass-roots level many years before the founding of the United Nations, the Organization moved quickly to affirm that the advancement of women was central to its work."[14] Within the first year of its existence, the Economic and Social Council established the Commission on the Status of Women (CSW) and the General Assembly unanimously adopted Resolution 56 (1) recommending that all member states adopt measures to grant women the same political rights as men in order to fulfill the aims of the Charter of the United Nations.[15] The earliest interna-tional meetings convened to support the work of the CSW were seminars to increase the participation of women in public life in 1957, 1959, and 1960,[16] although the first comprehensive statement of internationally accepted principles on the rights of women – which included a government commitment to foster women's full and equal participation in political and public life – did not appear until 1979 with the adoption of the Convention on the Elimination of All Forms of Discrimination Against Women (CEDAW).[17] These commitments were elaborated, as well as taken one step further, during the 1995 Fourth World Conference on Women in Beijing, when delegates composed the Platform for Action (PfA) outlining, among other things, a series of concrete proposals for governments to ensure women's equal access to and full participation in power structures and decision-making, as well as to increase women's capacity to participate in decision-making and leadership.[18]

Over the years, the United Nations has sponsored numerous meetings and conferences which have served as international fora for the discussion of issues related to women's social, economic, and political status. Indeed, as Keck and Sikkink note, the emergence of international women's networks is more intertwined with the UN system than other transnational networks, so that chronologies of the international women's movement are largely a listing of UN meetings – Mexico City, Copenhagen, Nairobi, Vienna, Cairo, and Beijing. Although international conferences *per se* do not create women's networks, they can foster their formation by legitimizing the issues and by bringing together unprecedented numbers of women from around the world. Not only do such face-to-face encounters generate the trust, the information sharing, and the discovery of common concerns that give the impetus to network formation, but they also facilitate the literal linking of activists: following the NGO meeting at the First World Conference on Women in Mexico City in 1975, a group of women founded the International Women's Tribune Centre, which used the mailing list generated at Mexico City to keep in touch with individuals and groups around the globe. The list has expanded over the years so that today the Tribune Centre is a communication link for 16,000 individuals and groups working on behalf of women in 160 countries.[19]

The international space afforded to gender issues by the UN has gradually expanded and changed over the years, as the institution has moved from emphasizing the legal foundations of equality towards recognizing women's role in development towards acknowledging the profound gendering of social, economic, and political life. While international conferences and legislation are the most tangible markers of these shifts, transnational networks and institution officials have together been the ones to introduce new concepts to the debate on gender equality, to conduct and to collect research on the situation of women worldwide, and to harness these new ideas and statistics as tools in the struggle for women's rights. One example of the innovative character of this exchange is the development of the concept of 'mainstreaming', a relatively new term in discussions of gender equality, which emerged in the years following the 1985 Third World Conference on Women in Nairobi and received definition and endorsement in 1995 at the Fourth World Conference in Beijing as a procedure whereby "before [policy] decisions are taken, an analysis is made on the effects on women and men, respectively."[20] A potentially revolutionary concept calling on all actors across a range of issue-areas and all stages in the policy process to consider the gendered impacts of policy-making and implementation, mainstreaming quickly became the official policy in many developed countries and among international organizations like the UNDP, the World Bank, and the European Union, largely due to "the efforts of women activists and entrepreneurs to increase the visibility of women and the importance of gender in the policies, programs and projects of international development agencies."[21] The stress on mainstreaming has gone hand-in-hand with the promotion of gender-balanced decision-making, now seen as key to women's empowerment, together elevating the role of the *political* in effecting social and economic change.

Inter-Parliamentary Union

Although a much less well-known international institution, the Inter-Parliamentary Union has played perhaps as crucial a role as the United Nations in promoting gender-balanced decision-making worldwide. Founded in 1889 to bring together parliamentarians across the globe, the IPU has focused more explicitly than the UN on advancing women's political participation and on providing networking opportunities for women parliamentarians. It has done this primarily through the collection and the distribution of statistics on women's political participation worldwide and annual Meetings of Women Parliamentarians, but the IPU has also sponsored a number of specialized conferences in recent years specifically on the topic of women and the decision-making process.

The IPU issued its first worldwide survey on the status of women in politics in 1975 to mark the start of the UN's Decade for Women and to follow up on the work of the First World Conference on Women, held that year in Mexico City. Ten years later, the UN again commissioned the IPU to carry out a statistical survey on the distribution of seats between women and men in parliamentary assemblies. Since 1987 the organization has conducted surveys every four years on women's participation in political life and the decision-making process, and it currently maintains a website with up-to-date information on the percentage of women in national parliaments, as well as a bibliographic database to facilitate research on women in politics worldwide.[22]

Women MPs began to meet informally during IPU statutory sessions starting in 1978, and in 1986 this practice was formalized as the Meeting of Women Parliamentarians, which assembles for a whole-day session on the eve of IPU Conferences in order for women MP's to coordinate their views and to agree on strategies for promoting their concerns during the session.[23] This network had the idea to organize a conference in Geneva in 1989, where delegates agreed that the more women are involved in the political decision-making process, the more the concept of democracy will assume true and tangible expression.[24] This discussion eventually led the IPU Council, the plenary policy-making body of the IPU, to link gender balance with democracy in 1992 and, consequently, to set up a group of six men and six women, representing the six main regions and the various political systems and cultural backgrounds of the world, to work on a full-fledged Plan of Action to Correct Present Imbalances in the Participation of Men and Women in Political Life,[25] which would represent the

IPU's contribution to the Fourth World Conference on Women in Beijing. This Plan of Action also provided for the holding of another IPU conference in New Delhi in 1997, as part of the follow-up to Beijing, on the theme Towards Partnership Between Men and Women in Politics.[26] This conference called for a new world comparative survey on women in national parliaments, as well as a study covering the various aspects of women's participation in political parties; their involvement in the electoral process both as electors and as candidates; and their presence, role, and functions in parliament. The IPU has since gone beyond numbers to analyze the root causes of women's underrepresentation and to design remedies by outlining concrete strategies to enable women to enhance their political input and impact on national and international political processes.[27]

Council of Europe

While UN and IPU documents and activities have put 'women in decision-making' on the international political agenda, Western European institutions and networks have contributed greatly to the further development of normative principles and practical strategies for effecting changes in patterns of representation. The Council of Europe, in particular, is credited with coining the term 'parity democracy' – the idea that representative assemblies be composed equally of women and men – which has spurred a number of national debates on women's political representation, most notably in France but also in other countries across Southern Europe.[28] While the main venues for constructing the claim to parity democracy in the COE have been a series of working parties of experts, colloquia, and specialist Conferences of Ministers held in Strasbourg in 1986, in Vienna in 1989, in Rome in 1993, and in Ankara in 2000, these meetings did not appear in a vacuum but often followed UN activities, which served "as a series of external prompts for actors within the Council of Europe and their non-governmental lobbyists to develop new initiatives in this issue-area at the European level,"[29] and as a consequence of the work of women and feminist movements to politicize the issue at the European level.[30]

The debate on parity democracy within the COE started with the Third Medium-Term Plan 1987-1991, *Democratic Europe: humanism, diversity, universality*, adopted in November 1986, which introduced a new policy frame on deepening democracy within Europe. One consequence of this new focus was the Council of Ministers' adoption of the Declaration on Equality of Women and Men in 1988, a declaration which presented women's presence and participation in public life as a *sine qua non* of democracy. To discuss ways of promoting this agenda, the Steering Committee for Equality between Women and Men (CEEG) convened a seminar of experts in Strasbourg in 1989 to re-examine the relation between gender and democracy in order to formulate strategies to guarantee equal representation of women and men in the democratic system. A report presented to the seminar by Elisabeth G. Sledziewski[31] was perhaps the first to use the term 'parity democracy' and to present many of the

4th World Conference on Women Beijing 1995. (Photo: Kirstine Theilgaard.)

basic ideas later repeated in national debates in favour of parity. Despite disagreements on objectives and strategies, most delegates to the meeting agreed on the legitimacy and the necessity of quotas for accelerating *de facto* equality between men and women. Indeed, "several speakers thought that international (European) channels would have to be used to bring about acceptance of this new approach. The concept of quotas...should be introduced as a legal argument into international texts."[32] Subsequent meetings sought to hammer out these various disputes in order to develop policy recommendations and to resolve larger theoretical and practical issues regarding the parity democracy project. Despite the enduring "absence of expert agreement over the theorisation of parity-democracy, or over its usage to legitimise the case for statutory measures to enhance the representation of women,"[33] however, the COE has continued to push ahead on the issue. In 1999 the Commission for Equal Opportunities presented a report entitled "Répresentation paritaire dans la vie politique," while the COE Parliamentary Assembly issued Recommendation 1413 on equal representation in political life, both of which urged national delegations to take concrete measures in their parliaments to correct women's underrepresentation by introducing parity in political parties and making state party financing conditional upon implementing this objective.

European Union [34]

Clearly influenced by developments within other international institutions – especially the UN – the European Union has engaged in a variety of efforts in recent years to try to increase women's representation both in the European Parliament and in local and national assemblies. Due perhaps to the more formalized connections between levels of governance with the EU, the configuration of meetings, agencies, publications, legislation, and networks dedicated to this issue within the EU is comparatively dense. Even before the advent of gender-balanced decision-making to the international political agenda, women's policy within the European Community/ European Union had been one of the few well-developed areas of European social policy. 'Gender equality' in the EC had long been confined, however, to issues relating to women as workers, since European integration was defined as a mainly economic project until the early 1990s. This changed in 1992 when member states ratified the Treaty of European Union, better known as the Maastricht Treaty, which introduced the concept of 'European citizenship' and thus transformed the EU into a political entity of sorts. Not coincidentally, around this time a major shift began to occur in EU gender equality policy to include the larger political, social, and economic context within which women operated as workers.

Women in decision-making first appeared on the EU gender equality agenda around this time in association with the Third Medium-Term Community Action Programme for Equal Opportunities for Women and Men for the years 1991-1995. Besides expressing a commitment to improving the involvement of women in the political decision-making process, this Action Programme funded nine expert networks on different aspects of women's policy, including the European Expert Network on "Women in Decision-Making," and inspired the Commission to fund the European Women's Lobby and the Council to issue various pieces of 'soft law' (Resolutions, Recommendations, and Communications that have little binding force) encouraging member states and European institutions to take steps to recruit more women. The Fourth Medium-Term Action Programme 1996-2000 slightly reoriented this activist focus: deeming member state action to be primary, it emphasized instead 'Community added value,' the notion that EU action should not replicate or replace what is, should, or can be done at the national level, but rather should add something to it, either by dealing with the EU level or by making connections between or extrapolations from diverse national practices. Consequently, the role of the Commission was now seen to be one of facilitating communication by gathering information, sponsoring research, encouraging transnational contact, disseminating 'best practice,' and monitoring developments.[35]

Pieces of 'soft law' passed by the Council during the same time period grew increasingly more detailed over time with regard to women in decision-making. Earlier legislation briefly mentioned decision-making as one element of the larger strategy for achieving gender equality. Legislation in the 1990s, in contrast, placed decision-making at the center of attention. "Council Resolution of 27 March 1995 on the balanced participation of men and women in decision-making"[36] highlighted gen-der-balanced decision-making itself as a goal meriting special attention. Among other things, it invited member states to promote balanced participation by developing an integrated global strategy that would include publishing reports; developing incentives and supporting measures for NGOs; supporting research; and devising, launching, and promoting information and awareness campaigns at regular intervals. "Council Rec-ommendation of 2 December 1996 on the balanced participation of women and men in the decision-making process"[37] integrated proposals and opinions from the Com-mission, the European Parliament, and the Economic and Social Committee to present a detailed set of normative arguments and practical measures to increase women's political representation, and it recommended that member states adopt a comprehen-sive, integrated strategy designed to promote balanced participation of women and men in the decision-making process. Such a strategy might include public campaigns to alert public opinion; the collection of statistics; education and training programmes; quantitative and qualitative studies on legal, social, and cultural obstacles to women's participation, as well as strategies for overcoming such obstacles; and the exchange of good practice. The Recommendation also called on the Commission to encourage and to organize a systematic pooling of information and experience between the member states on good practice and an assessment of the impact of measures taken to achieve a better balance between women and men in decision-making.

To operationalize these grand pronouncements of intentions, the Commission sought throughout the 1990s to establish its own contacts with women organizing outside the formal political arena, as well as to facilitate the establishment of networks of women's groups across Europe.[38] In 1990 it funded the creation of the European Women's Lobby (EWL), a non-governmental organization established to represent women's interests at the European level that acts as an umbrella organization for women's groups in the various member states. Europe-wide women's organizations with a commitment to equality have the right to direct representation on the EWL's General Assembly and national women's organizations or coordinations of women's organizations in each country have the right to four delegates each. The EWL's primary mission is not only to lobby for measures to compel member state governments on issues of gender equality, but also to exchange information and to develop transnational campaigns.[39] Under the auspices of the Third Medium-Term Action Programme, the Commission also established a European Expert Network on "Women in Decision-Making" in 1992. This Network, which had one expert in each Member State and a European Coordin-ator based in Brussels, was charged with the tasks of examining the hurdles that kept women from attaining decision-making positions, of informing and sensitizing the general public on this subject, and of devising strategies and instruments to achieve a larger participation of women and men in decision-making. While the EWL continues to exist, the Network of Experts was funded only for the years 1992-1996. The work it performed, however, has continued up to the present in the form of the European Database – Women in Decision-Making at <http://www.db-decision.de>.

Taken together, these efforts – the Action Programmes, the 'soft laws,' and the women's networks – have helped render gender equality one of the core goals of the European Union. The Treaty of Amsterdam in 1997 cemented its importance by declaring 'equality between women and men' to be one of the major missions of the Community on par with economic development and cohesion. The recent Finnish Presidency Report on European implementation of the Beijing Platform for Action argued, further, that this "concept of equality must be understood as including the task of the promotion of equality between women and men in power and decision-making."[40] In one further demonstration of its commitment, the EU has even started to conduct actions in third countries – especially the applicant countries – to encourage women's participation in the decision-making process. One such project is the Phare Democracy Programme, integrated into the European Initiative for Democracy and Human Rights in 1998, which seeks to train women as decision-makers in order to increase the participation of women from Central and Eastern Europe in politics and public life.[41]

Contributions and limitations of international and transnational activism

The recent worldwide surge of interest in gender-balanced decision-making, while perhaps most visible to citizens at the national and local levels, thus has notable international and transnational dimensions that have heretofore been overlooked in analyses of women's political representation. Most significantly, international institutions and transnational networks provide for the exchange of information – both descriptive and strategic – that domestic actors can use to wage campaigns at the national level. International and transnational actors do not privilege ideas necessarily by choice, or because they are more enlightened than national actors, but rather as a consequence of the limitations of their power. International institutions cannot enforce any of the resolutions they issue – at least not by coercive means – so their main purpose is to set new international norms and models of political organization.[42] Similarly, transnational networks cannot lobby national governments as effectively as domestic social movements, since they often lack a strong grassroots base to make their activism a credible challenge to any national *status quo*. Both international institutions and transnational networks, however, can use their position outside national debates and their lack of political-ideological baggage to devise and to diffuse new ideas and strategies for social change. Not weighed down by context, they can innovate conceptually and present these new understandings as more objective precisely because they are one step removed from the people they will effect. Taking the stand that ideas matter – that people are not simply motivated by material concerns – they privilege, moreover, the causal potential of *agency* to overcome structural inequalities. Although limited to statements of principles, their work can therefore help heighten state and social movement actors' awareness as to the political origins of exclusion and their own role in effecting change.

Inclusion will not occur, however, until domestic actors decide to take the necessary steps to challenge and to intervene into the processes that produce and reproduce inequalities. Doing so will require not only bringing, but also adapting, abstract international principles back into national contexts defined by cultural and historical particularities. In this the transnational exchange of information can prove a vital resource, as activists endeavour to learn from more and less successful attempts of activists elsewhere to bring more women into politics. Although no one 'magic formula' exists for how to do this most effectively, the sharing of strategies across borders can expose a variety of arguments and strategies that might not have occurred to domestic actors on their own. Most importantly, however, international and transnational activism reveals women's underrepresentation to be a *political problem with a political solution*, encouraging activists to *mobilize* to promote change.

Persuading governments to sign international documents that commit them to the goal of gender-balanced decision-making, nonetheless, constitutes only a first step in bringing the issue to the political agenda. Since "the intrinsic attractiveness of ideas plays only a limited role in their chances of gaining wide political resonance,"[43] citizens will ultimately have to target political parties, the organizations which engage in the actual recruitment of candidates for political office and, as such, present the most immediate barrier to women's increased representation, to demonstrate the potential electoral pay-offs of presenting more female candidates. For this, mobilization 'on the ground' will be indispensable. Because patterns of exclusion benefit certain groups over others, those in privileged positions must be shown the advantages they will accrue in expanding inclusion to out-groups. The election component of democracy provides this wedge: made aware of the political nature of exclusion, voters begin to notice when parties fail to recruit a diverse slate of candidates, compelling parties to seek to include previously-excluded groups. While categories will likely always exist in politics, "the importance of having more women in politics and in positions of influence [is] to engage in examining the uses of 'women' and other categories. Those whom the category is deemed to represent need to be present to debate its uses."[44] International and transnational activism helps de-naturalize these categories, but national actors will have to redefine them: inclusion, like exclusion, is a political process.

References

Bacchi, Carol Lee (1996). *The Politics of Affirmative Action: 'Women,' Equality and Category Politics*, Thousand Oaks, Sage.

Berman, Sheri (2001). "Ideas, Norms, and Culture in Political Analysis", *Comparative Politics*, 33. Vol. 33 no. 2., p. 231-250.

Boutros-Ghali, Boutros (1995). "Introduction by Boutros Boutros-Ghali, Secretary-General of the United Nations", United Nations (ed.), *The United Nations and The Advancement of Women, 1945-1995*, New York, United Nations Department of Public Information, p. 3-65.

Commission of the European Communities (2000). *Report from the Commission to the Council, the European Parliament and the Economic and Social Committee on the Implementation of Council Recommendation 96/694 of 2nd December 1996 on the Balanced Participation of Women and Men in the Decision-Making Process*, Brussels, Commission of the European Communities.

Dahlerup, Drude (1986). "Introduction", Drude Dahlerup (ed.), *The New Women's Movement: Feminism and Political Power in Europe and the USA*, Newbury Park, Sage, p. 1-25.

European Commission (2000). *Implementation of the Platform for Action Adopted at the Fourth World Conference on Women in Beijing 1995: Information Note on European Commission Activities Prepared for the ECE Regional Meeting on the 2000 Review of Implementation of the Beijing Platform for Action*, Geneva, United Nations.

European Women's Lobby (2000). "Women in decision-making", http://www.womenlobby.org/Document. asp?DocID=91&tod=01252.

Finnemore, Martha and Kathryn Sikkink (2001). "Taking Stock: The Constructivist Research Program in International Relations and Comparative Politics", *Annual Review of Political Science*, 4. Årgang, p. 391-416.

Hacia una Democracia Paritaria. Análisis y Revisión de las Leyes Electorales Vigentes (2001). Madrid, CELEM.

Hafner-Burton, Emilie and Mark A. Pollack (2000). "Mainstreaming Gender In Global Governance", paper presented at the "Mainstreaming Gender in European Public Policy" Workshop, Madison, WI, 14-15 October.

Helfferich, Barbara (1994). "Le Lobby Européen des Femmes", GisPle Halimi (ed.), *Femmes: moitié de la terre, moitié du pouvoir*, Paris, Gallimard, p. 165-169.

Hoskyns, Catherine (1991). "The European Women's Lobby", *Feminist Review,* Vol. 38, p. 67-70.

Hoskyns, Catherine (2000). "A Study of Four Action Programmes on Equal Opportunities", Mariagrazia Rossilli (ed.), *Gender Policies in the European Union*, New York, Peter Lang, p. 43-59.

Inter-Parliamentary Union (1994). "Plan of Action to Correct Present Imbalances in the Participation of Men and Women in Political Life", www.ipu.org/wmn-e/planactn.htm.

Inter-Parliamentary Union (1997). "Concluding statement by the President on the outcome of the Conference 'Towards Partnership Between Men and Women in Politics'" http://www.ipu.org/splz-e/Ndelhi97.htm.

Inter-Parliamentary Union (2001a). "Meeting of Women Parliamentarians", http://www.*ipu.org/wmn-e/meeting*.htm.

Inter-Parliamentary Union (2001b). "Specialized Conference in New Delhi", http://www.*ipu.org/wmn-e/nd-conf*.htm.

Inter-Parliamentary Union (2001c). "Studies and Surveys", http://www.*ipu.org/wmn-e/studies*.htm.

Keck, Margaret, and Kathryn Sikkink (1998). *Activists Beyond Borders: Advocacy Networks in International Politics*, Ithaca, Cornell University Press.

Krook, Mona Lena (2002). "'Europe for Women, Women for Europe': Strategies for Parity Democracy in the European Union", John p. Micgiel (ed.), *Democracy And Integration In An Enlarging Europe*, New York, Institute for the Study of Europe, p. 67-86.

Lister, Ruth (1997). *Citizenship: Feminist Perspectives*, New York, New York University Press.

Lovecy, Jill (2001). "Framing women's rights and gender policies in Europe: the Council of Europe and the construction of parity", paper presented at the European Community Studies Association International Conference, Madison, WI, May 31-June 2.

Permanent Representatives Committee (1999). *Presidency report: Review of the implementation by the Member States and the European Union of the Beijing Platform for Action*, Brussels, Council of the European Union.

Pintat, Christine (1998). "Democracy Through Partnership: The Experience of the Inter-Parliamentary Union", Azza Karam (ed.), *Women in Parliament: Beyond Numbers*, Stockholm, International IDEA, chap. 6.

Risse, Thomas, and Kathryn Sikkink (1999). "The socialization of international human rights norms into domestic practices: introduction", Thomas Risse, Stephen C. Ropp, and Kathryn Sikkink (ed.), *The Power of Human Rights: International Norms and Domestic Change*, New York, Cambridge University Press, p. 1-38.

Steering Committee for Equality between Women and Men (1992). *The democratic principle of representation – Forty years of Council of Europe activity*, Strasbourg, Council of Europe Press.

Subirats, Marina (2001). "Democracia Paritaria: recorrido histórico y planteamiento actual", *Hacia una Democracia Paritaria*, Madrid, CELEM, p. 43-52.

Tarrow, Sidney (1998). Power in Movement: Social Movements and contentious Politics, New York; Cambridge University Press.

Tarrow, Sidney (2001). "Transnational Politics: Contention and Institutions in International Politics", *Annual Review of Political Science* 4. Årgang, p. 1-20.

United Nations (1979). *Convention on the Elimination of All Forms of Discrimination Against Women*, New York, United Nations.

United Nations (1995a). *The United Nations and The Advancement of Women, 1945-1995*, New York, United Nations Department of Public Information.

United Nations (1995b). *Fourth World Conference on Women: Platform for Action*. New York, United Nations.

Notes

1 Clearly both trends have long existed, and indeed, this is a positive development, according to Drude Dahlerup, because "both movements need each other, even if many movement activists would dissociate themselves from the political compromises, and even if most politicians considered the new movement much too radical and outrageous. In conclusion, being outside is probably a condition of radical new thinking; but this redefinition must be absorbed by some inside the system in order for the movement to influence public policy" Dahlerup (1986), p. 15.

2 Quotas for women in politics often fall within the 20 to 40 percent range, while the demand for parity democracy often implies a 50-50 split between women and men. I treat them as similar bids for 'gender balance' because of the ambiguity that often attends this term in national and international documents (Commission of the European Communities 2000).

3 I concentrate on these four institutions because they have played a particularly visible role in developing and spreading the debate on gender-balanced decision-making.

4 Keck and Sikkink (1998), p. 8; cf. Bergman in this volume.

5   Tarrow (1998) defines a social movement as sustained contentious interaction between non-elites and elites.

6   This statement, of course, depends on the definition assigned to 'international institution.' I use the term broadly to denote bodies created by two or more independent states to coordinate their views or to facilitate their cooperation. I take 'transnational network' to signify a system – however loosely organized – linking actors in different states who typically share common ideas or beliefs.

7   Tarrow (2001), p. 1.

8   Tarrow (2001).

9   Tarrow (2001), p. 11.

10 Tarrow (2001), p. 12.

11 Keck and Sikkink (1998), p. 2.

12 Keck and Sikkink (1998).

13 Risse and Sikkink (1999).

14 Boutros-Ghali (1995), p. 3.

15 A/RES/56(1), 11 December 1946, reproduced in United Nations (1995), p. 103; Charter of the United Nations, 26 June 1945, reproduced in United Nations (1995), p. 93.

16 United Nations (1995a), p. 77.

17 United Nations (1979).

18 United Nations (1995b).

19 Keck and Sikkink (1998), p. 169.

20 United Nations (1995b).

21 Hafner-Burton and Pollack (2000), p. 6.

22 Inter-Parliamentary Union (2001c). <http://www.*ipu.org*>

23 Inter-Parliamentary Union (2001a).

24 Pintat (1998).

25 Inter-Parliamentary Union (1994).

26 Inter-Parliamentary Union (1997); Inter-Parliamentary Union (2001b).

27 Pintat (1998).

28 *Hacia una Democracia Paritaria* (2001).

29 Lovecy (2001), p. 9.

30 Subirats (2001).

31 Steering Committee for Equality between Women and Men (1992), p. 17-27.

32 Steering Committee for Equality between Women and Men (1992), p. 48.

33 Lovecy (2001), p. 15.

34 For a more detailed account of EU efforts, consult Krook (2002).

35 Hoskyns (2000).

36 *Official Journal* No C 168, 04.07.1995, p. 3-4, European Council.

37 *Official Journal* No L 319, 10.12.1996, p. 11-15, European Council.

38 Lister (1997).

39 Helfferich (1994); Hoskyns (1991).

40 Permanent Representatives Committee (1999), p. 2.

41 European Commission (2000); European Women's Lobby (2000).

42 Finnemore and Sikkink (2001).

43 Berman (2001), p. 235-236.

44 Bacchi (1996), p.13.

CHAPTER 12

Life Course in Move(ment): Finnish Romany Women

An Interview with Airi Markkanen[1] by Beatrice Halsaa

B: You have focused the life course of Finnish Romany women in your doctoral thesis – why did these women catch your interest?

A: Firstly because the Finnish Romanies is a group connected with many prejudices. At the moment the situation of the Roma people is a keenly debated question all over Europe. The German author Günther Grass has described their situation this way:

> "Everywhere Gypsies are the lowest of the low. Why? Because they are different. Because they steal, are restless, roam, have the Evil Eye and that stunning beauty that makes us ugly to ourselves. Because their mere existence puts our values in question. Because they are all very well in operas and operettas, but in reality … they are anti-social, odd and don't fit in. "Torch them!" shout the skinheads."[2]

Secondly because neither scholars nor politicians have paid much attention to the lives of Romany women. I wanted to learn more about them, most of all about their everyday life and the construction of ethnic identity. The main focus of my work is the life course of Romany women. I also highlight the potential conflicts between women's role in the Romany culture and issues of gender equality. The overall situation of Romany women in the European region is briefly discussed in relation to the topic of this book: the women's movement. There is not much of a Romany women's movement as such in Finland, but at the European level interesting things are happening.

Finnish romanies

B: How would you describe the Finnish Romanies as an ethnic group?

A: Let me start by clarifying various ways of naming them: The word Romany is used especially officially and in documents. I call them gypsies or Romanies interchangeably. The Roma themselves use the words romani (Romany), mustalainen (gypsy), tumma (dark) or kaale (dark in the Romany language).

There are about 10-12 millions Romanies living in Europe today. In Finland, there are about 10 000 Romanies, and in addition there are 3000 Finnish Romanies living in Sweden. They are classified as an ethnic group, unlike for instance Jews who are considered a religious minority, and the Finnish Swedes who are seen as a linguistic minority. The Romanies belong to the old ethnic groups in Finland, along with the Sami people and the Tatars. In addition to the old ethnic groups, new ethnic groups are making their impact on Finland as thousands of refugees have moved to Finland recently. Except for the Vietnamese, the Somalis and the Russians, these groups are not seen as ethnic minorities, however, because of their small numbers.[3]

The Roma people differ from the ethnic Finnish population in many ways, for instance concerning religious affiliation. Ethnic Fins generally belong to the Lutheran church, while most of the Romanies have chosen a revivalist movement, for instance the Pentecostalist church. Although 95 percent of the Romanies formally belong to the Evangelic Lutheran church, they prefer to go to Pentecostalist churches.

B: The Roma people have been associated with travelling. Is this still an adequate association, or is it merely a prejudice?

A: Generally speaking, the Romanies are definitely still a travelling group. To-day the pattern of movements are changing. For instance, Roma people travel in great numbers from Eastern and Central Europe to Finland, whereas the younger Finnish Roma population is significantly less inclined to travel than the older generations.

In his interesting generation study based on autobiographical material from the 1980's, the sociologist J-P Roos divides the Finns into four generations:[4] The first generation is the "generation of wars and poverty" (those who were born between 1900-1920), the second generation is "the generation of the rebuilding and growth after the war" (those who were born around 1920's to 1930's). The third generation is the generation of "the great transition" (the baby boomers born in the 1940s), and the fourth generation is "the generation of suburbs".

Roos' four categories of generations does not seem to fit the Romany culture in Finland, however. I have found only two clear categories in my study: Those Romas who have wandered, and those who have lived in flats all their lives. In fact, the great transition among the Romanies happened during just one period, the 1950s and 1960s. During those decades the Romany male trades, such as horse-trading and the work of handicraft, such as tinsmith, became unnecessary. At the same time, Romany women's work, such as the selling of lace works and scarves, diminished as mass production conquered the markets. Consequently, the big migration of Romany people from the Finnish countryside to towns and to Sweden started.

As I interpret the history, Romany people who were born between 1900 and 1950 can be labelled as the "generation of the travelling way of life". Quite opposite of the stereotype interpretation, it is important to underline that the travelling way of life was certainly not a purposeless wandering and travelling. It was quite the contrary, indicated by the fact that different families had very strict boundaries and places where they used to travel and carried on with their trades.

The Romanies born in the 1960s and later belong to another generation. Not the fourth one as Roos sees it, but rather the second generation. With respect to Romas, it is the second generation which meaningfully may be described as 'the suburban generation'. A large part of the younger Romanies live in suburban areas, mostly in rented flats and in poor areas. But then of course, there are important variations; generations are not strictly bound to certain decades

Romanies, just like the predominant population, live in a conflicting and changing world, not in an ahistorical vacuum. There are variations and exceptions, but I think that the following three features describe the problematic aspects of Romany lives in Finland: Firstly, financial problems. Only few Romanies have a steady job. Secondly, problems connected with the behaviour of the Romanies themselves, such as rows between families. And thirdly, prejudices and negative attitudes in the predominant population towards the Romanies. These problematic areas of life obviously have different implications for Romany women and men. Gender differences are also relevant, when it comes to some of the distinguished positive features of Romany life: the caring and looking after each other.

About field work with the Romanies

B: Being an ethnographer, you have conducted extensive field work over a number of years. What did you do?

A: My field work with Finnish Romany women started in 1992 and has not finished. During my field work I have gathered material by means of participant observation. When I started the field work I did not have much information about the Romany life, just an assumption that their life was not easy. Over the years I have made interviews with about 50 Romany girls and women from 4 to 89 years of age (most of them were between 35 and 60 years old). Of course, also men could have been interviewed about women's lives, but I felt it was more natural to be among women. In addition to the 50 formal interviews, a number of women, men and children have affected my study more "invisibly". They have made their imprint in the pages of my field diary, and take their individual part in my study.

The study of a person's everyday life can be very problematic, and I visited some of the informants a number of times.[5] Also, I travelled with them. This gave me a chance to get close to the core of the Romany culture and the lives of Romany women. I have made close and hopefully lasting friendships, and I have come to 'love the field'. Naturally, this may cause problems in the field work.[6] In the interview situations there have been many kinds of problems and also funny moments.

I think it is easier to get closer to "real life" by forgetting recorders totally and by throwing oneself into the situation. The material is then developed out of a succession of moments and feelings. On trips or when visiting people, this method has produced better observations of the Romany life than I would have made if I had started the tape recorder and asked for personal data or other things connected with the various topics. The interviewees have forgotten to "play gypsy" and have talked about their things and life freely. The sauna, for instance, has been one of the liberating places during my field work. One of my interviewees loves going to the sauna and has a good wood heated sauna in the rear building. There she has often bathed me with a birch whisk and prayed for herself, her children and me.

Initially it was not my plan to make friends in the field, but the number of years and my extensive field work with the Romanies inevitably brought about many friendships. Through my visits during the years I have experienced the joys and sorrows of the lives of my interviewees, as well as the normalities of their everyday lives. I am not indifferent to their lives, and neither are they when it comes to my life, because care and respect are interactive. This, of course, implies an ethical responsibility for the researcher, which I have elaborated extensively in my dissertation: What kind of sensitive information can you publish, how can you write about people who have become your friends, how do you narrate the lives of a very stigmatised minority group?[7]

Important issues: sexuality, cleanliness and respect

B: What kind of issues have you focused in your research?

A: It has been my aim to study ethnicity as a lived experience. This means that I do not see ethnicity as a ready entity, or as a clearly defined object. I have been concerned with how different aspects of identity change during a life course, to find out which features are connected with different phases of life, with childhood, youth, adulthood and old age. I have mostly focused Romany women's ethnic identity when they move from adolescence to adulthood and old age, and more specifically the changes in ethnic identity from women's point of view. My research document show identity and ethnicity are constantly negotiated. Despite the very strict Romany customs, there is always space for negotiating them.

The ethnic identity of the Romanies is gendered.[8] Women's lives are lived not only in relation to their husbands, children and the rest of their families. Their lives are also influenced by educational and employment opportunities, by the hobby environment as well as the surrounding society on the whole. I have tried to grasp the totality of features influencing identity. Generally I wanted to identify the important features in the lives of Romany women. Which are the important rules expressing the ethnic identity among Romany women? Who follow the rules, and who do not?

B: What kind of prominent features, in your material, are characteristic of Romany women's lives?

A: Shame is a most important feature when you grow up as a Romany woman. While shame is rather unfamiliar to the ethnic Finnish population, there are many shameful things connected with a Romany woman's course of life. Shameful things include for example sexuality, bodily functions, illnesses of internal organs, menstruation, birth and the relationship between men and women. These and other aspects of a woman's life are regarded as things so shameful that it is quite inappropriate to talk about them, and especially to write about such topics.

Woman's sexuality is considered dangerous to a gypsy man, and women have the responsibility to control every aspect of her sexual attributes. A Romany woman has to know how to behave. The customs are strict, and closely connected with shame and honour. Customs concerning women's hemlines are still very powerful, for example. A woman's skirt has to be long enough to cover her ankles. When she walks, she has to walk without making the hemline move too much. Also, a woman's hemline must not touch a man's shoes, especially if he is not her husband. Touching his shoe is a sign of very impertinent behaviour. And if a spoon falls to a woman's feet, the spoon is impure and has to be thrown away. Young women have to be extra careful concerning their sexuality. For instance, if a young woman's hemline accidentally touches a bag of food, she has to spoil the whole bag. An interviewee described such an incident in her own life, and told me that she had never felt so embarrassed in her life.

On the other hand, a Romany woman has some counter-power: With her own behaviour she can either increase a man's honour, or destroy his honour. A Romany woman often takes care of the home and also of the official relationships to the outside world. She is the one who visits the social security office, housing authorities and "walks" around selling handicraft, or works outside home. Many Romany women who work outside the home choose to work as kitchen workers in restaurants, and in nursing. Attending the social security offices and housing authorities has become one of the women's duties during the last 30 years. Earlier women begged for clothes and food for their families. It is a shame for a woman not to take good care of the household duties. One of the most important duties of a Romany woman is doing the laundry – and doing it well. There are very strict rules about the laundry, because the clothes of people of different ages and sexes have to be washed separately. All the interviewees mentioned tidiness as the most important thing in taking care of the home. They also regard themselves as successful in this respect, as declared by Miranda, 60 years old: "I always like it tidy and, not worn out and the home must be clean and neat and everything must be in order".

The woman also has the main responsibility for the family's finances. The men who used to be in the business of horse-trading, now sell cars or smaller items, such as watches and brushes etc. Traditionally a Romany would not necessarily want to have any big business. Nowadays young couples live very similarly to the predominant population's way of life, but in social situations the rules are strict and have to be followed. For some of them, following the rules may even be a duty created by the collectivity.

Respect for older people is an essential part of the Romany culture which all interviewees mentioned. When I asked them what they thought is the most beautiful thing in their culture, they answered: "Respect for older people." This sort of respect was used as a sort of measurement of whether the Romany culture has changed or not. When I asked the young about it, they said that the older people are absolutely still respected. For example sexuality cannot be talked about in their presence.

Finnish Romanies have preserved manners of purity and impurity, shame and honour, and respect for older people very tight during centuries. The same kinds of

(Photo: Airi Markkanen)

(Photo: Airi Markkanen)

manners are features of Romany cultures all over Europe, but they may vary a lot. In many societies the Romanies have assimilated into the majority culture, and they do not follow their old manners anymore.[9]

The Romanies are, however, still clearly different when it comes to respect for older people and the rules of purity and impurity. Respect for older people and following the purity and impurity rules are basic principles of the Romany way of life – and also among Finnish Romanies' to-day.[10]

Romany life in Finland: forced settlement, wandering, persecution, attempts of assimilation, the new Romany nomadism to Finland.

B: As you said, the Finnish Romanies is an old ethnic group. As elsewhere in Europe, their lot has not been easy, has it?

A: You are quite right, unfortunately. The Romanies have been met with forced settlement, persecution, and attempts of assimilation almost all the time since they came to Finland in 1559. At that time Finland was a part of the Kingdom of Sweden. The same laws applied to the Romany people in Finland as in Sweden. The contents of the laws concerned deportation, adaptation and monitoring. In 1809 Finland became a Grand Duchy of the Russian Empire, and the emphasis of the special laws was still to adapt and monitor the Romany population.

We do not know much about the history of Romany women. A proclamation issued in 1812, however, ordered "defective, wandering Tatars and gypsies as well as other ill-mannered vagrant people, who were not fit to common work", to be preserved. Men were to be preserved in the workhouse of Viapori (Sveaborg), and women in the spinning houses. But the women refused to be parted from their children, and the children were then allowed to follow their mothers to the spinning rooms. Apart from this, there were hardly any references to Romany women in the first Finnish public report on the Romanies, a Committee Report from 1900 which suggested ways and means to assimilate the Romanies.[11] We do know, however, that the church in the previous centuries denied the Romanies access to the sacraments of Baptism, the Eucharist, Confession, Holy Matrimony, and even to the funeral ceremony.

The suggestions of the Committee Report from 1900 did not succeed in assimilating the Romanies. The next state Committee Report, which was published in 1955, was motivated by more or less similar interests, and did not differ much from the previous one. The existence of the Romany minority was seen as a social problem and a burden, in spite of the contributions of for instance Romany men taking part in World War II, where they fought side by side with Finnish soldiers against Russian soldiers, a fact that has recently been noticed.[12] The traditional practices of Romanies, like the men's horse-trading and the women's trade with handicrafts and fortune telling, were still not seen as 'real' work. Consequently, the Romanies were gradually forced to give up their travelling way of life.

B: This history seems familiar – but the cultural attitude gradually changed in the latter half of the 20th century, did it not?

A: Yes, it did. During the 1960s big changes took place in the social and cultural atmosphere in Finland. The business structure changed dramatically, with the growth of the industrial sector and then the service sector. These material and economic changes triggered social protests, and around 1966 a new wave of social protest took off in Finland that also included a new wave of the women's movement. New kinds of organisations were established. By the end of the 1960s the new organisations and different pamphlets drew attention to the conditions of the Romany population and the discrimination of their lives.

This general change in attitudes was reflected also in the Reform of the Constitutional Rights from 1995. The new Constitution unequivocally condemns discrimination of all sorts: No-one can be placed in an unequal position on account of their sex, age, ethnic origin, language, religion, beliefs, opinions, state of health, disability or other personal factors. Of utmost importance in the new constitution was the right of the Sami and the Roma people – as well as other minority groups – to maintain and develop their own language and culture. The Roma's rights to their own language and culture are guaranteed also through amendments in the educational legislation, now allowing the teaching of Romany as a mother tongue in school. Legislation on children's day care is also amended to include the support of Romany children's own language and culture.

The report Strategies of Romany Policy from 1999 differs from the above-mentioned reforms in a significant way:[13] Romanies themselves have taken part in the making of the report. Thus, they have had a more direct way to influence the understanding of how to define and handle the problems of marginalisation and how to combat the marginalisation process. Problems connected with living, unemployment, low level of education, social problems and the marginalization resulting from all these are common phenomena among Romanies. These problems are the same all over Europe and even more serious.[14]

The Romano Mission publishes a magazine called Romano Boodos

B: What changes occurred within the organisations dealing with Romany issues – and what kind of new organisations emerged?

A: The oldest of the Romany organisations in Finland is *The Finnish Romano Mission* (previously The Gypsy Mission) founded 1906 by a priest who belonged to the majority population. The priest tried to assimilate Romanies to the majority. But anyway he and his organisation were the only ones that tried somehow to make Romany life better. Nowadays the organisation has Romanies in its council, and the chair of organisation is a Romany, Henry Hedman. There are many projects going on in co-operation with the Finnish State, for instance projects against marginalisation.

One of the active contributors to the magazine Romano Boodos is Tuula Åkerlund. She is a Romaniwoman, writer and activist. She has had great success with her guide-book The Romani and Health Services: Guide for the Health Professionals from 1993, and her guides about the Romany culture for parish employers and social security officers. Miranda Vuolasranta (a Romani woman and activist as well) has edited a new textbook of Romany, Romani tšimbako drom. This book has been published by the Ministry of Education, Unit of Romany Education in 1997. The education unit also publishes a bulletin called Latšo Diives.

One of the greatest accomplishments of these Romany magazines is their stress on the importance of education. For instance, during the years of my interviews I encouraged the Romany women to study, and some of the middle-aged in fact started to study again. Some have been released from their "awkward" husbands. In fact, approximately 40% of the Romany women are single mothers.

During the last few years there has also been articles about drugs, and how drugs are among the most threatening things facing the Romany culture and families. The drug problem is described as concerning young Romany boys mostly, but drugs are known also to disturb Romany girls.

The Finnish Free Romany Organisation (Suomen Vapaa Romaniyhdistys) was founded 1964. In the board of the organisation there are mostly Romanies who belong to the Pentecostal parish. This organisation was founded by the Romanies themselves, which was something quite new. The organisation has many active Romani women in its various committees. At the moment there are projects for child rearing and health care as well as projects against drugs.

There is also the *Gypsies' Future Organisation* – a support group for young Romans. It was set up in 1996 to provide support for Romany children and young people brought up or still living in institutions and foster families.

Equality issues

B: How would you describe the gender equality situation with respect to Romany women? I guess there are at least two ways of approaching this issue, one by compar-ing Romany women to Romany men, and another by comparing Romany women to ethnic Finnish women.

A: These are important questions, highlighting the ethnocentricity of the famous Nordic and Finnish gender equality agenda.

According to the Western and Nordic idea of equality, the Romany men have power to decide and control women's lives. This means that culturally, men have a legitimate right to subdue women. On the other hand, one has to consider, as I have done previously, that the Romany women are far from helpless because of their important role in the social and economic life of their group. Issues of gender and power are discussed in the 1999 report on strategies, as the report pays attention to the question of equality between Romany women and men. The report says that "the man is in the background when it comes to questions connected with the woman's role and status, and vice versa. If the Romany culture differs from the culture of the predominant population, the Romany culture must be respected, because the Romanies are entitled to respect. In a well-balanced Romany family the man and the woman do not compete with each other. The man is the head of the family and the woman is its heart". [15]

The Advisory Board On Romany Affairs In Finland (The Suomen Romaniasiain Neuvottelukunta), set up in 1956, has stated that the gender equality program of the Finnish Government has been drawn up from the dominant women's group's point of view. This is just one out of many examples of a general lack of ethnic sensibility, in Finland as well as in the other Nordic countries. In fact, the status of the Romany women, who belong to a national and ethnic minority, has never been sufficiently elaborated. We do know, however, that Romany women suffer from work discrimination and even racism with respect to salary and employment. The understanding of the category 'women' which is implicitly or explicitly used in public reports, is never sufficiently broad to cover all women. Certain groups are always excluded.

Miranda Vuolasranta, secretary general of *The Advisory Board On Romany Affairs In Finland*, and herself a Romany woman, has told me about her aspirations for equality in the Finnish society, as well as her own solutions concerning dressing:

> "(–) I want to show that a Roman is good enough and can be a Finn. To take part in the working life and society, no matter how traditionally Roman you dress or live. In a way this has been one of the basic messages of my life, about which I have wanted to tell to both to my own minority and to the predominant population all my life. And especially to Romany women I want to say that the traditional way of dressing does not stop you from educating yourself and participating in the working life: this is what I have experienced as a life-long mission for myself."

We cannot really speak of a women's movement among Finnish Romanies. In Britain, however, there has been a remarkable growth of the women's movement among Traveller-Gypsies in the late 1980s. Most recently Sylvia Dunn, a Romany woman and formerly Vice President of the Gypsy Council for Education, Culture, Welfare and Civil Rights, has founded the National Association of Gypsy Women (NAGW). The association is growing steadily. This is important, because the growth of the Gypsy women's movement has brought into focus the meaning of sensitivity to gender, age and ethnicity. This sensitivity is to serve the whole community, not to lock particular sections into a victim mode.[16]

We also see a significant Romany women's movement in Bucurest, Romania. The sociologist Nicoletta Bitu, herself a Romany woman, is one of the activists there. She told me that her activism was triggered about ten years ago, when Romany houses in her home village were burned down, along with many surrounding Romany villages. In her country, one of the most serious problems facing Romany women is violence, domestic violence. The women are also victims of discriminatory attitudes of the majority population. She says, too, that the level of feminist awareness is not high because there is no Roma or Gypsy women's movement at the international level.

There are some studies done on the census of Gypsies in Europe, but unfortunately there are few data about Roma or Gypsy women which can document their situation. At the local level, there are several successful projects for instance in Slovakia, Macedonia, Hungary and Romania. According to Nicoletta Bitu we see "a beginning of the building of a Roma or Gypsy women civil society".

Nicoletta Bitu is worried also about the trafficking of Romany women and girls, drugs abuse and prostitution. She says that traffic intensified after communism failed in Eastern European countries and the Roma or Gypsy women became "an exotic raw material". The traffic is not all the time associated with prostitution. It can be associated with the activity of begging for income on the streets. The attitude of the Roma or Gypsy is a silent one and if they speak about prostitution and the drugs abuse, in private, they all the time say "they are not from our group." Nicoletta Bitu wishes that "maybe the future women movement will face this cruel reality". In the public policies in Europe, for instance Spain has the most advanced components for Roma Women positions in its National program. The Federacion de Associaciones de Mujeres Gitanas "KAMIRA" is said to be one that should be taken as a model for all countries. This organisation is working in Torremolinos, Spain.

Romany activism on Pan-European level and in Finland

A: Poverty and violence have driven the Romanies away from the countries of Eastern Europe. To mention just one example: In June 1999 more than a thousand Romany refugees arrived in Finland from Slovakia. New refugee centres were founded. Later in the summer visa became obligatory between Finland and Slovakia. The Slovakian Government has been asked by the EU to improve the conditions of the Romanies, and the concern at the EU level clearly indicates that the position of the Romanies has become an important political issue in many Eastern European countries.

Some of the Finnish Romanies I have interviewed showed a positive attitude towards the refugee Romanies, while others displayed a very strict negative attitude. Quite interestingly, those expressing a negative attitude have chiefly appealed to the fact that the refugee Romanies do not follow the rules of purity and impurity. Thus, they are not conceived as 'civilized'. With this concept, civilization, the Romanies do not refer to formal school education, but to the Romany rules of respect for older people, and for purity and impurity, manners and clothing.

One of the activist Romany women told me that she had attended a public meeting with the Polish, Slovakian and Czech Romanies. She underlined the importance of discussing the basic issues in the Romany language. She says that it "feels great" to attend international seminars, just because the Romany language is the working language. Another active Romany woman says that she is familiar with the miserable situation of the Romanies of Eastern Europe (poverty, violence against them, bad housing, unemployment etc.) She has visited several Eastern European countries familiarizing herself with the situation, but she thinks that things should be settled on the spot and not "rush from one country to another with the children".

Roma migration has become a pan-European issue. The Romanies, having no state of their own, form "a genuine European minority" in need of particular protection. In January, the President of Finland, Tarja Halonen, proposed a European consultative assembly for the Roma to be set up.

Conclusions

A: In Finland some activist Romany women are working in some Romany organisations but there is not a Romany women's movement. Romany women have always worked and acted in the Romany community, with relatives and with their family. There has not been any need or space for a separate movement. Even if women do mostly everything to-day and are strong, they cannot be above men, neither concretely nor abstractly but I would not call them deprived. They have very strong positions within the families and in the Romany community.

In Helsinki there was a conference about Romany questions in October 2001 discussing a European consultative assembly for the Roma people. Also the Romany women's position is negotiated at the European level. The case of Romanies was also taken into consideration in the Durban 3rd World Conference against Racism. The Conference affirmed that the Roma has been and still is, a persecuted people that have faced racism, genocide and ethnic cleansing. Miranda Vuolasranta thinks that this recognition is of enormous importance for Romanies. Their problems have never before been so broadly discussed at the level of the United Nations. The conclusions contain all the major issues: the urgent need for equal development in education, housing, access to health care services and basic rights.

It is said that Romany women often suffer from double discrimination, as women and as Romanies at the same time. Governments in Europe should give special attention to the particular situation and needs of Romany women, and national strategies in favour of Romanies should include a specific action plan for women. Priority and financial support should be given to projects carried out by or involving Romany women. During the Helsinki meeting autumn 2001 many speakers asked: "How is it possible to trust Romanies, if we are not given trust", and they claimed that "we are not trusted". At the moment a lot of important things are happening between Romany activists, organisations and majority governments in many European countries. There is a lot to do to improve the Romanies' lives generally, and the position of Romany women in particular. NOW is the time to act.

References

Acton & Caffrey & Dunn & Vinson, (1997). "Gender issues in accounts of Gypsy health and hygiene as discourses of social control". Thomas Acton & Gary Mundy (eds.). *Romany culture and Gypsy identity*. University of Hertfordshire Press.

Banks, Marcus (1996). *Ethnicity: Anthropological Constructions*. London and New York, Routledge.

Basso, K. H. (1970). "To give up on Words: Silence in Western Apache culture". P. Giglioli (ed.) *Language and social context: selected readings*. Harmondsworth, Penguin Books.

Bauman, Richard (1982). *Let Your Words Be Few*. Cambridge, Cambridge University Press.

Clifford, James (1986). Introduction: Partial Truths. James Clifford & George E. Marcus (ed.) *Writing Culture*. Berkeley, University of California.

Clifford, James (1988). The Predicament of Culture. Twentieth-Century Ethnography, Literature and Art. Harvard University Press.

Clifford, James (1997). *Routes, Travel and Translation in the Late Twentieth Century*. Harvard University Press, Cambridge.

Coffey, Amanda (1999). *The Ethnographic Self. Fieldwork and the Representation of Identity*. London-Thousand Oaks-New Delhi, Sage Publications.

Douglas, Mary (2000). Puhtaus ja Vaara. Ritualistisen rajanvedon analyysi. Tampere, Vastapaino

Grass, Gunther (1992). Losses. Granta. N:o 42

Hall, Stuart (1990). Cultural Identity and Diaspora. Jonathan Rutherford (ed.): *Identity, Community, Culture, Difference*. London. Lawrence & Wishart.

Hastrup, Kirsten (1992). Writing ethnography: state of the art. Judith Okely & Helen Callaway (eds.), *Anthropology & Autobiography*. London, Routledge.

Hastrup, Kirsten (1995). *A Passage to Anthropology. Between experience and theory*. London & New York, Routledge.

Heikkinen, Kaija (1998a).The Role of Own and Other's Everyday in the Construction of Identity. The Case of Finnish-Karelian Families. Satu Apo & Aili Nenola & Laura Stark-Arola (eds.), *Gender and Folklore*. Helsinki, Finnish Literature Society.

Komiteanmietintö (1900). Keisarilliselle Majesteetille, N:o 3. Helsinki

Lucassen, Leo, Willems, Wim, Cottaar, Annemarie (1997). *Gypsies and Other Itinerant Groups. A Socio-Historical Approach*. Centre for the History of Migrants. University of Amsterdam.

Mustalaiskomitean mietintö (1955). Komiteanmietintö N:o 7. Helsinki.

Okely, Judith (1979). Trading Stereotypes, the case of English Gypsies. Sandra Wallman (ed.), *Ethnicity at Work*. London.

Okely, Judith (1983). *The Traveller-Gypsies*. Cambridge, Cambridge University Press.

Okely, Judith (1992). Anthropology and autobiography: participatory experience and embodied knowledge. Judith Okely & Helen Callaway (eds.), *Anthropology and Autobiography*. London, Routledge.

Okely, Judith (1994*). Constructing Difference: Gypsies as "Other"*. Anthropological Journal on European Cultures. 1994, vol. 3, nr. 2, p. 55-73.

Okely, Judith (1996). *Own or Other Culture*. London, Routledge.

Airi skal denne være med? Rao, Aparna (1975). Some Manus Conceptions and Attitudes. Rehfisch, Farnham (ed.) – *Gypsies, Tinkers and other Travellers*. London, Academic Press.

Roos, J. P. (1987). Suomalainen elämä. Tutkimus tavallisten suomalaisten elämäkerroista. Helsinki, SKS.

San Roman, Teresa (1975). Kinship, Marriage, Law and Leadership in Two Urban Gypsy Settlements in Spain. Rehfisch, Farnham (ed.), *Gypsies, Tinkers and other Travellers*. London, Academic Press.

Stewart, Michael (1997). *The Time of the Gypsies*. Colorado, Westview Press.

Stewart, Michael (1999). Brothers and "Orphans": Images of Equality among Hungarian Rom. Sophie Day & Evthymios Papataxiarchis & Michael Stewart (eds.) *Lilies of the Field. Marginal People who live for the Moment*. Colorado: Westview Press.

Suonoja, Kyösti & Lindberg, Väinö (1999). *Romanipolitiikan strategiat*. Sosiaali- ja terveysministeriön selvityksiä 1999:9. Helsinki.

Sutherland, Anne (1975). *Gypsies, the Hidden Americans*. New York, Free Press.

van Maanen, John (1988*). Tales of the Field*. Chigaco, University of Chigaco Press.

Viljanen-Saira Anna Maria (1979). *Mustalaiskulttuuri ja kulttuurin muutos*. Helsingin yliopiston suomalais-ugrilaisen kansatieteen yleisen etnologian linjan lisensiaatin tutkielma. Helsinki.

Viljanen Anna Maria (1994). *Psykiatria ja kulttuuri. Tutkimus oikeuspsykiatrisesta argumentaatiosta*. Stakes tutkimuksia 37. Helsinki Suomen Antropologinen Seura.

Notes

1 Airi Markkanen finished her PhD degree in 2003: *Luennollisesti etnografinen tutkimus romaninaisten elämänkulusta*. ("In a natural way – an ethnographic study of the life course of Romani women") University of Joensuu Publications in the Humanities no 33.

2 Günter Grass (1992) (transl. by Markkanen).

3 Viljanen (1994).

4 Roos (1987).

5 See Clifford (1986); Clifford (1988); Clifford (1997); Hastrup (1992); (1995); Okely (1996); van Maanen (1988).

6 About silence in different cultures Basso (1970); Bauman (1982).

7 Heikkinen (1998a); Coffey (1999).

8 Hall (1990); Banks (1996).

9 See Grönfors (1997); Kopsa-Schön (1988); Kornblum (1975); Miller (1975); Okely (1979); Okely (1983); Okely (1992); Okely (1994); Okely (1996); Rao (1975); San Roman (1975); Stewart (1997); Stewart (1999); Sutherland (1975), Viljanen (1979); (1994).

10 e.g. Mary Douglas, (2000).

11 Komiteanmietintö (1900) (Committee Report (1900)).

12 However, no Romanies were sent to concentration camps during World War II from Finland.

13 Report (1999).

14 Lucassen & Willems & Cottaar (1998).

15 Suonoja & Lindberg (1999), p. 130.

16 Acton & Caffrey & Dunn & Vinson (1997). The Finnish Free Romany Organisation.

Part IV

Addressing Violence and Care

CHAPTER 13

The problem of trafficking in women at the transnational and national levels

With the example of Russia and NIS

Natalia Khodyreva

In this paper I shall touch upon the problems of the latest history of transnational, international and national women's organisations combating trafficking in women. This will be done through an analysis of the aims and positions of these organisations, as well as their debates and contradictions.

It will be followed by a discussion of differences with respect to prostitution and of the ration of palliative and radical, tactic and strategic measures taken by the national and transnational organisations in their co-operation.

This is necessary for the realisation of perspectives that represent the aim of the women's movement, because these debates reflect the values and differences both within the feminist movement and within transnational and national interests.

Contemporary history

The enhanced interest in the trafficking problem on the part of the women's non-governmental organisations (NGOs) was recorded in the early 1990s. It was connected with the disintegration of the socialist block and migration of women from the Eastern block to Western Europe and America. In 1993 the laws "On entering and leaving Russia" and "On employment of the population" were issued. Based on these laws every citizen of Russia obtained the right to independently search for a job abroad.

The first information about trafficking victims reached the Russian organisations, in particular the St. Petersburg Crisis Centre for Women (CCW), in 1993.[1]

Later, in 1996, at the conference "Russia at Cross-roads: Human rights" the women's organisations located in Berlin, informed us about the help provided to a number of Russian women who suffered through trafficking. In November that year, at the conference in Brighton "Violence and women's citizenship", CCW outlined the concrete steps in co-operation with European and post-soviet women's organisations for the solution of the trafficking problem.[2] In 1997 in Utrecht, CCW discussed future co-operation with the Anti-Trafficking Fund (STV); we consulted the Global Network for Survival in the process of editing the film "*Bought and Sold*". In autumn 1997 CCW had a meeting with the "*Midnight Mission*" from Dortmund (Germany) initiating future co-operation. In November CCW spoke at the International Conference " Trafficking in women from CIS countries" held in Moscow. At that conference we were entrusted to develop a project against trafficking in Russian women.[3]

In 2000 CCW prepared a report for the European Parliament on the trafficking situation in Russia. CCW joined Estonia and Latvia in taking part in the development of the National Anti-Trafficking Plan at the seminar in Amsterdam; we had a meeting in Moscow with the representatives of the OSCE; we took part in the seminar on trafficking and prostitution within the framework of the Second International Conference "Women of the Baltic Sea: Gender Equality and the Future" held in Helsinki; we spoke before the American Senate in Washington D.C. on the anti-trafficking legislation;[4] in 2000 we hosted the international conference "Co-operation of the Public and Governmental Organisations on the Problem of Women's Migration and Trafficking".[5]

In autumn 1999, with the support of Miramed Institute and "La Strada – Ukraine", Russian women's organisations entered the "Angel" Anti-traffic International Coalition.[6] Now, the international Angel Coalition united about 40 organisations from Russia, USA and NIS countries.

A number of reasons for such co-operation among women's organisations can be pointed out such as: 1) the general problem of labour migration of women from economically low regions like Russia, NIS and Asia to Western Europe and the US; 2) poor legal international protection of human rights of women migrants.

Among the transnational/national/international organisations we could mention The European Anti-Trafficking Network, Transnet, La Strada Project, Angel International Coalition, North Network against prostitution, STV, Coalition against Trafficking in women (CATW), Global Alliance against traffic in women (GAATW), Anti-Slavery International, CHANGE etc.[7]

Contradictory problems

The most complicated problems of trafficking dealt with several contradictions: 1) between the liberal discourse regarding human rights to freedom of movement and choice of place for living versus national interests favouring protection of national labour market; 2) between the policy of restriction of migration flows by the EU and the U.S. and the needs of the destination countries' internal markets for cheap labour; 3) between the depopulation problems of Western Europe and migration of the reproductive force from Russia, NIS, Eastern Europe; 4) the attitude towards prostitution as a free choice, profession versus violence, discrimination of women. The latter contradiction indicates at its most serious conceptual differences within the women's movement.[8]

Among the aspects pertaining to trafficking the following ones are distinguished: labour-, violence-, migration-, prostitution-related, remedial, moral, criminal, unequal economical relations between the countries.[9] Different NGOs and state structures have their own priorities with respect to these aspects that deal with the situation between the countries, inside the countries and between transnational coalitions. All of the above-listed aspects can be viewed at strategic and tactical levels.

The situation in Russia

From the point of view of the country of origin the main motive of Russian women is labour – the desire to earn money and then return home. The second motive is migration. The women are looking for a permanent place for living in safer and richer countries. Most Russian women wishing to work abroad prefer the basic simple occupations.[10] Marital motives essentially lag behind, and in the main, they are just a strategy for migration. As to prostitution, only 2-7 % of the Russian women do not deny this possibility of earnings initially.

Russian migration services present only 10% of all information on labour migration of women; the main stream leaves as tourists. So the official data gives account only of about 2000 Russian women leaving to work legally. Informally 100,000 Russian women leave to work abroad annually. The number returning is also unknown.

According to the data of the Crisis Centre for women, one in five women willing to work abroad faces the violation of her human rights and becomes a victim of trafficking and a slave in the existing working conditions.

From our clients' point of view, the most important thing for them is safe migration conditions, valid job agreement and appropriate salary. They plan to return home or to send money home to their family in order to pay for their children's education for treatment of their relatives or to buy apartments.

As long as the economic conditions in the different countries are unequal and the professional discrimination of women remains the same (and this will not change for many decades), the temporary labour migration will remain the tactic of survival for many of the Russian women. In our opinion, only a radical anti-trafficking method will create proper conditions for safe labour migration, protection of migrants' labour rights. In order to achieve this purpose it is necessary to lobby to convince the Russian government to conclude the official bilateral agreements with other countries concerning temporary employment of Russian citizens abroad on a mass-scale basis. A problem of the so-called organised crime will automatically be mitigated with the realisation of these tactics.

The law against trafficking (as well as all the laws that are not complied with properly in Russia) is not a radical remedy against trafficking. Therefore the struggle for its approval is important, but it is concentrated mainly on punishment of traffickers but does not look into the reasons for the very phenomenon.

The Angel Coalition represents interests of diverse groups of Russian women. These women belong to practically all social strata of the society. We help all women who suffer through trafficking. These women all need a visa to enter Europe and the USA and they will not be able to work legally at any job. Also, 70% of the young Russian women have never been abroad. Often the Russian women became victims of trafficking just because they wanted to see Europe or the US. Without the "help" of pimps they would never have managed to move out. Among other anti-trafficking measures we run public prevention campaigns.

Contradictory results and difficulties in the realisation of preventive programs against trafficking

After the organisation of a preventive campaign in mass media the number of women calling our hot-lines and looking for an opportunity to go abroad increased. The risk of becoming a trafficking victim – which was the subject of the campaign – was less important for them than the hopeless economic existence and the high level of violence in Russia. They are interested in safe migration and finding a job in Western/Asian countries. The stories of our women-clients are striking; the experience they meet gave them a good lesson for the future, but still they strive to go abroad again to make earnings.

We also help the victims to handle the consequences of their journey through psychological and legal support and financial aid to women who returned, including being deported.[11] To a great extent, the international legislation is aimed at support for the victims and punishment of the traffickers. A huge amount of money spent on it is provided by governmental and private funds. Unfortunately, in Russia we do not have adequate legal measures and official programmes aimed at the improvement of the poor economic position of women that are being funded by state authorities.

Financing of activity of Russia and NIS organisations against trafficking and violence

It was interesting to observe how the activities of anti-trafficking organisations in Russia were financed. In 1997 the UNICEF and Ford Foundation turned down our anti-trafficking projects. As a matter of fact, it was a peak of women' recruitment abroad there. The information concerning trafficking was fragmentary; the preventive programmes did not yet exist in Russia and NIS. In 1999-2000 we had already had a lot of clients who suffered at that time. Moreover the USA is at the top of the list of preference countries for migration among the young women and accordingly of the level of trafficking incidents.

The policy of funding only a certain organisation and only one approach to their choice – or nothing at all – seriously hindered the realisation of anti-trafficking projects. Such funding policy was inefficient because it brings forward serious competition between the weak and poor, yet developing women's organisations and the established crisis centres in the Russian provinces. When the US government provides a large grant to one fund, this fund tends to transfer that money to a single subordinate organisation to maintain a substantial part of the grant to cover its own administrative costs.

According to the given tactic, the regional organisations (many of the numerous ones within huge Russia) received less than 50% of all grants, if not less. Small grants do not promote the stable development of any of them. Usually such centres arise by division of the already established old centres. But the fund takes a chance to report about its help to plenty of crisis centres set up all over Russia. Such tactics did not favour stability (which is extremely important for crisis centres) and adequate quality of work of crisis centres – the proper quality of work is possible only in the environment of stable development.

The tactics of middle European and private US funds are more flexible, more sensitive to regional interests and more effective for Russia. A good example is a Network of Crisis centres in the Barents Region. The last one consists of the representatives of different countries – Nordic and Northwest part of Russia with common territory, living condition and interests.

Fortunately, the German anti-trafficking women's organisations (for example, Midnight Mission of Dortmund) helped us a lot. They lobbied the German government to provide us with a grant, and we have received serious support from them. St. Petersburg Crisis Centre started its serious work practically at the end of 1998.

Now the US government is going to provide a grant against trafficking, to be distributed between different Russian organisations. But unfortunately, we have lost time, overlooked the situation, which was tragic. Too many Russian women have already suffered.

Sharing experience by transnational organisations and coalitions is an important part of the co-operation between us. But Russian NGOs are more dependent in financial matters, and it is important for them to define and realise the Russian women' needs and interests first of all. I shall not speak about the national interests: they may not be the same as the interests of ordinary women. Some countries pursue the so-called anti-trafficking policy by encroaching on the freedom of Russian and NIS young women, like not letting them come to the countries at all. The major funding policy of the European countries aims at supporting the independence of NGOs in the issue of trafficking, but there are the structures that make the financing directly dependent on the ideological position, in particular with respect to prostitution.

The positive aspect of funding was a possibility to influence the policy of the Russian government. At the beginning we did not rely at all on the aid of local government. Now these issues are already being discussed in the course of Angel Coalition's lobbying the regional and federal government (in Irkutsk, Kazan, Chelyabinsk, St. Petersburg, Murmansk, Petrozavodsk, Novgorod, Yaroslavl, Moscow, Far East etc.). And again we emphasise the interests of Russian women to be faced by the Russian government and the other states. The main problem still is legal and therefore safe labour migration. If the problem of legal labour migration is solved then the problem of the so-called organised crime, as far as trafficking is concerned, will disappear as such. The crime thrives first of all on the prohibitive and rigid visa and labour policy of the destination countries that defend their national labour markets. At the same time the private business in Western countries and the USA needs cheap labour. There is also a need in Western countries for reproductive import, with a view to improve the demographic and recreation situation. There have been a number of cases of import of reproductive materials registered, for example, import of Russian women's ovules to Finland and Cyprus.

Countries of destination

The countries of destination are known for another phenomenon – huge number of women from East Europe involved in sex-business.[12] This means that due to trafficking there are certain changes in women's lives. Most women from the countries of origin – those willing to work within normal professions – get involved in prostitution in the countries of destination. Following the traffickers' activities most of these women are forced into prostitution, forced labour and slavery practices.

The approximate numbers of these women are known from the statistics of police raids, including those on deported women, or/and from anonymous NGO organisations. Not much is known about successful women who illegally work in normal businesses (or in prostitution) or about those Western employers who gain large incomes based on the work of their illegal workers from Eastern Europe. The employer does not have to arrange medical and social insurance for such workers; he does not pay the taxes for them and does not pay any decent wages to these workers as compared with the locals. In the main, our migrants work in social service, tourism, the entertaining business, construction and agriculture. Thus in Europe and USA there is a quite a large group of people concerned about their personal interests and sex-business who are not principally interested in the legalisation of employment of migrants from Russia and NIS. Let us take, for example, the ads for mass-scale recruitment of nurses to American hospitals.

Despite certain appeals on the part of a number of European countries to legalise labour migrants, the policy of these countries still involves repression and control of these women-migrants.

Common features and differences in NGO positions in EU, USA and NIS.

Basically one may say that regarding most aspects of trafficking the different NGOs have much in common. For example, there is full unanimity with regard to preventive and social aid to trafficked women. Effective co-operation was achieved by different coalitions and organisations in the area of social support. Here it is really possible to speak about a transnational, or even global, approach, which approaches we certainly distinguish from each other.

As far as migration and labour aspect of trafficking are concerned, the accents are different here. Thus in the practices and goals of the European and American NGOs no tasks of lobbying local governments are mentioned with a view of conclusion of bilateral agreements between the countries on legalisation of women's labour. Very often we hear remarks on impracticability of this goal. In this aspect the interests of EU countries certainly affect the activities of local NGOs. It is worth mentioning that the latter reflects the transnational interests of the European Union countries. Therefore trafficking as a migrant labour-related problem is rather poorly represented in their activities. The Angel Coalition and the Crisis Centre for Women regard migrant labour actions as one of radical strategies to combat trafficking. The idea of legal employment of non-EU citizens in the countries of the European Union within popular occupations is commonly not included in the agenda of these transnational organisations. It was notable that in the course of my negotiations with STV in a 1996 regarding Russia joining La Strada project, I was told that the inclusion of Russia is not planned.

Meanwhile, the majority of organisations place accent on the human rights aspect in trafficking (excluding labour rights). We would like to mention the usual rhetoric concerning human rights issues, especially when we talk about women's right to choose the place of residence and place of work without obstruction. Moreover, this approach is understood by some organisations purely in the context of labour rights of women occupied in prostitution.

Despite the support for this (rather abstract) aspect we would like to mention the utmost difficulties related to its realisation in NIS and Russia, as generally there is a problem with realisation of any provision of crime laws in Russia and NIS.

It is necessary to note the existing differences with regard to these aspects between the transnational coalitions, European organisations and organisations within one single country. As an example, GAÀTW and CATW show principal differences in their attitudes towards prostitution. All of the heated debates are concentrated around three concepts: choice, freedom, work. According to the first approach, some women choose this occupation by their free will. The second position shared by Nordic organisations states that prostitution is discrimination and violence against women. Therefore all those involved in prostitution are regarded to be victims of trafficking. Both organisations tend to subordinate the Eastern organisations, and in particular, the Angel coalition, to their standards and frameworks. The funding of our projects depends on their policy as well.

Debate about prostitution and export of discourses

It was surprising for us that the prostitution aspect as a part of the trafficking problem was so important. One can observe that sometimes the interests of a small group of privileged prostitutes (and former prostitutes) dominate over the interests of most women for whom prostitution is just a strategy for overcoming economic and social hopelessness, as well as the interests of most migrant women planning to get employed at popular jobs.

On the other hand it is clear that the sex-business is extremely profitable, therefore it recruits large organisations and sometimes coalitions, and bribes the experts. The predominant position of patriarchal sexuality, promotion of it on the market, forming enormous groups of male consumers enjoying this system of entertainment is possible only in the conditions of a certain policy towards the Russian and NIS women. The destruction of the social-oriented (welfare) state in Russia, social polarisation of gender promotes feminisation of poverty. This policy has resulted in our underprivileged women being entrapped by the system of prostitution, both local and transnational.

But recognition of prostitution as work will never protect the human rights of illegal labour migrants coming from Eastern Europe and former USSR, because it does not provide permission for the relevant work in EU and USA (this concerns normal professions too).

Discourse of "free choice"

In a 1980 the discourse of choice was reviewed by many prostitute organisations. Its conservative basis was providently concealed. The women's right "to choose" prostitution as occupation was represented as a progressive and feminist view. In this context the issue of how and why female bodies are delivered to the market was absolutely not important for the market and its male consumers.

When the prostitutes apply the discourse of choice to their lives they use the neutralisation technique. In sociology the marginalised groups use this term to describe the rationalisation method which tries to help to overcome their status.[13] Any other type of reflection may be painful for their self-evaluation. Therefore the idea of free choice in prostitution involves a similar technique.

The phenomenon of protective strategy of choice[14], supposes the illusion of one's own choice, control over one's own life. Often women suffering from violence in prostitution report that they are responsible for the violence against them or that they have chosen prostitution by their free will. The specificity of human perception makes the recognition of external dynamic social factors (which influence and form the choice) very complicated. The perception is first of all concentrated on relatively stable features and behaviours that are easier to remember and analyse. It is worth pointing out the protective effect of this strategy which might be necessary at the first stage of coping with the trauma caused by the primary perception of the negative event (shock, disbelief, amnesia).

Here it is necessary to give an account of methodological problems that arise in the course of choice-discourse research. One of the problems is how far we can trust and take into account the victim's direct assessment or interpretation of her own behaviour. What are the political and social consequences of such interpretation?

On the one hand, the policy of free choice is the manifest of the market liberal philosophy which favours individualism for its competitiveness and consumerism. Therefore the struggle is at the level of individualism and free choice discourse. If these ideas are included in the concept of freedom, they will ultimately undermine feminism.[15] On the other hand, the choice might be used as a mechanism of getting distinguished from those women who "choose" to remain with the perpetrator or be a prostitute. The discourse of choice transfers all responsibility for prostitution to women. The ideology of victim blaming is very efficient. The concentration on choice is the updated version of victim blaming.

The export of neo-liberal discourse to Russia and NIS is supported by both sex-business and non-governmental organisations defending the prostitutes' human rights.

It is proclaimed as progressive feminism which opposes the obsolete ascetic feminism of the second wave.

This discourse of free choice, intentional job and free expression of sexuality in the form of prostitution is accepted in Russia by a number of non-governmental women's organisations and by some women in general, for many reasons.

Firstly, due to the conditions of many years of repression of female sexuality in the USSR it can be perceived as some kind of liberalisation. This kind of representation is promoted by mass media. Secondly, the sexual life of Russian women in the family is sometimes very frustrating for them. The matrimonial life leaves every third woman unsatisfied and many women experienced undesirable sexual contacts with their husbands and partners, involvement in a relationship similar to prostitution. According to our data, every fifth woman under 30 has had such an experience.

Apart from that, the newborn Russian sex-business also influences the formation of neo-liberal discourse by favouring prostitution, erotisation of violence. The Western feminists have already had the experience of confronting this discourse, but the Russian and NIS organisations have not had this experience yet. Furthermore, the traditional weakness of legal/human rights consciousness and contemporary women's movement affects the young women negatively. We do not have any known organised groups of prostitutes. We have distributed about 500 information stickers for different groups of prostitutes advertising our support, opportunities for legal help, training in self-defence groups, and so far we have not had any response.

Discourse of "work"

In the 20th century characterised by long and frequent periods of unemployment, cut in traditional male work in industry with the shift to the service industry, casual jobs, the work in the sex-business attracted ever more people. The need for sexual services for a large section of the male population caused the change in representation of prostitutes' work.

The neo-liberal-discourse idea of prostitution as an occupation is aimed at neglecting the difference between prostitution and other occupations. Its idea is to make pretence, but not to see the actual difference. As it is known, the patriarchal approach to knowledge is context-free. A normal worker sells his/her labour, but not his/her body, while in prostitution the body is a subject of the job contract. In this sphere one's own sexuality, identity and self-evaluation is damaged.[16] The problem is that engagement in prostitution affects the woman's personality, her values and motives, negatively. The value of human communication is belittled; the emotions and feelings are suppressed even if the woman does not use drugs or alcohol (from our information, 80% of St. Petersburg prostitutes are drug addicts[17]). Even if we extol prostitution, its psychological consequences will still have an effect on female sexuality, as the woman selling her body dissociates herself from it in order to escape the unpleasant manipulations.

It is necessary to note that the organisations of prostitutes who promote the neo-liberal discourse comprise a small number of privileged prostitutes, their customers and bosses of sex-business. The raising of the prostitutes' status by presenting their occupation as work has the purpose of raising their self-esteem in their own eyes and to force society to abandon its hypocrisy. The work in the sex-business, as an example, is compared with such socially significant occupations as social or sexual adviser or psychotherapist.

The social guarantees for prostitutes are viewed in the context of consequence of recognition of prostitution as normal work. Therefore the idea of struggle for the prostitutes' human rights can yield the expected results in the West.

However, this does not imply that such measure would affect the labour-related and social rights of the prostitutes leaving Russia and NIS. The universalisation of approaches in this issue will work against women's interests. Prior to the October Revolution Russia had its own experience of legalisation of prostitution. The idea of the state as a main pimp was supported by the increasing number of poor country girls and women working in the brothels of St. Petersburg. Currently the Russian prostitutes tend to conceal their income from taxation authorities in every possible way (just like other ordinary Russian people). The corruption in Russian law-enforcement structures that even fails to protect raped teenagers is well known. The sex-business is not interested in legalisation because of laundering its incomes and evading payment of taxes to the state. Even doctors are interested in legalisation of the sex-business to have illegal profits from treatment of HIV-infected patients in the environment of AIDS epidemics.

The research accounts pay considerable attention to the regional differences in prostitution, taking the East, West Asia.[18] The national discourses are also dissimilar. If the Western coalitions (the Netherlands, Denmark, Germany) consider prostitution in terms of choice, work or sex, the Philippine and Swedish organisations regard it as violence and exploitation. Moreover, only the Nordic countries pay great attention to another important aspect – the party buying the prostitute who is a man in most cases.

There are different positions with respect to prostitution within the prostitute groups (for example, WHISPER and COYOTE). Still many groups, so far, use the principle of universalism and over-generalisation tending to represent their own opinions as opinions of all women, prostitutes of all countries.[19]

Opinions about prostitution in Russia

In Russia the situation is very ambivalent.[20] Over a third of respondents (35%) regard prostitution as commodity-money relations where the woman's body, her sexual services are offered in exchange for money, other material values or services. The rating of this definition proves to be the first in popularity in all groups.

The second in popularity is the definition of prostitution as a phenomenon proceeding from poverty, dependence and other social and economic conditions unfavourable for women (9.5%). The third priority is the definition of prostitution as a job and profession (7%).

Next, sharing the fourth and the fifth positions are the definitions including moral appraisal of this phenomenon (mostly negative) and psychological reasons and motives inducing women to take up prostitution (7.5%).

There were some other versions of answers split into groups by the underlying factors: emotional reactions, violence against women, satisfaction of women's sexual needs, satisfaction of men's sexual needs, love for money, the way of life, the choice; some respondents had difficulty in answering; some respondents gave comprehensive reports referring to a number of external and internal factors.

About 20% of women who recognised or realised the fact of entering into sexual relations with a person indifferent to them for the sake of money, material values or services, gave a definition of prostitution as a sort of market relations, which was supported later by 35% of them. This indicates their realisation of their situation, its acceptance as a fact of life and life experience and its factual designation as prostitution.

There is a certain correlation between the level of income and the assessment of prostitution. The smaller the income, the more often prostitution is denoted as a profession and the fact of commodity-money relations. The older the respondents, the more they keep to liberal views of prostitution. The acceptance of prostitution as a trade or job is related with the past experience of sexual relations for money.

Thus, the experience of girls and young women demonstrates that every one in five women has already had an experience of emotionally non-reciprocal undesired partner relations in general, with the respective figure of 5% during the past year (0.5% of respondents refused to answer this question).

As to the perspectives, the women have built a rating of material and other values which, in their opinion, justify their entering into sexual relations with an unloved partner (in past or in future). The motives include escape from the threat of violence made with relation to herself or her family members; some noble intentions like earning money to pay for the medical treatment of family members; the third position in the rating is care for fundamental material values – own private accommodation, stable earnings, well-paid job, lots of money to spend. Then "the child" is mentioned, followed by the "desire to take revenge on some other man". The fifth position is taken by moving abroad for permanent residence, entertainment trips abroad. This is followed by other countless desires for material objects and services. All this is an indirect indicator of the fact that the stated pleasures and needs are not accessible to women and that they wish to obtain all this by way of entering into relationships with men they do not love.

Only a small group of women (below 0,25%) noted that they would enter into such contacts purely for the sake of their own sexual satisfaction. One can suppose, though, that women in general have difficulties finding sexual pleasure with men they do not care for; probably some other reasons of material character seriously affect their decision to enter such relationships.

As to the attitude to prostitution, one may note that within the past ten years the prevailing treatment of it is of a liberal character with references to market conditions.

At the same time most of the population express their attitude to prostitutes based on positions of moralising and contempt.

There are different opinions regarding prostitution among the young women of St. Petersburg, but the liberal market approach is prevailing. One's own experience of prostitution is of great importance here.

Some of the women's organisation and social services in Russia support the idea of raising the prostitutes' status (personal status). This movement is supported by a rami-fied system of support groups, consciousness-raising groups, by struggle for human rights and for the punishment of perpetrators. But in the given context this position cannot evade considering the status of prostitution as a phenomenon. This tactic is rather doubtful. For example, when the feminists regard domestic violence and rape as a violation of human rights they support the victims. We call them survivors. With regard to prostitution, the opposite tactic is used. Women are told that their practice has nothing to do with violation of human rights and sex-exploitation. The discourse is reduced to the idea of a very useful and highly qualified job, providing "social help" to men. The principal inconsistency is that violation of human rights is presented as work ("prompt assistance"). Would it not be better to develop an alternate system of compensation and reparation for the endured discrimination? Anyway, the Japanese women who, during the Second World War, suffered from being used as "women for comfort" insist on reparations, but not on "payment" for their work.

We understand the need of social work and support for women involved in pros-titution, but in our opinion the money intended for creating good working conditions for prostitutes should be spent on normal employment of young women.

The main tasks of the Russian and NIS organisations, in particular, Angel Coalition, involves practical help to trafficked women.[21] It does not matter through which obvious or latent motives the woman became a victim. We help all victims of trafficking. But the debates on prostitution are extremely important from the conceptual point of view.

In perspective the strategic approach should be maintenance of equal job opportun-ities for young women. The mainstream policy is relevant for this long-term aim. It is connected to the promotion of gender policy in Russia and NIS, the development of women's business, and the participation of women in the decision-making processes in economics. In the given context we adhere to the policy of women's NGOs in the Nordic countries.

Angel coalition position

We find that it is impossible to adhere to a single concept with respect to all women in all countries and regions. At the same time many differences, in our opinion, are rooted in the comparison of solutions of this problem at different levels and the criticism coming from both sides based on subjective interpretation of each other's positions. For example, the struggle against prostitution as a phenomenon cannot be treated as a struggle against prostitutes as personalities. It should be viewed from the point of view of long-term, that is, strategic goals. At the same time the struggle for recognition of prostitution as a job is just a palliative measure, a tactic for the improvement of the conditions of the prostitutes' work. We admit that there are a number of women in America and Europe who like this occupation. The Angel considers that the present socio-economic situation in Russia and NIS countries affects the increasing amount of women involved in prostitution on a mass scale. From the Angel's point of view, the principal and radical purpose is promotion of gender approach in the policy of equal job opportunities.[22]

Conclusion

The contemporary anti-trafficking activities of Russian and NIS-based non-governmental organisations are under the multi-sided influence of various Western and US coalitions, with the export of quasi-feminist neo-liberal and post-modern values. There is a common point of view on some of the aspects involving social help and prevention, and we adhere to transnational policy. But as far as prostitution is concerned, there are substantial intra-national and international differences. The abstractly viewed human rights aspect and debates related to prostitution predominate in the activity of Western and US coalitions.

Some Russian organisations accepted the discourse of prostitution as a free choice and work; whereas the Angel Coalition insists on taking into account the contemporary socio-economic context in Russia which does not leave the poor women any other "choice" than prostitution. The migration and labour aspects are treated differently by Western and Russian/NIS NGOs; in fact this issue is ignored by Western NGOs or is treated from a narrow angle. These NGOs are more interested in their own national interests and, generally, transnational interests within the framework of the EU-position concerning the issue in question.

References

The Amsterdam Intermediary Project. Ten years health and social care in prostitution (1999), Amsterdam.

An Angel Can Make a Difference (October 8-9, 1999) Anti-Sex-Trafficking Conference, IOM, Moscow.

Crossing Borders against Trafficking in Women and Girls. A resource Book for Working Against Trafficking in the Baltic Sea Region, (1999, November). Kvinnoforum, Stockholm.

Davidson, Julia O'Connel (1998). *Prostitution, Power and Freedom*, Cambridge, Polity Press.

Global Survival Network. Conference report from international conference "The Trafficking of NIS Women Abroad", November 3-5, 1997.

Jeffrews, Sheila (1997) *The Idea of Prostitution*, N.Melbourne, Spinifex.

Khodyreva Natalia (1996). 'Sexism and sexual abuse in Russia', in Chr. Corrin (ed.) *Women in a Violent World: Feminist analyses and resistance across Europe.* Edinburgh University Press, pp. 27-40.

Khodyreva Natalia (1996a) Violence against women in Russia. An International Conference. *"Violence, Abuse and Women's Citizenship"*, Brighton, University of Bradford, pp. 21-22

Khodyreva, Natalia (2000a): 'Statement of Natalia Khodyreva, NGO Representative, Foreign Relation Committee, Near Eastern and South Asian Affairs Subcommittee, Hearing on International Trafficking of Women and Children: Prosecution, Testimonies, and Prevention', November 4, 2000. Washington D.C, Harvard University, J.F.Kennedy School of Government.

Khodyreva, Natalia & Vasilieva, Larissa (2000b): Protection project's Seminar Series."What Victims of Sex Trafficking Need for Rehabilitation", December 6, 2000. Wash. D.C., J.Hopkins Univ.

Khodyreva Natalia & Cvetkova Maria (2000c): 'Russian Women and Traffic Phenomenon', *Sociologicheskie Issledovania (Sociological Research)* No. 11, pp. 141-144.

Khodyreva Natalia (2001): "Tolerance for What? Sexuality for Whom?" Paper presented at *"Sexualty in Transition – 2001"* Conference, Dubrovnic.

MacKinnon, Catharine A. (1994): "Rape, Genocide, and Women's Human Rights". Stiglmayer. Alexandra (ed.): *Mass rape: The War Against Women in Bosnia-Herzegovina.* University of Nebraska Press, Lincoln Nebraska.

Mansson S.-A. (1995): "International Prostitution and Traffic in Persons in Relation to Costs and Benefits of Europeanization". In Changing Faces of Prostitution, Helsinki, pp. 14-31.

Network in the North against prostitution and violence. International conference *"Prostitution is a Global problem"* (18-19 November, 2000), Murmansk.

One Year La Strada (1996) Results of First Central and East European Program on Prevention of Traffic in Women.

TRANSactions. Committee of Women Religious against Trafficking in women. (1 is., June 2000), The Netherlands.

Turukanova, Elena and Malusheva, Marina: The Legal and Institutional Promotion of Politic in the Women Migration against Trafficking in Women in Russia. Second International Conference on trafficking in women (23 October – 3 November, 2000). Angel Coalition, Moscow, Vol.1-2.

Some Mother's Daughter (1999). The hidden movement of prostitute women against violence. International prostitutes Collective (ed. Lopez-Jones, Nina), London.

Sykes, Gresham and David Matza (1957, December) Technique of Neutralisation: a Theory of Delinquency, *American Sociological Review*, 22, pp.664-70.

Vanderberg, Martina (November, 1997) Trafficking in women to Israel and forced prostitution. Report from the Israel Women's Network.

Vozvrashenie Domoi (Returning Home) (2000), INGI/Crisis Centre for women, St.Petersburg.

Wijers M., Lap-Chew L. (1997) Trafficking in Women. Forced Labour and Slavery-like Practices in Marriage Domestic Labour and Prostitution, STV, Utrecht.

Notes

1 Khodyreva (1996), pp. 27-40.
2 Khodyreva (1996a), pp.21-22.
3 Global Survival (1997).
4 Khodyreva (2000a); Khodyreva, Vasilieva (2000b).
5 Vozvrashenie (2000).
6 The Angel (1999).
7 The Amsterdam (1999); Crossing (1999); One Year (1999); Transaction (2000); Network 2000.
8 Davidson (1998).
9 Vijers, Lap-Chew, (1997).
10 Turucanova, Malysheva, (2000), pp. 11-96.; Khodyreva, Cvetkova, (2000), pp. 141-144.
11 Ibid. Vozvrashenie (2000).
12 Mansson, (1995), pp. 14-31; Vanderberg, (1997).
13 Sykes and Matsa, (1957), pp. 664-70.
14 McKinnon, (1994a).
15 Jeffrey, (1997).
16 Ibid.
17 Khodyreva, (2001).
18 Ibid. Crossing (1999); Mansson, (1995); One Year (1996); Wijers, Lap-Chew, (1997).
19 Some Mother's Daughter, (1999); Davidson O'Connel, (1998); Jeffrews, (1997).
20 Khodyreva, (2001); Khodyreva, Cvetcova, (2000).
21 Second (2000).
22 Khodyreva and Vasilieva, (2000b).

CHAPTER 14

Joining a Transnational Movement

– *Action Against Gender-based Violence in China[1]*

Cecilia Milwertz

In the 1960s and 1970s women's movements emerged, re-emerged and flourished in many parts of the world. Diverse and locally distinct, as they are now recognized, these movements were also linked and inspired across countries and continents. One important, though generally unrecognized, link of influence and inspiration was from the People's Republic of China (PRC) to Euro-North American women's movements. Not only were many young women in Europe and North America fascinated by images of the liberated, socialist Chinese woman. Moreover, the practice of consciousness raising used as a means to shift the locus of problems from the personal to the political, which was an integral part of Euro-North American women's movements, was inspired by the Chinese practice of 'speaking bitterness'. The sharing of personal experience is central to the practices of 'speaking bitterness' and consciousness raising. Through consciousness raising participants come to see that what was thought to be an individual problem is instead a social or political problem requiring a collective solution.[2] In this manner consciousness-raising also plays a role in activism against gender-based violence.

Based on an ideology of gender-equality, the Communist Party in China has made significant improvements in women's rights. The first PRC law was the 1950 Marriage Law, which in its latest revised version passed in April 2001, is also the most recent of a series of laws specifically related to gender equality issues. However, while importance has been attached to achieving gender equality, the approach applied by the PRC party-state has been based on promoting and controlling a top-down style of organizing *for* women that to a high degree defined solutions to what it saw as 'women's problems' on their behalf. The Communist Party created a rhetoric that prescribed male and female equality while denying gender difference. When there were discrepancies between this rhetoric and the actual experience of women, it was their experience that was denied and there was no language with which to express their experience.[3] Moreover, because legal equality had been granted by the party and was viewed as a favour bestowed upon women, they themselves were reluctant to criticize the Party.[4] In the mid-1980s the silence was broken when it became obvious that women were shouldering a disproportionate share of the burdens of transition following the initiation of economic reforms since 1978. As adverse effects of economic reforms began to be felt, the political climate allowed and even encouraged academics to meet to discuss the problems created by the reform process.[5] A dramatic change in women's organizing took place as a new wave of collective mobilization by women themselves from below started in China. Women began to organize on their own initiative in response to the negative effects of economic reforms on their lives as well as in reaction to a trend towards revival of traditional female submissive virtues. A relaxation of political control combined with a series of problems specifically or disproportionately confronting women led first to the establishment of women's studies at universities and subsequently to the emergence of various forms of self-initiated women's groups, networks and organizations.

Dissatisfaction was primarily articulated on behalf of other women confronted by specific problems (such as for example unemployment) by urban intellectual women who had themselves experienced a high degree of gender equality in pre-reform China. They embarked on a process of exploration of gender issues including the translation of books and articles on Euro-North American feminist theory leading to heated academic debates on the meaning of feminism in the Chinese context, and to the establishment of a new wave of the women's movement in China.[6] Urban academics began their self-initiated activities by setting up groups to discuss the gender inequality, which was becoming apparent in the reform period. The transformation from discussion groups aimed at addressing problems within the group to social movement activities aimed at turning public attention towards gender inequality and pushing for overall change in society was gradual. Ironically, the relatively free rein given to women-focused activities throughout the 1980s and on into the 1990s may in part be explained by the legitimization of women's liberation brought about by communist ideology. This has meant that discussions on equal rights between women and men have generally been viewed by the party-state as uncontroversial and unthreatening.[7] Since the 1980s women's organizing in the PRC has changed from a situation in which one organization – the All China Women's Federation, established by the party-state – represented all women in China, to the current situation in which many organizations are engaged in addressing issues of gender equality and representing various groups of women.[8] The Women's Federation system, which exists at all administrative levels of Chinese society, is by far the largest women's organization, while the new forms of organizing include smaller professional organizations (often linked to the Women's Federations) and tiny non-governmental type organizations.

The new wave of the Chinese women's movement has been fortunate to appear on the scene of the transnational and international context of women's organizing at a time when the previous deep divisions between Third and First World women's movements have been replaced by *improved* communication due to an acknowledgement of the profound diversity both in the lives of women based on differences of class, ethnicity, age and other factors and in the meanings of feminism cross-nationally.[9] And increasingly links and flows of inspiration and influence are being created between Chinese and other women's movements. One characteristic of the present phase of institutionalization of Euro-American women's movements is an increasing engagement in international activities, which makes them part of what Ruth Lister has defined as 'global civil society'.[10] The new wave of the Chinese movement is unquestionably rooted in issues originating in Chinese society. However, innovative practices and theories are often inspired through contact with women's movements in other countries and are facilitated by the gender and development programmes of international donor agencies that have developed as part of the institutionalization of the Euro-American second wave movements.[11]

This chapter examines some aspects of the transnational and cross-cultural links between China and Euro-North American women's movements. The focus is on two of the new organizations in Beijing – the Jinglun Family Centre and the Women's Research Institute – and their activities related to the issue of domestic violence. Domestic violence – also known as intimate abuse by male partners (husbands), wife beating and battering – is one of the most common forms of violence against women globally.[12] Although the term 'domestic violence' does not explicitly state whose violence against whom is being addressed, the term has been used internationally to denote men's violence against women. Only more recently has the term been questioned as being neutral and hiding gendered power relations. I use the term 'domestic violence' in this chapter because it was the term activists in China began to use in the 1990s when the introduction of this terminology represented growing awareness of an issue and increasing action against the practice.

The chapter points to some of the advantages and potential problems which the interaction between the Chinese organizations and the Euro-North American partners entail for the Chinese movement. Organizing is viewed as a transformational learning and action process. Activities employed by the two organizations have been inspired by practices in North America and supported by donor organizations. Some have succeeded, while others due to complex circumstances including among other factors domestic political constraints and the internal structures of the new organizations have failed. I argue that the activities of the two organizations – including both activities which failed in the sense that they never materialized or were discontinued, and activities which were continued and developed further, can be defined as successful because they have played a role both in the consolidation of activism against gender-based violence and in joining Chinese activism against violence against women to the global movement.

Organizing against domestic violence in Beijing in the 1990s

Men's violence against women, particularly within the family, is one of many issues addressed by the new women's groups, networks and organizations in Beijing and other parts of China. Although the criminal code forbade maltreatment and injury, men's violence against their wives was underreported, infrequently prosecuted and a certain amount of violence was also taken for granted as normal marital behaviour when the Women's Federation began to address the issue in the 1980s.[13] An article published in 1991 is one of the first major statements using the Chinese term "jiating baoli", which is a direct translation of "domestic violence" referred to by women's movement activists from the new women's organizations as an indication that new ways of understanding and defining men's violence, against women within the home were beginning to be introduced in China.[14] A couple of years later, a great deal of media debate was created by a case of a woman worker whose husband cut off her nose and ears. The case was widely publicized by the Women's Department of the Trade Union in co-operation with the newspaper *Workers' Daily* and despite the protests of the husband's work-unit, the Women's Department took the husband to court on behalf of the wife. Growing awareness and public recognition of the issue was also reflected in the early 1990s by surveys on women's status, marriage and family relations that included questions on violence within the family, and in other surveys specifically aimed at investigating the extent and background of such violence in China.[15]

The Women's Research Institute – counselling and studies of domestic violence

The first women's organization founded independently in Beijing with the aim of influencing public opinion and policy making on gender equality issues was the Women's Research Institute (WRI) established in October 1988 by a group initiated and led by Wang Xingjuan, a retired editor.[16] Initially, as the name indicates, the main aim of the Institute was to provide indirect support to women by investigating and documenting issues such as unemployment and prostitution, which the founding members viewed as insufficiently researched or totally ignored by the leadership and academia – although the new women's studies centres were also beginning to address such issues. In 1992 when the first Women's Hotline was set up the Institute began to provide direct psychological and legal counselling assistance to individual women. The Hotline led the WRI to become aware of the problem of domestic violence and to begin to collect data to document its nature and extent. Hotline counsellors were astonished to find that well-educated university professors, journalists, and company directors beat their wives. Prior to setting up the Hotline and undertaking the study they had thought that women being beaten in their homes by their husbands was not a problem in China and certainly not an urban one.

The Jinglun Family Centre – segments of the story of a domestic violence shelter

The Jinglun Family Centre (JFC) was formally established in early 1993 in Beijing by sociologist Chen Yiyun.[17] The Centre addressed the issue of domestic violence during a two-year period from 1994 to 1996 during which attempts were made to establish a shelter for battered women and a domestic violence telephone hotline was set up. At that time the concept of a shelter for domestic violence victims was almost unknown in China. Chen Yiyun had, however, visited shelters during visits to North America in the 1980s. Three actors were involved in the plans to set up a shelter: the Centre itself, the Chinese authorities and institutions with which the Centre co-operated, and the foreign donor organization that funded the activities. This segment of the story of an attempt to set up a shelter is based on the perspective of one of these three actors – the Jinglun Family Centre, more specifically that of director Chen Yiyun. According to Chen Yiyun the aim of setting up a shelter was first of all to investigate the problem of domestic violence by going beyond survey statistics to the actual experiences of women in order to achieve a better understanding of the problem than that provided by the quantitative results alone. On the basis of the in-depth knowledge and understanding of the problem that would be elicited by providing support directly to victims of domestic violence, it was hoped that policy makers could be made to acknowledge the serious nature of men's violence against women within the family and that a public debate on the issue could be initiated so as to change popular attitudes that accepted the violence. This is extremely important, for as Bo Wagner Sørensen has argued, a main reason that violence takes place is that it is viewed as socially acceptable.[18]

In order to set up a shelter Chen Yiyun contacted the local Beijing branch of the Women's Federation and the Beijing Bureau of Civil Affairs and invited them to join the endeavour. In the Chinese political context it would not be possible for a non-governmental organization such as the Jinglun Family Centre to set up a shelter without the support of party-state institutions. However, when an agreement had nearly been reached and a contract was about to be drawn up, the two collaborators withdrew their support arguing that a shelter was not a suitable solution when addressing the problem of domestic violence in China. It was said that too many people other than victims of domestic violence would be in need of a refuge and that a stream of people would overwhelm the shelter. Another, although contradictory, reason given was that in Chinese society the family and the work-unit can provide support to people who have problems, thus making outside interference unnecessary. A third reason was that none of the parties engaged in the plans to set up a shelter had any experience in handling domestic violence cases. How would they cope, for instance, if a violent husband turned up at the shelter? A final concern had to do with the complications involved if women brought children with them. While these misgivings were most likely motivated by the political sensitivity of openly acknowledging the existence of domestic violence (not least given the particular interest of Western media in such matters), the Jinglun Family Centre could not guarantee that it would be able to tackle all the problems that would potentially arise. In any case, as already mentioned, it was not politically or practically feasible to set up the shelter without the co-operation of party-state institutions and Chen Yiyun was forced to drop the plans.

The Jinglun Family Centre was caught in a complex situation including various actors and interests: the Centre was addressing the problem of men's violence against women in China – an issue which had been addressed previously although insufficiently. Inspiration and influence from women's movements in other parts of the world motivated the Centre to deal with the issue by setting up a shelter. Domestic political constraint blocked this initiative while a non-Chinese donor organization financially supported the initiative. On the one hand the Centre recognised the need to provide support to victims of violence although direct support was not the primary motive for setting up a shelter. The more overall aim was to create awareness of a problem in society among policymakers and the general public with a more long-term view to eliminating the problem. By adopting a practice inspired by women's movements in North America the Centre was in an initial phase of investigating how and whether this means of addressing the problem of domestic violence would function in China. These objectives were supported financially and were also influenced by an outside donor organization. On the other hand, domestic political concerns and constraints blocked the initiative and defined it as incompatible to Chinese cultural practice.

The domestic violence hotline

Following the aborted attempt at establishing a shelter, the Jinglun Family Centre set up a domestic violence telephone hotline in October 1994. This was made possible by finding other party-state collaborators. These would not have agreed to collaborate in setting up a shelter whereas a hotline was viewed as less politically sensitive. Moreover, as the Hotline was launched in October 1994, when preparations were well under way for the United Nations Women's Conference, a strategic move was made to link the hotline to the preparations by using the Conference logo in the *Workers' Daily* announcement and coverage of the hotline. The hotline was a politically feasible activity and the need for support to victims of domestic violence was documented by the many callers. Nonetheless, the hotline was in operation for less than two years before it closed. As was the case with the shelter this was due to a combination of internal (including both the Chinese domestic political context and the internal organization of the Centre) and external factors. To set up the hotline domestic political support and collaboration by party-state institutions and financial resources from the non-Chinese donor organization had been secured. One of the problems was that it became clear to hotline counsellors that to run a hotline it was often also necessary to be able to offer shelter to callers in need of immediate aid. Such help was only offered in a few cases where callers were offered shelter at the Centre. However, these few cases and the problems in recruiting counsellors for the hotline demonstrated the extent of activist resources needed to provide support to victims of violence. According to director Chen Yiyun it was relatively easy throughout the 1990s to find scholars who would write and lecture on the issues addressed by the Centre. However, it was comparatively more difficult to recruit volunteers for practical work such as hotline counselling – and especially difficult to recruit activists to do practical work such as helping victims of domestic violence. Although the Jinglun Family Centre is a non-governmental organization set up from below outside of party-state initiative, internally it is a top-down initiative in the sense that the organization has one central leader who is the main initiator and pivot of Centre activities. The Centre has not grown out of a collective initiative engaging a larger group of activists. Although many people were engaged in its activities, they were peripherally linked to the Centre. There was neither a large nor a constant base of volunteer activists to carry out an initiative such as a hotline or a shelter on a voluntary basis within the available financial framework.

The process of organizing – changing perceptions and success criteria

The example of activism related to the problem of domestic violence illustrates that once they came into direct contact with individual women through counselling, empirically-based studies and other activities, activists realized that the problems confronting women were often more complex and/or of a different nature than they had initially been aware of. In the process of providing services and engaging in research activists' perceptions of what constitutes 'objective, scientific' knowledge have changed (and are continuously changing) and dominant discourses in society are challenged. Terminologies have changed and 'new' perspectives and understanding of 'old' issues have emerged. Whereas political constraint and lack of activist resources led the JFC to discontinue its activities related to the issue of domestic violence the WRI has continued its activities and the Women's Hotline provides an example of how counselling attitudes are changing in the process of organizing. Activists did not start out with the intention of providing counselling based on a gender perspective. However, by the late 1990s what can be translated as 'women's awareness' had become a requirement when recruiting and training new volunteers for the Women's Hotline. In director Wang Xingjuan's words:

> … we require that counsellors must have women's awareness in their work.[19] This means that their work must be based on a women's standpoint. They must defend women's rights. They must help women to improve their self-confidence. Our counselling perspective cannot be based on the ideology of traditional society. The traditional ideology takes the view that in the case of domestic violence the woman is too fierce; she is always jabbering away, and finally the husband becomes anxious and impatient and has no other option than to hit her. In other words, it is the woman's own fault if her husband beats her. We do not agree with this. Regardless of how much a woman talks, it is wrong for a man to hit her. This is women's awareness.[20]

There are differences of opinion concerning the importance of this requirement among Hotline supervisors, and while some will give counsel based on 'women's awareness', others will base their responses to callers on what Wang Xingjuan calls a 'traditional ideology' of blaming the women who are the victims of violence.

International exchange

International exchange has provided inspiration for the setting up of activities such as hotlines and the attempt to set up a shelter. International exchange has also provided inspiration for changes of perspective and for the introduction of gender perspectives and awareness. In 1994 Wang Xingjuan talked of women being *beaten* by their husbands. A few years later she was talking of *domestic violence* – a concept introduced to China via the United Nations Women's Conferences and other international exchange – reflecting a change of understanding in which men's violence against women in the family was increasingly being viewed as unacceptable. Wang Xingjuan points to a meeting in India in 1998 as *the* event that led her to realize the importance of "women's awareness" and a view of men's violence against women as a gender-power relations issue. The fact that Wang Xingjuan had undoubtedly been introduced to similar perspectives at previous training workshops and visits to other countries illustrates how organizing for social change is a transformative learning process or as theorized by sociologists Ron Eyerman and Andrew Jamison a "cognitive praxis" of combined and continuous knowledge production and action.[21] A study of the early years of the Women's Hotline has questioned whether this new organizational activity is different from the All China Women's Federation in its approach and understanding of gender issues.[22] I would argue that the change of terminology from "beating" to "domestic violence" and the requirement that Hotline counsellors must have 'women's awareness' reflects a change of perspective or knowledge in which the violence women suffer from men in the family is being defined not as an individual problem for which the individual woman is to blame, but as a reflection of broader unequal gender relations in society and that marital violence was beginning to be viewed not as something 'natural' and acceptable but, on the contrary, as an unacceptable aberration. This may not have been happening in the early years of the Hotline, however it is what is being described as important in the late 1990s not only by the Women's Hotline but also by other groups within the new women's movement wave.

Success criteria – consolidation of activism against domestic violence

The two organizations, as well as other groups and organizations that have addressed the issue of domestic violence in the 1990s, have played a role in creating a greater openness and recognition of the issue of domestic violence as a gender equality and human rights issue over the past ten years. At the same time the individual experiences of the two organizations, the difficulties they have encountered and their exposure to the influence of women's movements in other parts of the world with new interpretations of and actions against gender-based violence have led the two organizations in different directions. For Chen Yiyun and the Jinglun Family Centre difficulties encountered in relation to the 1994-95 activities on domestic violence no doubt played an important role in the decision to downplay direct social service support activities and define the work of the Centre as primarily educational rather than interventional. The Centre lacked activist resources to engage in direct support to women and the issue of violence was seen as too politically sensitive. To have insisted on addressing that particular issue in the early and mid-1990s in the form of direct services funded by a non-Chinese donor organization might have risked jeopardizing all Centre activities. Early Women's Research Institute engagement in the issue of violence against women was less politically sensitive than Jinglun Family Centre activities. First of all, the Institute was not involved in providing direct support based on foreign funding to victims to the same degree as the Jinglun Family Centre. WRI Hotline counselling to domestic violence victims was one of many issues addressed by the Hotline and until the late 1990s, when Wang Xingjuan became involved in the plans to set up the Domestic Violence Network, the politically sensitive direct contacts to victims of domestic violence were limited.

In 2000, following two years of preparations, which were initiated following the previously mentioned meeting in India, the Network 'Domestic Violence in China – Research, Intervention and Prevention' (hereafter the Network or the Domestic Violence Network) was established. The Network consists of several Beijing-based non-governmental women's groups, organizations and networks and a few individual members and it has links to women's organizations, including provincial level branches of the All China Women's Federation, in several provinces. The Network is, as I have argued elsewhere, indicative of a consolidation and strengthening of collaboration between various organizations and groups in the new wave of the Chinese women's movement.[23] The Network aims, first, to undertake systematic research to understand the nature, cause and consequences of domestic violence in China. Second, it aims to explore effective intervention models against domestic violence through two community intervention initiatives in one urban and one rural setting. Third, based on research and community intervention, the Network aims to make policy recommendations to the government of China on how to better prevent domestic violence against women in order to better guarantee women's human rights in China.[24]

The Network reflects a consolidation of women's non-governmental organizing against violence against women, which might even be defined as the establishment of a movement within the women's movement similar to the crisis-centre movements in other parts of the world. The term crisis-centre movement has been defined as referring to units combating VAW in an institutionalised form through shelters or refuges and/or out-services like hotlines and consultation.[25] The links between organizations and groups from both Beijing and other parts of China, which form the Network, are indicative of a collectivity of activism and commitment and are a measure of movement success both as a visible organizational strengthening of the movement and in terms of what has been defined as fluid outcomes of women's movement activity.[26] Not all activities addressing the issue of domestic violence have survived. Especially attempts at setting up shelters, and this includes both the Jinglun Family Centre attempt, and a shelter in Shanghai which existed for a short period of time until it was closed by authorities, have not succeeded. Nevertheless, all activities – both those which failed and those which succeeded – have paved the way for later consolidation of activities addressing the issue of domestic violence. In the process of developing activism against gender-based violence within the Chinese women's movement, the Jinglun Family Centre has played the role of catalyst to other activities and organizations and as innovator. Suzanne Staggenborg argues for adopting a broad definition of movement success based on a long-range processual view of social movements in which success is measured not only in terms of policy outcomes but also in terms of the cultural consequences beyond the impact of their organized and public activities.[27] Movements need to first challenge existing ideas, cultural practices and means of socialization, before achieving more substantial goals, and these outcomes in the process of organizing should be treated as success. Movements can be successful in introducing new ideas and creating new norms – externally in society and internally within the movement – and these outcomes may produce subsequent achievements. Staggenborg emphasizes that this sort of cultural success can typically be attributed not to any one social movement organization, but rather to the movement as such. The Jinglun Family Centre attempt to set up a shelter and the short-lived domestic violence hotline as well as the changing ways of understanding domestic violence by Women's Research institute counsellors are examples of such successes. Some apparent failures are actually successes of a sort by contributing to later collective action because Feminist organizations can be effective at the same time as they self-destruct as organizations and fail to achieve changes in public policy. Groups that are unsuccessful in terms of organizational maintainance and policy outcomes may be effective as the centres of movement communities and as the originators of cultural changes. Although the successes of many feminist organizations tend to be hidden, they are likely to have an impact on subsequent rounds of collective action. Success includes pools of activists who remain involved in movement activities, models of collective action that are employed by subsequent activists and ideologies that continue to attract adherents.[28]

Transnational interaction – benefits and potential problems

In November 2000 the Domestic Violence Network held a meeting to mark the global women's movement annual '16 days of violence against women activism'[29] and to publicly announce the establishment of the Network to Chinese authorities and the general public thus demonstrating that activism against violence against women has become consolidated as part of the Chinese women's movement agenda and that the Chinese movement has become part of transnational and global women's activism on this issue. Chinese women's organizations have been influenced, inspired and also promoted by several Euro-North American 'partners'. In terms of institutions at least three outside actors directly involved in interaction with the Chinese women's movement can be identified. These are 1) governmental and non-governmental donor organizations, 2) women's NGOs, and 3) academic women's and gender studies. Their agendas and motives for interacting with the Chinese movement undoubtedly differ to some degree, but all are at the same time at some level part of or extensions of Euro-North American second wave women's movements and their aim is to work for social change and gender equality.

Contemporary feminisms are concerned with interacting (and theorizing) across and through the many differences of people and should therefore form an ideal basis for cross-cultural and transnational dialogue and activism between the Euro-North

American 'partners' and the Chinese women's movement. One of the benefits to the new wave of the Chinese women's movement of becoming part of transnational women's organizing around the issue of gender-based violence is that many years of second wave women's movement local, national and international experience is in a sense made instantaneously available to the new Chinese movement wave. The Chinese women's movement has become part of a 'ready-made' VAW agenda based on the following history: Since the 1970s women's movements in many parts of the world have addressed the issue of violence against women. In the 1980s they successfully placed the issue on the United Nations women-related agendas and in the 1990s VAW became a concern of the UN system as a whole.[30] While the occurrence of domestic violence in China is rooted in Chinese reality, large meetings such as the UN Women's Conferences in Nairobi (1985) and Beijing (1995) as well as smaller conferences and workshops have introduced new perspectives to interpretations of this particular form of violence in China.[31] Moreover, the activities of academics and activists in popular organizing have been inspired by their visits to organizations working on the problem of domestic violence in other countries. European and North American donor organizations are engaged in supporting the work of popular organizations in China on the issue of domestic violence and they have as such facilitated the process of transnational exchange.[32] Finally, because violence against women, and domestic violence, is addressed by United Nations women's conference and other documents, work on the issue has gained a certain legitimacy in an otherwise restricted political environment.[33]

On the one hand, there is no doubt that transnational and international engagement with women's movements has benefited the Chinese women's movement. On the other hand, the interaction is not unproblematic. Writing on the development of women's studies in China since the 1980s Nicola Spakowski is clearly sceptical of the degree to which indigenous Chinese women's studies are respected by the outside actors when she defines the interaction with western feminism as 'one-sided and dominated by the West'. Spakowski writes that 'The internationalisation of China's women's studies and women's movement is an actively promoted, well-directed and well-financed process of establishing Western (that is: American) feminist concepts among Chinese scholars and activists.'[34] In a similar vein Chinese women's studies scholar Li Xiaojiang has pointed out that some aspects of Western feminist discourse are irrelevant to the Chinese context and that some are even harmful to the movement in China.[35] Questions pertaining both to the usefulness of and interaction involved in transferring the 'ready-made' agendas to China need to be asked. Including among many relevant questions: To what degree do the non-Chinese and Chinese actors identified in this transnational interaction have similar or at least compatible interests and when and how do interests diverge? What roles do their different and, in relation to for example funding, unequal positions play in their transnational interaction?

Here we return to the example of the Jinglun Family Centre plans to establish a shelter. When Chinese authorities objected to the Centre plans, one of the arguments was that too many people in need of a refuge would overwhelm the place. The vast need for shelter was also something the Jinglun Family Centre had in mind as the main aim in setting up a shelter was not to help individual women – it was recognized that only a minority of those in need would be offered help – but rather to utilize knowledge of a few selected cases to make a problem visible and provide information to policy makers and the general public in order to change attitudes to the issue of domestic violence and to lobby policymakers to make changes in legislation and implementation of legislation. Was this choice on the part of the Centre based on common sense knowledge of what it is possible to achieve in a huge society with an enormous demand for support by many groups that are in various ways victims of the rapid economic reforms process? Did it not occur to activists to primarily provide support to individuals in a manner similar to the one adopted by the crisis centre movement in Europe and North America – that is directly supporting individual women in need – because they realized that such a task was impossible given the available resources and hence they opted for a strategy that focused on helping a selected number of representative cases in order to more generally address a problem in society and influence policymakers? Other new women's organizations have chosen similarly to focus on representative cases in order to base policy recommendations on these. What roles have the Euro-North American 'partners' played in directing Chinese activists towards such a choice? A choice which can have been motivated by a recognition of the actual problem, but which can also have been motivated by other more overall democracy and civil society establishing societal change agendas which are also included in their programmes? Where do the various interests of the two parts of the transnational interaction clash and when and where do they supplement each other?

Social movement activism is a continuous transformative learning and acting process – a cognitive praxis. Can the Chinese and Euro-North American transnational actors in this process be reciprocally open to each other's ideas, practices and choices? Was the adaptation of consciousness-raising by the Euro-North American women's movement a one-off incident of cross-cultural influence from China towards the West? Or are the Euro-North American partners open to the possibility that they can also learn from China in the sense that the 'ready-made' agendas are still being developed and should continuously be receptive to new input? Will the longer history of Euro-North American women's movement engagement with such issues as violence against women and the financial dominance of the 'partners' lead them to attempt to impose their experience and agenda on the Chinese movement? The donor organization may well have nudged the Jinglun Family Centre towards the attempt to set-up a shelter and run a hotline despite the fact that the internal set-up of the organization did not match the resource requirements needed for such activities and at a time when these activities were not yet politically feasible. However, even this 'failure' played a role in paving the way for future activities. One must also assume that not only the Chinese activists but also the outside partners are engaged in a learning process. There are examples in Beijing of women's organizations taking on a project mainly because a donor organization was offering funds for that particular activity. Based on appraisals of these activities made by activists my impression is that once they have tried such a project they are generally not willing to do so again. A major reason is that social movement organizing generally requires huge and exhausting amounts of voluntary work and this is just not feasible in relation to projects that do not fall within the field of what activists themselves are passionately and ardently engaged in. On the other hand, a project that was initially started because it offered funds can very well turn out to have extreme importance for the development of an organization. In fact one motive for starting the first Women's Research Institute Hotline was that it was an activity which would be able to attract donor funding. Subsequently, several additional hotlines have been established and they have become the core activity of the organization. It would seem that women's organization activists are able to both adopt *and* adapt from the theories and practices of Euro-North American movements based on what is feasible in their own political and cultural context simply because their activities have to function at a very practical level. Importantly, as this chapter has attempted to illustrate, transnational social movement interaction is part of a continuous learning process.

It is obvious that transnational interaction has played an important role in the process of Jinglun Family Centre and the Women's Research Institute organizing against domestic violence. Spakowski has pointed to the dangers of the dominance of the western actors in transnational interaction in relation to Chinese women's studies. Uma Narayan, on the other hand, notes how third world feminists are habitually accused of adopting Western ideologies and practices, which are seen as incompatible with their home culture when they attempt to challenge traditional patriarchal culture and create social change.[36] This chapter has pointed to a series of questions that merit further research in order to understand transnational relations between Chinese activists and donor organizations, the negotiations between them and the balancing acts both are engaged in in relation to Chinese authorities when promoting gender equality and human rights agendas in China.

References

Basu, Amrita (1995). "Introduction", Amrita Basu (ed.). *The challenge of local feminisms: women's movements in global perspective*. Boulder, San Francisco, Oxford, Westview Press, 1-21.

Barkey, Cheryl & Alexandra van Selm (1997). *Gender and development in China. A compendium of gender and development projects supported by international donors*. Beijing, United Nations Development Programme.

Bergman, Solveig (1999) "Kvinnor i nya sociala rörelser" (Women in new social movements), Christina Bergqvist et al. (eds.). *Likestilte demokratier? Kjönn og politikk i Norden (Equal Democracies – gender and politics in the Nordic countries)*. Oslo, Universitetsforlaget, 91-110.

Bonnin, Michel & Yves Chevrier (1991). "Autonomy during the post-Mao era", *The China Quarterly*. Number 127, September, 569-593.

Cai Yiping, Feng Yuan & Guo Yanqiu (2001). "The Women's Media Watch Network", Hsiung, Ping-Chun, Jaschok, Maria & Milwertz, Cecilia with Red, Chan (eds.), *Chinese Women Organizing – Cadres, Feminists, Muslims, Queers.* Oxford, Berg.

Cornue, Virginia (1999). "Practicing NGOness and Relating Women's Space Publicly: The Women's Hotline and the State", Mayfair Mei-hui Yang (ed.), *Spaces of Their Own – Women's Public Sphere in Transnational China.* Minneapolis/London, University of Minnesota Press, 68-91.

Croll, Elisabeth (1995). *Changing identities of Chinese women: rhetoric, experience and self-perception in twentieth-century China.* Hong Kong, Hong Kong University Press, London and New Jersey, Zed Books.

Erwin, Kathleen (2000). "Heart-to-Heart, Phone-to-Phone", Davis, Deborah P. (ed.). *The Consumer Revolution in Urban China.* Berkeley, Los Angeles and London, University of California Press, 145-170.

Eyerman, Ron & Jamison, Andrew (1991). *Social Movements. A Cognitive Approach.* Oxford, Polity Press.

Eyerman, Ron & Jamison, Andrew (1998). *Music and Social Movements.* Cambridge, Cambridge University Press.

Heise, Lori, Mary Ellsberg & Gottemoeller, Megan (1999). "Ending Violence Against Women". *Population Reports*, Series L, No.11. December.

Hester, Marianne (2000). "Domestic violence in China", Radford, Jill, Friedberg, Melissa & Harne, Lynne (eds.). *Women, violence and strategies for action. Feminist research, policy and practice.* Buckingham and Philadelphia, Open University Press, 149-166.

Honig, Emily & Hershatter, Gail (1988). *Personal Voices. Chinese Women in the 1980's.* Stanford, California, Stanford University Press.

Hsiung, Ping-Chun, Jaschok, Maria & Milwertz, Cecilia with Red Chan (eds.) (2001). *Chinese Women Organizing – Cadres, Feminists, Muslims, Queers.* Oxford, Berg.

Li Xiaojiang. 1989. *Nüren de chulu.* (A solution for women). Shenyang: Liaoning renmin chubanshe.

Li Xiaojiang (1999). "With What Discourse Do We Reflect on Chinese Women? Thoughts on Transnational Feminism in China", Mayfair Mei-hui Yang (ed.). *Spaces of Their Own. Women's Public Sphere in Transnational China.* Minneapolis and London, University of Minnesota Press, 261-277.

Lin Chun, Bohong, Liu & Yihong, Jin (1998). "China", Jagger, Alison & Young, Iris (eds.). *A Companion to Feminist Philosophy.* Malden, Massachusetts and Oxford, Blackwell, 108-117.

Lister, Ruth (1997). *Citizenship: feminist perspectives.* London, Macmillan.

Milwertz, Cecilia Nathansen (2002). *Beijing Women Organizing for Change – a new wave of the Chinese women's movement.* Copenhagen, NIAS Press.

Narayan, Uma (1997). "Contesting cultures. Westernization, respect for cultures, and third-world feminists", Uma Narayan. *Dislocating cultures. Identities, traditions and third world feminism.* New York and London, Routledge.

Pi Xiaoming (1991). "Jiating baoli – baipishu" (Domistic violence – whitebook), *Zhongguo funü (Chinese Women).* Number 12, 20-22.

Ryan, Barbara (1992). *Feminism and the women's movement: dynamics of change in social movements, ideology and activism,* New York and London, Routledge.

Spakowski, Nicola (2001). "The Internationalization of China's Women's Studies", *Berliner China Hefte*, 20, May, 79-100.

Staggenborg, Suzanne (1995). "Can Feminist Organisations Be Effective?", Marx Ferree, Myra & Martin Patricia Yancey (eds.). *Feminist Organizations*, Philadelphia, Temple University Press, 339-355.

Sun Xiaomei (1997). "The cause of violence in Chinese families and its prevention", Paper presented at *the Expert workshop on fighting domestic violence against women: social, ethical and legal issues*, Beijing 29-31 October, 1997.

Sørensen, Bo Wagner (1998). "Explanations for wife beating in Greenland." In Klein, Renate C.A. (ed.). *Multidisciplinary Perspectives on Family Violence*. London and New York: Routledge, 153-175.

Sørensen, Bo Wagner (2001) "Men in Transition": The Representation of Men's Violence Against Women in Greenland." *Violence Against Women*. Volume 7, Number 7, July, 826-47.

Sørensen, Bo Wagner (2002). "Vold som fænomen og begreb." (Violence as phenomenon and concept). Paper presented at Dannerhuset, Copenhagen, 31 January.

Wesoky, Sharon (2002). *Chinese Feminism Faces Globalization*. New York & London, Routledge.

White, Gordon, Howell, Jude & Xiaoyuan, Shang (1996). *In search of civil society*, Oxford, Clarendon Press.

Zhang Naihua (2001). "Searching for 'Authentic" NGOs: The NGO Discourse and Women's Organizations in China", Hsiung, Ping-Chun, Jaschok, Maria & Milwertz, Cecilia with Red Chan (eds.), *Chinese Women Organizing – Cadres, Feminists, Muslims, Queers*. Oxford, Berg.

Notes

1 This chapter was originally prepared for a Women's Movements and Internationalization Network meeting while the author was in receipt of a European Science Foundation research fellowship at the Institute for Chinese Studies, University of Oxford. Research visits to China were supported by the Nordic Institute of Asian Studies (May 1996), the British Academy (March-April 1997 and 1998) and the European Science Foundation (July-August 1997 and 1998). All visits were hosted by the Institute of Sociology, the Chinese Academy of Social Sciences.

2 Ryan 1992, 46-47. See Erwin 2000:165-66 for an explanation of the historical origins and contemporary use of the practice of 'speaking bitterness'.

3 Croll 1995.

4 Li 1989.

5 Bonnin & Chevrier 1991.

6 For an analysis of new forms of organizing as constituting part of a new wave of the Chinese women's movement see Milwertz 2002.

7 Lin, Liu and Jin 1998.

8 See Hsiung, Jaschok & Milwertz with Chan (2001), Milwertz (2002) and Wesoky (2002) for accounts of the development of a multiplicity of women's movement organizing. See Zhang 2001 on the All China Women's Federation.

9 Basu (1995), 3.

10 Lister (1997), 62-63.
11 See Heitlinger in this volume on the conceptualization of cross-border feminism.
12 Heise, Ellsberg & Gottemoeller (1999):1-2.
13 See Honig & Hershatter (1988).
14 Pi 1991. The article was published by the Women's Federation journal *Women in China* (*Zhong-guo Funü*) after having been rejected by a Beijing newspaper, see Cai, Feng and Guo (2001).
15 These studies have generally been preoccupied with social stratification related in particular to urban-rural locations, occupation, education, age and sex, and have not tended to take into consideration gendered or patriarchal relations Hester (2000).
16 See Milwertz (2002), chapter 3 for an account of the establishment and activities of the Women's Research Institute.
17 The following account of the Centre's early engagement with the issue of domestic violence is based on Centre documents, a series of talks and interviews with Chen Yiyun and interviews with Centre activists in the period October 1994 to August 1998. See Milwertz 2002, chapter 2 for an account of the establishment and activities of the Jinglun Family Center.
18 Sørensen (2002), See also Sørensen (1998) and (2001).
19 The Chinese term *funü yishi* literally translates to 'woman's awareness'. The term is used in the sense of 'women's subjective awareness' or 'women's self-consciousness' referring to women's regaining of a gender identity in terms of realization rather than denial of their difference as members of the female sex, a difference that was erased by equality politics.
20 Wang Xingjuan, interview (1998).
21 Eyerman and Jamison 1991, (1998).
22 Cornue (1999).
23 See Milwertz (2002), chapter 5.
24 The Network runs a website in Chinese, see http:// www.*stopdv.org*.cn
25 Saarinen in this volume, see also Bergman 1999.
26 Staggenborg (1995): 347.
27 Staggenborg (1995): 341.
28 Staggenborg (1995): 353.
29 Starting from 25 November – the UN International Day to end VAW, and lasting until 10 December – the UN Human Rights Day – see Saarinen (2000).
30 Saarinen in this volume.
31 Sun 1997, Hester 2000.
32 Organizations which have supported Beijing activism against VAW include for example the *Asia Foundation, the Ford Foundation, The British Council* (see Barkey and van Selm (1997)), *the Swedish International Development Cooperation Agency* (Sida), *the Danish International Develoment Agency* (Danida), *the Institute of Human Rights*, Oslo University and *NOVIB*.
33 See Khodyreva in this volume on the issue of outside funding and sharing of experience.
34 Spakowski (2001).
35 Li (1999).
36 Narayan (1997).

CHAPTER 15

Exercises in Transversalism

– *Reflections on a Nordic and NW-Russian Network for Crisis Centres in Barents**

Aino Saarinen

Prologue – travelling from the West to the East – crisis centres in Russia.[1]

When writing about globalisation, democratisation and women's movements, Donna Dickenson[2] presents the very inspiring term 'a global community of fate'. A global community of fate is something that arises from women's special experiences of injustice and unites them all over the globe, across a wide spectrum of differences and divisions concerning nationality, class, marital status, age, ethnic and religious belonging, and sexual orientation. It is not easy to find a more touching expression to describe and challenge the phenomena for which we now have a name from the perspective of women – violence against women or gendered, gender-based violence.[3] The first sign of political existence of a global community related to gendered violence was the International Tribunal on Crimes Against Women in Brussels in 1976. Formally it was identified ten-twenty years later, by the United Nations (UN) conferences on women in Nairobi in 1985 and in Beijing in 1995 and by the UN as a whole in 1993 when the General Assembly recognised violence against women to be violation of women's human rights.[4]

To return to the roots, the crisis centre movement grew out of the Second Wave of women's movements at the turn of the 1960s-70s.[5] It was committed to exposing women's everyday, even the most hidden and taboo-ridden dimensions of it through intimate consciousness raising groups working out painful and vulnerable experiences. The informal self-help forums that changed victims into survivors grew into the action groups that wanted to break the silence and to convert "the personal into the political". In a rapid pace, they were further transformed into institutions of support and advocacy, first in England and North America, then throughout the territory covered by the Second Wave.[6] Mobilisation for and around the crisis centres – a movement within a movement – soon became intertwined with the processes towards creating a global agenda with the Brussels tribunal as its initial turning point.

* The project on the crises centre movement in Barents is funded by the Academy of Finland.

The tribunal included women from the Nordic countries, Finland being an exception.[7] During the pioneering period of the late 1970s, autonomous crisis centres were set up in Scandinavia – Norway, Sweden, Denmark – and Iceland.[8] Soon, Finnish women joined the movement as well, but here the development took another route as the majority of the centres are affiliated with a federation for transitory homes for single mothers dating back to the 1940s. There exist also a few autonomous units and some centres within the public sector in Finland.[9] Today, the total number of centres in the Nordic countries is well over two hundred.[10]

During the initial phase, activists in the Western world were ahead of the others but the Brussels tribunal also attracted Third World participants.[11] The Soviet Union and other socialist countries were not familiarised with the issue until the Nairobi conference; finally, the preparations for the Beijing conference after the collapse of the socialist regime in 1991 represented a breakthrough.[12] As a result of these macro-level changes the crisis centre movement gained ground in the post-socialist regions within just a few years.[13] By the mid-1990s the first autonomous crisis centres had been established in central Russian cities. In no time, the movement was expanded throughout the huge country so that in the end of the 1990s, the first autonomous and public centres were set up even in peripheral areas, including the North of NW-Russia, a border region to the northernmost parts of Norway, Sweden and Finland. In addition, crisis centres can be found within the public administration. The number of public units is not known but there are currently around one hundred autonomous units in Russia.[14]

Responding to the East-West challenge – from bi-local diffusion of ideas towards trans-regional networking

Among women's East-West grassroots initiatives of the time, there is one of special interest here, namely the *Femina Borealis* network mobilising scholars and other grassroots-activists to work for woman-friendly trans-regional policies in the Barents region which comprises the subregions of Murmansk, Arkhangelsk and Karelia in Russia, Finnmark, Tromsø and Nordland in Norway, Norrbotten and Västerbotten in Sweden and Lapland and Oulu in Finland.[15] *NCRB – A Network for Crisis Centres in the Barents Region for 1999-2002* is the first Femina Borealis development project; it links the globalised crisis centre movement to the post-bipolar transformations in Northern Europe.

NCRB aimed at combating violence against women and children by working with crisis centres and at empowering crisis centre and women's movements locally and trans-regionally. Through this, it was to challenge the military-based and state-centred concepts of security safeguarded both by "malist" theories of international relations and 'high politics'[16] in an area that, during the Cold War, was one of the most highly militarised places on the globe[17]. To reach its aims, NCRB built up a network between the twelve existing centres in NW-Russia[18] and seven centres on the Nordic side of the border, one from each Nordic Barents province, and carried out the programmes for training, campaigning and information technology. The second NCRB project period will concentrate on the Russian units in 2002-2005.[19]

Self-evidently, the community-in-the-making in Barents calls for analysis of the three phases arising from the definitions of social movements[20] – from the response to the East-West challenges to drawing on trans-regional frameworks and joining in multilateral actions. The focus of this article is, however, more limited: it will explore the second movement phase by analysing the training programme. The data consists of various project material, the questionnaire sent to the crisis centres in Barents in 2000[21] and some focus group and individual interviews conducted in the respective localities in 2000-2002. As I am the co-ordinator of the NCRB project, these issues are approached from an insider's perspective through the dual position of being a scholar and a leading activist at the same time. This, naturally, points to participatory action research, in which the researcher and what is being researched are distinct but not separate. Quoting the words of Peter Reason[22], it is not about research on but *with* people, who are all engaged in opening new political spaces. From the researcher's point of view it is a question of twofold movements, looking from a distance and entering into relations of experience, reflection and, at its best, imaginary practice. At the same time, the other people involved participate as subjects in the actual processes as well as in the reflections upon them, which means that the evaluations of the participants and the joint Nordic-Russian project team are being used all the way to outline and understand the problems and to find solutions.[23]

This is all the more necessary because, ever since its beginning, the project has faced many basic problems arising from the earliest phases of East-West collaboration when the former opposition between women's movements across the bi-polar divide were transformed into a 'development invasion' from the West to the transitional East.[24] NCRB is, without any doubt, part of this invasion because in Barents, too, many of the Russian crisis centres have been set up with support from foreign actors, crisis centres and various sponsors, of which many, are located on the Nordic side of the Barents region.[25] In the late 1990s part of the Russian centres continued to receive Western training and financial support while, at the same time, they were not necessarily in contact with other Russian units in their own area. In sum, a timely challenge to NCRB was to develop the existing short-term, bi-local and sporadic East-West diffusion of ideas and institutions towards continual, more comprehensive and, most importantly, reciprocal networking.

When working for this qualitative change NCRB naturally confronted the issue now being discussed by the women's movements with actors from both sides of the East-West trans-regions throughout Europe, i.e. how to build a new type of unity between a multitude of actors in a region which has been deeply divided for the main part of the 20th century and the most intensive phases of the Second Wave? Following Nira Yuval-Davis' and Ruth Lister's[26] theory on mobilisation and politics in complex settings, I argue that transversalism, which was developed in the Italian women's movements for collaboration across the divide in the Mediterranean in the early 1990s, is a set of methodological tools worthy of thorough exploration. Essentially, transversalism is about changing perspectives with the help of techniques called 'rooting' and 'shifting'. Some suggestions by Elisabeth Porter concerning concepts of deliberative disagreements and transitional spaces also seem interesting in the northern context. They continue the debates on transversalism and give – even from the perspective of the insider – a fruitful contribution to reflections on the controversies and dynamics of women's movements today.

Another divide – institutional communalities versus differences, divergences and divisions

Due to the fact that NCRB was initiated within a pre-existing network, there were no habitual problems in getting access to the field. On the contrary, it was easy for me as the project co-ordinator and founding member of the Femina Borealis to contact the crisis centres through local network activists. But the following steps were a real challenge because, as it is well known from research on women's movements[27], problems increase along with the intensification of interaction. In our case, moving from networking towards collaboration and co-operation turned out to be more difficult than expected – at least not by me due to my lack of experience with the crisis centre movement. To put it simple, in accordance with my long-term involvement in the women's movements and the traditions of Femina Borealis, I worked within a broad understanding of feminism when outlining the project. When starting the action programmes I had to confront the fact that besides the East-West division, there was another dividing line within the NCRB network, namely the institutional variation that characterises the crisis centre movement in general. In brief, the practice of leadership in the development project as well as the simultaneous research conducted by myself and the NCRB project team[28] on the crisis centre movement in Barents confirmed that the centres in northern Europe are, as all over the world[29], characterised by minor differences and major divergences and, finally, fundamental divisions and oppositions[30] that all cut across both the ideological basis, the daily practices and the institutional structures.

In general, crisis centres everywhere operate in a dual way by providing clients with immediate help through consultation, self-help groups, hotlines and shelters and by working in society for long-term changes through awareness raising, training, exhibitions, research and documentation, and by campaigning and lobbying. In this way, they mix elements of cultural re-determination, protest and claims making.[31] In their activities the centres collaborate with multiple overlapping like-minded institutions, organisations, networks and groups run mainly by women. The limits to actions and actors are, as in social movements in general[32], open and floating both horizontally, in civil society and vertically, in relation to the public domain.[33] All in all, the individual crisis centres can be seen as links or connective structures for the crisis centre movement as a whole.[34]

Within these communalities, however, the centres also differ from each other in terms of various issues: firstly, the scope and background of problems are defined and secondly, from whose perspective they are approached and how gender and power comes into the picture.[35] In more concrete terms, the majority of autonomous units in Barents – located in the Norwegian, Swedish and Russian territories – work with violence against women or gender-based violence as their key concepts. Consequently, centres are declared to be women-only-domains where help is given from-sister-to-sister. Interventions in the world outside the centres challenge male power openly and directly, and, as so often within the Second Wave[36], the organisation is flat at least as long as the units are of small size.[37] Affiliated and public units – which are found in the Finnish and Russian parts of Barents only – operate under terms of family violence or domestic violence, which are gender-neutral from a feminist angle and pose questions concerning women's co-responsibility.[38] Furthermore, they rely on paid professionals and work on and with men as well. Awareness raising is preferred to open confrontation, and the centres are managed by formal boards comprised of collaborative organisations or they function as parts of their public organisations.[39]

Training in a transversal spirit

In conclusion, NCRB was in 'double trouble' – in addition to the problems arising from the a-symmetrical East-West relationships, the institutional boundaries turned out to have a problematic role in the network dynamics. In short, crisis centres do what has been called boundary work[40], whereby the actors, through inclusions and exclusions, divide each other into "us" vs. "them" and actually do this so effectively that the national associations are all over comprised of one institutional variant only.[41] All in all, it seems justifiable to speak about conflict vs. consensus models. At the same time, it should be stressed that the models are no bi-polar entities. On the contrary, and again according to the results of the questionnaire, all claim to be fighting for women's rights and reflect on the issue of violence in broad social contexts.[42] Thanks to these uniting elements, the original idea of bringing together all the existing variants finally worked in spite of the pitfalls.

Self-evidently – and contrary to the actors within the previous bi-local collaboration in setting up crisis centres – NCRB could definitely not speak for *the* Western model to be applied and further developed in all Russian units. Instead, increasing information of all of the models as intertwined sets of ideas, practices and institutional arrangements and as parts of the surrounding communities became the starting point for the project's internal development strategy. Consequently, there was a special call for a project methodology that would tackle the existence of multiple and partly opposed ways of thinking and acting.

Around this time, debates on transversalism had been started within the European women's movements and aroused my interest. Naturally, the ethnic and religious divisions in the Balkans and some other explosive parts of Europe are not the same as the divisions arising from the formerly bi-polar East-West, but I was, nevertheless, inspired by the idea of transversalism and presumed that its main techniques, the processes of rooting and shifting, would be of help in bridging the separateness and increasing mutual understanding in other contexts as well. In transversal rooting – in the words of Yuval-Davis[43] – the participants openly define their own positions by telling about their experiences, aims and values; in shifting, they are obliged to change the perspective in order to listen to the 'opposed' group and at least to understand, even if not to accept, the views of others, in our case, both across the East-West divide and across the institutional boundaries.

The first step of importance was the project organisation. To approach the problems from both perspectives across the East-West divide, NCRB relied on a bilateral Nordic-Russian project team located at Oulu and at Arkhangelsk. An additional element was the information technology programme. Femina Borealis had already been linked together by IT since its early years, because such networking was found to be a 'must' in a peripheral, vast area without good traffic connections. Within the NCRB, there were, at least in principle, no gatekeepers for communication either vertically between the project team and the centres or horizontally between the centres themselves.[44] In addition, the project's operational backbone, the series of training courses, was also organised to help to channel views and impulses from all directions. The main responsibility for the courses was shared by the Finnish-Russian NCRB team and the Northern Feminist University (NFU) at Steigen, Norway, which was one of the institutional founding members of Femina Borealis and specialised in training 'ordinary women' instead of academic women only.[45] Moreover, one institution from both East and West with previous experience in training crisis centres in the Russian Barents region, Iris at Luleå, Sweden, and INGI at St. Petersburg, Russia, were invited to join the course working group. In its final form, the group thus included all the four respective nationalities and experience and expertise in crisis centre work and women's movements and in academic and practice-oriented training.

However, for rooting-and-shifting, it was most essential that the courses were rotated from region to region across the borders. Rotation of the UN conferences on women has been shown by, for example, Cecilia Milwertz[46] to have had positive effects on balancing the flows of ideas across global divides. For NCRB, rotation was vital because it gave an important role to the grassroots units. The themes and topics discussed were decided in negotiations between the course group from above and the varying local teams representing the actors from below. Finally, the course participants visited local centres, met with their collaborators, politicians and media and were thus able to perceive their practices as complex realities and linked to the surrounding communities. At the end of the project period, all territorial and institutional variants had hosted a course, that is, been in a position of rooting, while visitors from other countries and other types of centres had mainly had the role of shifting, i.e. listening and trying to understand.[47]

Naturally, there is no reason to idealise the network method of organising activities. Decentralisation within NCRB, as elsewhere[48], lead to compromises in content. The lack of thematic coherence and continuity was, however, compensated for by the apparent enthusiasm of those allowed to make the choice. Undeniably, the delegation of

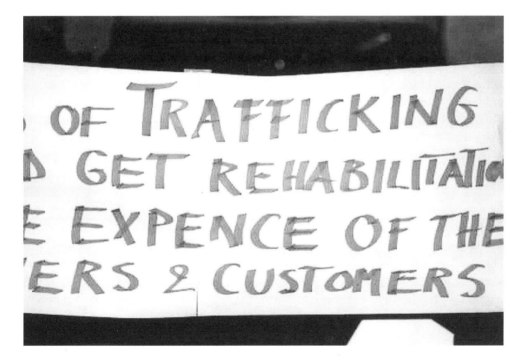

The International Day for Combating Violence against Women, start of the "16 Days of Activism" – a global annual campaigning period, Oulu, Finland, 25 November, 2001. Participants from Network for Crisis Centres in the Barents Region.

responsibility to many actors mobilised resources – views, insights and energies – from all over the network and had a positive impact on the project dynamics as a whole.

Limits in dialogue – deliberative disagreements

The series of courses was started with an overview of the global norms on gendered violence and human rights, the crisis centre models in use in Barents and reports on women's movements in the respective countries – all of which aimed to show that no single territorial or institutional model was prioritised over the others. As mentioned above, in the subsequent courses, navigations between the institutional divergences and divisions that cross the territorial borders played a more central role than the East-West divide. The most challenging thing in this respect was, without doubt, the 'man question' rooted in the outlined oppositional elements between the conflict vs. consensus models.

In more detail – there exists a sophisticated continuum in the practices of excluding vs. including men in the centres. Swedish autonomous centres strictly exclude men from the clientele and personnel, Norwegian centres may accept them occasionally, as some kind of 'distance clients' (contacted by phone), while Russian centres, both autonomous and public units, may let them in for consultations (sometimes in spite of principal reservations) and, finally, Finnish affiliated centres allow men to stay in shelters (as objects of violence) and help them (as abusers) with male-targeted programmes conducted by male co-workers.[49] With the two extremes at the background, the NCRB courses were begun as women-only-meetings in order to guarantee a safe space for the participants in the conflict position. Only later, a few male participants and a male lecturer to present views and activities related to men and preventive programmes were accepted to attend. Lastly, men were given a 'room of their own' in the form of a workshop at the closing seminar. Divisions and oppositions were, thus, made visible, but only half a step was taken to make those in the conflict position to shift, that is, to listen to consensus views. To keep all conflict-oriented units involved, no course was arranged directly around the man question. As a conscious sidestep, a bi-local Finnish-Russian mini-seminar was held close to the end of the project period with the man question on the main agenda.[50]

This was a hard choice because, firstly, one of the Finnish units had been awarded by the national council for equality in its pioneering efforts to help abusive men and because, secondly, there was evident interest in work on and with men among the Russian centres; this was indicated by the fact that the mini-seminar mentioned above was attended by a group in the process of starting the very first crisis centre for men in NW Russia[51]. And last but not least, putting the man question onto the course agenda was also supported by the fact that help to violent men is today included in all multilateral programmes at global and sub/regional levels.[52]

According to the 'guidebook' of the transversal dialogue, the movement-in-the-making should have confronted even the most controversial issues, which means that keeping the man question out of the main agenda can be interpreted as a failure. However, in line with Elisabeth Porter[53], a more positive alternative is to claim that it was put onto the agenda of deliberative disagreements. In this respect, Porter's notion is an essential addition to the praxis of transversal dialogue. It can be interpreted by claiming that in development work in complex settings with multiple actors with divergent and opposite views, it is important to agree upon what the partners, at that moment, do not agree upon in order to continue together around some selected uniting issues and aims. In the last instance, deliberative disagreements are necessary articulations between debating on frameworks and joining in action – tools for political alliances across differences, in entering from the second to the third phase in the life cycle of social movements[54].

Through 'Russian models' into a transitional space?

Both Nira Yuval-Davis and Elisabeth Porter[55] give a warning by saying that there is no promise for reaching any agreement at all. When reflecting on the exercises in transversalism for networking and institution building across the post-bipolar divide and the multiple institutional boundaries in Barents, it is not justified to boast about common identities and frameworks. All in all, the end results of the first NCRB project period are complex. No immediate fundamental changes took place concerning the pre-existing differences in ideas and institutional practices seen through the conflict vs. consensus models and especially the work on and with men, which divided, in the first place, the Scandinavian vs. Finnish units with their roots in different strands of the Western crisis centre movement. However, as to the East-West asymmetries, the bilateral project group[56] is assured that NCRB did take some steps towards making the one-way transmission of ideas and practices from the West into the East more multi-directional and, thereby, encouraging reciprocal flow of experiences.

This is confirmed by the evaluations received from the involved centres as well.[57] The Nordic units give credit to the work of Russian activists and experts, especially in the training of collaborative partners, active campaigning and fostering contacts with the local media. At the same time, the Russian units seem to be in a new position in relation to the Nordic units – they now consider themselves not merely receivers but also co-arrangers of training. Finally – in the words of Marit Stemland[58] – there is a shared feeling that the participants respect each other's reasoning, which transversalism is all about.

In my opinion, this makes a very good starting point for the second NCRB project period, which is centred around the Russian units. In transversal terms, they will now continue rooting but, at the same time, also engage in shifting in the form of personnel exchange across the Nordic-Russian borders and Nordic trainers at Russian courses. Here, again, I find Elisabeth Porter's contribution valuable.[59] The concept of 'transitional space' applies to the present state of the East-West crisis centre movement-in-the-making in Barents by pointing to the issue that was often taken up in 1999-2002 – the debates on the Russian models for crisis centres, which have, without doubt, found a lot of resonance among the Russian actors.[60] In the second project period, the debates have a chance of becoming reality and, as such, a turning point in the East-West crisis centre movement in Barents as a whole.

The NCRB course agenda for 2002-2005, now ratified by the Russian units by themselves, does suggest some openings in this respect.[61] Against the above background, the most interesting single issue on the agenda is the man question that had been put aside as part of deliberat disagreements. Well aware of some potential collisions, the Russian project team has, after consulting the involved units, decided to confront the issue. In the background, there is the crisis of masculinity in Russia – involving health, life style and identity problems – which has had serious negative effects on the lives of women and children.[62] In Russian Barents, moreover, the man question has the special dimension of being directly linked with the gradual post-Cold War de-militarisation and the following mass unemployment of men.[63] As a result, the first crisis centre for men now evolving in the Murmansk region[64] will have a chance of presenting itself as part of the Russian models without any veto from the Nordic – i.e. the Scandinavian – side. In the end, it is possible that the Russian units will challenge their Western 'mother institutions' for a new dialogue on alternative notions of feminism. At its best, a debate on feminism that does not contradict either working with men as allies or helping abusive men[65] will come out from this process to be put onto the main agenda of the second NCRB closing seminar to be held in 2005.

Epilogue: Beyond the East-West divide? The "Third Wave"?

Would it be too courageous to claim that NCRB has contributed to the deconstruction of the dualism of 'emancipated feminists in the West' vs. 'downtrodden sisters in the rest of the world'[66]? At any rate, all that has been said above is related to the heated debates on the traffic on feminism across global divides. Territorial expansion of the Second Wave and the crisis centre movement – starting in the West in the 1960s-70s, proceeding to the South in the 1980s and, finally, entering the post-socialist East in the 1990s – has been followed by consequent waves of criticism. Criticism first arose from within the West and was voiced by Nordic and continental European scholars, who began to question the Anglo-American frameworks.[67] It continued in the name of postcolonial critics challenging Westocentrism[68] as a whole, by coloured and indigenous women living both in the West and in the South.[69] By the late 1990s, critical voices from the post-socialist East, too, have become louder and the accusations of Western-feminism-as-cultural-imperialism 'colonialising' the transitional countries more terse.[70] In words spoken in Russian Barents, the 'euphoria'[71] is over.

Appraisals of how appropriate specific Western institutions and notions of gender are in post-socialist and transitional contexts will provoke demands for solidarities in difference, often repeated with the purpose of counteracting the lack of reciprocality; actually, the NCRB project itself can be seen as an expression of it. However, both Yuval-Davis and Lister advise us to be aware of the trap of *un*critical solidarity.[72] To them, transversal dialogue should not lead to losing oneself, as it is about enabling multiple viewpoints to be heard and, at its best, transformed and shared positions to emerge. In many ways, this makes sense. To take an example, Nordic women actors are satisfied with the fact that the Nordic authorities have, finally, made legislative reforms and carried out development programmes to eradicate the most intimate forms of male domination.[73] At the same time, interventions into the private domain have been met with evident suspicion in the transitional countries recovering from intensive state control of all dimensions and spheres of life.[74] To paraphrase *the* slogan of the Second Wave, it seems that in the post-socialist East the personal is, at least occasionally, being made a-political. This is a serious challenge to the Western feminist theories, in which the private/public distinction has been the cornerstone of criticism against "malist" political theories and practices in relation to eradicating violence especially.[75] In this respect, we are at the beginning of a 'long march'.

However, there are also numerous reasons for optimism. Along with the series of UN conferences on women discussing violence as a priority issue, the role of the United Nations Development Fund for Women (UNIFEM) in the implementation of the Nairobi and Beijing processes has been promising. Recent evaluations of development projects funded by the UN convince everyone that there is no reason to underestimate the achievements of actors at work on all the six continents.[76] We should also mention the global electronic working group *End Violence* co-ordinated by the UNIFEM, which has attracted more and more activists in the Third World and in the transitional countries. The annual 16 Days of Activism campaigning period, which brings together the grassroots actors and the formal multilateral institutions,[77] is a special highlight, not to mention the Global Videoconference that linked the grassroot sites around the world to the UN General Assembly on the last *International Women's Day* of the Second Millennium.

Thus, when the global community of fate related to violence, hopefully, convenes again at the Beijing Plus Ten conference in 2005, it will be fundamentally different from the tribunal in Brussels in 1976 in at least two ways. Firstly, it will be a more multi-voiced community than those operating in the mid-1970s, and secondly, it can rely on active support and interventions from multilateral democratic institutions at global and sub/regional levels.[78] Together, the transformations in the grassroots activities and the formal politics testify of both continuity and change. In short, combating gendered violence through the crisis centre movement is one of the best indicators of how well and alive – and simultaneously transformed – the women's movements are.

To reflect on these transformations, we should, in my view, move more consciously at the different levels of analysis to scrutinise the developments, not only through a close-up of the movements in their empirical variety, but also in relation to the nation-state order vs. the dynamics arising from the multilateral global, regional and sub-regional democratic bodies. From this perspective – maybe – a thesis on transforming of the Second Wave into a qualitatively new Third Wave by the late 20th century should be outlined? In a systemic macro context, the First Wave was about the nation-state as a political community excluding vs. including women and the Second Wave about the welfare state with a more vs. less women-friendly face, while, finally, the Third

Wave will be about the 'post-national' multi-level orders, in which global democracy on the one hand and global divides on the other are the key issues. Within globalised civil society, it would be fruitful to pay special attention to movements crossing the major divides – to approach them as laboratories, in which the commitment to fostering transversalism, multi-voiced dialogue and reciprocal collaboration is a sign of entering a transitional space on a global scale.

To explore these issues, the NCRB community is now seeking contacts with scholars and activists in the Mediterranean, which is the 'cradle' of the first debates on transversal dialogue. The Southern activists have already accepted the invitation to attend the second NCRB closing seminar in 2005, and we look forward to meeting with activists from the Baltic and Central European East-West trans-regions there as well.[79]

References

Danilova, Raisa & Liapounova, Olga & Novikova, Maria (2002). "Violence against women and responses to it in the Russian Federation: a country report", *Women against Violence, An Australian Feminist Journal,* 12, p. 29-45.

Davis, Kathy (2002). "Feminist Body/Politics as World Traveller. Translating *Our Bodies, Ourselves*", *The European Journal of Women's Studies*, 9:3, p. 223-247.

Dickenson, Donna (1997). "Counting women in: globalization, democratization and the women's movement", Anthony McGrew (ed.), *The Transformation of Democracy? Globalization and Territorial Democracy*, Cambridge, Polity Press, p. 97-120.

Drembach, Nikolai (2003). "The *Alternative* Crisis Centre for Men in Murmansk", Aino Saarinen & Olga Liapounova (eds.), *Crisis Centres and Violence Against Women. Report of the Nordic-Russian Network for Crisis Centres in the Barents Region 1999-2002*, Arkhangelsk, Pomor State University, p. 139-142.

Eduards, Maud (1997). "The Women's Shelter Movement", Gunnel Gustafsson (ed.), *Towards a New Democratic Order. Women's Organizing in Sweden in the 1990s*, Stockholm, Publica, Norstedts Tryckeri, p. 120-168.

Elman, Amy R. (1996). *Sexual Subordination and State Intervention. Comparing Sweden and the United States*, Providence & Oxford, Berghan Books.

Evans, Peter (2000). "Fighting Marginalization with Transnational Networks: Counter-Hegemonic Globalization", *Contemporary Sociology. A Journal of Reviews*, 29:1, p. 230-241.

Ezekiel, Judith (2002). "*Le Women's Lib*: Made in France", *The European Journal of Women's Studies*, 9: 3, p. 345-361.

Fábián, Katalin (2002). "Cacophony of Voices. Interpretations of Feminism and its Consequences for Political Action among Hungarian Women's Groups", *The European Journal of Women's Studies*, 9:2, p. 269-290.

Group of Specialist for Combating Violence Against Women (1997). *Final Report of Activities of the EG-SVL including a Platform of Action for Combating Violence Against Women*, Council of Europe, Strasbourg.

Halsaa, Beatrice in this volume

Heitlinger, Alena in this volume

Heininen, Lassi (1999). *Euroopan pohjoinen 1990-luvulla. Moniulotteisten ja ristiriitaisten intressien alue*, Acta Universitas Lapponiensis 21, Rovaniemi, Arktisen keskuksen tiedotteita/ Arctic Centre Reports 30, Lapin yliopisto.

Heinänen, Aira (1992). *Lapsen tasa-arvoa tavoittamassa*, Helsinki, Ensig ja turvakotien Liitto.

Jalusic, Vlasta (2002). "Feminism, Citizenship and the Possibilities of an Arendtian Perspective in Eastern Europe", *The European Journal of Women's Studies*, 9: 2, p. 103-122.

Joachim, Jutta (1999). "Shaping the Human Rights Agenda: The Case of Violence against Women ", Mary K. Meyer & Elisabeth Prügl (eds.), *Gender Politics in Global Governance*, Lanham & Boulder & New York & Oxford, Rowman & Littlefield Publishers, p. 142-160.

Johnson, Janet Elise (2001). "Privatizing Pain: The Problem of Woman Battery in Russia", *NWSA Journal* 13: 3, p. 153-168.

Khodyreva, Natalia in this volume.

Krook, Mona Lena in this volume.

Lister, Ruth (1997). *Citizenship. Feminist Perspectives*, Houndmills & Basingstoke & Hampshire & London, Macmillan Press.

Lønnå in this volume.

Milwertz in this volume.

Nash, Rebecca (2002). "Exhaustion from Explanation. Reading Czech Gender Studies in the 1990s", *The European Journal of Women's Studies*, 9: 3, p. 291-309.

Nordic Council of Ministers (2000). *Nordic Ministers for Gender Equality: Trafficking in women is a crime against human rights*, Press Release, Copenhagen 29 August 2000.

Pashina, Albina (2003). "The Movement of Crisis Centres in Russia: Features, Success and Problems", Aino Saarinen & Olga Liapounova (eds.).

Platform for Action and the Beijing Declaration. Fourth World Conference on Women. Beijing, China, 4-15 September 1995 (1996). New York, Department of Public Information, United Nations.

Porter, Elisabeth (1999). "Risks and Responsibilities: Dialogue Across Difference in Northern Ireland", A Paper Presented at the *European Consortium for Political Research*, University of Mannheim, 26-31 March.

Reason, Peter (1994a). "Human Inquiry as Discipline and Practice", Peter Reason (ed.), *Participation in Human Inquiry*, London & Thousand Oaks & New Delhi, Sage Publications, p. 40-56.

Rotkirch, Anna (2000). *The Man Question. Loves and Lives in the Late 20th Century Russia*, Research Reports 1/2000, Helsinki, University of Helsinki – Department of Social Policy.

Russel, Diana H. & Van de Ven, Nicole (1984). "Preface", Diana H. Russel & Nicole Van de Ven (eds.), *Crimes Against Women: Proceedings of the International Tribunal*, Frog in the Well, East Palo Alto (no page numbers).

Russian Association of Crisis Centres for Women (1993). *Violence Against Women in Russia. Research, Education, and Advocacy Project. A Report for the Non-Governmental Meeting. United Nations World Conference on Women, Beijing, China*

Saarinen, Aino (2000). "The transregional crisis centre movement in the Barents region. Background and context on a global scale", Aino Saarinen & Hilda Rømer Christensen & Beatrice Halsaa (eds.), *Women's Movement and Internationalisation: the "Third Wave"?*, Reports from the Faculty of Education, 82, University of Oulu, p. 81-91.

Saarinen, Aino & Huttunen, Arja (eds.) (1996), *Proceedings of the First Femina Borealis Research Conference, August 17-21, 1995*, Femina Borealis 3, Northern Gender Studies 3, Universities of Oulu and Lapland.

Saarinen, Aino & Liapounova, Olga (2002). "Building a Trans-Regional East/West Community of Crisis Centres in the Barents Region*", Taking Wing, Conference Report, Conference on Gender Equality and Women in the Arctic, 3-6 August 2002, Saariselkä, Inari, Finland*, Ministry of Social Affairs and Health, Helsinki 2002, p. 245-251; *Women against Violence. A Feminist Journal*, 12, p. 4-8.

Saarinen, Aino & Liapounova, Olga & Drachova, Irina (eds.) *NCRB – A Network for Crisis Centres for Women in the Barents Region. Report of the Nordic-Russian Development Project, 1999-2002*. Series "Gender research; methodology and practice", volume 5, Arkhangelsk, Centre for Women's Studies and Gender Research, Pomor University.

Saarinen, Aino & Liapounova, Olga & Drachova, Irina (2003). "NCRB Project Report", Aino Saarinen & Olga Liapounova (eds.), p. 5-60.

Saarinen, Aino & Liapounova, Olga & Drachova, Irina (2003). "Crisis Centres in the Barents Region Questionnaire Report", Saarinen, Aino & Liapounova, Olga & Drachova, Irina (eds.), p. 161-195.

Saguy, Abigail (2002). "Traffic in Sexual Harassment Policy", *The European Journal of Women's Studies*, 9: 3, p. 249-267.

Shtylova, Lybov (2003), "Gender Education Programme for Volunteers Improved the Work of the Crisis Centre in Murmansk", Saarinen, Aino & Liapounova, Olga & Drachova, Irina (eds.), p. 106-115.

Spindel, Cheywa & Levy, Elisa & Connor, Melissa (2000). *With an End in Sight. Strategies from the UNIFEM Trust Fund to Eliminate Violence Against Women*, United Nations Development Fund for Women, New York.

Steans, Jill (1998). *Gender in International Relations. An Introduction*, Cambridge, Polity Press.

Stemland, Marit (2003). "Evaluation of the Contribution of the Northern Feminist University to the Training Courses of the NCRB Project, 1999-2002", Aino Saarinen & Olga Liapounova & Irina Drachova (eds.), p. 61-74.

Säävälä, Hannu (2003). "Väkivaltaisten miesten auttaminen ja miesryhmät Suomessa", *Yhteistyöllä väkivallan ehkäisyyn lähialueseminaari – viranomaisyhteistyöllä kaupallisen seksin ja huumeiden torjunnassa*, Oulun lääninhallitus, 7-8.11.2002.

Tarrow, Sidney (1998). *Power in Movement. Social Movements and Contentious Politics*, Cambridge & New York & Melbourne, Cambridge University Press.

Taylor, Verta (2000). "Mobilizing for Change in a Social Movement Society", *Contemporary Sociology. A Journal of Reviews*, 29: 1, p. 219-229.

Weeks, Wendy & Gilmore, Kate (1996). "How violence against women became an issue on the national policy agenda", Dalton, Tony & Draper, Mary & Weeks, Wendy & Wiseman, John (eds.), *Making Social Policy in Australia. An Introduction*, Allen & Unwin, p. 140-153.

Williams, Fiona (1996). "Postmodernism, feminism and the question of difference, Parton, Nigel (ed.)*, Sociological Theory, Social Change and Social Work,* London, Routledge.

United Nations Economic and Social Council (2003). *Report of the United Nations Development Fund for Women on the elimination of violence against women,* E/CN.6/2003/11-E/CN.4/2003/121.

Yukina, Irina & Saarinen, Aino & Kudriashova, Elena (eds.) (2003), *Women's Strategies and Politics in Transition. Dialogue across the East-West Divide,* Series "Gender research: methdology and practice", volume 4, Arkhangelsk, Centre for Women's Studies and Gender Research, Pomor University.

Yuval-Davis, Nira (1997). *Gender & Nation,* London & Thousand Oaks & New Delhi, Sage Publications.

Notes

1   The term crisis centre covers all kind of units combating violence against women in an institutionalised form, be they called crisis centres, shelters, refuges, safe houses, hot lines, consultation units or emergency duties.

2   Dickenson (1997).

3   Spindel & Levy & Connor (2000).

4   Joachim (1999); Saarinen (2000).

5   Weeks & Gilmore (1996); Elman (1996).

6   Elman (1996), 33-60.

7   Russel & Van de Ven (1984).

8   Eduards (1997).

9   Heinänen (1992); Saarinen & Liapounova & Drachova (2003).

10   Eduards (1997).

11   Russel & Van de Ven (1984).

12   Russian Association (1993).

13   Also Heitlinger in this volume.

14   Saarinen (2000); Russian Association (1993); Pashina (2003).

15   Saarinen & Huttunen (1996).

16   Steans (1998), p. 7-9.

17   Heininen (1999), p. 82-86

18   The BEAR consists of the subregions of Murmansk, Arkhangelsk and Karelia in Russia; Finnmark, Tromsø and Nordland in Norway; Norrbotten and Västerbotten in Sweden; and Lapland and Oulu in Finland. In addition, St. Petersburg as the centre of NW-Russia was included into NCRB.

19   http://www.edu.oulu.fi/ktl/NCRB/.

20   Tarrow (1998), p. 4.

21   http://www.edu.oulu.fi/ktl/NCRB/; Saarinen & Liapounova & Drachova (2003).

22   Reason (1994)

23   See the two publications around NCRB that we are editing at present – the project report (Saarinen & Liapounova & Drachova (2003), which includes 13 articles from the involved NCRB units, and an anthology (Yukina & Saarinen & Kudriashova 2003) from the related Nordic-Russian and international research network funded from, for example, the Nordic (NorFA) research programme on Gender and Violence.

24   Heitlinger and Khodyreva, both in this volume.

25   Saarinen & Liapounova & Drachova (2003).

26   Yuval-Davis (1997), p. 55-60; Lister (1997), p. 78-84.
27   Evans (2000); Taylor (2000).
28   Saarinen (2000) on the crisis centre movement in Barents. See also the NCRB questionnaire report by Saarinen & Liapounova & Drachova (2003) and some reports on a comparative Norwegian-Russian and international project on social work at crisis centres (e.g. Danilova & Liapounova & Novikova 2003).
29   See e.g. Elman (1996), p. 32-60; Eduards (1997); Weeks & Gilmore (1996); Johnson (2001).
30   For a different conceptualisation see Williams (1996).
31   Nash (2002); Johnson (2001).
32   Evans (2000).
33   Saarinen & Liapounova & Drachova (2003).
34   Eduards (1997).
35   See also Johnson (2001); see also Weeks & Gilmore (1996).
36   Taylor (2000).
37   Saarinen & Liapounova & Drachova (2003).
38   See also Weeks & Gilmore (1996).
39   Saarinen & Liapounova & Drachova (2003).
40   Saguy (2002).
41   Due to this, we often hear from other Nordic activists that there exist only a few crisis centres in Finland. In this case, all affiliated and public units are excluded. Many activists in the crisis centre movement, who were interviewed by me for the NCRB project took up the boundary work as well. See also Eduard (1997).
42   Saarinen & Liapounova & Drachova (2003).
43   Yuval-Davis (1997), p. 130.
44   This was, paradoxically, most important to Russian women because, for example, travelling by train from Arkhangelsk to St. Petersburg and back takes 54 hours. A flight ticket costs more than the average monthly salary.
45   Irrespective of its name, the NFU is a non-academic institution – one of the Norwegian *kvinneuniversiteten* that have their origin in the feminist reflections of women's culture. See http://www.kun.nl.no; also Halsaa in this volume.
46   Milwertz in this volume.
47   http://www.edu.oulu.fi.ktl/NCRB/; http:www.kun.nl.no.
48   Taylor (2000); Evans (2000).
49   Saarinen & Liapounova & Drachova (2003).
50   http://www.edu.oulu.fi.ktl/NCRB/.
51   Drembach (2003).
52   Platform for Action (1996), p. 73-81; Group of Specialists (1995); Nordic Council of Ministers (2000); http://www.nl.oneworld.nl/ewlobby/en; United Nations Economic and Social Council (2003).
53   Porter (1999).
54   Tarrow (1998), p. 4.
55   Yuval-Davis (1997), p. 130; Porter (1999).
56   Saarinen & Liapounova (2002); Saarinen & Liapounova & Drachova (2003).
57   http://www.edu.oulu.fi/ktl/NCRB/.
58   Marit Stemland (2003) from the NFU had the main responsibility of the courses with the NCRB project team.

59 Porter (1999).
60 E.g. Shtyleva (2003).
61 http://www.*edu.oulu.fi/ktl*/NCRB/.
62 Rotkirch (1999), p. 264-273.
63 Saarinen & Liapounova & Drachova (2003).
64 Drembach (2003).
65 For an interesting approach see Hannu Säävälä (2003) from the Oulu crisis centre.
66 Davis (2002).
67 This challenge was mentioned in the first application for WMI funding from NorFA in 1996 as well. For continental criticism, see Ezekiel (2002).
68 Yuval-Davis (1997), p. 25.
69 Stoltz in this volume.
70 Davis (2002); Fábián (2002).
71 Shtyleva (2003).
72 Yuval-Davis (1997), p. 129-130; Lister (1997), p. 80-83.
73 Saarinen (2000).
74 Nash (2002); Jalusic (2002).
75 Jalusic (2002); Saarinen (2000).
76 Spindel & Levy & Connor (2000); United Nations Economic and Social Council (2003).
77 Spindel & Levy & Connor (2000), p. 9-10; Saarinen (2000).
78 Saarinen (2000); Joachim (1999); Krook in this volume.
79 An Italian and a Dutch institution are already part of the NCRB research network. http://www.*edu.oulu.fi/ktl*/NCRB/.

CHAPTER 16

Feminist Perspectives on Fathers' Leave. A Cross-country Comparison

Chiara Bertone

Introduction

Making the gender division of labour in the family a political issue has been one of the main, and more influential, aspects of the new feminist movement as an international phenomenon. As part of what Dahlerup, in this volume, refers to as the international connections characterising that movement, this issue, with keywords starting from "the personal is political", travelled across countries, and became part of the core of the national movements' activities and identities. However, besides a common radical framework, what changing the gender division of labour meant changed in each country.[1] It varied according to the specific ideological features and political strategies of the feminist movements and to its relations with women's organisations engaged in pressure politics. The different meanings acquired by this issue were also linked to each country's economic and institutional context, e. g. the levels of married women's labour market participation and the availability of child care services, as well as to the prevailing family ideologies.[2]

A measure which is largely identified as a fundamental one in the present political and feminist debates for improving gender division of labour in the family, supporting a more equal sharing of caring tasks, is fathers' leave. This measure has also been a transnational issue, object of debate in institutions like the European Union.[3]

I have therefore chosen to look at the different frameworks within which fathers' leave was discussed in two specific cases as a contribution to the understanding of the situated meanings and patterns of influence of the new feminist movements' positions and struggles. Building on detailed national case studies is actually a necessary condition for studying the international diffusion of an issue such as fathers' leave without loosing sight of its variable and context-specific meanings (see Kristmundsdóttir in this volume).

For this purpose I will contrast two national cases, Italy and Denmark. These countries represent two largely different settings under several fundamental dimensions: the features of child care arrangements (e.g. more extensive provision of child care services for children under three and better coverage of the costs of children in Denmark, strong tradition of protective legislation, in particular long maternity leave, in Italy), the normative bases of child care policies ("who should care for children?"), but also the features of, and the relations among, women's organisations.

The comparative strategy of contrasting two cases, as Bergman argues in this volume, helps to develop an understanding of interpretations of the particularity of each case, since they form a kind of commentary on one another.[4] Moreover, a comparative approach focusing upon few cases and based upon qualitatively oriented research methods appears more suitable to analyse aspects of social movements relating to issues like collective identity building and discursive strategies.

The analysis concerns in particular the debates on fathers' leave during the historical period witnessing the development of the new feminist movement[5] in those two countries, namely the 1970s and beginning of the 1980s. This same period also witnessed the introduction of fathers' leave in Italy (although here the right of the father was conditioned to the mother renouncing hers), within the Parity Act of 1977, and in Denmark, where it was to a greater extent the outcome of a heated political debate, in 1983. With fathers' leave I mean here any form of extension to fathers of the right (or the obligation) to take a leave after childbirth, including a part of the leave that was already available to mothers: it therefore also comprises what is generally referred to as parental leave, to be divided between mother and father, as well as the "daddy quota" of the leave which can only be taken by fathers. I analyse the claims voiced by women's organisations on this issue as part of their set of claims on state intervention on child care. The actors included are autonomous women's organisations, women's units in political parties and trade unions, groups of the new feminist movement.[6]

The variable meanings of fathers' leave

The equality/difference dilemma, or, as Pateman has called it, "the Wollstonecraft dilemma", has been used as a fundamental interpretative key for exploring the meanings of fathers' leave.[7]

Leira, for instance, referring to the dispute between cash for child care and leave for fathers in recent debates on child care policies in the Scandinavian countries, argues that fathers' leave represents the "sameness" side: "as carers for young children, mothers and fathers are generally assumed to be equally capable, although the ways in which they care for children may differ".[8] At the same time, as regards more specifically the "daddy quota" (i.e. the part of the leave that only the father can use), which has recently been introduced in Scandinavia with the outspoken aim of promoting a more gender equal sharing of caregiving, Leira suggests that its "underlying premise" is "perhaps rather the equal value of father's care and mother's care" than sameness.[9] In fact, it entails a recognition of a gender imbalance, which the law must counteract, in the distribution of care responsibilities and in mothers' and fathers' relative positions for negotiating them.

At a more general level, Fraser[10] sees measures like fathers' leave, if aimed at promoting equal sharing of caring tasks between women and men, as a fundamental challenge to the constraints of the Wollstonecraft dilemma. By challenging the gendered character of caregiving and deconstructing present gender roles, they represent steps towards a "universal caregiver model", where caregiving would be shared within the household by both women and men, but also partly carried by the public institutions as well as by actors located in civil society.

As the study presented here will show, however, it seems problematic to assign one of these general meanings to fathers' leave as a claim of the women's movement, independently from its definition in situated claims-making processes. In fact, seemingly analogous claims about fathers' leave can take different meanings, if they are placed within the broader range of claims about state intervention in child care, outlining different models of distribution of responsibility for child care and of its costs among the different care providers: the state, the family, the market and the third sector.

In analysing the claims, two aspects can be identified: the one given by the measures demanded, and the symbolic one, given by the arguments justifying the state's moral obligation to provide for them. These arguments define whose needs should be satisfied and on the basis of which entitlements. Fraser[11] has proposed in this respect to consider claims as interventions in the political struggle on needs interpretation, where demands for certain public measures also imply a claim for legitimacy of the needs of certain social groups as political issues, and for a certain interpretation of these needs. Although strictly related, the two aspects of the claims must be considered as distinct ones in the analysis, since different meanings can be attached to demands for the same measure.[12] In the case of fathers' leave, different relations can be established between children's, fathers' and mothers' needs, and the claims can be voiced on behalf of different groups of women (e.g. full-time or part-time working women).

I see therefore claims here as outcomes of processes by which women's organisations constructed common understandings and conflict dimensions on the definition of whose needs should be fulfilled with the introduction of leave for fathers, under its different forms, or with an alternative measure: e.g. housewives or women working outside the home, middle-class or working class women, children, fathers.

I will interpret these claimsmaking processes by reconstructing the strategic choices that have shaped them. I will point in particular to two elements. The first one is variation in women's organisations' positions and goals, in particular the different role played by the new feminist movements in the two countries. The second element is variation in the sets of opportunities and constraints that these actors found in articulating their claims, as well as the boundaries that they avoided to overcome. In this respect, I will refer to the general features of the distribution of responsibility of child care in the two countries and to the normative bases of child care policies.

The new feminist movement: new agendas on child care issues

The 1970s were marked in both countries by the appearance of a new actor, the new feminist movement, characterised by a strong collective identity and opposition to the established political system.[13] Its presence changed the relations among organised women, introducing new conflict dimensions, and between them and the other political and social actors.

In Italy, the feminist movement acquired growing visibility and political influence, and became the protagonist in setting the agenda of women's issues, in particular on the strongly conflictual issues of divorce, introduced in 1970 and confirmed by referendum in 1974, and abortion, legalized in 1978. It realised a fundamental shift in the way family relations and women's conditions were thematised. In the 1960s, women's organisations, both those belonging to the Catholic and to the Leftist political and cultural blocks, largely focused upon maternity, identifying women's problems in the difficult combination of work outside the home and child care and claiming for public support to make this combination possible, by extension of maternity leave and development of public crèches. These goals were partly achieved in the beginning of the 1970s. Some improvements of public child care services for children under three came after the 1971 law on public crèches, although their coverage remained limited and uneven throughout the country.[14] The 1971 reform of maternity leave improved an already comparatively high protection of the working mother's time to care for children after childbirth.[15] However, these reforms did not challenge the fundamental features of child care arrangements, which remained contradictory: the full-time housewife caring mother was the ideal model, but at the same time support to working mothers was the only kind of support to motherhood provided by the state.[16]

Women's organisations had discussed the need for public support to combining paid work and child care within a substantially unchallenged idea of the family as a harmonic unit, a site of solidarity. It was this idea that feminists challenged, by defining the relations between men and women in the family in terms of conflict and oppression, and by rejecting the family as an institution. This change can be synthesised as a move from emancipation in the family to liberation from the family, and it implied a shift in focus from parenthood – in particular motherhood – to relations within the couple.

In this shift, maternity was assigned a different meaning: feminists gave motherhood as pregnancy a central place, but they defined it as a question related to sexuality. The focus on gender power relations within the family also changed the place of child care in the definition of women's condition. The oppressive gender division of labour based upon women's unpaid work was referred to the family institution itself, defined by marriage. Against Catholics imposing housework, and Communists ignoring it, the solution proposed, at least by the more radical groups, was liberation from housework by liberation from the family.[17] Altogether, claims regarding public intervention on child care remained therefore marginal in feminists' activities.[18]

In Denmark as well, the emergence of the new feminist movement, called (*Rødstrømperne, the Redstockings*), marked women's politics in the 1970s. It was characterised by the combination of a radical and Leftist orientation, as opposed to gender equality feminism, mainly represented by the old cross-party women's organisation, *Dansk Kvindesamfund* (*The Danish Women's Society*). In the 1960s, Denmark had witnessed a largely consensual development of child care policies, whose main result was a great expansion of child care services and the recognition of a fundamental public responsibility in child care. This process had provided cross-party women's organisations with the possibility of preserving internal consensus upon their claims on child care, by keeping a double direction in their demands, both for services and for cash transfers as well as extension of maternity leave. At the same time, a condition for preserving this consensus was claiming for policies to be neutral as regards family models or caring arrangements, avoiding to define a preferred pattern for women with children, of permanence on the labour market or of full-time caregiving.

The *Redstockings* rejected the goals of these organisations, defining them as women's equality on men's terms: women's liberation required instead a radical societal change in all spheres of life, in the class structure as well as in family relations and sexuality.[19] Especially in the first years, the *Redstockings* did not usually address claims to the state, since they did not see state activity as a suitable means for the radical changes they struggled for. Their activity rather consisted in placing issues on the public agenda and influencing their definition.

Despite acting outside institutional politics, the new feminist movement deeply influenced, in both countries, women's organisations' claims regarding state intervention in child care in the 1970s, including maternity leave reforms and the introduction of fathers' leave.

First, the definition of women as a group, without other specifications, as the subject on behalf of whom claims were voiced, represented a move from more sectoral views, referring for instance to housewives or to working women, or to mothers working for choice or for need, etc. It also represented a shift from the centrality of children's needs which had marked in particular women's organisations' claims in Denmark.

Secondly, the new feminist movement's definition of the gender division of labour in the family as a political issue had to be dealt with also by the other organisations, although its relevance varied widely in the two countries and for the different organisations.

Finally, the presence of the new feminist movement introduced a stronger division between activity inside and outside political institutions, resulting in Italy mainly in conflicting positions on child care issues, and in Denmark rather in a division of labour, with the feminist movement often taking a more radical stance and parts of the established women's organisations and women's units in political parties a more moderate one on common issues.[20]

The claims for fathers' leave

The struggle to define gender relations and division in the family a public, political issue was a general trait of the radical feminist movements emerging in those years in the Western countries. What the focus upon women's emancipation through wage work had left unquestioned, namely the oppressive relations in the family that burdened women with domestic work and the responsibility for caring, was now identified as a central issue in the feminist struggle. Despite this common background, however, fundamental differences in feminists' politicisation of the gender distribution of child care tasks in the family emerged in the two countries, also involving claims for fathers' leave.

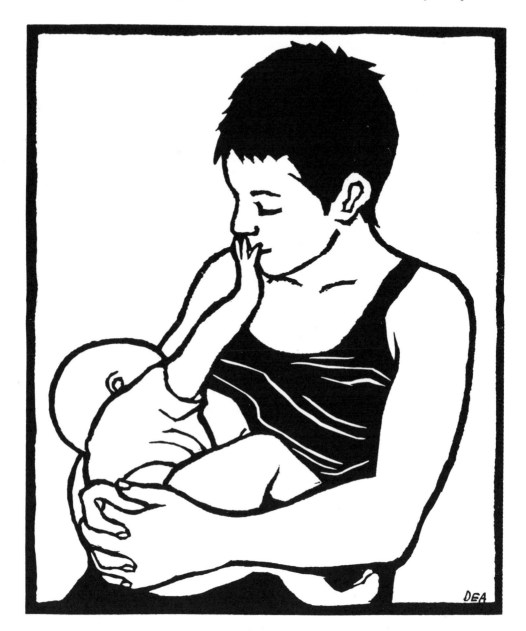

Italy

A form of fathers' leave was introduced in Italy under the 1977 Parity Act. This law was aimed at securing equal treatment in access to work and in working conditions, reducing the additional obstacles and costs of hiring women,[21] while it did not provide for positive action measures. The extension of optional leave to fathers was defined in this equal rights framework, rather than as an intervention explicitly aimed at changing the division of labour within the family.

The limited political discussion concerned the extension to fathers of the right to take the optional leave of six months, starting at the end of the third month after childbirth. The proposals differed in giving to the father an independent right or conditioning his right to the mother renouncing hers, and in whether to extend to the father the right to unpaid leave to care for sick children. The idea of an exclusive leave reserved for fathers remained substantially absent from the debate.

In the end, the law gave fathers the possibility of taking the optional period, but only in substitution of the working mother, and provided that both parents were wage workers. This limited coverage to a minority of families, also excluding those with self-employed women as well as with women working in the informal labour market. As a result, the number of fathers that took advantage of the measure was very small. Fathers were also given, in alternative to the mother, the right to take leave to care for sick children.

According to Beccalli, this law was not an outcome of mobilisation of the relevant social actors of the time, namely the trade unions and the feminist movement, but a symbolic measure wanted by the political élite, like most of the reforms passed those years of co-operation between the Christian Democratic Party in government and the Communist Party in the opposition.[22] In fact, during the 1970s and up to this law, leave for fathers did not become a main issue neither in the political debate nor among women's organisations.

In those years, feminists were strongly striving for releasing the gender division of work from its invisibility in the family and for making it a matter of public concern. Changes were not expected from state regulation, but from modifying power relations between women and men and improving women's self-determination. The demand for wages for housewives, supported by an important part of the movement, may partly be interpreted in these terms. Although it could appear directed to the recognition of family work, including child care, as a women's task, it was also presented as a way to provide women with the power lever to negotiate a fairer division of work in the family.

Moreover, although some feminist groups, including those acting within the trade unions, actually claimed leave for fathers in the second half of the 1970s, most of them could not share a positive view of the introduction of leave for fathers within a gender neutral "gender equality" framework, to which they opposed the need to break the boundaries between public and private. With their reference to women as a group, then, they rather tended to overcome the sectoral focus upon working mothers that had characterised claims in the 1960s, and that lay behind the focus on equal opportunities at work of the Parity Act. They pointed to economic independence as a crucial condition for women's self-determination and liberation from the family, but they included both women working on the labour market and housewives in the notion of women as a group, as illustrated again by the mobilisation for wages for housewives.

Most women's organisations supported instead an equal rights framework on fathers' leave. The largest one, namely the Leftist Union of Italian Women (*Unione Donne Italiane*), and women's units in Leftist parties shared this support, but at the same time they criticised the "formal" equality framework of the Parity Act, and demanded anti-discriminatory measures to be extended beyond the labour market, e.g. to schools or the media.

Reference to equal rights was also often integrated by other perspectives. Asserting the social value of motherhood remained an important basis of legitimacy for claiming public support to child care, both for Catholics and for the Union of Italian Women, although with different meanings. Catholic women's organisations placed it within the definition of the family as the fundamental unit to be supported.

> [leave for fathers] has been a consequence of (…) the persistence with which we have followed up the idea that man and woman are two persons with equal dignity, and therefore equal dignity at work, and therefore equal rights and duties. This is what has allowed us to (…) perfecting what was present in nuce in the law on maternity, namely that in order for maternity to be a social fact, it is evident that also the father is involved and thus he also has the right and duty to assist the child.[23]

The Union of Italian Women, which, during the 1970s, was approaching feminists' positions also on other issues, in particular on abortion, increasingly combined references to the social value of motherhood with an emphasis on the oppressive character of the social construction of motherhood.

> What do we mean by social value of motherhood? We do not want a 'mum-centred' society, which, while exalting motherhood in words, actually lays its burden upon the woman. In this way motherhood (…) acquires all the fixity of a social role, becomes object of ideology and mystification; it is surrounded by false privileges, to which however correspond elements of actual underestimation, subordination, marginalisation of the woman's figure.[24]

In any case, leave for fathers was conceived within an idea of harmonic composition of the needs and interests of mothers, fathers and children, without referring to power relations and negotiations of roles within the family. In the previous decades, Leftist women's organisations had largely endorsed the principles of socialisation of care, claiming for a move of responsibility for child care from the family to the state. Catholic women's organisations had rather supported, according to the principle of subsidiarity, the idea that child care should be kept as much as possible in the social sphere, primarily in the family, and the state should only intervene in case of need, e.g. in support of women having to work outside the home. Now, fathers' greater participation in caregiving in the family could be presented, under the Leftist perspective, as an integration of socialisation of care in relieving women of their burden. Under the Catholic perspective, it could be referred to the logic of subsidiarity, as an alternative to the need for moving care out of the family. In both cases, the question of the gender division of labour was related to a notion of the family as a harmonic, yet more democratic, entity, rejecting feminists' conflictual view.

Campaing for improved maternity leave.
(Courtesy of the Women's History Archives, Denmark)

Denmark

Compared to Italy, the Danish Redstockings politicised more clearly the question of men's obligation to share child care responsibilities, defining it not only as a fundamental social problem, but also as a matter of state intervention. Thus, despite their general diffidence towards the state, they claimed that it should actively promote a change in the division of work in the family, mainly by introducing mandatory leave for fathers and promoting shorter working hours.

The question of men's participation in child care was one of the issues debated within and across the established women's organisations, and leave for fathers was a main demand in this respect. This demand could thus represent a common ground for a broad mobilisation of women's organisations was realised, although without great direct co-operation: from the Redstockings, joining other grassroots organisations in a common campaign, to the cross-party umbrella organisation Danish Women's National Council (*Danske Kvinders Nationalråd*), but with the exception of trade union women. Unlike in Italy, the Redstockings did not support, instead, any demand for wages for housewives:

> That it *is* perhaps best for children to have a parent around them in their first years must imply that we claim for longer leave for both mothers and fathers, not that the MOTHER has to devote herself totally to a vocation as wife and mother (...) In Denmark we cannot be interested in a wage for housework because it will only make women's exclusion from the labour market faster and less painful for the employer and lock us all even more in the nuclear family and in men-women relationships, and all attempts in that direction must be turned down as far as possible from the start.[25]

Actually, leave for fathers was a main issue in the political debates on the reform of maternity leave throughout the 1970s, up to the 1980 Act. The controversy concerned in particular whether to give it the same (or greater) priority as the extension of leave for mothers and whether it should be optional or mandatory (in the sense that it could not be used alternatively by the mother).

A joint Committee of the social democratic government's Children's Commission and the Equal Status Council argued for a strict relation between concerns for children's needs, which remained the central reference in the political debates on child care, and for gender equality.

> [One has to discuss] the more moral way of presenting the problem 'Who has to 'pay' for improving children's conditions'? When this question is inserted in a gender equality perspective, the explanation has to be found in the actual conditions for gender equality – conditions that according to the Committee cannot endure any deterioration. The Committee will warn about and turn against initiatives and measures aimed at solving problems especially at women's expense.[26]

Conceiving fathers' leave as an active measure for inducing men to share responsibility for child care, the Committee proposed that it should be mandatory. This position, however, was not shared by all the supporters of the reform, and was strongly opposed by the main trade unions' confederation (*LO*). In the end, the 1980 law only included an extension of maternity leave.[27] The majority in the Social Democratic Party had decided to give up a more extensive reform, despite a strong internal opposition, especially by women. The debate continued until a further reform, introducing optional leave for fathers, was achieved in 1983.[28] In the following years, however, a very small percentage of fathers took advantage of the leave.[29]

Women's organisations' focus on fathers' leave was a consequence of the attention raised by the new feminist movement upon the need for changes in the gender division of labour in the family, and it entailed a questioning of the gender neutral equal opportunities framework. State intervention should be extended to the conditions for real equality, including a more balanced sharing of the burden of child care between mothers and fathers.

> What the Danish Women's National Council wants is to draw attention to the fact that we, the women will not tolerate being a reserve labour force – in periods of depression we have to divide the work that is there – and that the conditions under which children grow up are not a question we just can leave to the family. It is a social task. Our basic viewpoint is that if we have to obtain real equality (*ligestilling*) between women and men, women must obtain economic independence. Therefore, we must concentrate on education and occupation, but at the same time this means that women must face the fact that they have to surrender some of the power in the home.[30]

More than the demand for optional leave, mandatory leave incorporated a conflictual view of family relations and was more clearly conceived in terms of affirmative action, requiring state intervention explicitly aimed at conditioning the distribution of caring tasks in the family. Despite these differences, the notion of equality, in either a more moderate or a radical version,[31] represented a common framework for the arguments used in support of leave for fathers. The largely prevailing goal was that of de-gendering caregiving, and the model to be realised was that of the dual earner – dual carer family.

At the same time, the focus in claims turned from children's needs to women, as a result of the new feminist movement's construction of women as a group. Unlike in Italy, however, this construction referred to a model of women's permanent presence on the labour market. Women's caring role as mothers as a basis of legitimacy for their entitlement to public support remained instead very marginal, even among the more conservative organisations.

Finally, emphasis upon men's obligations to take their share in caregiving under an openly conflictual perspective tended to be limited to the Redstockings. Although it seemed to influence the definition of women's organisations' demands, their public arguments were mainly formulated in consensual terms, emphasising advantages for men. This might be an expression of women's organisations' search for legitimacy for their claims and for alliance with other grassroots organisations such as pedagogues' and parents' organisations.

Strategies and perceived opportunities

Several elements of the different context of opportunities in the two countries, as it was perceived by women's organisations, seem to have played an important role in the definition of their claims-making strategies.

In Italy, politicising the question of gender division of caregiving in the family had a disruptive effect upon a persistently strong notion of caring as belonging to the private sphere, and in particular to the family, especially for children under three. Besides, de-gendering caregiving entailed a difficult change in the meaning of care itself, given the strength still held by the idea of maternal care as the primary model. This might have been perceived as an obstacle to a greater involvement not only of the feminist movement, but also of organisations like the Union of Italian Women in demands for fathers' leave as means for balancing the gender distribution of caring tasks.

Given the extent of state intervention and the legitimacy held by the definition of child care as a public responsibility, the Danish situation opened instead to greater possibilities of setting leave for fathers not only within the framework of gender equality on the labour market, but also of state support to redistribution of responsibilities for care in the family. Furthermore, the professionalisation of care that had accompanied the development of child care services contributed to making an open challenge to its gender connotation relatively less disruptive. As a result, the possibility of a broader definition of the issue might have encouraged the involvement of a broad range of women's organisations and groups.

Another important difference concerned the actual relevance of fathers' leave for women's lives, and was related to the great variation in the patterns of women's labour market participation.[32] In Italy access to leave for pregnancy and childbirth was restricted to the limited number of women working in the regular labour market, while in Denmark it could more easily be represented as a universal question, and be identified as a basic point of departure for promoting changes in the gender division of labour. Moreover, in Italy, given the persisting strong presence of housewives, revaluing women's full-time caring could be more easily thought as a possible alternative to de-gendering caregiving. In Denmark, instead, where the dual breadwinner family was becoming the taken-for-granted norm, a better sharing of care responsibilities in the family could more easily appear as the only viable key for improving gender equality.

The different prevailing normative bases for child care policies also influenced women's organisations' strategies. In Italy, demanding fathers' leave within a framework of individual, gender-neutral citizenship rights might have been partly perceived as a cost by women's units in political parties and women's organisations, as it also appeared in the case of the Parity Act. In fact, none of women's organisations, neither Leftist nor Catholic, belonged to a liberal tradition of struggle for individual rights. The bases of entitlement on which they partly met in the previous decades were not originally citizenship rights (although especially towards the end of the decade they often tended to be reformulated as such), but women's entitlements as workers and as mothers. At the same time, as argued above, no bridging seemed to be possible between an equal rights framework and the new feminist movement's concern for women's self-determination.

In Denmark, instead, the definition of fathers' leave within an equal rights framework did not preclude a broad involvement of women's organisations, including the Redstockings, in the issue. Part of the actors in the political debate as well as part of women's organisations actually interpreted the introduction of leave for fathers as a modification of the gender equality framework, towards a notion of real equality needing positive action. At the same time, however, the concern for parents' right to free choice, grounded on a liberal notion of individual rights, limited the legitimacy of claims for mandatory leave.

Besides the perceived opportunities linked to the general institutional and political context, the claimsmaking strategies of women's organisations were also related to the conflict dimensions emerging in their mutual relations, including their different attitudes towards institutional politics.

As regards claims on fathers' leave, we could characterise the positions of the different organisations and groups in both countries as placed between two poles. On one extreme, those who supported a conflictual notion of the family, assuming that a redistribution of caring tasks would not be a product of free negotiations, but required an alteration of power relations in the family. The other pole was given by the positions assuming that securing equal opportunities on the labour market would foster by itself a redistribution of caring tasks in the family. This position entailed a limited politicisation of the issue of the gender division of labour, which should only indirectly become matter of state intervention. The relations between and within women's organisations and groups subscribing to these two positions were different in the two countries.

In Italy, the confrontation between these two positions was more conflictual, and corresponded to the divide between actors engaged outside and inside institutional politics. Feminist groups, in fact, were not only uninterested in engaging in demands on the state, but, even when they actually formulated demands for fathers' leave as trade union feminists did, they strongly argued against the framework within which the introduction of leave for fathers was proposed and supported by women acting in political institutions. For an organisation setting itself across this division, as was the Union of Italian Women in those years, approaching feminists' position also entailed, therefore, distancing itself from party politics and engaging on other issues, rather than bridging these different positions. As a result, leave for fathers did not become a shared issue and was only marginally debated on the occasion of the passing of the Parity Act, while the scene of women's politics was rather occupied by the struggle on abortion and on reproductive issues.

In Denmark, the two positions seemed to open to greater possibilities for common claims. The initiative to voice claims for fathers' leave, either optional or mandatory, mainly came from above, having as protagonists women in political parties and established women's organisations. Although not directly co-operating, the Redstockings and the Danish Women's Society shared the demand for mandatory leave for fathers. Moreover, this position was not in complete opposition to the supporters of optional leave: despite being based on a more conflictual view of the family, it was at the same time an expression of a more radical version of the same gender equality orientation.

Thus, the Redstockings' pragmatic attitude towards the state and the fact that their claims on child care did not substantially depart from the gender equality framework, although with emphasis on radical societal changes as conditions for real equality, provided a ground for some form of division of work with established women's organisations in claiming for leave for fathers. A strong conflict line divided instead supporters of leave for fathers and the trade unions, including the women's union, that gave priority to the class perspective upon concerns for gender equality and endorsed instead longer leave for mothers.

In sum, in the Italian case two distinct strategies, one of bargaining and one of opposition, can be detected, on which organisations and groups were divided along the inside/outside dimension. The Danish case showed instead the prevalence of bargaining strategies, with conflict lines regarding not so much the inside/outside dimension, but other dimensions of differentiation among organisations.

Conclusions

In both countries, the new feminist movement played a fundamental role in making the general issue of division of work, including responsibility for child care, and distribution of power between women and men in the family a public, political issue, requiring state intervention. At the same time, I have argued that the connection between politicisation of this issue and claims for fathers' leave is highly variable, and that its presence and features must be investigated in the specific contexts, in relation to the features of the women's organisations involved and to the perceived opportunity structure.

In order to grasp the different meanings attached to fathers' leave, rather than referring to the equality/difference dilemma, I have proposed a perspective which investigates the variable relations between demands for fathers' leave and their justifications, i.e. the arguments referring to the needs of different social subjects to be met by this measure. A crucial element in this respect appears to be the more conflictual or harmonic representation of family relations, with assumptions about convergence or assessments of differentiation between women's, men's and children's needs.

Claims for fathers' leave can be aimed at promoting state intervention in support of a more balanced sharing of caring tasks between mothers and fathers, as part of a more conflictual view of family relations, as it happened under many aspects in

Denmark, but this is not always the case. In Italy, fathers' leave was not conceived, especially by the new feminist movement, as a main means for promoting a greater gender balance in caring tasks. On the contrary, the conditioned form of fathers' leave was introduced as part of legislative measures going in the direction of the realisation of a "universal breadwinner model", making the gendered character of caregiving in the family more invisible rather than challenging it.

The comparative approach used in this article has thus proved useful to highlight national specificities in an issue which the new feminist movement apparently shared across countries. Moreover, it points to the importance of taking account of the national contexts, and the specific historical backgrounds of national women's movements, when we look at how issues such as fathers' leave are taken up in the agenda of women's organisations at an international, for instance European, level.

References

Ballestrero, Maria Vittoria (1979). *Dalla tutela alla parità*, Bologna, Il Mulino.

Beccalli, Bianca (1985). "Le politiche del lavoro femminile in Italia: donne, sindacati e stato tra il 1974 e il 1984", *Stato e mercato*, n.15, pp. 423-459.

Bertone, Chiara (2002). *Whose needs? Women's organisations' claims on child care in Italy and Denmark*, Aalborg, FREIA, Aalborg University.

Bergqvist, Christina (1999). "Childcare and Parental Leave Models", in Bergqvist, Christina et al. (eds.) *Equal Democracies? Gender and Politics in the Nordic Countries*, Oslo, Scandinavian University Press.

Dahlerup, Drude (ed.) (1986). *The new women's movement. Feminism and political power in Europe and the USA*, London, Sage.

Dahlerup, Drude (1998). *Rødstrømperne. Den danske Rødstrømpebevægelses udvikling, nytænkning og gennemslag*, Copenhagen, Gyldendal.

Dalla Costa, Mariarosa (1988). "Domestic labour and the Feminist Movement in Italy since the 1970s", *International Sociology*, 3(1), pp. 23-34.

Ergas, Yasmine (1986). *Nelle maglie della politica*, Milano, Franco Angeli.

Fraser, Nancy (1989). *Unruly Practices,* Cambridge, Polity.

Fraser, Nancy (1994). "After the Family Wage. Gender Equity and the Welfare State", *Political Theory*, 22(4), pp. 591-618.

Geertz, Clifford (1973). *The interpretation of Cultures*, New York, Basic Books.

Hoskyns, Catherine (1996) *Integrating Gender*, London, Verso.

Istat (1986). *Sommario di statistiche storiche 1926-1985*, Roma, Istat.

Leira, Arnlaug (1998). "Comments on 'Social Care and Welfare State Restructuring' by Mary Daly and Jane Lewis", in *Women's Empowerment and Political Presence*, Seminar 4 of the EC-Programme "Gender and Citizenship: Social Integration and Social Exclusion in European Welfare States", Denmark, October 16th-17th.

Naldini, Manuela (2002). *The Family in the Mediterranean Welfare States*, London, Frank Cass.

Pateman, Carole (1989). *The Disorder of Women*, Stanford, Stanford University Press.

Pedersen, Susan (1993). *Family, Dependence, and the Origins of the Welfare State*, Cambridge, Cambridge University Press.

Rostgaard, Tine, Mogens N. Christoffersen & Hanne Weise (2000). *Parental leave in Denmark*, Copenhagen, The Danish Institute of Social Research.

Saraceno, Chiara (1998). *Mutamenti della famiglia e politiche sociali in Italia*, Bologna, Il Mulino.

Skocpol, Theda and Margaret Somers (1980). "The Uses of Comparative History in Macrosocial Inquiry." *Comparative Studies in Society and History*, 22(2), pp. 174-195.

Notes

1 Dahlerup (1986).

2 On the question of transnational interaction and cultural diffusion, on the ways in which women's movements adopt and adapt ideas and issues developed by movements in other countries, see Bergman and Milwertz in this volume.

3 The question of parental leave has been discussed at the European Union level since the Commission proposal for a Directive on parental leave made in 1983 that included a non-transferable part of the leave reserved to fathers with the outspoken aim of improving the sharing of family responsibilities between women and men, but was rejected (Hoskyns 1996). The Directive on parental leave was then passed in 1996, provided instead the right for parents to be given up to three months' unpaid parental leave.

4 Skocpol and Somers (1978), p. 178, identify three distinct logics of comparative history: *parallel demonstration of theory*, used in researches applying a general model to different historical cases in order to demonstrate its fruitfulness; *contrast of contexts*, when comparison is used "to bring out the unique features of each particular case (…) and to show how these unique features affect the working-out of putatively general social processes"; *macro-causal analysis*, when comparison is aimed at making causal inferences about structures and processes. See also Geertz (1973).

5 I have chosen this term on the basis of the contextual meanings of feminist movement in the two countries compared, and of the self-perception of that movement's actors. In Italy, one could simply use the expressions "feminist" and "feminism", since the distinction between the new feminist groups, calling themselves feminists (*femministe*), and the already existing women's organisations (*organizzazioni femminili*), corresponded to the self-perception of both of them (Ergas 1992, p. 568). In Denmark, instead, the term "feminist" was not used to distinguish the radical feminist groups developing during the 1970s from the old women's organisations (Dahlerup 1998). The feature of being "new" appears therefore necessary for identifying the 1970s movement.

6 Published and archive material by and on these organisations, as well as interviews with some of the protagonists, were the sources for the analysis, which is extensively described in Bertone (2002).

7 According to Pateman (1989), p. 14, assumptions about gender that are implicitly present in the political discourse in modern democracies expose feminists to the following dilemma: first, "it is taken for granted that for women to be active, full citizens they must become (like) men. Second, although women have demanded for two centuries that their distinctive qualities and tasks should become part of citizenship – that is, that they should be citizens as women – their demand cannot be met when it is precisely these marks of womanhood that place women in opposition to, or, at best, in a paradoxical and contradictory relation to, citizenship".

8   Leira (1998), pp. 374-375.

9   See also Bergqvist (1999).

10 Fraser (1994).

11 Fraser (1989).

12 Pedersen (1993).

13 Ergas (1986); Dahlerup (1998).

14 Kindergartens had instead traditionally been much more widespread and increased in the 1970s, with a trend towards universal coverage.

15 A four-week maternity leave had been introduced in 1902, and fascism improved protective measures in order to discourage women's employment. The post-war reforms partly built upon that tradition of protective legislation, but they also became a means for supporting mothers' harmonisation of paid work and care responsibilities. The 1950 law on protection of working mothers, an advanced law in this field in Europe, extended the period of compulsory leave to three months before and eight weeks after childbirth, and raised the financial compensation to 80 percent of the normal wage. The 1971 reform added an optional leave of six months, with a financial compensation of 30%, and introduced an unpaid leave to care for a sick child under three.

16 Saraceno (1998); Naldini (2002).

17 Dalla Costa (1988).

18 This marginality emerges from the studies on feminism, but also from those on the political debates surrounding laws regarding child care (Naldini 2002), and from the primary sources analysed in Bertone (2002).

19 Dahlerup (1998, Vol. II).

20 Dahlerup (1998) argues that women's political influence in the 1970s and early 1980s, also in the field of welfare and family policies, was grounded on this kind of combination of different roles.

21 An enactment of EC directives, this law was also aimed at adapting labour regulation to the more symmetrical model of family relations introduced by the family law reform of 1975 (Ballestrero 1979).

22 Beccalli (1985).

23 Interview with Alessandra Codazzi, former head of the Women's Office in the CISL, the Catholic trade union. June 23rd, 1998.

24 UDI, *Libera nella maternità Autonoma con il lavoro Protagonista nella società*, Campagna emancipazione 1976, p. 9.

25 The same article compares the voicing of this claim by feminist movements of other countries with its marginality among the Redstockings, finding an important reason in women's "different condition – a much bigger part of women are only housewives in, for instance, England than in Denmark", 'Løn for husarbejde – nej, men det er svært at sætte opofrelse i banken!' *Kvinder*, no.26, 1979, pp. 18-19.

26 Børnekommissionen, *Børnefamiliernes økonomi og arbejdsforhold*, Udvalgsrapport no.1, København, 1980.

27 The 1980 reform added a paid leave period of four weeks before childbirth to the previously existing fourteen weeks overall for women wage earners.

28 The 1983 reform included a further extension of the paid leave period, up to twenty-four weeks. Fathers were given the possibility to take up to ten weeks after the fourteenth week, and a specific fathers' leave of two weeks after childbirth (or counting from the moment when the child came home) was introduced. Paid leave for the care of a sick child was not obtained by law, but leave for the first day of the child's sickness was introduced during the 1980s in collective contracts.

29 Although increasing in the following years, it only reached 4% of fathers in 1996 (Rostgaard, Christoffersen and Weise (2000)).

30 'Kvindeformand: Vi har glemt børnene' *Berlingske Tidende* 30/11/1975.

31 According to Dahlerup (1998), the radicalised version of equality feminism, resulting from the influence of the Redstockings movement, was centred on a notion of *real* gender equality requiring, besides or rather than formal equal rights, active promotion of social change.

32 In Italy, in the 1970s women's activity rate began to rise: from 31.5 in 1970 to 34.3 in 1977, the year of the Parity Act (Istat 1986). However, it remained very low compared with most other European countries, and its rise was accompanied by growing women's unemployment rates. In Denmark, women's already high activity rate continued to grow throughout the 1970s: from 53.7 in 1970 to 67.6 in 1983, when fathers' leave was introduced.

Part V

Multiculturalism – Globalisation

CHAPTER 17

Who are 'we' to tell...?

Black, Immigrant and Refugee Women and the Politics of Analysing Feminist Movements

Pauline Stoltz

The focus of this book on global identities and transnational networks invites us to think about the political activism of groups of women (and men) in feminist movements in different parts of the world. The chapters at the same time not only address feminist movements in several countries, but also activities related to the national, as well as the international level of politics. In this often described as more and more globalised world, we can wonder if these political activities in any way have changed?

Thinking about globalisation we are often invited to forget about or 'overcome' borders and boundaries between states, genders, 'cultures', 'races, 'ethnicities', etcetera. One can wonder if there is something inherently good about globalisation, about more contact between peoples and/or social movements, about international co-operation in general or if there are any fallacies, which we should watch out for. An implicit call for *solidarity* between peoples, states and social movements could be recognised in the above. *Citizenship rights* (including political rights) are part of the mechanisms that define and thereby close the category of citizens in a specific state. By forgetting or 'overcoming' these borders and boundaries between states, citizenship rights could end up in the background of our attention. In this chapter I would like to claim that there is a danger in doing that when having a focus on the political activities of different actors within feminist movements.

The above line of reasoning opens up for a discussion of the categories we are talking about. When we are talking about feminist movements, whom then, are we talking about? Feminist movements can *analytically* be described as closed categories. Who, at the same time, belongs to the Swedish feminist movement(s)? What issues and characteristics do these actors represent? And who are 'we' to tell...? Have recent developments in world politics led to any change in the political activities of different groups of feminist actors? A focus on *waves*, on continuity and change, often invites us to focus on the *mainstream* of political activists. But who then, is left out? Why? And is this exclusion desirable or not? Power relations *between* women suddenly become important to disclose.

We can think of the well-known critique by Black, Third World and Postcolonial feminists. They have claimed that the way, in which the concept of 'women' in feminist contexts is described, although it often does not seem to have a racial denomination, nevertheless assumes to indicate a white woman. It is only when the word *Black* is put in front of the word *women* that *Black women* seem to become visible.[1] Black and postcolonial feminists have therefore raised demands for a more differentiated use of the word *women*, as well as a reconsideration of the consequences of its different uses in political theory and practice.

The aim of this chapter is to discuss the movements of closure we, as feminist academics, use, in order to discuss the political activism of groups of women (and men) in feminist movements in different parts of the world. Taking a starting point in the above mentioned critique by Black, Third World and Postcolonial feminists a special focus will be given to the political activities of Black, migrant and refugee women in Europe (more about these problematic categories below).

In visualising we use language as an aid. Unfortunately we cannot capture everything 'in a word'. There is probably no way we ever will be able to, since it appears to be an aspect of the phenomenon of language itself. This raises a number of political problems though: when is it interesting for scholars investigating feminist movements – to 'define', to 'identify', to 'name' women (or men)? And when does it simply just not matter? What are the reasons for the 'defining', the 'identifying', the 'naming'? These reasons can be political, and not only question injustices and inequalities but also emphasise and reinforce them. When does our choice of words become problematic? What presumptions do feminist political theorists have, when they use words like 'individuals' or 'political community' or what the characteristics are of the actors involved in deliberative processes? Those are also the boundaries of the meanings of the words *women* and *feminist movement* that are of interest.

The moments of closure we create in our analysis around these words can influence our thinking about the political arenas for solidarity within and between social movements. In this chapter I would like to claim that notions of *citizenship* and *solidarity* are important foci for those interested in the political activism of groups of women (and men) in feminist movements in different parts of the world. The solution to some of the problems that might arise due to *unwanted* exclusionary mechanisms, I would suggest could be found in a discussion of the concepts of the political, of political community and of feminist solidarity and alliance politics. I would like to suggest the notion of 'political solidarity' as a theoretical tool in this last discussion.

Black, migrant and refugee women

We can start by taking an example of a category of women that is politically active in a feminist fashion, although rarely recognised as such by other feminist actors or for that matter by feminist academics. The question becomes why?

Reading Julia Sudbury's *'Other Kinds of Dreams' – black women's organisations and the politics of transformation* (1998) raises many important questions about the construction of racialised groups and the usefulness of political organising around racialised gendered identities. Her category of 'black women' is recognised as an outspokenly problematic category, which attempts to capture women of African (sometimes specified as African-Caribbean), Asian and Middle-Eastern heritage living in a British context. This is a heterogeneous category, which Sudbury intentionally attempts to keep open. The (feminist) political activism of these women has not often been documented. One could even claim that 'black women' (in whatever ways they are constructed in different contexts) and equally problematic categories as 'migrant women' or 'refugee women' in for example different Nordic or European contexts are quite invisible as political actors as a whole.

This invisibility is (amongst others) an academic miss, which according to Sudbury partly finds its explanation in the often very limited definition of political activism, which is used by many researchers. If one limits one's focus to only investigate political activism in the realm of party-political and parliamentary constructions of politics, then one misses the creative strategies, which these groups of women show.

'Black', migrant and refugee women in the United Kingdom as well as in the rest of Europe are active in numerous migrant organisations, anti-racist and anti-fundamentalist organisations, as well as within the more traditional feminist movements. They work together with 'black' and/or 'white' men and with 'white' women, in both interest organisations and sometimes in political parties. They work mainly with issues related to legal status, citizenship rights and human rights. They also concentrate on issues of both racism and sexism. They do this at the same time *not primarily* within the realm of political parties, but rather within that of interest organisations.[2] This is partly due to the general hindrances to women's political activities on both a national level of politics, as well as for example on the international level of the European Union or the United Nations, but these constraints have certain specific characteristics.

There are two political arenas with different structural constraints that can be identified when discussing the political activities of 'black', migrant and refugee women in Europe. These are, roughly speaking:

1) Constraints in terms of political activity as expressed through party politics, in both a national as well as a European context. That is, within political society;
2) Constraints in terms of political activity as expressed through interest organisations, in both a national as well as a European context. That is, within civil society.

In the first political arena there are hardly any 'black', migrant or refugee women at all. This stands in sharp contrast to the hindrances and possibilities which these groups meet within the realm of the second arena.[3]

The constraints on the party political activity of these groups of women can be said to stem from matters of citizenship and weak legal status. This insecure legal status is seen as one of the main barriers confronting 'ethnic minority' women. At least that is the conclusion drawn by Jyostna Patel, who, on behalf of the European Women's Lobby, investigated which strategies were used to empower Black, ethnic minority and migrant women in a number of organisations in six of the member states of the

European Union. The focus on the insecure legal status was a recurring theme, which these organisations strikingly often worked with.[4]

Without a citizenship that includes political rights, one can maybe become a member of a party, but the possibilities to become an active representative in a political institution will be limited. 'Black' women with full citizenship rights can at the same time face problems of racism. The constraints on the political activities of refugee and migrant women in that sense overlap with those of 'black' women with full citizenship rights. In spite of this type of reasoning, it is still always doubtful to put these different heterogeneous categories under one heading. What definitions of not only political activism, but also of politics one uses, is in any event important to investigate in a discussion of this open category of active, but more or less invisible political actors and their possibilities of politically representing themselves.

Within (feminist) political philosophy this invisibility has in my eyes, amongst other things been dependent on some generalised assumptions, which we will discuss in the remainder of this chapter. These include assumptions on (1) what we mean by politics (mainly as a phenomenon), (2) on the gender neutral political rights bearing individual (the assumption being that voting and representing rights are present for all political actors), and (3) on the boundaries and character of political communities (in which the political community of a social movement also amongst feminist thinkers often has a nation-state as its territorial boundaries).

The solution to some of the problems that might arise due to *unwanted* exclusionary mechanisms as they are described above, I would suggest could be found in a discussion of feminist solidarity and alliance politics. I would like to suggest the notion of 'political solidarity' as a theoretical tool in this discussion. But let us first develop our argument on citizenship, rights and universality some more, since these are intrinsic to the problem.

Citizenship, rights and universality

When women in general have rights which differ from each other, co-operation between women is influenced. In a situation in which 'white' women have rights which 'black' women lack, 'white' women have a privilege of speech and representation. 'White' women then have a stronger voice in the formulation of common demands. This has some problematic aspects related to it. The differences in rights also puts a pressure on the way the different actors use channels and means of communication with other actors in the feminist movements. Somewhere along the line we can imagine deliberative processes with actors involved who lack official political rights. This can for example be in the context of ideas about the role of civil society, and thereby of feminist movements, in deliberative processes. But even then, citizens with full rights do the final decision making and the implementation of the decision.

These differences in formal and substantial *rights* therefore give us reason to question presumptions about the *universality of citizenship* in a more general context. Taken to its extreme we can ask: is universality possible or even desirable to achieve? Also,

Bell Hooks

it can make us question the subject positions of actors in a deliberative democracy. Let us discuss this for a moment, since it is related to the presumptions feminist political theorists have in their thinking.

A presumption exists in democratic theory about deliberative processes that actors who engage in dialogue and deliberation have all existing rights in place – if not in a substantial manner, then at least formally. Many of the discussions about deliberation (understood as different types of dialogues and negotiations between political actors) concern this difference between actors having formal rights but not being in a position to give substance to these rights. This argument derives from both a general political theoretical[5] as well as a feminist theoretical discourse. Feminist theorists like Iris Marion Young, Nancy Fraser and Anne Phillips have initiated and partaken in these discussions. The problems they have highlighted concern issues of presence for groups like women, gays and lesbians or Black people who are in the possession of political rights, but who are in spite of many observed improvements still rarely found amongst the ranks of professional politicians, parliamentarians, ministers or presidents. Their discussions also concern the *effects* of being present in terms of the content of politics, the possibilities of influencing policy processes when being in a minority position and, related to all of this, the meaning of concepts like 'oppression' (Young), 'recognition' (Fraser) or 'difference' (Young; Phillips; Fraser). Social movements are in these discussions seen as political communities, which represent the particular interests of Blacks, women, gays and lesbians, etcetera.

In these often very thought provoking and influential theories, a presumption of existing rights being in place is still found: a presumption of territoriality and of a formal status as a citizen in a specific state. For migrant women, these rights are not always in place. Only in some European countries do migrants have voting rights. This is often in the form of local voting rights. In even fewer countries this will also extend itself to the regional level. Furthermore, for anyone currently residing within the European Union, we can put question marks behind the *detailed* content of the presumptions of territoriality and of all rights being in place.

This limitation to the discussion is very common, and to a certain extent theorists such as Young also admit that the lack of an international focus is a problem. In spite of emerging literatures on cosmopolitanism, globalisation and transnationalism, few of these works have followed this up in full. Recent attempts by Held and others[6] are exceptions to the rule.

There is always a risk that issues of membership end up in the background, while the main focus is on states and the blurring of territorial boundaries. Two aspects can be highlighted. First, in *cosmopolis* membership would have no meaning. Everybody would be a member. Therefore nobody could identify herself or himself as a member. Again, the construction of membership needs its binary opposite of non-membership to produce meaning. Second, there would also be a danger of a world government with, because there is no escape other than guerrilla warfare and/or asylum out in space, authoritarian powers. Therefore suggestions of a *transnational* type of citizenship have been made.[7]

There is a danger of a somewhat naïve euphoria over global citizenship. In this version the possibility of not everybody being a member, or a full citizen, is not an option. A certain hegemonic 'we' have already decided that 'we' are all members. Unwanted exclusionary mechanisms or unwanted inclusions are not visible in this discourse. We can instead wonder how the word 'global citizen' comes into meaning. What are its boundaries?

Ideas about differences between citizens and how these should be dealt with often have an idea of universalism behind their solution. For example, in the traditional deontological view is the ability to articulate universal and impartial rules of importance. It is claimed that these are necessary to create unity out of diversity, or, put differently, to solve the problem of conflict among different, even mutually exclusive wills. To judge impartially, from a position outside and above the conflict itself, is in this context seen as important.

In a discourse in which existence is ordered through general rules, actors and actions are defined by these rules. This is also the case when actors are only defined partially, such as when migrants have a limited number of rights and lack certain political and/or other rights. A position of impartiality has received criticism for being disembedded and disembodied in a problematic way, not taking into account the specificities and particularities of actors and actions. This results in a tendency for *differences in power* and, following our discussion, in *rights*, to *disappear* into the background.

In the reasoning around the individual citizen's relation to the state, many exclusions are taken for granted. Those of women and of Black people in European politics can be seen as examples of this. The institutions of the European Union and their ways of excluding different groups tell us something about the boundaries of the universalistic standards to which they have professed to adhere. At the same time as the institution of the European Union has opened internal borders for the free movement of people, a substantial process of strengthening of its external borders by means of the Schengen Agreements has taken place. However, all of this has still been done in the name of universal standards. The boundaries of the idea of the European Union are here brought into play by a strange economy of inclusions and exclusions. Universalism is at the same time never achieved.

If the concept of citizenship is taken to have an aim of equality and universality, then this can, in a European context, still only mean that this (European and/or national) notion of citizenship can only be created in relation to the others of the citizens of the European Union. In relation to *what* is outside of Europe (the relation between the EU and the rest of the world) and to *who* is outside of Europe, as well as in relation to its others *inside* of Europe. The European Union is, by means of the Schengen *acquis,* well on its way of developing these ideas of citizenship in a rather undesirable way.

The universalist democratic project of the European Union can be questioned for its universalism and version of democracy. It should at the same time in my eyes still be possible to reason around citizenship, not without any exclusions at all (this does not seem conceivable), but without *unwanted* exclusionary mechanisms. A substitution of a new order of inclusion and exclusion might not in itself be a bad idea, and might be a big step towards correcting particular wrongs. After all, we need to answer the question of how citizenship in territorially bounded polities can remain equal and inclusive in globalising societies.

That is, in light of our discussion of the concepts of citizenship and universalism, it can be suggested that an aim of freedom and equality for the citizens of Europe should also include an element of *power* in its analysis. The stereotypical representations of 'black' and migrant women and men and of notions of nationality and 'Europeanness', which are part of the discussions about citizenship and migration in Europe, are reinforcing the already existing inequality of, amongst others, 'black' women in Europe.

In the context of this chapter, the question becomes how notions of citizenship are created, notions which enable feminist researchers focused on the political activities of feminist actors to pay respect to both the people residing on European territory, and to those outside of it. This cannot be done without a notion of universal human rights or without a view of Europe as being part of the world and of an international system of states.

Human rights are important tools of rights for both male and female refugees and migrants. The ways human rights and national rights intersect with each other, or not, can be said to be of increasing importance to feminist thinking about the ways unwanted exclusionary mechanisms can be addressed.[8]

Universality can never be fully obtained. At the same time we cannot do without it. This does not diminish the importance of universalist projects like democracy or human rights. These projects are flawed with problematic aspects, but are still important in themselves. Both citizenship rights and human rights are for example important for the social and political position of 'black', migrant and refugee women in European societies. They are part of the content of their political struggles, they are important for their possibilities to be present on different political arenas and they are crucial for our thinking on the feminist struggle in Europe in general.

The political and the political community

As mentioned earlier our thinking on feminist movements relates to discussions in democratic theory about deliberation and the difference between having formal rights and not being in a position to give substance to these rights. Social movements are in these discussions seen as political communities, representing the *particular* interests of certain groups like women. These categories of citizens should be listened to specifically or given special attention to, due to their lack of substantial rights. Let us now concentrate on the construction of these political communities. How do we imagine this to happen? And what is the relation between political communities and the political as a phenomenon?

If universality never can be fully obtained in a democratic project or within the project of human rights, what then is the *alternative* to an all-encompassing universality in which exclusionary mechanisms are denied, dismissed or ignored?

The *opposite* position could be described as an extreme acknowledgement of different identities, in neatly ordered tiny small categories. That is, we turn to the problems of particularism. In this position, the gap between formal equality and its actualisation or implementation is fully acknowledged. It is even addressed by means of a network of measures, identifying the specific problems of each group and subgroup, and proposing a set of measures, like affirmative action, that can rectify the wrong. *What* is marked as particular in this process and *why* are questions of importance to us in this context.

The creation of categories and subcategories can, by some, be seen as creating no problem whatsoever. In a democratic political process, categories are always re-negotiated, it could be argued. This process at the same time becomes a problem, when certain categories are more or less institutionalised as permanent others. When groups are never in the centre and always in the margins, then this is an issue. Universalism can never be totally obtained. This cannot be done in the context of a political community of a social movement, or in that of a state. The question then, as indicated above, becomes what strategy to use? How to keep a category open? How to be able to address universal 'wrongs'? How to relate categories to political agency and identity? How to re-negotiate the (stereotypical) representations which function to naturalise and exclude certain groups?

We could take as our starting point that a detailed catalogisation is in place. What then still could be lacking is the possibility of a 'metaphorical' elevation of the specific 'wrong' into a stand-in for the universal 'wrong'. An individual could argue that 'I am *not* merely that specific individual exposed to a set of specific injustices. I am more

Michelangelo Sibyl.

than that', in a longing to be part of a universal discourse. What we are looking for then, is a clear gesture of *politicisation* proper.[9]

Or differently put, the problem is that the political has become invisible. Conflicts and power relations disappear and politics is reduced to a rational process of negotiation among private interests under the constraints of morality. An example of this could be found in John Rawls' idea of political liberalism[10], in which an overlapping consensus brings us the political stability about the fundamentals of political order.

Rather it could be argued that reasoning around the notion of consensus in this context is not the answer. Preaching a global tolerance of differences and an all-encompassing unity might cover up what universalism should be or could be about. Let us for a moment not take struggle against sexism or racism as our starting point, but instead class struggle. Zizek argues in relation to class struggle that subjectivity and universalism are two sides of the same coin: it is precisely because 'class struggle' encourages individuals to adopt the subjective stance of a 'proletarian', that its appeal is universal. The division it mobilises is not between two well-defined social groups (Us and Them) but the division that runs between those who recognise themselves in the call of the Truth-Event and those who deny or ignore it. The existence of the true Universal is that of an endless and incessantly divisive struggle.[11]

Instead of 'proletarians' we could instead take the example of 'women' as 'feminists'. The women's struggle encourages (often, but not exclusively) 'women' to adopt the subjective stance of a 'feminist'. By doing this, the *appeal* of feminism becomes universal. Those who recognise themselves in the call of the analysis of feminism and those who deny or ignore it can be viewed as belonging to two different groups. But the question: 'who belongs to what group?' is part of a constant struggle.

This line of reasoning implies that in order for the *political*, as phenomenon, to become *visible*, a moment of antagonism and struggle needs to be present. The political could, following Carl Schmitt, in that sense be described as in need of this antagonism and this struggle in order to exist. Schmitt describes this in terms of a friend and enemy relationship.[12]

A radical democratic politics, as suggested by Chantal Mouffe and others, emphasises the friend/enemy distinction of the political. It takes place within a multiplicity of political spaces always linked to specific 'subject positions'. These can never be conflated with social agents. That is, in order to struggle against sexism or racism, one has to destroy racist or sexist subject positions and the institutions in which these are embodied, not concrete human beings. Social agents are constituted by a multiplicity of subject positions. The articulation of these is always precarious and temporary. A decentred view of the subject such as this can enable us to theorise the multiplicity of relations of subordination in which a single individual can be inscribed. It can also enable us to understand that one can be dominant in some groups while subordinated in others.[13]

If the question: 'who belongs to what group?' is part of a constant struggle for the feminist movement, then this could be followed by questions like: 'who is a friend?', 'what is a friend?' and 'can enemies become friends?' Several political philosophers have discussed the question of friendship throughout history, like Aristotle and Montaigne. Recently Jacques Derrida (1997) investigated what he called 'the politics of friendship'. As his startingpoint he used a remark attributed to Aristotle by Montaigne: *'o my friends, there is no friend'*. Although in the context of 'global sisterhood' and the perceived importance of the coherence of the notion of 'women' for the feminist struggle, maybe it is better to start from the remark: *'o my sisters, there is no sister'*. This brings us to our earlier mentioned discussion of feminist solidarity and alliance politics.

Political solidarity

Say that we analytically want to capture all the actors involved in the heterogeneity of the political community of a specific feminist movement. We then need to consider *the political process* that *precedes* the creation of this movement in order to see who is a friend or an enemy. To act in a manner which can be recognised to be as a friend and out of solidarity is complicated. I would like to suggest the use of the notion of *political solidarity* in this context. When doing that, we can focus on both the notions of the *political* as well as on that of *solidarity*. Let us start with the discussion of the notion of solidarity. We could see this term in relation to primarily different actors within the feminist movements.

Solidarity requires hard work. It is not a given or can be presumed to exist without a problem. Neither is it something that can be demanded. We can preferably distinguish *demanding* solidarity from making an *appeal* to solidarity, which is something totally different. The notion of an appeal gives the impression that we can be obliged to act out of solidarity. This is not the case, since the demand itself reveals the lack of solidarity. Solidarity is therefore always something that we can only make appeals to.[14]

Solidarity should not be taken too lightly or be viewed in a 'naïve' way. It is not safe, it cannot be assumed and it requires hard work. This is why it is important to emphasise the political aspect behind the notion of political solidarity. The political should here be related to a process of dialogue and deliberation, as well as to antagonism. Since we can only make *appeals* to solidarity, is it hard work and the element of dialogue between different actors is of the utmost importance in this process.

The problem with naïveté in the context of a discussion of solidarity is that there seem to be situations in which co-operation cannot be achieved without some form of compromise. Compromises that are made without one of the parts (typically the more powerful one) being aware of it happening, or solely on one of the parts' terms, are undesirable. They will lead to the unwillingness of the other part to co-operate. This is something that in my eyes is expressed by 'black' women in relation to 'white' women.[15] It could also be expressed by for example unionist and nationalist women in the context of Northern Ireland[16] or by other groups with an unequal power relationship. The notion of political solidarity can be used in order to capture the process of political co-operation between different groups of women as well as men in a feminist project. It enables us to focus on and address power dimensions that can be at work in this process. The naïveté in the context of certain discussions of solidarity has led Ien Ang to suggest a politics of partiality. She states that:

> A politics of partiality implies that feminism must emphasize and consciously construct the limits of its own field of political intervention. While a politics of inclusion is driven by an ambition for universal representation (of all women's interests), a politics of partiality does away with that ambition and accepts the principle that feminism can never ever be an encompassing political home for all women, not just because different groups of women have different and sometimes conflicting interests, but, more radically, because for many groups of 'other' women, other interests, other identifications are sometimes more important and politically pressing than, or even incompatible with, those related to their being women.[17]

I am very sympathetic to the thoughts behind the idea of a politics of partiality as suggested by Ien Ang, especially concerning her insistence on a changed starting point for discussion. Instead of the assumption that ultimately a common ground for women to form a community can be found, based on the a priori successful communication between women, Ien Ang suggests an alternative. She prefers a starting point in the realisation that there are moments at which no common ground exists whatsoever. There are moments when any communicative event would be nothing more than a speaking past one another. It is therefore better to start with a focus on the very limits of the idea of sisterhood (and thus the category 'women') and on the necessary *partiality* of the project of feminism as such. This includes a very concrete focus on how the gulf between mainstream feminism and 'other' women is constructed and reproduced.[18]

Acknowledging incommensurability does not have to result in political paralysis. It can be the starting point for common political pursuits. When the feminist movements strive to develop a politics based on group identity, it is preferable to avoid the dangers of fragmentation, which can leave some fragments isolated and ignored. At the same time the tendency towards the subordination of minority group interests within the articulation of those of larger groups should be avoided. In order to accomplish this, argues Lister, a politics must be rooted in a broader commitment to solidarity. This should be a form of solidarity that recognises a commonality of interests with the potential to unite the fragments. Lister calls this a 'politics of solidarity in difference'.[19] Nira Yuval-Davis uses the notion of 'transversal politics' in a slightly similar vein.[20]

Whereas Lister's notion is oriented towards the politics which come out of a process of deliberation, my notion of *political solidarity*, which is perhaps a shorter and therefore less clumsy terminology, has a slightly different focus and starting point. As opposed to Lister, I have divided the discussions of the constitution of a community from that of the content of a politics. The community should in this sense be seen as the feminist movement and the politics that of a feminist politics.

I do agree with Lister that the identities individuals choose to identify with politically cannot be taken as given or static. Political identities emerge and are expressed through an ongoing social process of individual and collective 'identity formation'. Asking the individual to identify with only one aspect of a many faceted identity runs the same risk of fragmentation at the individual as at the group level. Lister also points out that a citizen has a plurality of sites of citizenship participation. This makes a commitment to dialogue of importance.[21] If we accept that politics does not have to be premised on the construction of a solid, unified 'we', and we focus on the unstable part of the word 'we', a different picture emerges from the political paralysis described above. In most conventional conceptions of politics, including identity politics, we accept that politics is premised on a construction of a unified 'we'. In an anti-essentialist mode, this could be questioned.

Instead we can take as a starting point the notion of the political. Feminists can make an appeal to solidarity as an expression of the political as a phenomenon, characterised by a starting point of incommensurability and antagonism. They then identify who their friends are and who their enemies are. As a consequence an unstable community arises: the community of feminists. The question 'who is a friend and part of the community?' thereby constitutes a problem, a *political* problem.

Regarding the notion of the political, this can be compared to the work of Carl Schmitt. He has pointed out that the concept of the state, as a political community, presupposes the concept of the political. That is, states arise as a means of continuing, organising and channelling political struggle. Political struggle gives rise to political order, not the other way around.[22]

The same could be said in terms of the feminist movements and the phenomenon of feminist struggle. The concept of a social movement like the feminist movement, which is also a political community, presupposes the concept of the political, as can be recognised in the political struggle of feminism. That is, feminist struggle gives rise to a community of feminists, not the other way around. After all, as Chantal Mouffe has pointed out, why restrict the political to a certain type of institution or envisage it as constituting a specific sphere or level of society?[23]

The advantage with this view of the political is that the political representation and agencies of Black, migrant and refugee women become visible. Matters of power relations between women can be addressed in a different way, when the discussion does not start from the presupposition of the feminist movement as a stable community, but instead starts from the political antagonisms, which create unstable and temporary communities.

Still, through my insistence on the terminology 'political solidarity', I seek to stress the combination of the words *political*, as in 'fought over', and *solidarity*, as in a 'commitment to shared goals and interests'. The 'we' of the feminist movements is a 'we' that constantly is and has to be re-invented and re-negotiated in order to act within a political discourse. This is also important for feminist researchers to remember. Our analysis should help to address racist and sexist expressions directed at all women and men. The question 'how?' is as important as the questions 'by whom?' and 'with whom?'

Conclusion

There is a paradox in the way feminists, who work for the inclusion of women, themselves create and sustain exclusionary mechanisms that exclude parts of the selfsame categories they claim to promote. The theory of waves, discussed elsewhere in this volume, seems often to focus on the mainstream of social movements. Drude Dahlerup for example, focuses explicitly on 'the common core of feminism' in her discussion of waves in the context of New Social Movement theories. She argues that if we cannot identify a common core, it follows that we cannot talk about one continuous feminist movement or about feminism as an 'ism', a political ideology. As mentioned in this chapter, the social construction of women as a group or a category which is part of the *raison d'etre* of feminist movements, can at the same time be seen as problematic.

This is in this volume agreed upon by both Drude Dahlerup and Elisabeth Lønnå, who on the other hand is much more critical of the use of the image of the wave as a basis for a theory or a model. Both of them acknowledge but do not emphasize or discuss the invisibility of the activities of those who do not belong to this mainstream, a position which can be said to be characteristic for much of the Nordic mainstream women's movement research.[24]

The differences between women, notably in terms of the intersections of gender and 'race', have been the focus of many feminist debates during the 1980s and 1990s. If certain groups, like those of 'black' women, are systematically excluded from political debate, and their political representation remains 'invisible', unnoticed or implicit in both ethics and politics, then this *can* be a problem. Not all groups need to be represented, or desire this inclusion. When on the other hand we, feminist researchers, can identify political activities (actions, organisations and debates) which point toward an *unwanted* exclusion, we must pay attention. Regardless of whether this concerns the exclusion of 'black' women from the political communities of a sovereign state or of a social movement like the feminist movement, or whether this concerns their exclusion from the ethical notion of the self.

We can make an analytical distinction between civil society and political society. Politics happens at both arenas. Actors within feminist movements work at both arenas. Black, migrant and refugee women as political actors within feminist movements can mainly be found in civil society. This has to do with developments of globalisation, the blurring of the national and international levels of politics and the related tension around notions of citizenship and human rights.

The consequence of this is that Black, migrant and refugee women have fewer channels to public debate and to established social networks than white, indigenous women, in a way that strains their political activities. Also, this questions our ways of visualising feminist movements. The possibility of capturing the activities of different actors within feminist movements is easier when the categorisation of the political community of a feminist movement is kept open. To, as Mouffe suggests, picture the phenomenon of the political to precede political community helps us keep this category open. Mouffe's suggestion helps us visualise the activities of constantly new actors in constantly re-negotiated and re-invented feminist movements. That is, if we are willing to not only say we keep this category open, but also focus our attention on power inequalities in feminist movements. The notion of political solidarity, as I suggested, can help us imagine the political process, which precedes the formation of the social movement.

This suggestion to define the political and political communities in this way on the other hand only helps us imagine social movements. States are another type of political community, as used in a definition of political communities within an international relations discourse. Although neither are stable in character, states are much less fluid and unstable in character, as compared to social movements. States as political communities in an increasingly globalising world therefore need a separate discussion. Considering the earlier discussion on the blurring of the national and international levels of politics and the related tension around notions of citizenship and human rights, it would be a good idea if feminist academics took part in this.

References:

Ang, Ien. (1995). "I'm a feminist but…"Other" women and postnational feminism." Barbara Caine and Rosemary Pringle (eds.) *Transitions. New Australian Feminisms*. St Leonards: Allen & Unwin.

Bauböck, Rainer (1994). *Transnational Citizenship. Membership and Rights in International Migration*. Aldershot. Edward Elgar.

Bell Hooks (1981). *Ain't I a Woman. Black women and feminism*. Boston: South End Press.

Davis, Angela Y (1981 – 1983 new edition). *Women, Race and Class*. New York: Vintage.

De los Reyes, Paulina, Irene Molina and Diana Mulinari (eds.) (2002). *Maktens (o)lika förklädnader – kön, klass och etnicitet i det postkoloniala Sverige*. Stockholm: Atlas.

Dean, Jodi (1996). *Solidarity of Strangers – Feminism after Identity Politics*. Berkeley: University of California Press.

Derrida, Jacques (1997). *Politics of Friendship*. London: Verso.

Fraser, Nancy (1997). *Justice Interruptus – Critical Reflections on the "Postsocialist" Condition*. London. Routledge.

Fraser, Nancy (1989). *Unruly Practices. Power, Discourse and Gender in Contemporary Social Theory*, Cambridge. Polity Press.

Held, David (1995). *Democracy and the Global Order – From the Modern State to Cosmopolitan Governance*. Cambridge. Polity Press.

Hirst, Paul (1999). Carl Schmitt's Decisionism. In Chantal Mouffe (ed.), *The Challenge of Carl Schmitt*. London. Verso.

Hoskyns, Catherine (1996). *Integrating Gender – Women, Law and Politics in the European Union*. London. Verso.

Hull, Gloria T. et al. (1981). *All the Women Are White, All the Blacks Are Men, But Some of Us Are Brave: Black Women's Studies*. Old Westbury, N.Y.. The Feminist Press.

Linklater, Andrew (1998). *The Transformation of Political Community – Ethical Foundations of the Post-Westphalian Era*. Cambridge. Polity Press.

Lister, Ruth (1997). *Citizenship. Feminist Perspectives*. London. Macmillan.

Moraga, Cherríe and Anzuldúa, Gloria eds. (1981 – 1983 second edition). *This Bridge called my Back – Writings by Radical Women of Color*. New York. Kitchen Table.

Mouffe, Chantal (1992). Democratic Citizenship and the Political Community. In Chantal Mouffe (ed.), *Dimensions of Radical Democracy – Pluralism, Citizenship, Community*. London. Verso.

Mouffe, Chantal (1993). *The Return of the Political*. London. Verso.

Mouffe, Chantal (1996). Radical Democracy or Liberal Democracy? In David Trend, ed. *Radical Democracy: Identity, Citizenship, and the State*. London. Routledge.

Mouffe, Chantal (1999). *The Challenge of Carl Schmitt*. London. Verso.

Nussbaum, Martha C. with respondents, ed. Joshua Cohen (1996). *For Love of Country – Debating the Limits of Patriotism*. Boston. Beacon Press.

Patel, Jyostna (2000). *Overcoming Discrimination – selected strategies empowering black, ethnic minority and migrant women*. Brussels. European Women's Lobby.

Peters, J. and A. Wolper (eds.) (1995). *Women's Rights, Human Rights: International Feminist Perspectives*, London. Routledge.

Peterson, V. Spike and Laura Parisi (1998). Are women human? It's not an academic question. In Tony Evans (ed.) *Human Rights Fifty Years On – A Reappraisal*. Manchester: Manchester UP.

Phillips, Anne (1995). *The Politics of Presence*. Oxford. Clarendon Press.

Rawls, John (1993). *Political Liberalism*. New York, Colombia UP.

Rawls, John (1971). *A Theory of Justice*. Oxford. Oxford University Press.

Rooney, Eilish (1995). Political Division, Practical Alliance: Problems for Women in Conflict, *Journal of Women's History*, winter/Schmitt spring, Carl (1987) *Der Begriff des Politischen*. Text von 1932 mit einem Vorwort und Drei Corollarien. Berlin. Duncker & Humbolt.

Stoltz, Pauline (2000). *About Being (T)Here and Making a Difference – Black Women and the Paradox of Visibility*. Lund Political Studies 115. Lund. Dept. of Political Science.

Sudbury, Julia (1998). *'Other Kinds of Dreams' – black women's organisations and the politics of transformation*. London. Routledge.

Trend, David ed. (1996). *Radical Democracy: Identity, Citizenship, and the State*. London. Routledge.

Walzer, Michael (1983). *Spheres of Justice: A Defense of Pluralism and Equality*. New York. Basic Books.

Young, Iris Marion (2000). *Inclusion and Democracy*. Oxford. Oxford UP.

Young, Iris Marion (1990). *Justice and the Politics of Difference*. New Jersey: Princeton UP.

Yuval-Davis, Nira (1997). *Gender and Nation*. London. Sage.

Zizek, Slavoj (1999). Carl Schmitt in the Age of Post-Politics. In Chantal Mouffe ed. *The Challenge of Carl Schmitt*. London. Verso.

Notes

1   Bell Hooks (1981); Moraga and Anzaldúa (1981); Davis (1981); Hull et al. (1981)
2   Sudbury (1998); Stoltz (2000), chapters 3 and 6
3   See Stoltz (2000); Patel (2000); Sudbury (1998); Hoskyns (1996)
4   Patel (2000), p. 17-18
5   Rawls (1971); Walzer (1983)
6   Nussbaum (1996); Lister (1997); Linklater (1998); Young (2000)
7   see also Bauböck (1994)
8   For examples of feminist human rights studies, see Peters and Wolper (1995); Peterson and Parasi (1998).
9   Zizek (1999), p. 34-35
10 Rawls (1993)
11 Zizek (1999), p. 35-36; see also Mouffe (1993), esp. chapter 3 and Mouffe (1996)
12 Schmitt (1987)
13 Mouffe (1996); see also Trend ed. (1996) and Mouffe ed. (1992)
14 Dean (1996), p. 21
15 see for example Bell Hooks (1981)
16 see for example Rooney (1995)
17 Ang (1995), p. 73
18 Ang (1995), p. 60-61
19 Lister (1997), p. 80
20 Yuval-Davis (1997)
21 Lister (1997), p. 80-81
22 Schmitt (1987); see also Hirst 1999
23 Mouffe (1993), p. 3
24 For an alternative position see for example several of the contributions in de los Reyes (2002)

CHAPTER 18

Women's Movements
and the Contradictory Forces
of Globalisation

Sigríður Dúna Kristmundsdóttir

Introduction

The 20th century has been described as the "age of extremes", harbouring as it did both unprecedented progress and extraordinary acts of cruelty.[1] It can also be characterized as "the age of women's movements", as never before in recorded history have women's movements been as prolific or exerted comparable influence on society and culture. During the 20th century women gained rights they did not previously possess and their lives became in many instances quite different from what could be expected when the century dawned.

Yet, at the turn of the 21st century researchers have portrayed women's movements as having become more diffused and less focused than during their recent heyday in the 1970s and 1980s.[2] Emphasis on what differentiates women like race, sexuality, class or politics is seen to have contributed to this decline of movement coherence or unification. Such a lack of coherence is certainly true for Iceland. Since the decline of *Kvennalistinn (The Women's Lists Movement)* in the 1990s there is no one dominant women's movement in the country.[3] Instead there are many small groups each with their own agenda. Diversity and multivocalism rather than sameness and speaking in one voice is the observable pattern. This process of fragmentation is contextualised by globalisation that penetrates all areas of social life including that of feminist activities. It is also in important respects parallel to certain of the effects of globalisation. It therefore seems pertinent to view feminist activities in the context of globalisation in order to understand what is happening to women's movements at the beginning of the 21st century.

Another reason why globalisation necessarily contextualises our studies of present day feminism is that this pervasive phenomenon can bring about an emphasis on local cultural traits, which in turn can have negative effects on the social position of women. Of special note in this respect is the enhanced emphasis on difference, which I argue is one of the effects of globalisation. Cultural contradictions are considered, both the ones we find in cultures generally and the contradictions we find as a result of globalisation. That in turn leads to the sketching of a pattern in which the levelling forces of globalisation are seen to create a need to re-differentiate women and men. In order to substantiate such a pattern as well as generally understand current feminist activities I argue that we have both to employ intensive studies of particular women's movements or feminist groups and cross-cultural comparison. To illustrate my argument I discuss the recent history of women's movements in Iceland and, finally, draw some conclusions.

The effect of globalisation on the social position of women

Globalisation is of course both a real and an abstract phenomenon. It is real in the sense that it has effectively changed our world. The way we perceive these changes belongs on the other hand to the realm of the abstract and that is how I address the issue. One aspect of how people perceive of globalisation is that of a pervasive diminishing of the multiplicity and diversification of human society and culture. To many the known world seems to be becoming smaller every day and the individual appears both insignificant and powerless in the face of global processes.[4] The reality of this is perceived in people's daily lives in various ways. To take a few examples, in Europe organizations such as the European Union enact rules and regulations that determine details like the acceptable ingredients in manufactured food products or where people can buy a bottle of wine. The same brand names, be it for cars or ice cream, can be found wherever people go. Technology in mass communication and international business interests allow the transmission of the same news, movies and advertisements worldwide so that wherever people switch on the television they get the same information and entertainment. The world is not only perceived as having become smaller as a result, it also seems to be a less secure place. Once sharply defined boundaries between countries and nations have become blurry, and into the bargain the globalised transmission of information brings news of terrorism which respects no boundaries.

Anthropologists have found that people tend to react to this perception of sameness and lack of boundaries by emphasizing what it is that makes them different from the big global mass out there. Local traditions in food, clothes, festivals and so forth are revived and used to create boundaries. They are used to saying: This is us and we are different from you, we are not a faceless global mass, we are Estonians, Icelanders, Catalonians, Muslims, Christians or whatever people size upon as their defining characteristic.[5] Globalisation therefore involves the creation and incorporation of locality and of difference, which counteracts the levelling influence of globalisation. Hence the local becomes an integral part of the global as is neatly expressed by the concept of glocalisation, which refers to the simultaneous and interactive processes of homogenisation and heterogenisation taking place within globalisation.[6]

As I have argued elsewhere the importance of the local and different in globalisation can lead to renewed emphasis on women's traditional roles, especially their roles as mothers and housewives.[7] In these roles women are symbolically at the very center of their culture, they are the nurturers of children on which the continuation of culture and society depends, a holy centre just like the womb is the magical centre where children are formed and from where they emerge as human beings. Cultures communicate themselves in symbols and women as a gender group are therefore eminently situated symbolically to communicate what a culture has to say about itself. When this happens, women themselves, their role, behaviour, dress and so forth are being used as a kind of communication device to express how one social group differs from another. It is not a coincidence that in war, raping women is seen as a means to subjugate the enemy. Raping the enemy's women defiles what is central to the enemy's definition of themselves and is therefore a means towards winning a war. In this context it is also not surprising that women who willingly consorted with occupying soldiers during World War II were punished as traitors after the war.[8]

If women in their traditional roles can be perceived to be a symbolic means to express a culture, then it follows that globalisation can serve to increase emphasis on these very roles as a means to communicate cultural difference and defy the homogenising effect of globalisation. Re-emphasis on women's traditional roles and place in society can be widely observed in different societies, for instance in various Islamic societies of which the former Taliban regime is perhaps the most blatantly obvious example. It can be found in the East-European societies now in transition as well as in non-transitional societies such as Austria where the Freedom Party, which strongly advocates women's traditional roles, enjoyed popularity in national elections and became part of Austria's coalition government. Women often take extreme pride in their traditional roles. The symbolic baggage these roles carry means, however, that when it becomes necessary to emphasize the culture in question and, in an ever increasing global space of sameness, to create boundaries and differences, it also becomes imperative to control women and make them comply with their traditional roles and their inherent values. This inevitably restricts women's social freedom, mutes their voices in the public sphere and makes it more difficult for them to use the rights they have by law.

Contradictions

Touraine has argued that while globalisation is by no means a new phenomenon, the globalisation that we are now experiencing involves a rupture between the economic, social and political elements of society and their respective values. Therefore the integration of society, as we know it in the West, is threatened.[9] Our reaction to that, says Touraine, is that we size on ascribed status instead of achieved status to define ourselves as individuals. A person's gender can therefore become a more important defining characteristic than social status indicators such as professional specialization or earning power. In other words, what we can achieve or become in this ruptured society of disconnected values has become uncertain as an indicator of the individual and at times devoid of meaning. What continues to be meaningful is what we unquestionably are, women or men, young or old, Christians, Muslims or Jews, to name a few categories of identity. Hence it is women's ascribed status as women that is becoming more important in our globalised world, not what women can make of themselves by using the rights they have by law.

Touraine sees this rupture between societies' main elements and their respective values as the destruction of tradition. Tradition he takes to mean that the meanings of a culture all stick together, or that the elements of a culture are mutually meaningful. I disagree with him. First, we have plenty of examples in anthropology of the cultural contradictions people live with around the world. Why is it, for example, accepted in the Nordic countries that women should have the same right as men to a professional career, but at the same time it is also accepted that women should take care of their children and homes to a greater degree than the fathers of the children? This is a contradiction individual women wrestle with it in their daily lives trying to make things work, and feminism can in one respect be seen as a response to an inconsistency such as this. There is no culture, traditional or not, that is devoid of contradictions.

Secondly, there may be no such thing as tradition in the conventional sense. At some point tradition is invariably invented, it is made by human beings, not given by an omniscient god as a law of nature.[10] And it is made or invented to serve a purpose of some kind, symbolic or practical. Hence what is emphasized as an important tradition at any given time has meaning first and foremost at that time, not in some past historical time. In tradition the past is used to legitimate the present, as is the case with the re-emphasis on women's traditional roles I have outlined. If the social sciences see the revival of tradition, or the reinvention of the meaning of traditional elements, as a means to reintegrate the ruptured meanings of our globlised societies, they are simply reacting to globalisation in the same manner as those they study and have lost a necessary critical grasp of their subject matter.

Yet another kind of contradiction is that while globalisation can be seen to disempower women by leading to an emphasis on women's traditional roles, the spread of women's rights during the 20th century is also a result of globalisation. The global spread of western, liberal 19th century ideas about the rights of women was essential in securing for women the emancipatory legal rights that empower them in the public sphere of society. As the twentieth century progressed, the rights of women became a standard against which to measure the relative modernization and progress of individual societies (for much the same reasons as today, i.e. women's symbolic importance in the identification of groups such as nations) and they were widely adopted.[11] Examples of the globalisation of women's rights can also be seen in agreements issued by such transnational bodies as the United Nations and the European Union.

There are examples of local reaction to the globalising of women's rights which counter its homogenising effects by re-emphasizing difference in much the same way as has been observed for globalisation generally. One such example is the Latin-American *Marianismo*. When women in Latin-American societies were given the legal rights that made them by law equal to men, the difference between women and men that had until then been legitimised by the law was swept away and women and men became the same kind of citizens. Then emerged the phenomenon of *marianismo* which is the association of women with the figure of the Virgin, suggesting that because of their role as mothers, women are, like the Virgin, morally good and as such superior to men. By emphasizing women's importance as mothers and placing that role on a religious pedestal alongside the mother of God, women were effectively re-confined to the domestic sphere and sexual control over them was reinforced. *Marianismo* thus subverted the proclaimed intentions of women's legal emancipation by re-differentiating women and men as cultural beings and, in the process, limiting women's newfound legal emancipation.[12]

This process corresponds to what I have already described as the effect of globalisation and indicates an interesting pattern. It suggests that when the differences between women and men are in some sense levelled out there is a reaction which attempts to re-differentiate the gender groups. It is as if a world without two clearly defined genders is unthinkable, be it in terms of rights or more readily apparent things such as dress and behaviour. In a globalised world where sameness is perceived as pervasive and where emphasis on women's traditional roles is used to re-differentiate groups such a reaction is perhaps not surprising.[13] However in order to ascertain to what extent such a pattern is localised or culturally determined rather than general, we need more and detailed studies of specific societies.

If we accept that feminist activities today are to an extent contextualised by the larger phenomenon of globalisation, we have obviously to broaden our scope of investigation to include transnational comparisons. Such comparisons do not extend only to women's movements but also to the general social and cultural processes that form them. Because of this larger scope we have to be able to work with generalisations, which is not always comfortable. Anthropology has a methodological tradition of trans-cultural comparisons yet cautions that generalisations have to be based on intensive, detailed and localized studies of the phenomena compared. Only then can we claim that our generalisations, or the broad view we have to adopt, has a sound basis in an "on the ground" reality. Intensive studies of particular women's movements, or women's rights activities, are therefore essential to the broader scope we have to employ. To exemplify this connection between studies of local phenomena and the broader context of globalisation, I shall now briefly consider the case of Icelandic women's movements.[14]

Icelandic women's movements

In the 1890s and the first decades of the 20th century Icelandic women successfully fought for and won their basic emancipatory legal rights, such as the right to vote and the right to education. They were organized into movements, which co-operated with women's movements in the other Nordic countries and their representatives attended various international women's movement meetings. Although the Icelandic movements were to an extent shaped by local social and cultural elements such as Iceland's struggle to gain independence from Denmark and the relatively recent formation of urban areas in Iceland, they were very much part of the globalisation of women's rights occurring at the time.[15]

Once basic rights were obtained and women had successfully demonstrated that they knew how to use them, there followed a period of fragmentation. Feminists worked in various groups on issues of concern to women but were not united into a movement with defined goals. It is tempting to view this period as one of reaction to the levelling out of the status of men and women inherent in women's newly obtained rights. It is characterized by emphasis on women's role as mothers and housewives to the extent for example that although women had all the same rights to education as men only very few used them. Most women who could afford further education attended women's schools where they were prepared for their role as mothers and housewives. By the end of the 1950s, women were firmly entrenched in their gender defined role and it reflected unfavourably on husbands if their wives sought work or a career outside the home. In spite of comparable legal rights the gender groups were again clearly defined and differentiated.[16]

In the 1960s changing economic conditions in Iceland meant that women were increasingly needed on the labour market and many took a job, often part-time, outside their home. New contraceptive devices made this transition easier as it allowed women to control their pregnancies to a greater degree than before. Again rumbles were heard from abroad where women were forming women's movements and maintained that women did not only need rights, they also needed to be liberated from their traditional roles. In 1970, Rauðsokkahreyfingin, the Icelandic Redstocking or Women's Liberation Movement was founded, initiating a new phase or wave in feminist activities in Iceland. And as with the former phase or first wave of feminism around the turn of the century, this movement was both shaped by Icelandic social and cultural conditions and a part of a western phenomenon that spread quickly around the world. Again Icelandic women were part of a globalising process.

The Redstocking Movement had considerable impact during its first few years culminating in the women's strike in 1975, which made headlines around the world. The strike, which brought Icelandic society virtually to a standstill for a day, was held in connection with the United Nations International Women's Year and took place on Oct. 24, The United Nations Day. It was thus part of a global phenomenon, that of the United Nations emphasis on the rights and liberation of women. In spite of the success of the women's strike it seems to have created a vacuum in movement activities. The Redstocking Movement slowly petered out in internal, mostly leftist dissension, and by 1980 there was no single vigorous women's movement in Iceland. Again it is as if the contradictory forces of globalisation were at play. A successful globally connected action resulted in local fragmentation.

Yet the vacuous period was short. In 1980 Vigdís Finnbogadóttir was elected president of Iceland. In her campaign she emphasized the importance of the women's strike in 1975 for her candidature, and her election gave Icelandic feminists a new lease on life. Two years later *Kvennalistinn* (*The Women's Lists Movement*) came into existence.[17] Interestingly in its ideology Kvennalistinn emphasized women's gender specific culture and maintained that because women were culturally different from men they should be elected into public decision-making institutions such as the Althing and municipal councils. After the homogenising period of the Redstocking Movement, which argued that women could and should do all the same things as men, Kvennalistinn in effect re-differentiated women and men. Again we have the pattern of levelling out of gender differences followed by re-differentiation.

Kvennalistinn had considerable impact during its first decade or so, successfully putting forward women's lists in municipal and national elections. However, during the late 1990s it lost its votes and influence in Icelandic society and politics. There are at least two reasons for this decline. First, the political context in which Kvennalistinn operated changed. The number and prominence of women politicians had greatly increased which made Kvennalistinn seem redundant to voters who perceived of the list as being first and foremost concerned with having women elected. In a sense Kvennalistinn was the victim of its own purpose to increase the participation of women in politics. The re-differentiation of women and men it set out with did not work once women were successfully elected on behalf of the traditional male-dominated parties. Secondly, Kvennalistinn lost a basic feminist feature when it teamed up with other political parties in the 1994 Reykjavík municipal elections, diffusing its political focus. It became in a sense like the traditional parties levelling out the difference between them and itself. Both the change in the political context and Kvennalistinn's assimilation with traditional political parties diffused the differentiation of women and men in politics, which initially gave the movement its leading impetus.

The political system in Iceland has now absorbed this movement and at the dawn of the 21st century there is no single dominant women's movement in Iceland. That does not mean that feminist activities have disappeared in Iceland. What Dahlerup defines as the common core of feminism, an elementary continuous ideology made up of partial visions of the ideal, is very much there.[18] But organizationally feminism in Iceland has become diffused and fragmented. It is tempting to fit the present state of feminist activities in Iceland into the pattern I have indicated. Once Kvennalistinn was seen to contribute to the levelling out the difference between women and men it lost its force and a period of fragmentation followed.

From a feminist point of view it is debateable whether fragmentation need be all-bad. It allows small feminist groups easier access to the social discourse as they are not overshadowed by a dominant women's movement. A number of such groups have been formed and feminists have also become active within traditional patriarchal institutions like the university and the church influencing institutional policy. Specialized activities such as combating violence against women are well organized if not adequately funded. Businesswomen have united into a movement of their own and young women are on the move. In 2000 a novel written by three young women, exemplifying the resistant fashion formed by feminist ideas in which young women today engage with the choices of everyday life, became a bestseller.[19] International women's clubs have become popular in Iceland and international institutions concerned with women's issues such as The United Nations Development Fund for Women have gained a foothold in the country, emphasizing the international character of feminist issues. Yet, if there is need for concerted feminist action of some kind, there is no obvious venue, such as a strong women's movement, through which it can take place.

As this listing indicates, feminist activities in Iceland have become organizationally diffused and ideologically multivocal. Icelandic feminists have different views on basic ideas such as what sort of social persons women are or should be and contend that they need not agree on every issue. It remains to be seen whether traditional twentieth century women's movements are a thing of the past in our globalised world. That need not be and as this article is going to press it seems that a new movement might be emerging in Iceland.

On March 14th 2003 *Femínistafélag Islands* or *The Icelandic Society of Feminists* was founded by a number of women connected with the University of Iceland and other feminists both male and female. Gender studies and gender perspectives in teaching and research have proliferated at the University in recent years and the initiative for the new society came from the group of scholars concerned. In its first few months the society has provided a channel for concerted action on various issues and it remains to be seen if it will develop into a fully-fledged women's movement in the tradition of the 20th century or into something else in tune with a changed world. In any event it will be interesting to observe how and if the contradictory forces of globalisation will influence this new organization. Perhaps the fact that men are active within the society and the emphasis it places on issues of direct concern to men signals a period of levelling out of the differences between women and men after a period of fragmentation and differentiation described above.

Conclusion

The present is hard to decipher simply because we are still living it. To aid us in that task we have created concepts such as the ones of globalisation and glocalisation, which I have applied here in order to make sense of current feminist activities in Iceland and, by implication, elsewhere. By using these concepts I have identified a pattern, that of a globalised levelling out of cultural difference between men and women followed by local reaction that attempts to re-differentiate women and men culturally. I have indicated the symbolic importance of women in creating cultural difference and its effects on women's possibilities to use the rights they have by law. Furthermore I have maintained that although a general pattern can be discerned, as in the history of Icelandic women's movements, we need more detailed and intensive studies of particular movements or feminist activities to further substantiate such a pattern.

Another concept commonly used to decipher feminist activities is that of waves implying that women's movements occur in swells that rise and fall like the waves of the sea.[20] The movements themselves are seen as the crests of such waves, preceded and followed by more diffuse activities. Two waves have commonly been identified in the history of western feminism; the first wave, that of the women's rights movement arising in the second half of the 19th century and subsiding towards the middle of the 20th century, and the second wave, that of the women's liberation movement from the 1960s onwards.[21]

Women's movements in Iceland in the 20th century fit neatly into the concept of waves. The first wave arose in the 1870s with the establishment of schools for women and subsided once women had won the same civil rights by law as men in the first half of the 20th century. The second wave, that of women's liberation, stirred in the 1960s and crested with the Redstocking Movement and Kvennalistinn in the 1970's and 1980s. Interestingly these two waves of feminist activities in Iceland have an identical pattern; they begin by women's movements presenting a defined set of ideas and goals and are followed by women's lists that in both instances succeeded in having women elected into municipal councils and the Althing.

But where does the concept of waves leave us with regard to explaining current feminist activities in Iceland? Can the multivocalism I have described for Iceland be characterized as a new wave in feminist activities? Or is it simply a new phase in the second wave characterized by the absence of a coherent women's movement? Clearly feminist activities are taking place simultaneously on more than one political level of society, but does that constitute a new "wave"? The concept of waves creates questions like these but does not answer them simply because it is too soon to say. Hence it seems that the concept may primarily be useful *after the fact*, to decipher what has already happened rather than what is happening.

As I have argued the concepts of globalisation and glocalisation can aid us in deciphering what is at present happening to women and their movements. That does not exclude the concept of waves, far from it, but these concepts contextualise current activities within the larger framework of contemporary social and cultural processes that necessarily shape feminist activities and ideology. Apart from the fact that globalisation can radically change women's social environment calling for new perspectives and new solutions, certain parallels can, as I have indicated, be seen between the processes of globalisation and glocalisation and that of current feminist activities. The multivocalism I have identified for feminist activities in Iceland and of which others have written for other countries is clearly based on the idea of difference, the idea that women are different and can have different views on diverse issues although they can all be feminists.[22] Difference has thus become an acceptable internal element in feminist ideology as opposed to the idea of sameness or unification on which traditional women's movements to an important extent depend.

As I have argued difference is an important factor in globalisation. By seeming to level out differences, globalisation brings about increased emphasis on difference. Hence what has happened to feminist activities both parallels and is part of that of globalisation; perceived sameness, be it that of women and men or that of a globalised world, has created an emphasis on difference. Global social processes are thus reflected in local social processes such as feminist activities, which accordingly need to be viewed in the wider context. And as I have repeatedly argued, detailed and intensive studies of feminist activities will continue to be the backbone of our insights but we need to place the knowledge gathered from such studies within an international perspective where working with generalizations is unavoidable. There the ubiquitous and contradictory forces of globalisation are bound to play an increasingly important role.

References

Bauman, Zygmunt (1995). "Searching for a Centre that holds", in Featherstone, M., Lash, S., and Robertson, R. (1995). *Global Modernities*, London, Sage, p. 140-154.

Björnsdóttir, Birna Anna, Sturludóttir, Oddný and Hauksdóttir, Silja (2000). *Dís*. Reykjavík, Forlagið

Budgeon, Shelley (2001). "Emergent Feminist (?) Identities: Young Women and the Practice of Micropolitics", *The European Journal of Women's Studies*, vol. 8, issue 1, p. 7-28.

Coward, Rosalind (1999). "Do we need a New Feminism?", *Women: A Cultural Review,* vol. 10. no. 2, p. 192-205.

Dahlerup, Drude (2002). "Continuity and Waves in the Feminist Movement – a Challenge to Social Movement Theory", in this volume.

Ellingsen, Dag, Björnsdóttir, Inga Dóra and Warring, Anette (1995). *Kvinder, Krig og Kjær-lighed*, Oslo, Cappelen Forlag A.S.

Gledhill, John (1994). *Power and Its Disguises*, London, Pluto Press.

Goddard, V. (1994). "From the Mediterranean to Europe: honor, kinship and gender" in *The Anthropology of Europe: Identities and Boundaries in Conflict*, (eds.) Goddard, V., Llobera, J., and Shore, C. Oxford, Berg, p. 57-93.

Hobsbawm, Eric and Ranger, Terence (1983). *The Invention of Tradition*, Cambridge, Cambridge University Press.

Hobsbawm, Eric (1994), (1999). *Age of Extremes: The Short Twentieth Century 1914-1991.* Reykjavík, Mál og menning.

Humm, Maggie (1992). *Feminisms: A Reader*, London, Harvester.

Kristmundsdóttir, Sigríður Dúna (1997). *Doing and Becoming: Women's Movements and Women's Personhood in Iceland 1870-1990*. Reykjavik, University of Iceland Press.

Kristmundsdóttir, Sigríður Dúna (1999). "Father Did Not Answer That Question: Power, Gender and Globalisation in Europe", Cheater, Angela, (ed.), *The Anthropology of Power: Empowerment and disempowerment in changing structures*, ASA Monographs 36, London, Routledge, p. 42-57.

Líndal, Amalia (1962). *Ripples from Iceland*. Akureyri, Bókaforlag Odds Björnssonar

Lönnå, Elisabeth (2002). "Waves in the History of Feminism", in this volume.

Mcdonald, Maryon (1996). "Unity in Diversities: Some tensions in the construction of Europe*"*. *Social Anthropology* 4, 1, 47-61.

Robertson, Roland (1995). "Glocalization: Time-Space and Homogeneity-Heterogeneity", Mike Featherstone, Scott Lash and Roland Robertson (eds.), *Global Modernities*, London, Sage, p. 25-44.

Rose, Jacqueline (2000). "What does Feminism Want?", *Women: A Cultural Review*, vol. 11, no 1/2, p. 139-144.

Styrkársdóttir, Auður (1998). *From Feminism to Class Politics: The Rise and Decline of Women's Politics in Reykjavík 1908 – 1922*. Department of Political Science, Umeaa University.

Touraine, Alan (1998). "Economic Globalisation and Social Fragmentation – Is There a Way Past This Opposition?", Public Lecture, University of Iceland, Sept. 26.

Touraine, Alan (2001). *Beyond Neoliberalism*. Cambridge, Polity Press.

Notes

1 Hobsbawm, [1994], (1999).
2 See e.g. Rose, (2000), and Budgeon, (2001).
3 Kvennalistinn is variously referred to in English as The Women's Lists Movement or The Women's Slate Movement. Its full name in Icelandic is Samtök um kvennalista. In this article the abbreviated Icelandic version, *Kvennalistinn*, will be used.
4 See e.g. Bauman, (1995). Also Mcdonald, (1996).
5 For a fuller discussion on anthropologists' examination of globalisation and the effect globalisation can have on women's position around the world see Kristmundsdóttir, (1999).
6 Robertson, Roland (1995).
7 Kristmundsdóttir, Sigríður Dúna (1999).
8 See e.g. Ellingsen, Björnsdóttir and Warring (1995).
9 Touraine, Alan (1998) and (2001).
10 See e.g. Hobsbawm, Ranger (1983).
11 Goddard, (1994).
12 Gledhill, (1994).
13 It is for instance tempting to ask whether recent international and globalised agreements on women's rights can themselves be one of the causes of the re-differentiation that we observe? Could their homogenizing message filter down from their elated institutional status into everyday lives in such a manner that people feel all the more keenly the need to redefine women and men as separate cultural groups?
14 The account is based on my study of Icelandic women's movements. See Kristmundsdóttir, (1997). See also Styrkársdóttir, (1998), for an analysis of the first women's lists 1908-1922.
15 See also Christensen and Halsaa in this volume.
16 A perceptive account of gender differentiation in Icelandic society at this time is to be found in Líndal, (1962). Amalia, who was from Boston where she had attended university, came to live in Iceland with her Icelandic husband in 1949.
17 A forerunner of Kvennalistinn was Kvennframboðið, which put forward women's lists in the 1982 municipal elections. Kvennaframboðið is here merged with Kvennalistinn, which came into being a year later, as it was founded by many of the same women and put forward the same ideology.
18 See Dahlerup, Drude in this volume.
19 Björnsdóttir, Sturludóttir and Hauksdóttir (2000). For a discussion of how feminist ideas form the choices of young women see Budgeon, (2001).
20 See Dahlerup and Lønnå in this volume.
21 ibid. and also e.g. Humm (1992).
22 See e.g. Rose (2000) and Coward (1999).

Diversity and Internationality

Ute Gerhard

Containing such a large number of different approaches and individual studies the volume at hand "Crossing Borders. Re-mapping Women's Movements at the Turn of the 21st Century", displays a remarkable variety of new and inspiring insights, thus giving a multifaceted and colourful picture of women's movements past and present. These studies show once more the importance of not generally speaking of women's movements and feminisms in the singular but in the plural form. This also means that there are no universally valid criteria nor any one definition which is suited to label women's movements, their beginning or end, and the extent to which a movement is coming closer to its political objective, i.e. to create more justice in gender relations and hence, a truly democratic society. This is not just a shortcoming or, rather, a characteristic of women's movements but a typical feature of all social movements. They are – as the term "movement" suggests – motors and actors of social change that interfere with history, wanting to change the status quo, i.e. the existing structures and institutions of a society, and by doing so, "liquefy" what formerly appeared to be stable and permanent. It is because of "the fluid concept of social movements"[1] that sociologists and social analysts have been having so much difficulty in forming a concrete idea of them and in developing ways of analysing the various movements. Social movements have no fixed form or structure which is why they are also called mobilised or mobilising networks; they come into existence without prior warning, develop into a broad current, then they remain silent for a long time and dissolve, while it is practically impossible to predict whether or not they will be revived. Neidhardt has coined a phrase to describe this phenomenon: "The powerful have difficulties with them, and even the intelligence service is in the dark."[2]

Any attempt to define feminism is therefore bound to encounter similar difficulties since so many different opinions are associated with this term – which often enough leads to a certain degree of dissociating oneself, depending on the respective historic, cultural or national context. Commonly, there are two meanings connoted with the term "feminism": On the one hand, feminism marks the social movement of women; in English or French it is used synonymously with the term "women's movement"[3]. In other languages, as for instance in German, the term "feminism" instead of "women's movement" was only introduced during the second women's movement in Germany. Here, it commonly suggests a certain degree of radicalism. On the other hand, feminism is also a social theory or concept that takes a critical stance towards society, its social structures and the prevailing world view, and thus has been leading, founding and supporting women's social movements like the other "isms" or "grand narratives" of modernity.

It was French women who invented and propagated the term in the late 19th century, giving it a meaning that constituted the foundation for feminist political theories of the 20th century[4]; however, speaking of "feminisms" means to take into due account the many diverse approaches and the lack of uniformity among the various movements, and to reconsider feminism as a controversial and highly contentious issue. Still, I believe it is necessary to draw the line somewhere in order to distinguish feminist from other political actions by women that use the issue of "being a woman" as a common denominator: If the latter were also defined as feminist action we would implicitly accept gender differences as being natural and essential while modern feminism came into existence to question, overcome and deconstruct these very differences.

Although researchers of social movements have also included conservative, reactionary, in particular totalitarian and extremist movements in their analysis[5], I would like to impose a normative restriction with regard to modern feminist movements: The significance of feminist politics lies in its fundamentally radical democratic approach and its concern with human rights as being women's rights – this is what I believe links the history of modern feminisms since the Declaration of the Rights of Woman by Olympe de Gouges in 1791 with global campaigning in the late 20th century: Their common aim is to end or prevent paternalism, discrimination and oppression of women on account of their gender in political and private relationships.

As the studies at hand suggest in a variety of ways, there are two points that are particular to women's movements, both of which I would like to address in my commentary: First, their fundamental and remarkable internationality, in particular the discussion of transnationality and globalisation; second, the discussion of the concept or the metaphor of "waves" in women's movements. Both are issues that most of the contributions in this volume deal with.

Internationality of women's movements

Even before the buzzword of globalisation had started to dominate our thinking about the changing world order and its economies, we became aware that today women's movements, too, mainly appear in the form of international networks, transnational campaigns and in the new media i.e. the internet, which is why this kind of mobilising is also being called "third wave feminism". It is the great merit of the volume at hand that it not only discusses the broad range and diverse levels of feminist issues and problems but, at the same time, also analyses their relation to local, national and international politics. There are many different examples and approaches, be it "Religion as a Source of Activism" (Christensen in this volume), "Women's Movements in Sports" (Laine ibid.), "The Problem of Trafficking in Women" (Khodyreva ibid.) or the possible "unintended consequences" which the Women's World Conference in Beijing had for women or a women's movement in China (Zhang ibid.); all of these contributions have as central themes internationality, transnational links and national repercussions. Evidently, bi-national or international comparison enables a productive and enlightening analysis of one's own country; this is methodologically reflected with particular regard to qualitative national studies (Bergmann, ibid.). Also, it seems that the closer cultural and political coherence in the Scandinavian countries – where glancing across borders in order to detect differences and commonalities is done as a matter of course more frequently than elsewhere – proves to be particularly suitable for comparative studies. However, since the introduction and several other contributions address the historical dimension, I would like to find out how women's movements of the early 20th century and their international orientation differ from feminist initiatives and projects at the beginning of the 21st century, and whether today we have to imagine feminist movements as being new or different because so-called globalisation has turned the world into a smaller and, at the same time, a wider place.

In two ways, international initiatives and influences by women's issues in other countries have indeed been playing a crucial role for all women's movements since the 19th century: On the one hand, knowing about the existence of identical problems and the exchange of similar or the same experiences of injustice helps to learn that it is possible to change one's own situation and encourages similar actions and political interference; on the other hand, international women's organisations have been giving practical aid in organising women's interests at the national level. This is especially true for the International Council of Women (ICW) which was founded during a conference of the National Women's Suffrage Association in the U.S. in 1888 on the occasion of the 40th anniversary of the Declaration of Women's Rights of Seneca Falls. The ICW was founded with the goal of merging the many women's groups already existing in other countries and encouraging the formation of national women's councils. By 1914, 23 national organisations had already joined the ICW; by 1939 women from 63 countries had joined.[6] Based on the principle of non-interference, in order not to touch national interests and to avoid political and religious conflicts, the objectives of this international umbrella organisation were deliberately formulated in a vague manner: promoting solidarity among women from "all parts of the world", "for the good of humankind", "service to the family and the state" (from the preamble of the statutes, back-translation)[7] Since this self-imposed political restriction meant that women's suffrage could not be put onto the agenda, in 1904, the suffragettes founded a new international organisation following the world congress of the ICW in Berlin: the Inter-national Women's Suffrage Alliance (IWSA, later generally shortened to IAW). This alliance was a political association of the more radical feminists, soon encompassing as many member countries as the ICW, and having spun a co-operation network that extended far beyond Europe and America. Missing in both organisations, however, were the socialist women who from a classist point of view refused to work together with middle-class feminist. Instead, they founded the Socialist Women's International under Clara Zetkin's strict leadership.[8]

However, when international feminist solidarity was put to test with the outbreak of World War I, the actual fragility of the empathic bond of international sisterhood became apparent. With the beginning of the war, the ICW froze all international rela-tions. Lady Aberdeen, the president, expressed her deep chagrin to the chairwoman of the Federation of German Women's Unions, Gertrude Bäumer, while at the same time emphasising: "All of us are glad that women all over the world have responded to the call of duty and sacrifice in such a wonderful manner [...] and that it is the best guide to us if women of each nation do what they believe to be their duty as citizens of the respective country." [9] Only a small minority of convinced pacifists among the suffragettes, initiated and led by Dutch Aletta Jacobs and American social reformer Jane Addams, dared to invite to a women's world conference of neutral and warfaring nations during the war in The Hague.[10] 1200 delegates from 12 countries were present, with many demonstrations of solidarity by intellectuals and celebrities from all over the world. This at first loosely-knit network later became the Women's International League for Peace and Freedom (WILPF) while maintaining its loose structure and, at a national level, worked not in associations, but in problem-oriented or subject-specific committees. Although both the ICW and IAW eagerly took up again their international co-operation in the 1920s, it had become clear that this union of international sister-hood, organised efficiently and on the basis of national associations, could not seriously overcome the limitations of national politics. At most, they could be ambassadors for international peace and understanding at a personal level.

The new "wave" of women's movements that spread almost simultaneously in various European and American countries in the late 1960s was also significantly influenced by the outside world. From the very beginning, it also had an international orientation, yet it worked in a different manner than the "old" women's movements.

This new women's movement was not organised in associations i.e. in a strict hierarchical structure of representatives, but was rather made up of an informal net-work of groups. Like the other *new* social movements, feminists opposed established organisations and parties with their policies, and instead searched for alternative and non-parliamentary strategies of interference, thus developing a new public sphere of civil society, and putting topics like violence against women on their political agenda. However, the relationship between new feminist movements with their respective state and its institutions were evidently different in the individual countries – either coined as patriarchal or women-friendly. Hence, also progress and achievements were not only diverse but also non-simultaneous, according to their political, social and cultural context. Moreover, gains and losses were also perceived in a variety of ways. This would explain why radical French feminists in the 1970s were already speaking of the end of the feminist movement, while West German feminists in the 1980s were still fighting over the first institutional achievements by the new women's movement in equal opportunities politics, which some also called a betrayal of the autonomy principle or an "incorporation of autonomous politics".[11] At the same time, the equality-oriented welfare politics of Scandinavian countries prepared the ground for a so-called state feminism which partly took the edge off radical feminist ideologies, as Bergman has shown for Finland.[12] Despite these differences the new feminist movements have something in common: Because the role of national state has fundamentally changed with growing global economic interdependencies, international treaties, transnational organisations and new state communities like the European Union, these movements are generally more critical of and less oriented at state policies. In this context, it is all the more surprising how late feminists in the Western countries, while bemoaning the stagnation or backlash of women's movements in their respective countries, have come to realise the changes at the international level and the significance of international women's policies.

Almost coinciding with the end of the East-West conflict, while priorities of global politics are being rearranged and a market-oriented neo-liberalism is winning the day under the heading of 'globalisation', local and global women's movements and feminist initiatives are coming into existence – independent of Western feminisms – that have lately been labelled as "third wave feminism".[13] Their point of departure was the United Nations Decade for Women from 1975 to 1985. In particular, the World Conferences on Women, regularly held by the United Nations since that time, increasingly became a platform for women from the "Third World", constituting a basis for their international networking and an empowerment for political action in their regions.

These worldwide initiatives comprise a large variety of networks such as *Women Living under Muslim Laws* which has 1997 activists from 18 countries with a Muslim population[14], *Women in Black* starting their demonstrations during war in Yugoslavia or *Madres de la Plaza de Mayo* in Argentina, and, in particular, the campaign organised by the *Center for Women's Global Leadership* under the motto "Women's Human Rights". [15] This campaign, supported by hundreds of thousands of signatures from 120 countries, held a tribunal on "Violence against Women" in Vienna in connection with the UN World Conference on Human Rights in 1993. The publication and documentation of the violations of women's human rights all over the world has greatly contributed to the fact that "Women's Human Rights" during the Women's World Conference in Beijing in 1995 gained new attention and jolted the world's public. By recognising "gender-specific violence as discrimination against women" on the Beijing platform women have claimed "general" human rights and also redefined the latter with regard to the special significance of oppression in the private sphere.[16] Thus, the international campaign addresses the feminist criticism of androcentrism in law and human rights that deplores the lack of human rights protection for women. Furthermore, it attempts to redefine the facts of cases with regard to women-specific experiences of injustice and to rigorously extend these with regard to (private) violence imposed or tolerated by the state. Claiming human rights as women's rights refers back to an unsettled matter of women's movements that has been accompanying modernity ever since the "Declaration of the Rights of Woman", drafted by Olympe de Gouges in 1791.

Here, the question arises whether this long line of tradition in the struggle for rights actually stands for the achievement or the problem of this approach. Even after the explicit legal recognition of women's rights in the Universal Declaration of Human Rights of the United Nations in 1948, their – imperfect – validity and effect is a contentious issue. The Convention on the Elimination of all forms of Discrimination against Women (CEDAW) which was passed by the UN General Assembly in 1979 was ratified with reservations by many states and has not been able to prevent the daily violation of women's human rights.[17] Still, the legal form of this declaration gives a voice to those who have experienced injustice. This declaration offers a legal guarantee beyond applicable national law that each woman can claim and that translates her experience of injustice into a legal language. Since, however, injustice against women and violations of personal integrity and autonomy are still taken as a matter of course in the gender order, i.e. women's role of most cultures, this translation requires triggering by a movement that publicly raises the issue of women's rights. It remains to be seen whether this "third wave" of feminism will truly become a women's human rights movement.

In the volume at hand the interesting question is raised whether national and international women's politics are possibly positioned in a dialectic or contradictory context. Using Iceland as an example, Kristmundsdóttir discusses the impact of globalisation processes on the position of women in the various societies. There the author depicts a prevailing pattern that is not at all defined as an assimilation process or as recognition of equality as a "victory of the principle"; quite to the contrary, difference is being emphasised. In threshold countries, social insecurities as well as the awareness of critical economic developments may lead to an emphasis on cultural difference and, hence, to a "renewed emphasis on women's traditional roles, especially their roles as mothers and housewives" (in this vol.), just as new political priorities in the developed industrial countries take the wind out of the feminist movement's sails. Here, too, the repercussions of globalisation, international co-operation and economic dependency cannot be concealed any longer, requiring new forms of "political solidarity", as Stoltz points out (in this vol.), in particular between the majority population, migrants, refugees and women of 'colour'. The insistent claim for women's human rights also proves to be an indispensable normative benchmark that can give a voice to women and enable them to assert their claim to citizenship rights as women. Feminist researchers have extensively dicussed and concretised the various necessary elements of citizenship for women. However, being experts for recognition and the significance of difference, they do not plead for cosmopolitanism but for "a differentiated universalism" that includes and requires a "politics of solidarity in difference" and "a commitment to dialogue".[18] Collecting a multitude of comparative analyses, varied stimulations and political statements, this book constitutes a valuable contribution to the dialogue to be led at an international level.

The "wave" metaphor with regard to women's movements

Since the contributions in this volume consistently refer to 'waves' of women's movements, I cannot but briefly address this concept. It seems to me that this term not only demonstrates the many different ideas of this physical description of a fluid or mobile state but that the concept as such is being overstrained in its explanatory power. First, I would like to emphasise that the term cannot be used for defining a category of analysis but at most for the purpose of describing a phenomenon. This means that it would make no sense to understand the metaphor of 'waves' with regard to women's movements as a theory or model that seems to include only one dominant "mainstream of political activists". Especially as the term has probably been construed in the everyday speech of mostly British or American English,[19] such a theoretical presumption would indeed be misleading (cf. Lønnå in this vol.). Reservations of this kind against the use of the term are apparently based on the idea of a linear wave movement spreading across space in ups and downs, considering the continuity of *one* triggering stream or of the aims of women's movements. Similar to Drude Dahlerup, I assume that the different feminisms of modernity can be followed back to "a common core" of experienced injustice (cf. Dahlerup in this vol.), but the term leads me to have different associations: I believe that the wave metaphor aptly describes the fact that the various protest movements of women originate from similar problems or, figuratively speaking, come from a sea of contradictions and injustice. These waves come and go very irregularly, sometimes, depending on their thrust and the storms of protest, into various directions; they grow or break and remain unpredictable. In order to explain why gender relations sometimes become so virulent that a movement of women is formed under the common denominator of gender, several conditions have to be fulfilled. As the research of social movements has often enough proved, merely structural contradictions such as social inequality or relative deprivation do not suffice for emergence of a movement.[20] Rather, the coming together of women as women in spite of their social, cultural, "ethnic" etc. differences is quite unlikely.[21] Women as "half of humankind" are neither a demographic minority nor a homogeneous social group; they are members of social classes and ethnic groups or different sexual and religious orientations, often intimately living together with those against whom they revolt. Therefore, mobilising women as members of the female sex is not an easy endeavour. In addition to structural contradictions, this task also requires political opportunities, an availability of resources, and incentives for mobilising as well as instances where contradictions and experiences of injustice can be articulated and framed in the public sphere. Furthermore, it needs a convincing common political objective or social utopia and, last but not least, an avantgarde of intelligent and courageous female activists who succeed in establishing groups and networks while gaining public attention and political power. When taking the above prerequisites into due consideration it is not the failing of women's movements that we should lament; instead we should be surprised that despite so many barriers and set-backs, it has been possible to mobilise women again and again not only for their own sake, but "for the sake of humankind"[22], turning their unsettled matter of concern into a political agenda. From this perspective, the term "long waves" in women's movements allows for doldrums[23] or breathing spaces[24], thus helping us to interpret current backlashes or obstructions in a less pessimistic or in a cooler manner.

References

Bergmann, Solveig (2002), *The Politics of Feminism – Autonomous Feminist Movements in Finland and West Germany from the 1960s to the 1980s*, Åbo: Åbo Akademi University Press.

Braun, Lily (1895), *Bürgerpflicht der Frau*, Berlin: Dümmler.

Buechler, Steven M. (1990), *Women's Movements in the United States. Woman Suffrage, Equal Rights and Beyond*, New Brunswick et al.: Rutgers University Press.

Cook, Rebecca (1994), *Human Rights of Women. National and International Perspectives*, Philadelphia. University of Pennsylvania.

della Porta, Donatella/Mario, Diani (1999): *Social Movements. An Introduction*, Oxford. Blackwell.

Evans, Richard J. (1979), *Sozialdemokratie und Frauenemanzipation im deutschen Kaiserreich*, Berlin: Dietz.

Friedman, Elisabeth (1995): *Women's Human Rights: The Emergence of a Movement*, Peters, Julie, Wolper, Andrea (ed.): *Women's Rights – Human Rights. International Feminist Perspectives*. New York/London. Routledge, p. 18-34.

Gerhard, Ute (1994): "National oder International. Die internationalen Beziehungen der deutschen bürgerlichen Frauenbewegung", *Feministische Studien*, 12 (2): p. 34-52.

Gerhard, Ute (1999), *Atempause. Feminismus als demokratisches Projekt*, Frankfurt/M. Fischer.

Internationales Frauenkomitee für dauernden Frieden (ed.): Internationaler Frauenkongress in Haag vom 21. April bis 1. Mai 1915, Amsterdam (1915).

Klejman, Laurence/ Rochefort, Florence (1989), *L'Egalité en marche. Le feminisme sous la Troisième Republique*, Paris: Pr. de la Fondation Nationale des Sciences Polit.

Kontos, Silvia (1989): "Von heute an gibt's mein Programm" – zum Verhältnis von.

Partizipation und Autonomie in der Politik der neuen Frauenbewegung, *Forschungsjournal Neue Soziale Bewegungen*, Sonderheft. p. 52-65.

Mayer Ann E. (2003), "Die Konvention über die Beseitigung jeder Form von Diskriminierung der Frau und der politische Charakter "religiöser" Vorbehalte". Rumpf Mechthild/Gerhard & Jansen, Mechtild M. (Ed.), *Facetten islamischer Welten. Geschlechterordnungen, Frauen- und Menschenrechte in der Diskussion*, Bielefeld, transcript, p. 103-122.

Neidhardt, Friedhelm (1985): "Einige Ideen zu einer allgemeinen Theorie sozialer Bewegungen", in: Hradil, Stefan (ed.): *Sozialstruktur im Umbruch*. Opladen: Leske + Budrich.

Offen, Karen (1988): "Defining Feminism. A Comparative Historical Approach", SIGNS, 14 (1). p. 119-157.

Offen, Karen (2000), *European Feminisms 1700-1950. A Political History*, Stanford: Stanford University Press.

Rammstedt, Otthein, Soziale Bewegung, Frankfurt/M. Suhrkamp (1978).

Rupp, Leila & Taylor, Verta (1990), *Survival in the Doldrums. The American Women's Rights Movements 1945 to the 1960's*, Columbus: Ohio State University Columbus.

Rupp, Leila J., "Zur Organisationsgeschichte der internationalen Frauenbewegung vor dem Zweiten Weltkrieg"; *Feministische Studien*, 12. Jg., 2/1994.

Rupp, Leila J. (1998), *Worlds of Women: The Making of an International Women's Movement*, Lawrenceville. Princeton University Press.

Smelser, Neil J. (1972), *Theorie kollektiven Verhaltens*, Köln: Kiepenheuer & Witsch.
Wichterich, Christa (1995), *Frauen der Welt. Vom Fortschritt der Ungleichheit*, Göttingen. Lamuv.

Notes

1   Gusfield (1981) London: p. 317-339.
2   Neidhardt (1985).
3   Klejman, Rochefort (1989).
4   Offen (1988). p. 119-157.
5   Smelser (1972). Rammstedt, Otthein (1978).
6   Rupp, Leila J. (2000) (1998); Offen.
7   Cf. Rupp (1994). p. 53-65; cf. also in Gerhard (1994). p. 34-52.
8   Evans, (1979) p. 142-144.
9   Letter from Isabel Aberdeen to Gertrud Bäumer, April 1915, Helene-Lange-Archiv Abt. 17, IV, 84-330 (8); see also Thébaut, Francoise, Der Erste Weltkrieg, in: Duby, George/ Perrot, Michelle (ed.), Geschichte der Frauen, 20. Jahrhundert, Frankfurt/New York, Campus, p. 33-91.
10 Cf. in detail Internationales Frauenkomitee für dauernden Frieden (ed.) (1915): Internationaler Frauenkongress in Haag vom 21. April bis 1. Mai 1915, Amsterdam (1915) in the languages, Comité International de Femmes pour une Paix Permanente.
11 Kontos (1989) p. 52-65.
12 Bergmann (2002).
13 Wichterich (1995), Lamuv; cf. also Basu (1995):
14 http//www.wluml.org.
15 Cf. on this Friedman (1995).
16 Cf. Cook (1994).
17 Mayer (2003).
18 Lister (2003).
19 Furthermore is is not clear whether this metaphor can really be transposed into other languages. In German the term is not really translatable: First, the terms "historic" and "new" women's movement were not coined until – probably due to the English expression – we started speaking of an first and a second women's movement. What about the Scandinavian languages?
20 della Porta & Mario (1999).
21 Cf. this Buechler (1990).
21 Braun (1895).
22 Rupp, Taylor (1990).
24 Gerhard (1999).

Time and Tide:

Memories and Metaphors –
Moments and Movements

Sasha Roseneil

As I settle down to write the epilogue for this book, Britain is preparing for the state visit of US President George W. Bush to London. A week of demonstrations is just beginning, with marches and rallies, an ironic "tea party" outside Buckingham Palace and the symbolic toppling of a statue of Bush planned to protest the visit. All police leave has been cancelled, and it is expected that large parts of central London – around Parliament and the government buildings of Whitehall – will be sealed off, to try to prevent the demonstrators – and terrorists – getting close to the President and his entourage.

Exactly twenty years ago, in November 1983, all eyes were on the protests generated by the arrival of another United States Air Force aeroplane – bringing Cruise missiles to Greenham Common. The evening the first missiles arrived, Whitehall and Trafalgar Square were blockaded by tens of thousands people, and eighty km away, at the Greenham Common airbase, hundreds of women living at the women's peace camp witnessed their arrival with tears and keening. A few weeks later, on December 13, fifty thousand women gathered at Greenham to register their objection to the stationing of American nuclear weapons in Britain. Equipped with boltcutters and fuelled by anger, they tore down long sections of the perimeter fence. Hundreds were arrested.

Right wing Presidents in the White House, millions of peace protesters mobilized across Europe, acts of civil disobedience and moral outrage, a tangible collective anxiety about the future of the world. Snapshots of these two moments suggest many similarities.

But much has changed since 1983, in geo-politics, economy, culture, technology, and gender relations... With state communism over, neo-liberalism appears triumphant, and the revolution in information and communication technology connects the planet in ways unimaginable two decades previously. The "war on terrorism" is a very different beast from the Cold War – Al Qaeda is understood as a fundamentally different enemy for the west from communist Russia. Tony Blair, not Margaret Thatcher, is Prime Minister of Britain, and New labour stakes a claim to a social democratic, third way politics that construes the role of government very differently from Thatcherism. And, notwithstanding the ongoing protests of Women in Black[1] and a number of other local women's actions[2], there is no substantial women's peace movement in 2003 which is in any way comparable with that which rocked the ship of state in the early 1980s. Women have taken part in the anti-war demonstrations in Europe, North America and Australia in great numbers, but they seem to be less ready to engage in collective identification *as women* now than twenty years ago. If further evidence is needed of the key assertion of this volume that women's political activism must be studied in its temporal and spatial specificity, a comparison between these two moments provides it. Drawing on analyses developed in this volume of the relatively less prevalent autonomous organizing by women in the Nordic countries as being related to the strength of popular discourses of gender equality and common interests, it might be speculated that a Nordic-style gender discourse has spread well beyond the Norden in recent years. Alternatively, it might be suggested that processes of individualization and women's increased economic, social and cultural independence might be militating against the claiming of the gendered identifications which mobilized, and were mobilized by, the women's peace movement of the 1980s.

An Auto/biographical excursion

I return in my mind's eye to the heady days of the early eighties because that was the moment of my activation, the time when I became a political activist. Whenever I reflect upon social movements I am drawing, in a range of ways, on experiences which date from then. Listening to a radio interview earlier this week with a 16-year-old student involved in organizing a school strike against Bush's visit – hearing her profound sense of moral purpose, her anger at the geo-political situation, her passionate belief that joining the protest was more important than being at school – I was transported back twenty years, to my days organizing Youth CND[3] in Northampton, to my interviews on local radio about why I had decided to miss school to join the blockades at Upper Heyford and the fence-cutting at Greenham. And I remembered the heated discussion I had with my dearly beloved and inspirational history teacher, a Quaker and a pacifist, as she endeavoured to persuade me not to drop out of school to go to live at Greenham, but rather to stay and take my exams. One day, she said to me, you can write about Greenham. You will be more use to the movement as a writer than as a participant.

I won that battle of wills. My sense of urgency was too great – and the lure of Greenham's queer feminisms to a seventeen year old "tortured" lesbian too powerful – to compete with well-intentioned advice to defer my political and personal gratification. I left school in December 1983, six months before my A' Levels, and went to live at Greenham. Like many thousands of others, I had the whole gamut of Greenham experiences – the exhilaration of being part of a dynamic, transformatory community of strong-minded, politically engaged women, of taking action against the base, arrests, court appearances, imprisonment... a life-changing, life-enhancing experience that has provided me with personal resources that I draw upon daily. Once you have stood up to the United States military at the age of seventeen, and been imprisoned by the British state for doing so, no authority figure or power structure in a university ever has much chance. And the lessons in deliberative, consensus-building political process, in valuing individuality, difference and diversity, whilst seeking to create shared understandings and projects, were amongst the best lessons I have ever learnt. My teacher was right that I could, and would, eventually write about Greenham.[4] But I never bought her belief that intellectual work is more valuable than activism. As I turned myself, and was turned by postgraduate study, into a member of the feminist academy, researching, thinking and writing about Greenham, I moved iteratively between the bodies of thought and texts of sociology, political science and feminism, and grounded, experiential knowledges – mine and my interviewees – of political activism.

I chose to spend over a decade of my life immersed in a scholarly engagement with Greenham because I believed it mattered, it needed to be recorded, analyzed, understood, critiqued, taken seriously, in all its complexity and contradictions. As a sociology undergraduate in the second half of the 1980s, the feminist scholarship which I encountered tended to focus on women's oppression and victimization, and there seemed to be a notable lack of attention to women's agency, to women's movements and feminist politics, and to the many ways in which women sought to challenge and resist dominant gender and social relations. A burning desire to redress the balance carried me through many years of working on an unfashionable topic, in the post cold war days when Greenham seemed like pre-history (or perhaps, pre- "the end of history"[5]), before twenty year anniversaries, September 11 and the outbreak of war against Iraq put peace politics back on the agenda of the left-leaning intelligentsia and the media.

****

For me, this book's vital importance rests in its contribution to feminist understandings of women's political agency. Those who chose to research women's movements seem to me to be the optimists in the feminist academy – and their writings offer critical resources for thinking about how social relations can be transformed. There is an energy and a vitalism in this collection which challenges the reader to think differently about the history of women's struggles and thus, about the potential for social change. This is in contradistinction to much mainstream social movement research, which too often has a managerialist, technocratic feel to it, and which seems to be driven by an impetus to understand how movements work, to taxonomize, categorize and label, with no real interest in the passions which animate them, or the changes they effect. If we take seriously the post-structuralist notion of the "performativity" of social representations – the ways in which representations construct that which they seek to describe – we can register the significance of analyzes and accounts of women's political agency.[6] They contribute to bringing into being that which they analyze.

I would like to suggest that research and writing on women's movements, such as that gathered together here, are important too for the ontological work that they perform. In their collective emphasis on exploring dynamic fields of conflicts, contestations and co-operations, on different modes of, and motivations for, activism, and different articulations of women's interests, needs and identity, and how these have changed across time and space, they constitute an ontological intervention within feminist scholarship. Social movements are notoriously difficult to study, due to the fluidity inherent to their constitution, and the impossibility of delineating their boundaries definitively. In her essay Solveig Bergman insightfully draws attention to the metaphorical nature of the notion of *movement*, and suggests that it be understood as an analytical rather than an empirical concept. Extrapolating from this, if we were to treat movement as a metaphor, to think in terms of the *movement* of the social, of women's *movement*, rather than focusing on movements as things, the study of movement becomes an approach, an analytical perspective, a lens through which to look at the social formation. Such an approach is, I believe, considerably more productive, both as a representation of social relations and as a tool for feminist theory and praxis, than other metaphors which have occupied central positions within feminist theorizing.

To illustrate my point, let me juxtapose the metaphor of "standpoint", a notion that has occupied an almost uniquely important place in the recent history of feminist thought, with the metaphor of "movement".[7] *Standpoint* references an idea of statics, stillness, grounded-ness, solidity, of a single, unitary, fixing, reaching down through the ground, through a narrow, defined end. A *point* is an end, a tip. To *point* is to gesture, in one direction. To *stand* is to position oneself upright. To take a stand is to take a position. To stand up and be counted is not to sit down, lie down, crouch, or cower. There is a brave, confrontational, oppositional character to standing. One stands up for what one believes in; one stands up and faces the music, and faces one's enemies. One doesn't turn one's back when taking a stand. Politically and ethically there is much that appeals about this metaphor. But there are problems with the metaphor which are rooted in the ontology of the social which it conjures. It sees the world in terms of fixed points and positions, of still points, and standpoint theory goes on to understand the world as composed of a social structure of hierarchically organized, dichotomous groups – men and women, "the rulers" and "the ruled", "the haves" and "the have nots", "the oppressors" and "the oppressed", who stand in opposition to each other, facing each other, confronting each other.[8]

The metaphor of *movement* offers a radically different way of looking at the world. A concern with social movements, and women's movements, enables the study of the terrain of collective conflicts and actions, and their dynamics of power, as does standpoint theory, but rests in a social ontology which stresses not social structure but movement within the social. The disciplines of sociology, philosophy and geography have all recently been awash with metaphors of movement, of mobilities, flow, fluids and travel, and with powerful arguments that these metaphors better capture the constitution of the social in a globalizing, networked, individualizing era than the modern notion of social structure: Bachelard's imagery of sea, river, flux, waves and liquidity, Deleuze and Guattari, and Braidotti and Bauman's notions of the vagabond, the nomad and the traveller, and Bauman's "liquid modernity".[9] Urry[10] has recently argued for a "sociology of fluids", which emphasizes heterogeneous, uneven, unpredictable mobilities, in which there are no fixed points of arrival and departure. His model of the social imagines routeways or channels which guide these flows, and his understanding of power sees it diffused through these fluids into minute capillary-like relations of domination and subordination. The fluids move at different speeds, and possess different properties of viscosity, and so move in different shapes, and do not always remain contained by the walls which channel them – like white corpuscles, they can seep into smaller and smaller capillaries. To Urry's notion of the movement of fluids I would wish to add a notion of the flow of energy through the social formation. Drawing on a neo-Durkheimian conceptualization of the creative energies, the collective effervescences, which constitute the social order[11], and Maffesoli's[12] theorization of the historical shift from *pouvoir* – the power of institutional politics and ruling elites – to *puissance* – the inherent energy and vital force of the people – we can understand *movement* as the flow of collective energy for social transformation.[13]

Embracing the metaphor of movement as a key trope in feminist research can facilitate a mode of thinking in which the constant flow of difference is a central analytical focus, as Pauline Stolz's chapter demands. Moving beyond dichotomous models of friend and enemy, oppressors and oppressed, to nuance the complex flows of power, the dynamic energies, and the fluidities of the social connections which constitute the social, and which produce transformation therein, can enable a feminism which destabilizes fixed understandings of "women's" history and its political activisms. These are moves to which many of the authors in this volume have contributed groundbreaking analyses, and which feminist scholars of the future would do well to share. The metaphors we live by matter.[14] At this historical moment, in the post-September 11 world, metaphors of movement, and sustained analytical attention to movement in the social, have never been more important.

References

Bachelard, G. (1983) *Water and Dreams: an essay on the imagination of matter Farrell,* TX: Pegasus.

Bauman, Z. (1993). *Postmodern Ethics,* Oxford: Blackwell.

Bauman, Z. (2000). *Liquid Modernity,* Cambridge: Polity.

Braidotti, R. (1994). *Nomadic Subjects,* New York: Columbia University Press.

Collins, P. Hill (1986). "Learning from the Outside Within: the sociological significance of black feminist thought", *Social Problems*, 33: 14-32.

De Landa, M. (1997). *A Thousand Years of Nonlinear History*, New York: Swerve Editions.

Deleuze, G. and F. Guattari (1986). *Nomadology.* New York: Semiotext(e).

Durkheim, E. (1915). *The Elementary Forms of the Religious Life.* London: George Allen and Unwin.

Fukuyama, F. (1992). *The End of History and the Last Man.* London: Penguin.

Gibson-Graham, J.K. (1996). *The End of Capitalism (as we knew it): a feminist critique of political economy. Oxford: Blackwell.*

Harding, p. (1986). *The Science Question in Feminism.* Milton Keynes: Open University Press.

Harding, p. (2003). How Standpoint Methodology Informs Philosophy of Social Science. Paper presented to Research Symposium on Feminist Knowledge and Politics: A Dialogue, University College Cork, 4-5 April 2003.

Hartsock, N. (1983). "The Feminist Standpoint: Developing the Ground for a Specifically Feminist Historical Materialism", in p. Harding and M. Hintikka (eds.) *Discovering Reality: Feminist Perspectives on Epistemology, Metaphysics, Methodology and Philosophy of Science*, Dordrecht. Reidel.

Jaggar, A. (1983). *Feminist Politics and Human Nature.* Brighton: Harvester.

Lakoff, G. and M. Johnson (1980). *Metaphors We Live By. Chicago,* IL. Chicago University Press.

Maffesoli, M. (1996). *The Time of the Tribes: the decline of individualism in mass society.* London: Sage.

Rose, H. (1983). "Hand, Brain and Heart: A Feminist Epistemology for the Natural Sciences", *Signs*, 9, 1.

Roseneil, p. (1993). "Greenham Revisited: Researching Myself and My Sisters" in D. Hobbs and T. May (eds.) *Interpreting the Field,* Oxford. Oxford University Press.

Roseneil, p. (1995). *Disarming Patriarchy: Feminism and Political Action at Greenham,* Buckingham. Open University Press.

Roseneil, p. (2000a). *Common Women, Uncommon Practices. The Queer Feminisms of Greenham.* London: Cassell.

Roseneil, p. (2001). "A Moment of Moral Remaking: The Death of Diana, Princess of Wales", in F. Webster (ed.), *Culture and Politics in the Information Age. A New Politics?* London: Routledge, p. 96-114.

Smith, D. (1987). *The Everyday World as Problematic: A Feminist Sociology.* Boston. Northeastern University Press.

Smith, D. (1990). *The Conceptual Practices of Power: A Feminist Sociology of Knowledge.* Boston. Northeastern University Press.

Urry, J. (2000). *Sociology beyond Societies: Mobilities for the Twenty-First Century,* London. Routledge.

Notes

1 http://www.womeninblack.org.uk/
2 For instance, a naked protest by 750 women outside Byron Bay in New South Wales, Australia http://www.commondreams.org/headlines03/0208-06.htm, and demonstrations at Menwith Hill in Yorkshire http://cndyorks.gn.apc.org/mhs/wpc/wpchistory.htm
    See also http://www.womenagainstwar.net/
3 Campaign for Nuclear Disarmament
4 Roseneil (1993, 1995, 2000).
5 Fukuyama (1992).
6 For an excellent example of a text inspired by the belief in the performativity of social representations see Gibson Graham's (1996) exercise in feminist political economy, which recognizes the importance of challenging representations of societies and economies as hegemonic formations.
7 Standpoint theory began with the work of Smith in the late 1970s (e.g.1987; 1990), and developed with contributions by Hartsock (1983), Rose (1983), Jaggar (1983), Collins (1986) and Harding (1986; 2003).
8 Harding (2003).
9 Bachelard (1983); Deleuze and Guattari (1986); Braidotti (1994); Bauman (1993; 2000).
10 Urry (2000).
11 Durkheim (1915). For a longer discussion of the uses of a neo-Durkheimian cultural sociology for the study of collective action see Roseneil (2001).
12 Maffesoli (1996).
13 A similar notion of energy is utilized by De Landa (1997).
14 Lakoff and Johnson (1980).

Abstracts

Contextualising and Contrasting Feminism: Studying Women's Movements from a Cross-country Perspective

Solveig Bergman

Comparative studies face major theoretical and methodological difficulties and challenges. The article highlights a number of these problems with particular reference to cross-national comparisons of the recent women's movements. The 'methodological turn' in sociology and in social movement research with an emphasis on qualitative methodology has not yet been fully reflected in comparative social research. Instead, macro-level structural analyses and e.g. studies using the 'political opportunity structures' approach have been popular. The author argues that a contextual and contrastive approach, where two or more case studies are used as frames of reference for each other, provides a fruitful methodological basis for a comparison of feminist strategies and practices in different political and cultural settings. Yet, an emphasis on contextually defined diversity may lead us to overlook the obvious affinities between feminisms across countries. Classical comparative approaches may not be suitable to catch the processes of international diffusion and cross-national cultural influences. A further challenge to research is the growing permeability of national borders resulting from globalisation and the transformation of nation-states. As a consequence, it may become less relevant to view the nation-states as the primary units of comparison. Also women's movements are in a process of developing networks and communities of interest across the international arena.

Waves in the History of Feminism

Elisabeth Lønnå

This article concerns itself with the term "waves" with regard to its usefulness within feminist history. Examples from Norway and Denmark show that through searching for "waves of feminism" we may be blinded to activities that may have been important to the development of women's rights and status. Because they were not able to break through to create or be part of a "wave" of activity in their own times, women activists may not be considered important. By examining the periods between the great "waves" of activity, we may discover and appreciate other aspects of feminist history. Such a view encourages an open perspective which can affect how we meet feministic groups today and in the future.

Continuity and Waves in the Feminist Movement – a Challenge to Social Movement Theory

Drude Dahlerup

In the chapter "Continuity and Waves in Feminist Movement – A Challenge to Social Movement Theory", Drude Dahlerup discusses the wave metaphor that is usually used to describe the rise and fall of feminist mobilization: the first wave of feminism, the second wave, and maybe the third. However, she points out that the theoretical foundation as well as the empirical base of this *continuity thesis* need to be clarified.

Three dimensions of continuity are discussed in this chapter. It is argued that it is possible to speak about one continuous feminist movement in terms of shared identity and ideology, even if organizational continuity is discussed. This discussion of continuity in the feminist movement challenges social movement theory, especially the New Social Movement theory. Lastly Drude Dahlerup presents a different perspective, that of a long tradition of "emancipation movements". The methodological consequenses for social movement research is discussed.

No Bed of Roses: Academic Feminism 1880-1980

Beatrice Halsaa

The article examines academic feminism as a social movement, underlining the importance of meaning-making politics. The history of Norwegian academic feminism is outlined from women's struggle for access to higher education in the 1880s until the institutionalisation of women's studies during the 1970s. A horizontal perspective is applied in the sense that Norwegian academic feminism is discussed within a broader Nordic and international framework. Social Movement Theory and efforts to combine political opportunities, cultural framing and women's agency inspire the approach.

Religion as a Source of Activism. The YWCA in Global Perspectives

Hilda Rømer Christensen

The YWCA, *the Young Women's Christian Association*, both nationally and internationally contributed to the modernisation of revivalist and missionary projects to also encompass women and their demands, for housing, financial independence and decent working conditions. Due to spiritual commitments – the idea of "extension in all lands" and skilled organisation the YWCA was one of the few women's associations that successfully settled in metropolitan centres as well as in the so-called colonial peripheries.

The article unfolds and problematizes what appears to be a story of successful integration and cooperation at the global level. Also it addresses the implications of studying a religious based women's association in transnational and global perspectives.

Women's Movements in Sports:
National and International Issues

Leena Laine

In this article possibilities in and restrictions for women's organising in the very area of modern sport and physical culture will be discussed, on a national and specially on an international level. Starting with a presentation of a larger frame of the modern sports culture, controlled by men and based on socially defined, gendered wievs of the body, the article analyses the activity periods of women there and compares them with the activity waves and crests in other women's movements. Of special interest are the periods of 20s-30s and again 40-50s where women's activities, after the "mobilisation start" in earlier decennies, were both growing, widening and diverging, but also saw serious backlashes, specially in competitive sports and there areas of central symbolic importance for men's culture (track and field, skiing).

   After the Second World War women in the Nordic countries challenged the male power in the sport's structure more systematically, by founding a women's committee organisation. After a new backlash in the 60s, a new equality movement supported by governmental equality politics since the 70s was started. A short description of the latest decennies is given, with a broader wiev on globalised sports. In the sports area women's gymnastics movement with social aims meant continuity, the equality fights in competitive sports, or on organisational level, were shorter, a generation long. Still there has been shown a basic continuity in the whole history, based on the demand of democratizing and equalising the sports system.

Contested Ideological Issues of Early Russian Feminism

Irina Yukina

The paper discusses the ideology of the Russian feminism of the first wave, which the author defines traditionally as the struggle for the suffrage at the period from the end of 19th till the beginning of 20th century. The disagreement with the prevailing ideology leads to the creation of an alternative ideology, which unites people interested in changing their status. The challenges are the decisive fact in the development of any movement. The article explores two directions in Russian feminism ideology of the first waves, which determined its development.

Contrasting Discourses of Gender-Equality. Local Women's
Groups Facing Established Politics

Malin Rönnblom

In this chapter, the relationship between women's organising and established politics in a rural context is highlighted, based on the assumption that a study of women's organising is also a study of the construction of politics. The aim is to focus on the limits of established politics and democracy by analysing how feminist activists and local politicians respectively argue how gender equality should be defined. In this way, studying women's organising is seen as a strategy to analyse "normal politics" and "normal democracy". The chapter also includes a theoretical discussion of gender and rurality, where also the relationship between women's organising and the state is brought up.

Unintended Consequences of Hosting a Women's Conference: Beijing and Beyond

Naihua Zhang

In 1995, China hosted the UN Fourth World Conference on Women amidst great international controversy. Did China deserve to host the event? What was its impact on Chinese women and the women's movement? This paper critically examines these questions first by reviewing the history of Chinese women's contact with the outside world to illustrate that the event marked China's full integration into the international women's movement. The effect of the conference was explored through the interaction between local and international women's movements. It demonstrates that the conference resulted in the changing social and political environment in which the women's movement is carried out in China and facilitates its expansion and development. The paper concludes with the author's observations of the dynamics of the local/global exchange and interplay.

Cross-border Connections of Czech Women's groups: The Role of Foreign Funding

Alena Heitlinger

The article explores the nature of cross-border links involving women's groups in post-communist Czech Republic. It describes and analyzes local and transnational women's organizations and networks, documents their sources of funding, and evaluates the impact of foreign funding and cross-border networking on the legitimacy and empowerment of local women's groups.

Promoting Gender-balanced Decision-making: The Role of International Fora and Transnational Networks

Mona Lena Krook

This article examines the role of international organizations and transnational networks in politicizing and promoting the issue of gender-balanced decision-making. It presents a genealogy of international and transnational efforts to target "decision-making" as an area vital to promoting substantive equality between women and men, focusing on the United Nations, the Inter-Parliamentary Union, the Council of Europe, and the European Union as international fora in which transnational networks interact with institution officials to develop new ideas and strategies for gender equality.

Life Course in Move(ment): Finnish Romany Women
Airi Markkanen

The interview is concerned with Markkanen's field work among Finnish Romany Women in the 1990s and 2000. It describes the everyday life of Finnish Romany women and the marks of ethnicity which they carry, such as dress, and the cultural factors such as purity/impurity, customs, shame and honour questions that the women have to think of in their everyday lives.

Markkanen writes about the women's lives in their own society and in Finnish modern life. The article is also concerned with the questions facing Romany life in today's Europe with Romany nomads coming across the borders from former Eastern Europe. Finally it deals with how the life circumstances of the Romanies have become a political question too.

The Problem of Trafficking in Women at the Transnational and National Levels With the example of Russia and NIS*
Natalia Khodyreva

The article discusses the problems regarding international, transnational and national women's organisations combating prostitution and trafficking in and from Russia since the disintegration of the socialist block and the Soviet Union in the early 1990s.

A key problem is that there are different and even opposite views on prostitution, even among women's movements themselves. In some countries (e.g. Sweden) women's organisations are strongly against it and see it as violence against women while in some other Western countries (e.g. the Netherlands) they have worked (successfully) for its legalisation. Another up to date problem are the neoliberal debates around competitiveness and consumerism, in which prostitution is linked to choice, freedom and work. This cannot, as the author argues, apply to the situation of women in economically poor and turbulent countries. More dialogue and collaboration is thus needed within transnational networks to link together actors in Russia and NIS and Western countries for joint actions in order to further legislation in Russia.

---

* NIS, the Newly Independent States – the countries that until 1991 were constituent republics of the USSR, Armenia, Azerbaijan, Belarus, Georgia, Kazakhstan, Kyrgyzstan, Moldova, Tajikistan, Tuskmenistan, Ukraine, Uzbekistan and Russia.

Exercises in Transversalism. Reflections on a Nordic and NW-Russian network for Crisis centres in Barents

Aino Saarinen

The article is an analysis of the crisis centres for women that have arisen from the "Second Wave" of women's movements in Barents, the northernmost parts of Norway, Sweden, Finland and NW Russia at the turn of the 1990s-2000s. The transition from bi-local and sporadic collaboration into trans-regional networking and institution building across the East-West divide and the institutional boundaries between autonomous, affiliated and public units is followed through the NCRB – A Network for Crisis Centres in the Barents Region development project (1999-2002; 2002-2005). The article concentrates on the training courses, which are analysed within the framework of the transversal dialogue that has developed in women's movements to bridge various dividing lines and to promote dialogue and reciprocality. The article is based on experiences in running the development project, various project materials, a questionnaire sent to the crisis centres in Barents and focus group and individual interviews in the 19 NCRB localities.

Joining a Transnational Movement – Action against Gender-based Violence in China

Cecilia Milwertz

This chapter examines transnational and cross-cultural links between China and Euro-North American women's movements. The focus is on two of the new organizations in Beijing – the Jinglun Family Centre and the Women's Research Institute – and their activities related to the issue of domestic violence in the 1990s. The chapter points to some of the advantages and potential problems which the interaction between the Chinese organizations and their Euro-North American partners entail for the Chinese movement. It is argued that the activities of the two organizations, including both activities which failed in the sense that they never materialized or were discontinued, and activities which were continued and developed further, can be defined as successful because they have all played a role both in the consolidation of activism against gender-based violence and in joining Chinese activism against violence against women to the global movement.

Feminist Perspectives on Father's Leave.
A Cross-country Comparison

Chiara Bertone

Fathers' leave has been identified as one of the main means for promoting changes in the gender division of labour within the family, a crucial issue for the new feminist movement as an international phenomenon. This article looks at the different frameworks within which fathers' leave was discussed in two specific cases, as a contribution to the understanding of the situated meanings and patterns of influence of the new feminist movements' positions and struggles. By analysing the claims voiced by the women's movement on this issue during the debates preceding the introduction of some forms of fathers' leave in Italy (1977) and Denmark (1983), I show its different strategic framings in the two national contexts, arguing that it was not always aimed at promoting an equal sharing of caring tasks.

Who are "we" to tell…? Black, Immigrant and Refugee Women and the Politics of Analysing Feminist Movements

Pauline Stoltz

In this chapter the movements of closure are discussed which we, as feminist academics, use, in order to discuss the political activism of groups of women (and men) in feminist movements. A special focus is given to the political activities of Black, migrant and refugee women in Europe. These can mainly be found in civil society, due to developments of globalisation, the blurring of the national and international levels of politics and the related tension around notions of citizenship and human rights. The consequence being (1) that these groups have fewer channels to public debate and to established social networks than white, indigenous women. Also, (2) this questions our ways of visualising feminist movements with a limited focus on the mainstream of feminism. Power relations between women become important to disclose, as do the presumptions we have in our thinking on social movements as political communities.

Women's Movements and the Contradictory Forces of Globalisation

Sigridur Dúna Kristmundsdóttir

The article discusses how the fragmentation of women's movements at the turn of the 21st century is related to globalisation. It outlines the effects globalisation can have on the position of women and the contradictions it embodies and creates. It is argued that in order to make sense of current feminist activities they need to be viewed in the context of this cultural phenomenon and that intensive studies of particular women's activities have to be placed within its context. The argument is illustrated by the history of women's movements in Iceland.

Biographical Statements

Solveig Bergman

D.Soc.Sc. Solveig Bergman has worked as researcher and lecturer at the Department of Sociology, Åbo Akademi University, Finland. Since November 2003 she is Director of the Nordic Institute of Women's Studies and Gender Research (NIKK) in Oslo. Her publications focus on women's movements in Finland and Germany, new social movements in the Nordic countries, women and politics and the institutionalisation of women's studies in the Nordic countries.

Chiara Bertone

Chiara Bertone is lecturer at East Piedmont University, Italy, where she teaches Sociology of the Family. With a Ph.D. in Women's and Gender Studies from Aalborg University, Denmark, she is currently researching in gender and sexualities. She is author of *Whose needs? Women's organisations' claims on child care in Italy and Denmark* (Aalborg University 2002) and co-author of *Diversi da chi? Gay, lesbiche, transessuali in un'area metropolitana* (Guerini, Milano 2003).

Hilda Rømer Christensen

Hilda Rømer Christensen, associate professor and national research co-ordinator of Gender Studies in Denmark, Department of Sociology, University of Copenhagen. She holds a Ph.D. degree in history from University of Aarhus, Denmark and has been a visiting fellow at Universities in Europe and the USA. Hilda Rømer Christensen is editor-in-chief of *Kvinder, Køn og Forskning*, the Danish journal in the field of gender research. She has research specialisation social, cultural and gender history as well as theory and methodology in historical and gender analysis.

Drude Dahlerup

Drude Dahlerup, professor of Political Science, University of Stockholm. Has published extensively about women in politics and about theory and history of the women's movements, e.g. *The Redstockings. The Development, New thinking and Impact of the Danish Redstocking Movement 1970-1985, vol. I-II*. Gyldendal 1998 (in Danish). Editor of *The New Women's Movement. Feminism and Political Power in Europe and the USA*. Sage 1986.

Ute Gerhard

Ute Gerhard, Prof. Dr. Phil., at the Johan Wolfgang Goethe-University Frankfurt am Main.

Ute Gerhard's main field of study is history and feminist theory, social policy, women's rights, history and sociology of law. Since 1997 she has been the director of the Cornelia Goethe Centrum for Women's and Gender studies (Frauenstudien und die Erforschung der Geschlechtsverhältnisse). Among her recent publications are *Debating Women's Equality. Toward a Feminist Theory of Law from a European Perspective* (New Brunswick, NJ 2001: Rutgers University Press); *Atempause. Feminismus als demokratisches Projekt* (Frankfurt, Fischer 1999); and *Frauen in der Geschichte des Rechts. Von der Frühen Neuzeit bis zur Gegenwart* (München, Beck 1997).

Beatrice Halsaa

Beatrice Halsaa is professor of gender studies, and has been involved in women's studies since the 1970's. She has published extensively, and her major fields of interests are feminist theory, gender equality politics, the women's movement, feminist utopias and women's studies. She is now writing a historiography of feminist research in Norway. At present she is Research Director at the Center for Women's Studies and Gender Research, University of Oslo. She is been head of the board of KILDEN – Norwegian Information and Documentation Centre for Women's Studies and Gender Research.

Alena Heitlinger

Alena Heitlinger is professor of sociology at Trent University, Peterborough, Ontario, Canada. The author of six books and numerous articles, she has published extensively on feminist, demographic, health, employment, and child care issues in the former Soviet Union, former Czechoslovakia, Canada, Great Britain, Australia, and post-communist Czech Republic.

Natalia Khodyreva

Obtained her Ph.D. in Psychology from St. Petersburg State University in 1988. Presently she lectures Gender Issues in Psychology, Health Psychology, Management in non-governmental organisations. Since 1988 she is involved in the Independent Women Movement of Russia; she is the founder of the first crisis centre for women in St. Petersburg. Her research interests are the epistemological styles and values on feminism among psychologists and other specialists, as well as strategies of gender programs in social justice.

Sigríður Dúna Kristmundsdóttir

Dr. Sigríður Dúna Kristmundsdóttir is professor of anthropology at the Department of Social Sciences, the University of Iceland. She was a founding member of Kvennalistinn and served as its representative in the Althing from 1983 to 1987. Her works include an analysis of the Icelandic women's movement from its beginnings in 1870 to 1990. In 2001 she was awarded the Icelandic Literature prize for her biography of dr. Björg C. Þorláksson, the first Icelandic woman scientist.

Mona Lena Krook

Mona Lena Krook is a doctoral candidate in Political Science at Columbia University. Her dissertation examines campaigns to increase women's parliamentary representation worldwide.

Leena Laine

Leena Laine is a researcher in history since 1976, and has published, co-published and edited several books in sports history and women's history. Specific areas have been sports organisations in Finland, women's sport and worker sports movement. She is finishing her dissertation on women's sports movements in Finland and Sweden at the university of Stockholm. Recently she has started a new large project on women's gymnastics movement in Finland.

Elisabeth Lønnå

Teacher and writer. Dr. philos. from the University of Oslo, 2003 with a thesis about Helga Eng, one of the early female pioneers within Norwegian academia: *Helga Eng. Psykolog og pedagog i barnets århundre* [Helga Eng. Psychologist and Educator in "The Childrens' Century"], published 2002. Cand. philol. with the thesis "DNA, Lo og striden om gifte kvinner i lønnet arbeid i mellomkrigstiden" [The Norwegian labour Movement and the Conflict Regarding the Employment of Married Women]. In 1996, published the book *Stolthet og kvinnekamp. Norsk Kvinnesaksforenings historie fra 1913* [Pride and Feminist Struggle. The History of the Norwegian Association for Women's Rights after 1913].

Airi Markkanen

Airi Markkanen. PhD.lic. Joensuu University, Finland. Cultural researcher. Doctoral theses in 2003 about "Ethnicity in the Finnish Romany Women's Life course": Luonnollisesti – etnografinen tutkimus romaninaisten elämänkulusta Joensuun yliopiston humanistisia julkaisuja no. 33 (University of Joensuu Publications in the Humanitles 33), Joensuun yliopisto (University of Joensuu) 2003. Joensuun yliopistopaino.

Cecilia Milwertz

Cecilia Milwertz is Senior Researcher at the Nordic Institute of Asian Studies in Copenhagen. She has a hybrid educational background in sinology and cultural sociology. Her current research deals with non-governmental women's organizing in the People's Republic of China. Her recent publications include *Chinese Women Organizing – Cadres, Feminists, Muslims, Queers* (2001) co-edited with P. Hsiung, M. Jaschok and R. Chan and *Beijing Women Organizing for Change – A New Wave of the Chinese Women's Movement* (2002) – a book that is very much inspired by the author's participation in the Women's Movement and Internationalization Network.

Sasha Roseniel

Sasha Roseneil is Professor of Sociology and Gender Studies and Director of the Centre for Interdisciplinary Gender Studies at the University of Leeds. She is a member of the ESRC Research Group for the Study of Care, Values and the Future of Welfare, and is the author of "Disarming Patriarchy" (1995, Open University Press), and "Common Women, Uncommon Practices: The Queer Feminisms of Greenham" (2000, Cassell). She is also editor or co-editor of "Stirring It: Challenges for Feminism" (1994, Taylor and Francis), "Practising Identities" (1999, Macmillan), "Consuming Cultures" (1999, Macmillan), "Globalization and Social Movements" (2000, Palgrave), and special issues of Citizenship Studies (2000), Feminist Theory (2001, 2003), and Current Sociology (2004).

Malin Rönblom

Malin Rönnblom has a PhD in political science from Umeå university, Sweden. She presented her dissertation in 2002, and it was called A room of One's Own? Women's Organising Meets Established Politics. She has earlier published in English, in 1997, the chapter 'Local women's projects' in the book Towards a new democratic order. Women's Organizing in Sweden in the 1990s, edited by Gunnel Gustafsson. Malin Rönnblom is active as a teacher and researcher at the Centre for Women's Studies at Umeå University. Her main research interests concern critical studies of gender-equality in national and regional politics, mainly in the Nordic countries but also in a global perspective.

Aino Saarinen

DSocSc, sociologist and political scientist, is senior scholar at the Aleksanteri Institute, University of Helsinki and one of the WMI co-ordinators and, at the same time, director of the Nordic and NW-Russian Network for Crisis Centres in the Barents Region development project and related research network. In 1996-1998, she worked at NIKK, the Nordic Institute for Women's Studies and Gender Research at Oslo. For 1999-2002, she was appointed to be the Nordic (NorFA) visiting professor in Women's Studies at the Nevsky Institute, St. Petersburg. Aino Saarinen has published on feminist theories and women in politics. Her present research deals with the crisis centre movement in Barents and Russian women as immigrants in Finland, Sweden and Norway.

Pauline Stoltz

Pauline Stoltz (PhD) is a senior lecturer in Political Science and the vice dean of the school for Technology and Society at Malmö University, Sweden. She has amongst others written 'About Being (T)here and Making A Difference – Black Women and the Paradox of Visibility' (2000) and 'Politisk Solidaritet' in 'Maktens (o)lika för-klädnader – kön, klass och etnicitet i det postkoloniala Sverige', red. de los Reyes et. al (2002). Currently she is working on a project on Swedish Development Policies, ICTs and the re-negotiation of differences in gender, ethnicity and class and on a project on gender and ethnicity in higher education. Her research areas are gender, ethnicity/'race', globalisation, development, higher education, postcolonialism and feminist political theory.

Irina Yukina

Historian and sociologist, PhD in sociology. Since 1999 she is the Chair of Department of Gender Studies of Nevsky Institute of Language and Culture (St. Petersburg). Her research area is Women's History and the Sociology of Social Movement, Russian Women's Movement in Historical Perspective and Russian Feminism of the First Wave.

Naihua Zhang

Naihua Zhang received her Ph.D. in sociology from Michigan State University and is now an Associate Professor at Florida Atlantic University. Her research interest includes social movements and sociology of development, and she has written on contemporary Chinese women's movement and women's organizations. Through her scholarship and association with Chinese Society for Women's Studies, an academic organization aimed at promoting the study of Chinese women, she plays a part in the development of women's studies and the women's movement in China.

Index of names